Readings in the Psychology of Gender

Exploring Our Differences and Commonalities

Anne E. Hunter

Lincoln Memorial University

Carie Forden

Clarion University of Pennsylvania

Allyn and Bacon

Boston • London • Toronto • Sydney • Tokyo • Singapore

To Matthew Donato and David Perry
for helping us to realize our dream of
egalitarian relationships between women and men

Editor in Chief: *Karen Hanson*
Series Editor: *Carolyn Merrill*
Editorial Assistant: *Jonathan Bender*
Editorial Production Administrator: *Bryan Woodhouse*
Editorial Production Service: *Chestnut Hill Enterprises*
Composition and Prepress Buyer: *Linda Cox*
Manufacturing Buyer: *Joanne Sweeney*
Cover Administrator: *Kristina Mose-Libon*
Electronic Composition: *Modern Graphics*

Copyright © 2002 by Allyn & Bacon
A Pearson Education Company
75 Arlington Street, Suite 300
Boston, MA 02116

Internet: www.ablongman.com

Between the time Website information is gathered and then published, it is not unusual for some sites to have closed. Also, the transcription of URLs can result in unintended typographical errors. The publisher would appreciate notification where these occur so that they may be corrected in subsequent editions.

Library of Congress Cataloging-in-Publication Data

Readings in the psychology of gender : exploring our differences and commonalities / [edited by] Anne E. Hunter, Carie Forden.
    p. cm.
Includes bibliographical references and index.
  ISBN 0-205-30594-6
 1. Sex differences (Psychology)   I. Hunter, Anne E. II. Forden, Carie.

BF692.2 .R43 2001
155.3—dc21

                                              2001053957

Printed in the United States of America

10 9 8 7 6 5 4 3 2 1   RRD-VA   06 05 04 03 02 01

Contents

8 *Gender and Violence* **208**

9 *Gender and Caregiving* **244**

10 *Gender and Work* **280**

Preface

Perspective

Why have we chosen the title *Readings in the Psychology of Gender: Exploring Our Differences and Commonalities*? First, despite the fact that most research in the psychology of gender highlights the differences between females and males, it is important to remember that we are alike in at least as many ways as we are different. Therefore, to provide a more accurate picture of gender, we have included readings that emphasize commonalities between females and males, along with those that focus on differences. Second, because we live in a culturally diverse society, it is essential that a collection of readings explores the unique ways that people of different races, ethnicities, social classes, and sexual orientations may experience gender. Historically, the bulk of writing and research in the psychology of gender has focused on white, middle-class, heterosexual males and females. We have tried to provide the opportunity here for people of non-dominant groups to see research on their experiences of gender. At the same time however, it is important not to place so much emphasis on the differences in the ways that diverse groups experience gender that we lose sight of the many similarities across groups of females and males.

We have adopted a dialectical model of gender. This model views gender differences and similarities in thinking, feeling, and behaving as the result of a complex interplay among biological, psychological, social, and cultural processes. Given the flexible human brain, the model also assumes that social and cultural processes can outweigh biological ones as influences on gender. This dialectical perspective is elaborated in the introduction to this book, along with an analysis of the ways that group differences in privilege and power affect the experience of gender. This introduction, because it provides a comprehensive theoretical framework for understanding the complex origins of gender, is well-suited to supporting a variety of approaches to teaching a course on gender.

This collection of readings is intended as a supplementary text. As such, it is relatively short in length, with ten chapters containing two to three readings each. The readings are challenging enough for an upper-level course in the psychology of gender yet also accessible to students in a lower-level course. Several of the readings we have chosen cover topics of importance to the study of gender that tend to be covered only superficially in textbooks, if at all (e.g., male circumcision). Other readings complement and extend topics typically covered in textbooks (e.g., interpersonal communication). We have also selected readings that represent a variety of research methodologies, with the goal of exposing students to the wide range of qualitative and quantitative methods that are typical of psychology.

Organization

This reader is flexibly designed so that it can supplement existing textbooks on the psychology of gender with diverse topical organizations. That is, chapters can be used independently from one another, allowing instructors to vary the order in which they assign chapters and to assign some chapters and not others. Furthermore, each reading within a chapter is preceded by a short summary of important points. This also gives instructors the flexibility to assign some readings and not others within a particular chapter, and in the order that best suits their needs. For instructors who wish to assign whole chapters, chapter summaries and integrative chapter questions are provided.

Pedagogical Features

The reader contains several pedagogical aids to assist students in the understanding and integration of the material:

1. Themes: the book introduction concludes with five themes that summarize our theoretical perspective on the psychology of gender. These themes provide an integrative framework that guides students' reading and helps organize their thinking. Themes are highlighted in boldface type in the summaries that introduce each reading, and are featured in the questions that open each reading and close each chapter.
2. Chapter Summaries and Integrative Questions: each chapter opens with a short summary that serves to introduce the readings. A series of "Putting It All Together" questions at the end of each chapter help students synthesize diverse readings.
3. Reading Summaries and Critical Thinking Questions: each reading is summarized in order to focus students and alert them to the main ideas and themes. Several "Questions to Consider" at the beginning of each reading help students to interact with the main ideas and themes, to relate them to their own lives, and to develop critical-thinking skills.

Acknowledgments

Many people have contributed to our understanding of gender. We would like to thank Betty Rosoff and Ethel Tobach, founders of the Genes and Gender Collective, for introducing us to the dialectical model of behavior, and Ronald

Friend, Brett Silverstein, Dana Bramel, and Beverly Birns of the State University of New York at Stony Brook, for teaching us about the importance of societal and feminist analyses. Thanks also to the authors who have contributed to this book for the ways they have expanded our understanding of gender issues, and to our students who constantly challenge us to reconsider our assumptions. The reviewers who read earlier drafts of this book provided us with many helpful suggestions, we thank Mary Ballard, Appalachian State University; Susan A. Basow, Lafayette College; John Batka, Cameron University; Judi Beinstein Miller, Oberlin College; Sylvia Beyer, University of Wisconsin-Parkside; Gail Cabral, Marywood University; Janet Kuebli, Saint Louis University; Angela Lipsitz, Northern Kentucky University; Laura Madson, New Mexico State University; Amy J. Marin, Phoenix College; and Jo A. Meier-Marquis, Unviersity of Texas at San Antonio. We also appreciate the people who contributed in practical ways to the completion of this book. Thanks to Patricia Harris Hunter for her help with editing and proofreading, Ethel Branson and Phyllis Owens for their loving care of young people, and the staff of the Clarion University Library, especially Brenda Sturtz, for their help with inter-library loans. We thank the staff at Allyn & Bacon for their enthusiastic support, particularly senior editor Carolyn Merrill and editorial assistant Lara Zeises, and the production staff who helped to get it into print. Finally, the loving support of our family and friends (you know who you are!) has made it possible for us to meet the challenges of writing this book. And we also thank our children—Alexander Hunter Donato, Elizabeth Donato Hunter, and Gray Thomas Lewis—for their persistent reminders to take joy in the present moment.

Introduction

As you read this book, you will learn that it is necessary to go beyond simple biological or environmental explanations to understand how gender differences develop and are maintained. We have chosen readings that are compatible with a *dialectical* model of gender. Dialectical theorists recognize that many gender-related differences are both biological and environmental in origin. That is, each component of gender (biological, psychological, social, and cultural) is seen as both the cause and the result of the other components. For example, our learning experiences influence our brain structure, such as the connections between nerve cells and cell size. In turn, changes in brain structures contribute to certain skills and abilities, which may motivate us toward additional similar experiences. In this example, learning both causes brain changes and is the result of brain changes. This dialectical process of reciprocal influence results in continuous change in the behaviors, thinking, and feelings of females and males, rather than fixed traits and behaviors. As you will see, this is why gender-related differences tend to vary over time and across cultures.

We are feminist social psychologists. To us, this means that the flexible nature of our brains enables social and cultural processes to override genetic and biological ones. That is, even though chromosomes and hormones may predispose the brains of females and males to develop somewhat differently, they do not direct the pattern of development. From the moment of conception, we exist within a broader social environment that exerts considerable influence on our hormones, neurotransmitters, and brain structure. Gender differences and similarities in thinking, feeling, and behaving must be situated in their social, historical, and cultural contexts—without ignoring critical biological contexts.

Biology in Society

A dialectical model of gender goes beyond models which discuss gender as the result of either biology OR environment (deterministic models) and beyond models which discuss the relative contributions of biology AND environment (additive models). Instead, the dialectical model recognizes that many gender-related differences are both biological and social (e.g., math skills)—that biological and environmental processes mutually affect one another and are, in fact, inseparable. It also acknowledges that the social environment has considerable impact on the production of hormones, and also on behaving, thinking, and feeling.

Sex and Gender

Some psychologists use the phrase *sex differences* to refer to biological factors—chromosomes, hormonal chemistry, brain structure, and reproductive organs that differentiate females and males. Each society can then take these biological differences and create its own set of expectations for femininity and masculinity. The phrase *gender differences* is often used to refer to these socially constructed expectations. Other psychologists, however, view this distinction as useful but oversimplified (Hyde, 1994; Lips, 2001). They view it as useful because it calls attention to the social and cultural influences on female-male behavioral differences. They view it as oversimplified because sex and gender are overlapping concepts, which means that the effects of biology and social environment on behavior are virtually impossible to separate. Hubbard (1990) describes how biological and social processes act on one another in a dialectical or reciprocal process to produce an outcome. For example, gender-specific toys and games (such as dolls for girls and trucks for boys) not only teach children gender role behaviors, but they also influence the structure and chemistry of the developing brain. In turn, the structure and chemistry of the developing brain affect the play activities selected by the child. Because we also view sex and gender as overlapping rather than as distinct concepts, we have adopted the definitions provided by Lips (2001): *sex* refers to male-female differences that are related to anatomy; *gender* refers to male-female differences that are a result of the complex interplay between biological and social processes, as well as the cultural expectations of masculinity and femininity.

The Flexible Human Brain

Unlike most other animals, we have considerable freedom to create and recreate ourselves. Instead of being constrained by our biology to engage in fixed, instinctual behaviors, our flexible and evolving brain allows us to continuously alter our behavior patterns to meet the ever-changing demands of our physical and social environments. Therefore, characteristics such as female deference and male dominance are not rooted in our genes (although they may be *influenced* by them), but are assigned to females and males to meet the needs of a particular society at a particular point in history. For example, the meaning of femininity and masculinity can vary considerably across historical time and place. This becomes apparent when we look at the evolution of male and female roles. Each culture's definition of femininity and masculinity is tied to its unique history, geography, economy, and natural resources (Wade and Tavris, 1994). These material conditions present challenges that demand solutions, and gender roles may be constructed as solutions. For example, during the fifties and sixties, the majority of middle class white women in the US were homemakers. In this role, images of women's natural domesticity prevailed, while men were assumed to be naturally suited to the workplace and its demands for competition and assertiveness. However, changing economic conditions that began in the seventies made it increasingly difficult for most two parent families to survive on one income. This economic situation, along with a new women's movement that began at about the same time, led the majority of women to expand their roles back into the workplace (the majority of women worked during World War II also). Although most of these women are concentrated into low status service jobs where they provide the same support and nurturance functions that they provide in the home, enough are making it into positions of power to challenge old notions about the natural domesticity and passivity of females (Forden, Hunter & Birns, 1999). At the same time, new images of nurturing fathers are taking shape. Thus, it is our malleable (flexible) brain that allows us to recreate our gender roles and ourselves in a variety of ways in response to our changing environments.

Learning Difference: Gender Roles

How do we learn and adopt a gender role? What developmental experiences shape our identity as male or female? According to socialization theory (e.g., Lips, 1995), parents, peers, media, and other agents of socialization teach us what is appropriate behavior for our gender. We then internalize these messages and act out our appropriate gender roles. For example, when children receive gender-specific toys, they learn what is expected of boys and girls. If a boy plays with a doll, he is often given the message that this is inappropriate behavior for him, and he learns that dolls (and by implication, caregiving) are not part of his masculine role.

Another perspective, based in psychoanalytic theory (e.g., Pollack, 1995), argues that gender identity emerges as infants struggle to develop a sense of "self" that is distinct from their caregivers. This process is different for males and females because in US society, caregivers are generally female. As a result, female infants cannot establish a sense of self that is completely separate from their caregiver because they must identify with her and be like her. Their sense of self develops "in relation," or in connection to another person that they love. As a result, females become skilled at relationships, but have difficulty with separation and independence from others. Male infants, on the other hand, cannot identify with their caregiver because she is unlike them. Their sense of self develops "in separation," or disconnection from another person that they love. As a result, males become skilled at being independent, but may experience difficulty with intimacy.

Children themselves are also active participants in constructing their gender roles. According to gender schema theory (e.g., Bem, 1983), children organize their experiences by creating mental models (or schemas). When a society sees gender as important, and draws distinctions between boys' and girls' clothes, toys, activities, and so on, children construct schemas of what males and females are like (for example that only males can be doctors). Children then approach situations expecting males and females to behave in ways that are consistent with their models, and will ignore behaviors that violate the models. They may be cared for by a female doctor, but will continue to believe that only males can be doctors. Gender schemas also serve as guides for children in evaluating and regulating their own behavior, as they strive to act in ways that are consistent with their concept of gender.

The Context of Difference: Unequal Power

Gender and sex differences are not just interesting variations in human behavior, they occur in a social context of privilege and power. While it can be painful to acknowledge that privilege and power are part of the experience of gender, it is essential to understand this social context, particularly if we wish to bring about change. We live in a hierarchical society where economic, political, and social power is distributed unequally. This means that gender, as well as race, ethnicity, economic class, sexual orientation, age, and other social categories can impact on our access to resources and opportunities. We see gender inequality in the workplace, for example, when women, especially women of color, experience a "glass ceiling" which makes it difficult for them to advance past middle management. Men, on the other hand, even when working in occupations that are traditionally female, may find themselves on a "glass escalator," because it is expected that they will move up into management positions (Lorber, 1994).

When this system of inequality is tied to sex and gender differences, it is called *sexism*. Under conditions of sexism, male power is supported and maintained not only by the prejudiced behavior of individuals, but also to a much greater extent by institutional rules and customs that restrict opportunities for women. Typically, these institutional practices are not openly sexist, but still operate in a way that makes it more difficult for women to succeed. Thus, the glass ceiling occurs in part because individual managers do not take responsibility for sponsoring women or people of color, but primarily because institutional recruitment policies which depend upon networking and referrals favor white men. (Lorber, 1994). These institutional practices may make it difficult for even well-intentioned managers to find women or people of color to mentor.

As Hubbard (1994) describes, in a sexist society, the fact that we are born with female or male genitals means that we will live different lives. The way we live our daily lives in turn affects our biology. For example, because of gender segregation in the workplace, men and women generally hold different kinds of jobs. People who spend eight hours a day in an office doing word processing (typically women) will be biologically different than people who spend their day working on a construction site (typically men). These two different types of work can contribute to creating differences in brain structure and chemistry as well as differences in physical power (Hubbard, 1990). And these biological differences then reinforce gender segregation.

The Defined Norm.   When power is divided unequally in a society, the ideas, experiences, and behaviors of the privileged group become the standard for "human" behavior, or the *defined norm* (Pharr, 1988). The way in which this group of people views and experiences the world is considered "normal," and the minds and experiences of people in other groups are often seen as lacking or defective because they are different from this norm. When the standards for the defined norm are male, female differences are often seen as deficits: women and girls are identified as being less intelligent, less capable, and less psychologically healthy (Forden, Hunter & Birns, 1999). Men of color, gay men, and working class men may also be seen as inadequate because they fail to meet the defined norm of masculinity set by white, middle-class heterosexual men (Kimmel and Messner, 2001). Even members of the defined norm themselves may be seen as inadequate when they fail to meet its unrealistic standards (Pleck, 1995).

Psychological research and theory generally reflect the bias of the defined norm because it has taken the white, middle-class male as its standard and failed to acknowledge that gender, race, and social class may impact on the human experience in important ways (Bing & Reid, 1996). For example, Miller (1991) claims that the models of personality development described by Erik Erickson and Daniel Levinson may not be applicable to females. Like the male gender role which emphasizes independence, these models describe healthy personality development as a process of separating from others in order to become a unique individual. Miller points out that this is difficult for females because they are encouraged to develop relationship skills, and so they must construct their sense of self through the process of connecting with others. This would be "unhealthy" development according to the standards of the defined norm, but Miller argues that the inclusion of women's experience opens up a new vision of healthy personality development for both females and males, where the quest for a sense of self does not entail forfeiting relationships.

Traits attributed to the female gender role are often judged to be inferior, but these differences may in fact be strengths. For example, as Donelson (1999) discusses, women are stereotyped as being compliant and more easily influenced than men, and research does show a small trend in this direction. When evaluated from a male standard, compliance is seen as undesirable evidence of women's dependency and indecisiveness. An alternative explanation, however, is that compliance reflects women's sensitivity to situational factors and greater concern with preserving group harmony. It may be that men are acting in nonconforming ways to protect their status because the male gender role requires that they be independent and not easily influenced. Interpreted in this way, women's compliance may be seen as the result of relational abilities rather than as dependency, as a strength rather than as a weakness.

Psychological Consequences of Unequal Power

Internalized Oppression.   The experience of low social and economic power becomes a part of individual psychology as *internalized oppression.* Because they are continually told that they are inferior and unworthy, members of low status groups may come to believe that they are incapable, that they deserve their low status, and that they are powerless to effect change (see Healey, 1993, for an account of a personal struggle with internalized oppression). For women and girls, internalized oppression can lead to self-destructive behaviors (such as eating disorders), difficulty with assertiveness, deference to boys and men, and the tendency to settle for less in life. It can also cause women to devalue and distrust each other, and to see men as more deserving of respect than women. These symptoms of internalized oppression may be reflected in female biology as well. For example, feelings of powerlessness are a contributing factor to clinical depression, and clinical depression is accompanied by imbalances in brain chemistry. Because internalized oppression then causes girls and women to behave in powerless ways and to mistrust each other, it plays an important role in maintaining women's low status.

Male Entitlement.   The experience of privilege and power can also be internalized, so that members of high status groups are likely to take for granted that they are inherently worthy, to believe that they deserve their opportunities, and to see themselves as capable of effecting change (Forden, Hunter, and Birns, 1999). Further, because their experiences are used to define what is "normal" (the defined norm), unearned advantages inherent in the social system are often invisible to members of privileged groups (McIntosh, 1993). For example, a white man is likely to assume that he has fairly earned his management position and may have difficulty recognizing that he has benefited from the institutional networking and referral policies that favor white men (see Davies-Netzley, this volume). Because the privileged group feels entitled to their advantanges and takes their institutional power for granted, they are also likely to experience feelings of anger or defensiveness when their privileges are pointed out (Johnson, 2001). For example, men may have difficulty understanding the need for programs to assist women with institutional networking and referral and feel that they are being disadvantaged when such programs are offered.

Male Gender Role Harm & Restricted Functioning.   Although men benefit from the privileges and power they are granted by sexism, they are also seriously harmed by their gender role. They experience restricted functioning as their gender role places limits on their ability to express the full range of human behavior. Males have been described as experiencing "gender role strain," (Pleck, 1995) when they: 1) fail to fulfill male gender role expectations, 2) are traumatized by their socialization into the male gender role, or 3) experience the negative consequences of fulfilling the male gender role. For example, one aspect of the male gender role is that men are not supposed to cry. If a man cries, he may evaluate himself negatively for being weak and unmanly. Boys may be traumatized as they grow up being taunted and teased for crying. And, not being able to cry may interfere with physical health and psychological well-being.

When males and females are successfully socialized into their respective gender roles, unequal power relations between the two are reinforced. Women reinforce male dominance when they see their subordinate status as deserved and behave in subordinate ways; men reinforce male dominance when they treat women as subordinates and act in ways that affirm their dominance. Gender roles are also harmful because they require that each gender express only half of the whole range of behaviors, feelings, and needs available to human beings. There are positive qualities in both masculinity and femininity that we all can claim.

Differences and Commonalities

Commonalities Across Gender. As Hyde (1994) points out, studies which demonstrate gender differences are intriguing and receive a great deal of attention, while studies which demonstrate gender similarities tend not to be reported. In addition, studies which find only tiny gender differences, or report findings which others are unable to replicate, also may receive an unmerited level of attention. As a result, gender differences may be overemphasized while gender similarities are ignored. In reality though, females and males are more alike than they are different. As members of the human race, males and females share similar abilities, behaviors, needs, desires, and fears. And even though gender role socialization may push us to develop different behaviors and abilities because we are male or female, there is more variation within a gender than there is between the genders. In addition, differences in behaviors or abilities that are interpreted as being the result of gender roles may in fact be displayed inconsistently and only in specific situations. For example, Aries (this volume) argues that gender differences in interaction occur not because males and females have consistently different communication styles, but because situational factors such as stereotyped expectations, status differences, and social roles evoke particular behaviors. It is important, then, not only to try to understand how females and males may be different, but also to look at the ways in which we are alike.

Differences Within Gender. While it is common to overemphasize differences between males and females, it is also common to overemphasize similarities within a gender. We assume that all women or all men are alike. This ignores the variety of other social factors that may influence an individual's experience—race, ethnicity, age, social class, religion, sexual orientation, and so on. These factors may profoundly affect how gender roles are constructed. For example, although men of color in this country are exposed to the same gender role expectations as white men, they also must deal with the particular gender role expectations held by their own culture. As a consequence, their experience of masculinity is unique (Lazur and Majors, 1995). So, while males have many experiences that they share, their experiences can also differ in important ways. To understand gender then, we must acknowledge these differences. There are many masculinities and femininities.

Conclusion

To summarize, our perspective on gender includes the following interrelated themes:

1. **Dialectical model.** Genetic, hormonal, and brain differences in males and females are significant influences on behavior. However, these biological fac-

tors are inadaquate to explain the vast differences in social and economic power and in gender roles. Furthermore, power differences and gender roles may themselves change hormonal and brain development. These biological changes in turn reinforce power differences and gender roles.

2. **Defined norm.** Males have more social and economic power than females, and this is especially true for males who are white, economically privileged, and heterosexual. Male dominance means that the psychological characteristics of the white, economically privileged, heterosexual male become the standard against which both males and females are measured, so that characteristics that differ from this standard are viewed as deficiencies.

3. **Gender role effects.** Females (and other low power groups) often experience internalized oppression and behave in powerless ways, but they also resist their oppression. Males benefit from their privileged status, but also are damaged by their gender role through restricted functioning and gender role harm.

4. **More alike than different.** Females and males are more alike than different because as human beings, we share similar behaviors, abilities, needs, desires, and fears. This is true even though gender role expectations influence us to a) develop different abilities and behaviors; and to b) act in gendered ways in certain situations.

5. **Cultural diversity.** Females and males are each culturally diverse groups. This means that although members of each group have many experiences in common, they also have many different experiences. Therefore there are many "femininities" and "masculinities."

Keep these themes in mind as you read through the selections for this book (to assist you, they are highlighted in the summary that precedes each reading.) These themes provide you with a framework for understanding the various gender differences and similarities addressed by the authors. As you read, also keep in mind that because of our adaptable human brain, social and cultural influences can override biological ones. The dialectical theory offers an optimistic view of human nature because it says that we have the capacity to choose among behaviors. Although our present social system is one of male dominance and rigid gender roles, we have the ability to create a new social system of gender equality and behavioral flexibility.

References

Bem, S. L. (1983). Gender schema theory and its implications for child development: Raising gender-aschematic children in a gender-schematic society. *Signs: Journal of Women in Culture and Society, 8,*(4), 598–611.

Bing, V. M. & Reid, P. T. (1996). Unknown women and unknowing research: Consequences of color and class in feminist psychology. In N. R. Goldberger, J. M. Tarule, B. M. Clinchy, and M. F. Belenky, Eds., *Knowledge, Difference and Power.* New York: Basic Books.

Donelson, F. E. (1999). *Women's Experiences: A Psychological Perspective.* Mountain View, CA: Mayfield Publishing Company.

Forden, C., Hunter, A. E., and Birns, B. (1999). *Readings in the Psychology of Women: Dimensions of the Female Experience.* Needham Heights, MA: Allyn & Bacon.

Healey, S. (1993). Confronting ageism: A must for mental health. In N. D. Davis, E. Cole & E. D. Rothblum, Eds., *Faces of Women and Aging.* Binghampton, NY: Haworth Press, Inc.

Hubbard, R. (1990). *The Politics of Women's Biology.* Rutgers, NJ: Rutgers University Press.

Hubbard, R. (1994). Race and sex as biological categories. In E. Tobach & B. Rosoff, Eds., *Challenging Racism and Sexism: Alternatives to Genetic Explanations.* New York: The Feminist Press at The City University of New York.

Hyde, J. S. (1994). Should psychologists study gender differences? Yes, with some guidelines. *Feminism and Psychology, 4,*(4), 507–512.

Johnson, A. G. (2001). *Privilege, Power, and Difference.* Mountain View, CA: Mayfield Publishing Company.

Kimmel, M. S. & Messner, M. A. (2001). *Men's Lives, 5th edition.* Needham Heights, MA: Allyn & Bacon.

Lazur, R. F. & Major, R. (1995). Men of color: Ethnocultural variations of male gender role strain. In R. F. Levant & W. S. Pollack, Eds., *A New Psychology of Men.* New York: Basic Books.

Lips, H. M. (1995). Gender-role socialization: Lessons in femininity. In J. Freeman, Ed., *Women: A Feminist Perspective.* Mountain View, CA: Mayfield Publishing Company.

Lips, H. M. (2001). *Sex and Gender: An Introduction.* Mountain View, CA: Mayfield Publishing Company.

Lorber, J. (1994). *Paradoxes of Gender.* New Haven, CT: Yale University Press.

McIntosh, P. (1993). White privilege and male privilege: A personal account of coming to see correspondences through work in women's studies. In A. Minas, Ed., *Gender Basics: Feminist Perspectives on Women and Men.* Belmont, CA: Wadsworth.

Miller, J. B. (1991). The development of women's sense of self. In J. V. Jordan, A. G. Daplan, J. B. Miller, I. P. Striver, and J. L. Surrey, Eds., *Women's Growth in Connection.* New York: Guilford Press.

Pharr, S. (1988). *Homophobia: A Weapon of Sexism.* Inverness, CA: Chardon Press.

Pleck, J. H. (1995). The gender role strain paradigm: An update. In R. F. Levant & W. S. Pollack, Eds., *A New Psychology of Men.* New York: Basic Books.

Pollack, W. S. (1995). No man is an island: Toward a new psychoanalytic psychology of men. In R. F. Levant & W. S. Pollack, Eds., *A New Psychology of Men.* New York: Basic Books.

Wade, C. & Tavris, C. (1994). The longest war: Gender and culture. In W. J. Lonner & R. S. Malpars, Eds., *Psychology and Culture.* Needham Heights, MA: Allyn & Bacon.

1

A Framework for Understanding the Psychology of Gender

The two readings in this chapter provide a theoretical framework for thinking about and for researching the complex underpinnings of gender-related differences and similarities. The first reading highlights the importance of the scientific study of gender differences, even though the findings may be misused to perpetuate harmful stereotypes about women. In viewing the scientific method as an essential tool for distinguishing myth from fact, the author calls for models that allow for the mutual and interacting effects of biological, psychological, and sociological factors. The second reading, written by the editors of this book, describes such a model of gender—the dialectical model—and shows how it overcomes the limitations of current models.

1

Stereotypes, Science, Censorship, and the Study of Sex Differences

Diane F. Halpern

According to Halpern, psychologists have an obligation to contribute to news media reports concerning whether, when and how much females and males differ in behavior and abilities. She asserts this despite her concern for the media's tendencies to oversimplify and to misinterpret scientific findings concerning sex-related differences* and to ignore findings that reveal no differences. Although Halpern is sympathetic toward those who oppose sex-difference research on the grounds that it contributes to negative stereotypes about females and to the popular tendency to interpret sex differences as female deficiencies, she does not support their position. She claims that the suppression of the truth about legitimate sex-related differences does not advance women. She views the scientific study of sex differences as a tool for dispelling false stereotypes by helping us to understand the complex underpinnings of legitimate differences, while avoiding simplistic explanations. She argues that when a society views the characteristics associated with females as inferior to those associated with males **(defined norm),** the problem lies in the patriarchal values of that society, not in the scientific research that reveals sex-related differences. Halpern further claims that avoiding sex-difference research might return us to an undesirable and recent past when males were often the exclusive participants in psychological research, based on the assumption that the male experience was the norm for all human experience **(defined norm).** However, Halpern acknowledges the inadequacy of current models for studying the psychology of women, and calls for new and more complex research

*Although we use the term "gender" to refer to differences between females and males that result from the interplay between biological and social factors, Halpern uses the term "sex" to refer to these differences. Our use of this term is explained in the book introduction.

models that reveal the reciprocal and interactive effects of biological, psychological, and sociological factors on sex-differences and similarities **(dialectical model).**

Questions to Consider:

1. Why does the news media tend to ignore scientific findings that reveal no sex-related differences? In what ways, if any, has this bias distorted your thinking about sex-related differences and similarities?
2. What, according to Halpern, underlies the tendency to view sex-related differences as female deficiencies in US society?
3. Do you agree with Halpern that the scientific method is a potential tool for advancing women? Explain your answer.
4. According to Halpern, how are current scientific models for studying gender inadequate, and how does the psychobiosocial (dialectical) model address these inadequacies?
5. What question would you like to see answered by scientific research on gender?

Research on sex differences is front-page news, often in the prestigious 'above the fold' section that is visible when the paper is folded. This is where the general public learns about studies like the one that found few females among mathematically-gifted youth (Benbow, 1988) and the one that found that women's fine motor and cognitive performance vary over the menstrual cycle (Hampson and Kimura, 1988). The bold headlines that proclaim these differences are based on the belief that news of sex differences, like sex itself, sells. The news media treat complex issues—like whether, when and how much females and males differ—simplistically, with a heavy emphasis on controversies (they're more interesting than agreements) and colorful quotes that are typically unrelated to their merit. The reports of these studies often bear little resemblance to the actual findings of the research because the usual rules of scientific evidence and reasoning don't apply in the media world, where deadlines and interest value reign supreme and rebuttal is frequently absent. Should reputable psychologists be contributing to the media circus that molds public opinion with sound bites and simplistic analyses of complex problems? Yes, we not only should, but we must.

Stereotypes and Science

Critics of sex-differences research argue that such research legitimizes negative stereotypes of women by creating an emphasis on the way the sexes differ while slighting the multitude of similarities. These critics often propose that psychologists should study only similarities because similarities are more important than differences. But, when we examine this argument closely, we find that it contains several unstated assumptions that don't hold up under scrutiny and tell more about negative stereotypes about women than the research that it criticizes. Stereotypes about any group (e.g., women, Latinos, men in college fraternities, New Yorkers) are not created as a result of systematic studies of group similarities and differences. Stereotypes about women and men existed long before psychologists applied their research skills to understanding the unique and shared aspects of group membership. Empirical research doesn't create stereotyping, as its critics imply; the systematic study of sex differences using scientific rules of evidence is the only way to dispel stereotypes and to understand legitimate differences.

The argument against research on the many questions of sex differences ignores the fact that we cannot study similarities without also studying differences. If we had not studied the way the sexes respond in different situations, we would not know, for example, that situational variables are more important in determining how a person will respond in most situations than individual variables like sex (Eagly, 1987). The insistence that we study only similarities creates a false dichotomy because research on similarities is not separable from the study of differences.

The 'Women Have Less' Fallacy

Another unstated assumption often implied by those opposed to the study of sex differences is that, if the truth were known, the results would reveal female deficiencies. This sort of unstated assumption can often be found in arguments against the biological bases of female and male differences. In my recent book on this subject (Halpern, 1992), I called this belief 'the women have less' fallacy. Many researchers have found that there are sex differences that are unrelated to reproduction that have large and practically-significant effects, and some of these differences cannot be completely explained without recognizing the biological differences between females and males. There are numerous examples of carefully controlled research where the data clearly show the effect of biological variables on non-reproductive differences between females and males. Although the literature on such differences is too large and too technical in nature to summarize here, I will briefly list some of these studies. I will limit my examples to those that pertain to cognitive abilities be-

cause this is the area that I know best, but there are numerous other areas where large sex differences are found that have, at least in part, a biological component (e.g., the overwhelming majority of acts of violence are committed by males; the ratio of males to females diagnosed with Attention Deficit Disorder is 10:1; and eating disorders are much more likely in females than males [American Psychiatric Association, 1987]). Because of space limitations, my summary is very brief and interested readers will need to consult the original studies and literature reviews for a more complete understanding.

Several researchers have found that certain cognitive abilities vary in a cyclical fashion over the menstrual cycle. For example, in a series of carefully controlled studies of normal women (using women without cyclical variations in 'sex hormones' as controls), Hampson and Kimura (Hampson, 1990a, 1990b; Hampson and Kimura, 1988) found that performance on visual-spatial tasks declined during the period in the monthly cycle when quantities of estrogen and progesterone are low, and verbal fluency and manual dexterity tasks improved during the portion of the monthly cycle when quantities of estrogen and progesterone are high. Many other studies have shown that perception also varies as a function of monthly changes in female hormones (e.g., Goolkasian, 1980). Although the magnitude of these differences is small, the systematic covariation with the ebb and flow of monthly hormones cannot be explained without acknowledging that these hormones can affect cognition.

Numerous studies involving individuals with hormone abnormalities also show the involvement of biological variables on cognition. Males with androgen deficiencies at puberty show severe deficits in spatial abilities with normal functioning on other cognitive tasks (Hier and Crowley, 1982).

Similarly, females with Turner's syndrome, an abnormality in which they have very low levels of 'sex hormones', have severe deficits in visual-spatial abilities with normal abilities on verbal tasks (e.g., Hines, 1982). Females who have been exposed to high levels of androgens during pre-natal development show increased aggression and activity, preference for 'boy-typical' toys and high levels of spatial ability (Berenbaum and Hines, 1992; Newcombe et al., 1983; Reinisch, 1981).

There is also clear evidence that there are some differences in the brain structures of normal females and males and that these differences are evident *in utero* (e.g., de Lacoste-Utamsing and Holloway, 1982; Kimura, 1987). Of course, the fact that there are brain differences doesn't imply that these differences *cause* sex-related differences in cognition, but there is a large body of other sorts of data that support this contention. For example, cognitive abilities vary as both a function of one's sex and one's preferred hand. Handedness (extent to which an individual is right- or left-handed) is a rough indicator of brain organization, and there are sex differences in handedness (see, for example, Casey and Brabeck, 1989; Coren and Halpern, 1991; Halpern and Coren, 1993). Careful manipulations of pre-natal and post-natal hormones with non-human mammals clearly show that these hormones affect a wide range of non-reproductive behaviors (e.g., Denenberg et al., 1988). Ancillary evidence that supports this viewpoint was recently presented by Masters and Sanders (1993), who found that the extremely large effect size for some spatial tasks (close to one standard deviation between female and male means) has remained stable over the past 17 years, despite substantial changes in the number of women in higher education and changes in sex roles. The ability to produce

fluent speech is much more likely to be a problem for males than females. There are three to four times more male stutterers than female stutterers (Skinner and Shelton, 1985). Males are also 10 times more likely to be severely dyslexic than are females (Sutaria, 1985). Finally, there have been numerous replicated studies that show that sexual orientation also covaries with specific cognitive abilities in predictable ways (e.g., Gladue et al., 1990; Sanders and Ross-Fields, 1986).

Although there is a huge body of evidence showing that sex-related differences do exist, there is nothing in these studies to suggest that either females or males have the overall advantage. Differences are not deficiencies, and there is no logical reason for labeling those characteristics that are associated with being female as 'less' valuable than those that are associated with being male. For example, girls are, on the average, more cooperative (less aggressive) than boys and score much higher, on the average, on tests of manual dexterity and the production of fluid speech (Hines, 1990). Thus, from an abilities perspective, we might expect that a majority of surgeons, mechanics and politicians would be female. That they are not is unrelated to their abilities and must have its origin in social variables. Boys, on the average, excel at other tasks such as the mental manipulation of shapes (see Halpern, 1992, for a review of these studies). If society labels those traits that are associated with being female as negative and those associated with being male as positive, then the problem lies in societal values, not in the fact that females and males differ or in the fact that researchers found these differences. We need to separate differences from the evaluation of the way in which people differ. This is an important message because we live in a diverse world where sex is only one way in which people differ. It makes no more sense to argue over which sex has the better intellectual skills than to argue over which sex has the better genitals or which race has the best skin color or shape of their eyes. Sex differences research is not a zero sum game with a winner and a loser. We can learn to appreciate differences and to value the uniqueness of individuals without denying the fact that males and females differ in many ways including some aspects of nature, nurture and their interaction.

Knowledge is Power

It is a fact that males score an average of 47 to 50 points higher than females on the mathematics portion of the Scholastic Aptitude Test (SAT-M), a difference that has remained constant for the last 25 years. If any part of this huge difference is due to sex-related differences in abilities, it is extremely small because the sex differences on other tests of mathematics ability are much smaller. Thus, sex differences research is critical in understanding and improving female performance on the SAT-M. The SAT-M is an important test because it is used in making decisions about college admissions in thousands of colleges in North America. We can and should argue about the reasons for, and consequences of, this huge difference, but this is an argument that we could not have if psychologists had never studied sex differences on the SAT-M. We could not address, or redress, the fact that this test results in lower scores for girls if the studies that show this difference had not been conducted. The only alternative to the knowledge that studies of sex differences provide is ignorance, and ignorance will not advance females or any other group.

A Psychology of Women

Like many of my feminist colleagues, I have taught a course entitled 'Psychology of Women' for many years. If we were to abandon the study of sex differences, then we would lose the theoretical underpinnings of courses like this one and all of the other women's studies courses. When we talk about the psychology of women, or their history, or literature, or women's 'place' in other academic disciplines, we are always putting women in some context and making comparisons with men, just as studies of minority groups make implicit and explicit comparisons with other ethnic groups. The notion of sex differences is at the heart of these courses because if there were no differences then there would be no need for a psychology of women. The alternative to the study of differences is to conclude that there is nothing distinct about women's psychology. The alternative is a return to the normative use of males for studies designed to explore human nature, an alternative that few feminists would advocate. This would be a giant step backward to a not-too-distant past where males were used as subjects in almost all areas of research including psychological and medical research. For example, it was only a little over 15 years ago when all of the studies on ageing conducted by federally-funded United States agencies used only male subjects despite the fact that a majority of the elderly is female. The exclusive use of male subjects was based on the tacit assumptions that sex differences should not be studied and males would yield data that would be applicable to all people. Of course, statistics about any group cannot be applied to individuals, especially when there is a great deal of variability in the data. We can only make group-level statements about 'on the average' differences, and it is important that this fact be clearly communicated whenever sex differences are discussed.

Psychobiosocial Models

Despite the fact that I believe that we must encourage the study of sex differences, I also understand the concerns of those who hold opposing opinions. We must all remember that research takes place in a social context and every aspect of our work, ranging from the types of research questions that we consider important, to the way we interpret data, is influenced by this context. Turn-of-the-century scientists found 'evidence' for the intellectual inferiority of women and it was 'well established' that intellectual tasks would drain the blood needed for menstruation which would somehow be harmful to women's health: sexist conclusions that were acceptable because of the social context in which they were presented (reported in Shields, 1980).

A feminist perspective on sex differences research is crucial for proposing new models and research paradigms for the study of women's psychology. Such models and paradigms recognize the reciprocal and interactive effects of psychology, sociology and biological factors—a model in which the influence of environmental factors on biology, and the way biological variables influence environmental factors, work jointly with a host of other variables to create sex-related differences and similarities. The answer to the questions about sex differences can never be 'either-or'; we must seek answers that allow for multiple determinants. There is ample evidence that biological and environmental variables exert mutual effects—the types of activities in which we engage alter brain structures and brain

structures, in turn, are likely to influence those activities in which we choose to engage (e.g., Diamond, 1988; Greenough et al., 1987).

Toward a New Model of Feminism

Like many of my colleagues, I shudder every time I hear a female college student proclaim that she is not a feminist. After many lengthy discussions and informal 'focus groups', I have concluded that so many young women eschew feminism because they believe that much of it is rigid and conformist. To some extent, I have also seen this drift toward a single admissible point of view. For example, there are many colleagues who refuse to consider the possibility that some women might lie about rape, incest or abuse. The importance of the issue of violence against women cannot be overemphasized, and it is feminists who must ensure counseling, medical care, legal assistance, education and shelter for the many victims whose only crime is being female. But this does not mean that no woman ever lies about violence. Similarly, feminists must ensure that cultural and other environmental factors are considered in our understanding of the ways in which females and males are similar and different. We must also fight vigorously against the misuse and biased interpretation of data. But this does not mean that we must reject the substantial body of evidence that says that biological variables are also involved in some of the differences. In other words, we must move toward a more tolerant and more inclusive feminism. We cannot pretend that data supporting biological factors do not exist. We also cannot ignore the overwhelming body of evidence showing that, while some sex differences are non-existent or very small, there are also some extremely large and meaningful differences.

The new feminism I am calling for will welcome debate and will encourage a careful and open-minded analysis of all the evidence that pertains to important issues. This would be a healthy change, signalling that feminism is strong enough to allow dissent and that 'truth' is not predetermined before the data are collected. Otherwise, we run the danger of becoming as myopic and dogmatic as those who believe that all sex differences are due to biological factors.

I hope that at least half of those future scientists who will propose and test these new models will be females who are proud to call themselves feminists, and I hope that they will understand that the misuse of research in the past is not a reason for censoring the science of the future. Censorship, even self-censorship, is the wrong response to past abuses. If we do not conduct research on sex differences, then we are left with stereotypes and the status quo.

References

American Psychiatric Association (1987). *Diagnostic and Statistical Manual of Mental Disorders*, 3rd rev. edn. Washington, DC: American Psychiatric Association.

Benbow, C. P. (1988). Sex Differences in Mathematical Reasoning Ability in Intellectually Talented Preadolescents: Their Nature, Effects, and Possible Causes, *Behavioral and Brain Sciences* 11: 169–232.

Berenbaum, S. A., & Hines, M. (1992). Early Androgens are Related to Childhood Sex-typed Toy Preferences, *Psychological Science* 3: 203–6.

Casey, M. B., & Brabeck, M. M. (1989). Exception to a Male Advantage on a Spatial Task: Family Handedness and College Major as Factors Identifying Women who Excel, *Neuropsychologia* 27: 689–96.

Coren, S., & Halpern, D. F. (1991). Left-handedness: A Marker for Decreased Survival Fitness, *Psychological Bulletin* 109: 90–106.

de Lacoste-Utamsing, M. C., & Holloway, R. L. (1982). Sexual Dimorphism in the Human Corpus Callosum, *Science* 216: 1431–2.

Denenberg, V. H., Berrebi, A. S., & Fitch, R. H. (1988). A Factor Analysis of the Rat's Corpus Callosum, *Brain Research* 497: 271–9.

Diamond, M. C. (1988). *Enriching Heredity: The Impact of the Environment on the Anatomy of the Brain.* New York: Free Press.

Eagly, A. H. (1987). *Sex Differences in Social Behavior: A Social-role Interpretation.* Hillsdale, NJ: Erlbaum.

Gladue, B. A., Beatty, W. W., Larson, J., & Staton, R. D. (1990). Sexual Orientation and Spatial Ability in Men and Women, *Psychobiology* 18: 101–8.

Goolkasian, P. (1980). Cyclic Changes in Pain Perception: An ROC Analysis, *Perception and Psychophysics* 27: 499–504.

Greenough, W. T., Black, J. E., & Wallace, C. S. (1987). Experience and Brain Development, *Child Development* 58: 539–59.

Halpern, D. F. (1992). *Sex Differences in Cognitive Abilities,* 2nd edn. Hillsdale, NJ: Erlbaum.

Halpern, D. F., & Coren, S. (1993). Left-handedness and Life Span: A Reply to Harris, *Psychological Bulletin* 114: 235–41.

Hampson, E. (1990a). Estrogen-related Variations in Human Spatial and Articulatory-motor Skills, *Psychoneuroendocrinology* 15: 97–111.

Hampson, E. (1990b). Variations in Sex-related Cognitive Abilities Across the Menstrual Cycle, *Brain and Cognition* 14: 26–43.

Hampson, E., & Kimura, D. (1988). Reciprocal Effects of Hormonal Fluctuations on Human Motor and Perceptual–Spatial Skills, *Behavioral Neuroscience* 102: 456–95.

Hier, D. B., & Crowley, W. F. Jr (1982). Spatial Ability in Androgen-deficient Men, *The New England Journal of Medicine* 306: 1202–5.

Hines, M. (1982). Prenatal Gonadal Hormones and Sex Differences in Human Behavior, *Psychological Bulletin* 92: 56–80.

Hines, M. (1990). Gonadal Hormones and Human Cognitive Development, in J. Balthazart (Ed.), *Hormones, Brain and Behavior in Vertebrates. Vol. 1. Sexual Differentiation, Neuroanatomical Aspects, Neurotransmitters and Neuropeptides,* pp. 51–63. Basel: Karger.

Kimura, D. (1987). Are Men's and Women's Brains Really Different?, *Canadian Psychology* 28: 133–47.

Masters, M. S., & Sanders, B. (1993). Is the Gender Difference in Mental Rotation Disappearing?, *Behavior Genetics* 23: 337–41.

Newcombe, N., Bandura, M., & Taylor, D. G. (1983). Sex Differences in Spatial Ability and Spatial Activities, *Sex Roles* 9: 377–86.

Reinisch, J. (1981). Prenatal Exposure to Synthetic Progestins Increases Potential for Aggression in Humans, *Science* 211: 1171–3.

Sanders, G., & Ross-Field, L. (1986). Sexual Orientation and Visual–Spatial Ability, *Brain and Cognition* 5: 280–90.

Shields, S. A. (1980). Nineteenth-century Evolutionary Theory and Male Scientific Bias, in G. W

Barlow and J. Silverberg (Eds.), *Sociobiology: Beyond Nature/Nurture,* pp. 489–502. Boulder, CO: Westview Press.

Skinner, P. H., & Shelton, R. L. (1985). *Speech, Language, and Hearing: Normal Processes and Disorders,* 2nd edn. New York: Wiley.

Sutaria, S. D. (1985). *Specific Learning Disabilities: Nature and Needs.* Springfield, IL: Charles C. Thomas.

2

The Origins of Gender Differences in Behavior: A Dialectical Model

Anne E. Hunter and Carie Forden

In this reading, Hunter and Forden challenge the popular tendency to attribute gender differences in behaviors, abilities, attitudes and feelings solely to biology, claiming that it is overly simplistic and serves to disempower both sexes. They also caution against environmentally based explanations that ignore biology, insisting that they too are incomplete. Arguing that gender differences and similarities have complex origins, they present a model that considers all biological and social influences on gender, as well as their reciprocal relationships **(dialectical model).** According to the dialectical model, all behaviors involve the simultaneous occurrence of both biological and social processes. Therefore, attempts to separate out the relative contributions of biology and environment to observed gender differences are viewed as misguided. Because of the highly flexible human brain, we are never constrained by our biology to act in fixed, instinctual ways. Instead, from conception to death, we continually alter our behavior to meet the changing demands of our environments.

We also help to create our environments. Thus, we both shape and are shaped by social conditions. This is reflected in our biology which, in turn, influences subsequent behaviors. Hunter and Forden view the dialectical model of the origins of gender as a highly optimistic model in that it encourages a vision of society where gender equality is achievable and where both sexes have the opportunity to develop their full potential, unconstrained by myths of sex-related biological limitations **(more alike than different).**

Questions to Consider:

1. Why, according to Hunter and Forden, do biological explanations of gender differences disempower both sexes? Are there ways in which you have been disempowered by this thinking? Explain your answer.
2. How does the concept of brain flexibility challenge biological explanations of gender?

3. According to the reading, how might sexism contribute to gender differences in physical power? Is it possible to eliminate this difference? Explain your answer.

4. Use the dialectical model of gender to critique the claim of evolutionary psychology that females are genetically programmed to be more nurturing than males.

Two biological theories of gender differences in behavior dominate the scientific literature and media—evolutionary psychology and prenatal hormone theory. Both theories emphasize the impact of biological factors on gender differences in behavior while minimizing the complex interactions between biology and society. Evolutionary psychologists (e.g., Buss, 1995) begin with the assumption that males are genetically predisposed to be aggressive, competitive, dominant and sexually promiscuous, while females are predisposed to be nurturant, passive, sexually selective and monogamous. They claim that these particular behavioral differences have evolved because they maximize the likelihood of getting one's genes into the next generation. The theory further claims that, since males are able to produce millions of sperm with minimal investment of energy, they have evolved with an innate strategy to fertilize as many females as possible. On the other hand, because females are limited in the number of offspring they can produce due to the time and energy demanded by each pregnancy, they have evolved with an innate strategy to be selective when choosing a sexual partner.

Prenatal hormone theorists (e.g., Collaer & Hines, 1995) propose that female and male brains are organized differently due to the presence or absence of testosterone during a critical period in prenatal development. In turn, these differently organized brains lead to different female and male hormonal and behavior patterns.

To date, there is no scientific research that demonstrates that gender differences in human behavior are coded in the genes (see Angier, 1999; Bem, 1993 and Eagly & Wood, 1999 for concise summaries and thought-provoking critiques of evolutionary psychology research). Similarly, there is no scientific research that demonstrates that biological differences in brain chemistry, structure and organization *cause* gender differences in human behaviors, abilities, feelings and attitudes (see Angier, 1999 and Bem, 1993 for excellent summaries and critiques of this research). In spite of this lack of evidence, the myth of biologically based differences is etched deeply in the popular consciousness. Unfortunately, the news media contributes to the widespread acceptance of this myth when it sacrifices scientific reporting for sensationalism. Research demonstrating gender differences sells, especially if these gender differences can be attributed to biological differences between females and males.

The belief in biologically based gender differences is disempowering for both females and males. When we overlook or minimize the role of environmental factors (situational, social and cultural) in explaining the gender differences that we observe in our everyday lives, we are likely to conclude that these differences are preordained by our genes and are therefore immutable (unchangeable). Some common examples of this pessimistic thinking are as follows: "There will always be wars, rape and other violent crime because males have a biological imperative to be aggressive." "Females are at a biological disadvantage for math ability, so they should be discouraged from classes and occupations that require math skills." "Females are naturally cooperative and nurturing, while males are naturally competitive and aggressive. Therefore, females are best suited for service jobs and caretaking roles, and males for positions of leadership and power." The widespread belief in these and similar deterministic statements may severely limit our life options and prevent us from achieving our full potential as individuals. For example, people who do not fulfill the behavioral expectations for their sex may come to the conclusion that they are abnormal. Subsequently, they may adjust their behaviors and interests to fit these expectations.

The belief concerning biologically based aggression in males is particularly tragic in that it perpetuates violence of all kinds—even the most deadly—by apologizing for it. The reasoning goes like this: "After all, boys will be boys," and "They can't help themselves." What an insult to males to suggest that their behaviors are more under the control of their biology than their capacity—tied to the adaptable human brain—to choose one behavior over another! Biological thinking is also disempowering when it is misused to justify and to maintain social and economic inequality between the sexes in our society. As long as women are viewed as naturally nurturing and lacking in leadership ability, patriarchy (a social system constructed around male dominance) will remain firmly rooted in place.

It is crucial then that we distinguish myth from reality in our thinking about the relationship between gender differences and biology. We have three main objectives in writing this article. First, we hope to challenge the popular tendency to accept without questioning the endless media reports that claim a mainly biological basis for observed gender differences in abilities, behaviors, feelings and attitudes. Similarly, we hope to challenge the environmental bias of many of those who are concerned about the misuse of biological theories to justify and to maintain the subordination of women. Understandably, such awareness may motivate one to explain gender differences solely in terms of environmental factors, or to minimize biological factors. Like biological approaches, this approach oversimplifies the origins of gender. The rapidly growing body of research on biological influences should not be ignored. Instead, it should be placed in proper perspective. Therein, our final objective is to present a *dialectical* model of the complex origins of gender differences and similarities. It is a model that considers all biological and environmental factors that might contribute to these differences, as well as their reciprocal and ongoing influences. We argue that a dialectical model provides the most accurate picture of how gender develops and is maintained. It is our hope that, from this point onward, you will be frustrated by any simplistic explanations of gender (both biological and environmental), and that you will attempt to challenge them whenever they surface.

Brain Flexibility

Hormonal and evolutionary theories of gender leave little room for the main biological feature that distinguishes humans from most other animals: our highly flexible or adaptable brain. Because of this flexible brain, humans are not constrained by their biology to act in fixed, instinctual ways. Instead, we are able to continually alter our behavior patterns to meet the needs of our environment. From the time we are conceived until we die, our biological processes (e.g., the production of hormones and neurotransmitters) are influenced by the social contexts (interpersonal, social, cultural and historical) in which they are embedded.

Because of this, it is impossible to disentangle biology from society. At any given moment, biological and societal processes are shaping us simultaneously (Hubbard, 1990). There is never a simple, direct pathway between genes, hormones, brain structures and behaviors (or between environment and behavior). This means that a behavior can never be genetically preordained, even though it may be partially inherited. Instead, our social environments and experiences can alter the direction of our genetic and other biological processes from the moment we are conceived. This is true even for characteristics that we tend to think of as dictated entirely by genes, such as height. For example, a child may be predisposed by his or her genes to be tall, but may never achieve that genetic potential because of prenatal exposure to tobacco, or because of poor nutrition during gestation, infancy or childhood.

Rollins (1996) provides an example of how the environment can modify genetic predispositions in positive directions. A child who has inherited a recessive gene for PKU (phenylpyruvic amentia) is at risk for retardation and an abnormally small head. However, because the enzyme that causes PKU can be detected at birth through a urine test, its biological pathway can be interrupted through close adherence to a prescribed diet. In a supportive environment, the child is able to overcome its genetic predisposition, and to develop normal intelligence and head size.

The well-established link between testosterone and dominance and aggression provides a gender-related example of our brain's responsiveness to the environment. Although it is commonly assumed that observed gender differences in dominance and aggression are explained by genetically-based differences in testosterone levels, this relationship is also subject to social influences. For example, dominance and defeating behavior has been shown to boost testosterone levels in human males (Gladue, Boechler, & McCaul, 1989). Given that our society heavily socializes males to compete and win, the male gender role may be influencing male biology in potentially destructive ways. On a more optimistic note, however, were we to eliminate aggression and competition as core components of the male gender script, their brain chemistry would be less likely to facilitate these behaviors.

Reciprocal Influences

As demonstrated above, our social environments—which determine the nature of our experiences—can exert powerful influences on our biology (genes, hormones, brain chemistry, structure and organization). However, as several theorists point out (Angiers, 1999; Bem, 1993; Fausto-Sterling, 1985; Halpern, 1997; Hubbard, 1994; and Rollins, 1996) there is no linear (one-way) relationship between our social environments and our biology. Instead, our experiences can alter our biology, and our biology can alter our experiences. The relationships are circular, not linear. For example, in part, we select and create our own environments based on proclivities that are biologically influenced. At the same time, our environments shape our proclivities. Therefore, we are simultaneously creating our experiences and being created by them. To illustrate, an infant born with an easy temperament tends to draw people towards her. Thus, she constructs for herself a responsive social environment (biology shapes environment). In turn, this responsive environment enhances the initial sociability of the infant (environment shapes biology). Our behaviors and abilities, therefore, are the result of the joint action of genetic blueprints and life experiences (Halpern, 1997). The nature-nurture dichotomy is meaningless within this dynamic psychobiosocial model of behavior. According to Halpern (1997, pg. 1097), nature and nurture "are as inseparable as conjoined twins who share a common heart."

From a dialectical perspective, it is also meaningless to attempt to determine the relative contributions of biology and environment to gender-related differences in behaviors and abilities. Like differences in temperament, gender-related differences result from the simultaneous influences of biological and social processes. Halpern (1997) illustrates this well from the perspective of cognitive psychology. According to her, learning is both a biological and a social event. This means that individuals are biologically predisposed to learn some skills more easily than others. It also means that social processes influence whether or not one's biological potential is realized. For example, even though several stereotypes about gender differences in skills are supported by research data (e.g., some forms of visual-spatial skills favor males), because individuals learn and frequently internalize these stereotypes, they may unconsciously select experiences that increase these gender differences. Using the example of visual-spatial skills, females may avoid opportunities to develop the skill, while males may seek out such opportunities. Several psychological variables, such as motivation to learn and expectations for success may also be affected by these stereotypes. Thus, beliefs about gender differences can have a powerful impact on cognitive development (and on physical, emotional and social development).

Given these simultaneous influences, it is impossible to sort out the biological and social components that create the observed gender difference in visual-spatial skill (or in any other skill, behavior, attitude or emotion). Nevertheless, since we know that experiences can change biology, identification of the environmental factors that best develop this skill becomes essential. There is abundant research demonstrating that training in spatial tasks improves performance, yet spatial reasoning is rarely taught in schools (Halpern, 1997). This may cause girls, in particular, to fall short of their biological potential for this skill. On the other hand, reading comprehension and writing—tasks on which females obtain higher average scores (Halpern, 1997)—receive a heavy emphasis in school, providing both sexes the opportunity to maximize their biological potential.

Hubbard (1990) provides us with another example of the simultaneous influence of biology and society in shaping gender. This example powerfully challenges the popular "male as naturally strong; female as naturally fragile" stereotype.

> If a society puts half its children into short skirts and warns them not to move in ways that reveal their panties, while putting the other half into jeans and overalls and encouraging them to climb trees, play ball, and participate in other vigorous outdoor games; if later, during adolescence, the children who have been wearing trousers are urged to "eat like growing boys," while the children in skirts are warned to watch their weight and not get too fat; if the half in jeans runs around in sneakers or boots, while the half in skirts totters about on spike heels, then these two groups of people will be biologically as well as socially different. Their muscles will be different, as will their reflexes, posture, arms, legs and feet, hand-eye coordination, and so on (pp 115–116).

If we create such distinct environments for our children, where is the logic in genetic explanations for male strength and female fragility, or for any other gender-related difference? As Hubbard (1990, pg. 116) argues, "We cannot sort nature from nurture when we confront group differences in societies in which people from different races, classes, and sexes do not have equal access to resources and power, and therefore live in different environments." According to her, even where biologically-based *average* differences between men and women exist, they are always interwoven with differences in social experiences from which they are impossible to separate.

Because of the dynamic relationship between biological processes and social experiences, gender differences and similarities often shift over time and from one culture to another. For example, as more and more women are gaining economic and social power in industrialized Western societies, earlier notions of innate female domesticity, nurturance and passivity are undergoing serious challenges. Evidence for cross-cultural differences in emotional expressiveness provides another example of the instability of gender-related differences and similarities. In Western cultures, women are considered the emotional sex. However, in many Mid-Eastern and South American cultures, men are expected to be at least as emotionally expressive as women. And, many Asian cultures discourage the open display of emotion in both sexes (Wade & Tavris, 1994).

Conclusion

In presenting a dialectical model of gender, we have argued that all abilities, behaviors, emotions and attitudes are the result of interlocking biological and social events. We have also argued that humans help to create the social environments that shape them. This has implications for our biology and in turn for our subsequent experiences. It is an ongoing cycle. In reality, gender-related differences in behaviors, abilities, emotions, and attitudes do exist, and many of these differences have a biological component. These differences are not fixed, however. In fact, our brains remain flexible throughout our lifetimes in response to all kinds of environmental events and experiences. The highly malleable (adaptable) human brain is our greatest source of hope for creating the opportunities for both sexes to develop their full emotional, social and intellectual potential, and for replacing a male dominated society with one where females and males experience social and economic equality. In pursuit of this vision, we must critically evaluate every media and scientific report concerning gender differences in behaviors—always mindful of all possible interlocking biological and social pieces of the complex puzzle we call gender.

References

Angier, N. (1999). *Woman: An Intimate Geography.* New York: Houghton Mifflin Company.

Bem, S. L. (1993). *Readings in the Psychology of Women: Dimensions of the Female Experience.* Boston: Allyn and Bacon.

Buss, D. M. (1995). Evolutionary psychology: A new paradigm for psychological science. *Psychological Inquiry, 6,* 1–30.

Collaer, M. L., & Hines, M. (1995). Human behavioral sex differences: A role for gonadal hormones during early development? *Psychological Bulletin, 118*(1), 55–107.

Eagly, A. H., & Wood, W. (1999). The origins of sex differences in human behavior: Evolved dispositions versus social roles. *American Psychologist, 54*(6), 408–423.

Fausto-Sterling, A. (1985). *Myths of Gender: Biological Theories About Women and Men.* New York: Basic Books.

Gladue, B. A., Boechler, M., & McCaul, K. D. (1989). Hormonal responses to competition in human males. *Aggressive Behavior, 15,* 409–422.

Halpern, D. F. (1997). Sex differences in intelligence: Implications for education. *American Psychologist, 52,* 1091–1102.

Hubbard, R. (1990). *The Politics of Women's Biology.* Rutgers, NJ: Rutgers University Press.

Hubbard, R. (1994). Race and sex as biological categories. In E. Tobach & B. Rosoff, Eds. *Challenging Racism and Sexism: Alternatives to Genetic Explanations.* New York: The Feminist Press at The City University of New York.

Rollins, J. H. (1996). *Women's Minds, Women's Bodies: The Psychology of Women in a Biosocial Context.* Upper Saddle River, NJ: Prentice Hall.

Wade, C., & Tavris, C. (1994). The longest war: gender and culture. In W. J. Lonners & R. S. Malpars, Eds., *Psychology and Culture,* Boston: Allyn & Bacon.

*Chapter 1: Putting It All Together*_____

1. Why might gender researchers be motivated to ignore biology when exploring the origins of gender differences in behaviors, abilities, attitudes, and emotions?
2. Is the dialectical model of gender a tool for advancing the status of women? Explain your answer.
3. What is meant by the concept "reciprocal influences" in the dialectical model of gender? Include an example with your explanation.

2

Gender in the Context of Power Relations

To have power is to have the capacity to make an impact or to have an effect (Lips, this chapter). From early childhood, some groups (particularly white, economically privileged males) receive strong cultural messages of their power while others receive consistent messages of their relative lack of power, or even powerlessness (for example, poor women of color). These messages are often internalized and can have a profound effect on feelings, behaviors and abilities. The first reading discusses the effects of the cultural construction of female powerlessness on the psychology of girls and women, and the contrasting effects of lessons in mastery for the psychology of boys and men. The second reading sensitizes readers to the struggles of Puerto Rican males in the US as they, too, deal with issues of power and powerlessness. That is, they must attempt to reconcile their traditional patriarchal gender-role identity with the conflicting gender role norms of the US mainland. Furthermore, this struggle occurs within a context of social and economic discrimination, or a loss in status and power. Puerto Rican conceptions of masculinity (particularly machismo) are disparaged in the dominant culture, and Puerto Rican males are often denied access to economic opportunities that would allow them to fulfill a central aspect of their gender identity—as provider. These experiences can profoundly affect their ability to adapt constructively to US mainland culture.

3

Female Powerlessness: Still a Case of "Cultural Preparedness"?

Hilary M. Lips

According to Lips, because girls and women have low power in society relative to boys and men, they are at high risk for "clipped wings" and consequently, for internalized powerlessness. That is, they tend to accept the cultural message that a powerless stance is often the best strategy for females **(gender role effects).** This "cultural preparedness for powerlessness" involves early and strong messages about the limited circumstances in which girls can take charge of a situation. The message is delivered with such consistency that girls and women actually become increasingly prepared to give up their power in any new situation. Lips eloquently refers to this training as a "well-nurtured habit of silence and self-doubt" and "an abiding path of acquiescence." To support her analysis, she reviews research that reveals that girls are socialized early in life to accept powerlessness in two major areas: mastery over tasks and influence over other people. Males, on the other hand, are socialized to expect power in these two

areas. These early and continuous messages about which sex is entitled to power are transmitted by parents, schools and peers. However, Lips claims that this gender difference in preparedness for power—though widely supported—is not inevitable. The many small and large ways that girls and women resist wing-clipping for themselves, and for their daughters, set in motion the possibility of far-reaching change.

Questions to Consider:

1. According to Lips, how does the school environment prepare girls for powerlessness? How might schools be changed to make them places where both boys and girls become powerful?
2. What is meant by the phrase "girls are encouraged to develop roots; boys are encouraged to develop wings?" According to Lips, how do parents en-

Revised and updated by the author. An earlier version of this article appeared in H. L. Radke, H. J. Stam, eds., *Power/Gender: Social Relations in Theory and Practice*, 1994. Reprinted by permission of Sage Publications, Ltd.

courage these different paths for females and males? Which have you been encouraged to develop—roots or wings? Explain.

3. What are some implications of Lips' analysis of gender and power for the wings of poor women and women of color?

4. In the last paragraph, Lips claims that "females use their own strength and the support of others to refuse—in small or large ways—to accept a powerless state." If you are female, give at least two examples of how you have refused (or could refuse) to be powerless. If you are male, give at least two examples of how you have supported (or could support) the empowerment of a female.

5. Are there ways that Lips' analysis can be applied to men who have low power because of their racial, ethnic or economic background? Explain.

For many years, I have been engaged in two projects that, though separate, continually produce overlapping themes. One is a study of the academic choices young women and men make with respect to mathematics and science (Lips, 1989; 1992; 1993; 1995); the other is an examination of issues surrounding gender and power (Lips, 1991; 1998; 2000; In press, a).

Though I did not particularly look for it, the theme of power and powerlessness often echoes through the data I gathered on the academic choices and career plans made by college students. With regard to mathematics, the physical sciences and, especially, engineering, female students often show a lack of confidence in their ability that belies strong past performance—equal to or exceeding that of their male peers. More generally, a surprising number of graduating female students, when asked to list their ca-

reer goals, leave the space for their answer blank—as if the space itself represents the horizon they see. I have been struck by the repeated observation that, in an era when there is an abundance of talk about choices for women, women of college age often do *not* take control of their lives, avoid making strong choices, and project a stunning lack of security in their own abilities.

It appears that girls and women are at high risk, first as targets of a 'wisdom' that clips their wings, and then, eventually, as recipients of a strong message that a powerless stance works best for them in many situations. This is not a new insight. What is lacking, however, is an analysis of the means whereby this clipping, even crippling, is actualized: the mechanisms through which that message is conveyed and incorporated in ways to be and, especially, ways not to be. For many of us, the larger factors supporting this view are obvious: sex discrimination, other forms of coercion at work, at school, and at home, and the ever-present threat and reality of violence against women. What is not so obvious, however, are numerous socialization practices that enhance girls' sense of powerlessness, and the ongoing patterns of social control in ordinary interaction made possible by these practices. Thus, the focus here is on the manner in which these routine practices and controls underlie the more obvious factors and prime or prepare girls and women to accept powerlessness.

An examination of the research on social interactions reveals a theme that I have labeled 'cultural preparedness for powerlessness'. It is as if girls are taught from the start that they can exert control over a situation only in certain limited circumstances. The message is so consistent that girls and women become increasingly *ready* to learn the lesson of powerlessness in any new situation. The effect is analogous to what psychologists have labeled 'biological preparedness'—a biologically based readiness to learn particular behaviors or associations (for example, Diener et al., 1975). In a similar fashion, as my reading of the research on social interaction suggests, early and continuing socialization 'primes' girls and women to accept powerlessness.

A generally accepted definition of power, in psychology, is the capacity to have an impact or produce an effect. Research has accumulated showing that girls receive strong and consistent indications of their powerlessness in two major areas of power: mastery over tasks and influence over people.

Childhood Socialization: Mastery vs Helplessness

Much of the research evidence suggests that, from childhood onward, females, in contrast to males, are taught that their actions frequently do not make a difference. Jeanne Block (1984), summarizing a lifetime of longitudinal research into the socialization of girls and boys, characterized the difference thus: girls, she said, were encouraged to develop *roots*, boys were taught to develop *wings*. Girls, in other words, were given few chances to master the environment, and their socialization tended toward "fostering proximity, discouraging independent problem solving by premature or excessive interventions, restricting exploration, and discouraging active play" (Block, 1984: 111). Boys, on the other hand, were encouraged to "develop a premise system that presumes or anticipates mastery, efficacy, and instrumental competence" (1984: 131). Other research supports Block's claim: parents and teachers, often unwittingly, are teaching girls not to try things (because their efforts either do not make any differ-

ence or may result in failure or danger) and not to speak (because no one will pay serious attention to them). Boys, by contrast, are being taught that their outcomes depend on their own efforts and that their concerns are taken seriously by adults.

Parents

While parents do encourage their female and male children to engage in sex-typed activities, they do not treat their sons and daughters as differently, at least during childhood, as gender norms might suggest (Crouter, Manke, & McHale, 1995; Lytton and Romney, 1991). However, small differences in early childhood treatment of girls and boys may lay the groundwork for the construction of far larger gender differences. The projection of small early differences in treatment to equally small later consequences implies a perhaps unjustified assumption of linearity in the relationship between socialization and outcomes. With the emergence of chaos theory and non-linear modelling, evidence has emerged, within psychology as in other social sciences, that linear relationships between behavioral antecedents and consequences may be the exception rather than the rule (for example, Chen, 1988; Grebogi et al., 1987; Guastello, 1988; Mende et al., 1990; Richards, 1990; Sterman, 1988). Seen within the framework of non-linear dynamics and catastrophe theory, the presence of small, seemingly trivial differences in the initial positions and development of two groups (in this case, females and males) does not imply continued similarity of paths in later stages of development. Thus, a mild or modest differential emphasis on mastery may foster subsequent gender divergences totally disproportionate to initial treatment differences.

Studies of parent-child conversations show consistently that parents, particularly mothers, emphasize emotions more and are more elaborative when talking to their daughters than to their sons (Eisenberg, 1999; Eisenmann, 1997; Fivush, 1993; Fivush, Brotman, Buckner, & Goodman, 2000). It appears that parents are preparing their daughters more than their sons to be sensitive to their own feelings and to those of others, to place a higher priority on negotiating and understanding relationships than on simply getting what they want without regard to the feelings of others. An interesting illustration of this phenomenon can be found in a study by Barbara Eisenmann (1997), who analyzed the mother-child conversations in which mothers told children of an imminent temporary separation. Mothers tended to pre-announce the separation to daughters and to discuss it cooperatively with them until reaching some kind of understanding and tacit agreement. Mothers of sons were less likely to prepare their children for their departure, apparently because they believed their sons would resist and that it would not be possible to reach an agreement through joint discussion. These mothers were demonstrating a *bilateral* influence strategy with their daughters: one in which the would-be influencer engages with the influence target. They were using a *unilateral* strategy: one in which the would-be influencer does not engage the target but simply takes action, with their sons. Years ago, Toni Falbo and Anne Peplau (1980) found that unilateral influence strategies tended to be used, in couples, by influencers who saw themselves as having less power in the relationship than their partner. If such a pattern can be generalized to mother-child pairs, mothers are operating as if they have less power with respect to their sons than their

daughters—and perhaps communicating this very message to their children.

Furthermore, in conversations about emotions, parents are more likely to discuss sadness with girls than with boys (Fivush et al., 2000). This may serve the important function of teaching girls how to deal with sadness. However, it may also teach girls more than boys to ruminate on sadness, a practice that has been linked to depression (Nolen-Hoeksema, 1987). Beginning in adolescence, girls and women are significantly more likely than boys and men to be depressed, and depression is correlated with feminine role identification (Wichtrøm, 1999). Feelings of depression are antithetical to feelings of power.

Parental behavior shows a relationship to the development of mastery, and that relationship may differ for female and male children (Yarrow et al., 1984). From the time when parents describe newborn infant daughters as 'softer' and 'finer' than their newborn infant sons, who are comparable in size and strength (Rubin et al., 1974), to the times when young boys are given toys that require skill and perseverance to assemble and use while girls are given dolls (Miller, 1987; Rheingold & Cook, 1975), the message sent by parents to their children is that boys can make things happen and can take care of themselves, while girls cannot or should not. Masculine-stereotyped forms of play train boys in instrumental and dominance-oriented behaviors; feminine-stereotyped play trains girls to be cooperative, accommodating, and supportive (Leaper, 2000). This message is underlined in early adolescence when girls' dating behavior is watched and circumscribed while that of boys is granted more latitude (Katz, 1986).

Studies of parent-child interactions show quite consistently that parents are more likely to encourage dependency in daughters than in sons (Lytton and Romney, 1991). In one study (Frankel and Rollins, 1983), parents worked with their 6-year-old children on jigsaw puzzle and memory tasks. The parents of sons and daughters used different strategies: parents of sons were more likely to suggest general problem-solving strategies and let the boy figure out how to apply them to the task at hand, while parents of girls were more likely to suggest specific solutions rather than waiting for their daughters to work out the solutions themselves. With a daughter, parents were more likely to work cooperatively; with a son, they were more likely to remain physically uninvolved, but to praise him for good performance and scold him for inattention. The parents in this study offer an example of the different messages about mastery that are communicated to girls and boys: it is communicated more strongly to the sons than to the daughters that it is important for them to learn to solve this problem and others like it—and that they do it as far as possible on their own.

The pattern described here may emerge very early. A study of parents attempting to teach their 8-month-old infants to put a small cube into a cup showed differences among the behaviors they directed at females and males (Brachfield-Child et al., 1988). Parents were more directive of their female than their male infants. They aimed more utterances, particularly negative, imperative and exhortative utterances, at girls than boys. Another study, focusing on parents' involvement in communication between their children, also showed parents of very young children being more directive of daughters than sons. Parents made more utterances encouraging girls than boys to interact with a sibling (Austin, Summers and Leffler, 1987). In this study, which in-

cluded pairs of siblings aged 18–26 months and 4–6 weeks, fathers were especially active in directing the interactions between their children, particularly the interactions involving girls. Other studies have shown that fathers are less compliant toward their preschool daughters than sons, that mothers try to control the behavior of young daughters more than that of sons, and that fathers may be more willing to listen to sons than to daughters (Maccoby, 1998).

Although parents in various cultural groups differ in the rules they attach to gender, it is not unusual to find that parents, particularly fathers, pay more attention to boys than to girls, and emphasize cooperation and nurturance more for girls and achievement and autonomy more for boys. For example, Phyllis Bronstein (1984) showed, in a study of Mexican families, that when interacting with their school-aged children, fathers listened more to boys than to girls and were more likely to show boys than girls how to do things. These fathers treated their daughters especially gently, but they seldom gave them their full attention and were quick to impose opinions on them. These fathers too were communicating a message of mastery to boys and helplessness to girls: what boys have to say is more important than what girls have to say, and boys are more capable than girls of learning new skills.

This conclusion is reinforced by findings that parents react to the achievements of their daughters and sons differently. For example, they tend to credit their sons' success at mathematics more to talent and their daughters' success more to effort (Yee and Eccles, 1988). A longitudinal study linking the influence of mothers to academic expectations of young children illustrates that, particularly in middle-class families, mothers may unwittingly produce gender differences in their children's expectations for success (Baker and Entwisle, 1987). The effects of mothers' expectations are generally positive for boys and tend to favor boys over girls in arithmetic and in beginning reading. It appears that mothers, through their day to day interactions with young children, subtly support the creation of a gender-differentiated academic self-concept by giving girls and boys different messages about the perceptions and expectations they should have of themselves. This process, note the researchers, is distinct from the abstract opinions mothers have about gender, which tend to be egalitarian.

Parents, through their encouragement of sex-typed activities, may encourage girls less than boys toward the sense of power that accompanies physical self-efficacy. Girls learn that they are weaker than boys, that they cannot depend on their bodies for certain strength-related tasks. They are less likely than boys to be steered towards sports, and such early socialization messages have an impact. Girls who play with "masculine" toys or games are more likely than their counterparts to later become college athletes (Giuliano, Popp, & Knight, 2000), but cross-national research shows that boys are more likely than girls to endorse sports activities as possible for themselves (Gibbons, Lynn, & Stiles, 1997). These messages to girls continue despite research suggesting that some of the female-male strength disparity that appears in adolescence is due to a lack of sufficient muscle use by females (O'Hagan, Sale, McDougall, & Garner, 1995). When girls do participate in strength or self-defense training, they show gains in self-efficacy that generalize beyond confidence in physical abilities to a sense of general life effectiveness (Holloway et al., 1988; Miller & Levy, 1996; Vaselakos, 1999).

Especially as they approach adolescence, girls may be taught by parents to

think of their bodies as sources of vulnerability and danger. Concerns about sexual activity and pregnancy often cause parents to place new restrictions on girls at adolescence, so that growing up is associated with a feeling of decreasing, rather than enhanced, freedom (Golub, 1983; Katz, 1986). Moreover, for the significant minority of girls who are victims of childhood sexual abuse by an adult family member, sexuality as a source of vulnerability takes on a sinister aspect. Researchers estimate that at least 20% of American girls experience some form of sexual abuse as children; one-third to one-half of the perpetrators of this abuse are family members (Finkelhor, 1994). For these girls, a long-term outcome is a persistent sense of powerlessness (Briere and Runtz, 1986; Edwards and Donaldson, 1989; Lowery, 1987).

Finally, parents may push daughters toward powerlessness by putting direct pressure on adolescent females to conform to gender-related expectations and to emphasize social relationships at the expense of academic achievements (Updegraff, McHale, & Crouter, 1994). Such pressure is less likely to come from parents with higher levels of education; in particular, having a highly educated father is associated with less adherence by adolescent girls to rigidly stereotypical femininity (Deslandes, Bouchard, & St-Amant, 1998).

Teachers

The gender-differentiated patterns of emphasis on mastery initiated by parents may be enhanced by teachers and school environments. Girls get higher grades in school than boys but show less confidence than boys in their scholastic abilities (Kimball, 1989). Even though girls *do* master academic tasks, often more quickly and easily than do boys, such mastery often does not translate into confidence in their own abilities. Preschool classrooms are characterized by a greater frequency of interactions between teachers and boys than between teachers and girls; one study of 2,183 such interactions found the ratio to be 60/40 (Ebbeck, 1984). Attention and feedback in classrooms from elementary school upwards are dispensed differently to girls and boys—and the differences are such as to reinforce feelings of mastery and control in boys and helplessness in girls. Teachers pay more attention to boys than girls and allow boys to talk and interrupt them more than they do girls (Sadker and Sadker, 1985; Serbin and O'Leary, 1975). This pattern ensures that more time will be spent on boys' than on girls' questions and that children will learn that male concerns take first priority. Apparently heeding this message, girls ask fewer questions than boys (Pearson & West, 1991).

Thus, though sharing instructional situations, girls and boys may nevertheless encounter very different educational experiences. For example, studies of elementary and secondary school mathematics classes show that boys receive a greater share of the teachers' attention in class than do girls, are more active than girls in providing answers, have more non-academic conversational contact with teachers and may be more likely to be considered the best, or as possessing high potential (Becker, 1981; BenTsvi-Mayer et al., 1989; Brophy, 1985; Koeler, 1986; Marshall and Smith, 1987). When teachers consciously try to direct equal amounts of attention to the boys and girls in their classrooms, they may elicit outraged reactions from boys, who are so used to getting most of the attention that they experience "equal attention" as less than their share (Orenstein, 1994).

These patterns are not limited to white, middle-class students. A pair of studies by Irvine (1985, 1986) show that, in the first two grades of elementary school, European American girls received less total communication from teachers than did European American boys or African American children of either gender. However, as the African American girls moved from lower to upper elementary school grades, there was a significant decline in total amount of teacher feedback, the amount of positive feedback, and the number of opportunities they received to respond in class, culminating in a situation where they were as inconspicious to the teachers as the European American girls. As African American girls progress through school, they apparently receive less and less attention from their teachers (Nelson-LeGall, 1990). African-American girls seem to enter the school system with more self-confidence, perhaps drawn from their families and communities, than do their European American counterparts. However, once in the school system, they are the targets of attempts to mold them into the 'quiet girl' ideal favoured by white, middle-class culture. These attempts may succeed less well with African-American girls than with their European American counterparts, perhaps because they get fewer rewards for being quiet and compliant, and feel an urgent necessity to speak up (Way, 1995). A survey of self-esteem among adolescent girls showed that African-American girls maintained their self-esteem at higher levels during the transition to adolescence than did European American or Hispanic girls (AAUW, 1991); however, this may be because they manage to disidentify with their school performance (Robinson & Ward, 1991).

These patterns are not limited to elementary school. Even at the college level, the classroom atmosphere and interactions may be less comfortable in general for females than males (Constantinople et al., 1988; Crawford and MacLeod, 1990; Schnellman and Gibbons, 1984).

Research by Carol Dweck and her colleagues (Dweck et al., 1978; Dweck and Leggett, 1988; Elliot and Dweck, 1988) shows that elementary school classrooms may introduce gender differences in the contingencies of performance feedback—with mastery orientations being more strongly encouraged for boys than for girls. The differences in feedback take three forms: the amount and diffuseness of feedback, the type of response on which the feedback is contingent, and the type of attribution for performance that is delivered along with the feedback.

Boys receive more negative classroom feedback than do girls, and that negative feedback is also more diffuse (that is, not focused narrowly on whether the answer is correct, but also on broader issues such as neatness, boisterousness, etc.). Girls, by contrast, get more, and more diffuse, *positive* feedback than do boys. When girls get negative feedback it is usually in response to a wrong answer; when they get positive feedback it may often be for behaving well, looking nice, handing in something that is neat and attractive. By contrast, when boys get negative feedback it is as likely to be for sloppiness, inattention, or disruptive behavior as for poor performance; when they get positive feedback, it is usually for good intellectual performance. Boys, under a steady stream of negative feedback, get used to criticism and learn not to be crushed by it. Girls, for whom negative feedback is rare, take that negative feedback to heart and maintain a sensitivity to failure.

Contributing to the tendency for girls and boys to respond differently to feedback from teachers are the explicit attributions teachers make when delivering feedback. For boys, negative feedback is often accompanied by an attribution to lack of effort or motivation. For girls, there is often no such attribution, since teachers apparently see girls as motivated and diligent. Negative feedback is often delivered to girls with *no* accompanying attribution, leaving them to infer that they are simply not very good at the task. Positive feedback may be delivered with an ability attribution, such as "you're so smart"—but while this type of feedback may build temporary confidence, it can backfire, as discussed below.

According to Dweck (1999), the end result of these different patterns of feedback is that girls and boys learn to make different causal attributions for success and failure. Boys are more likely than girls to learn that failure means that they are just not trying hard enough. Boys learn to think of their skills as improvable and to focus on that possibility of improvement as a goal. They learn, in other words, that their efforts make a difference, that, by trying harder, they can master a difficult situation. Girls, particularly high-achieving girls, are more likely than boys to learn that success means the task was easy for them because they are smart, or that the teacher likes them. Girls learn to adopt what Dweck (1999) calls an *entity approach to ability:* the idea that each individual has a fixed amount of ability, which is revealed by her performance. Thus, they feel that it is important to demonstrate their ability by performing well. They learn to avoid challenging, difficult tasks unless they are extremely confident of success, because failure threatens their own and others' opinions of their ability. Failure may, in fact, reveal that they are "not smart" after all.

Reinforcing the conclusions reached by Dweck and her colleagues are a variety of other findings. For example, teachers' judgment of girls' intellectual competence is predicted by girls' compliance to the teacher; however, teacher ratings of boys' competence is unrelated to compliance (Gold et al., 1987). Even in the first grade, girls and boys indicate that they have learned different things about what is important in school: boys' academic self-concept includes a strong focus on being able to learn quickly; girls are focused on the importance of obeying rules a'nd being honest (Entwisle, et al., 1987). Such teacher influences may provide some of the underpinnings for the frequently reported observation that girls enter many achievement situations with lower expectations of success than do boys (Crandall, 1969; Parsons and Ruble, 1977).

The result of girls' socialization toward the entity approach to ability may be a stronger predisposing tendency for females to seek favorable judgements of their competence—and avoid negative judgements—by avoiding the risks associated with publicly trying to master difficult material. Indeed, one study suggests that by the time students are in college, females and males show differences in their approach to learning that appear to reflect Dweck's predictions. Female college students report an emphasis on demonstrating that they knew the material; male students focus on the challenge of learning and emphasize feedback and exchange with the instructor (Magolda, 1990).

Such differential beliefs and orientations may have no obvious consequence in a number of classroom settings. However, they may cause girls and young women to be more vulnerable to uncertainty and failure when specific competencies are challenged and confused. In intellectual achievement situations fostering confusion and uncertainty about success, girls' self-views of abilities suffer and confidence falls; difficulty and confusion are interpreted as failures documenting an inadequate and unchangeable ability (Dweck, et al., 1980). When vulnerable individuals with performance-oriented achievement goals lose confidence in their level of ability, the result is a pattern of helplessness (Dweck and Leggett, 1988; Dweck and Licht, 1980).

Given these predisposing differences in implicit ability beliefs and motivational goals, boys may tend to display more confidence than girls in academic areas where opportunities for success seems most uncertain (Dweck and Licht, 1980). Such expected differences in confidence are in agreement with earlier work showing that girls' lower confidence is most likely to emerge on tasks that are unfamiliar, for which no clear feedback has been given about previous performance (Lenny, 1977), and for which success is very uncertain (Licht et al., 1989). Congruent with the evidence concerning confidence are findings such as those by Tapasak (1990): by the eighth grade, females with mathematics averages equivalent or better than males tended to underestimate their own future performance, while males tended to overestimate theirs. Significantly more females than males exhibited a negative expectancy-attribution pattern: they attributed success in mathematics to variable factors and failure to stable factors, and were less likely than males to persist at tasks and courses in mathematics (Tapasak, 1990). As with many other studies (for example, Dweck and Leggett, 1988; Licht et al., 1989), the Tapasak study demonstrates that reported gender differences in implicit views and beliefs about ability are not merely gender differences in self-presentation style. Females and males differ not only in their self-reports, and self-presentations, but also in their behavior with respect to the achievement areas in question.

As students progress from elementary school, they face an increasingly challenging and difficult instructional environment (Eccles et al., 1989). This occurs at a time when classroom environments and student-teacher relationships are salient and important to student achievement. With transfer to middle school, relative performance comparisons and self-assessments of ability intensify, effort and ability begin to be differentiated, and grades tend to be lower (Feldaufer et al., 1988). For mastery-oriented persons, the encounter with novel and confusing material in this less supportive, more uncertain climate would still remain a challenge to seek and overcome; for performance-oriented persons, it would represent an increasing confusion and threat to avoid. Such situational increases in the uncertainty of success in areas such as mathematics and the physical sciences, coupled with differences in predisposing beliefs and goals may explain girls' and young women's reluctance (relative to males') to continue taking mathematics courses, even when they have done well in the past (Dweck, 1986).

Regardless of talent, as challenges and obstacles increase from late elementary school to college, females seem likely to receive less parental and teacher encouragement than males. As early as elementary school, female students, more than males, have been encouraged to develop and maintain implicit beliefs and motivational orientations that allow failures to have a detrimental effect on their self-perceived abilities. In contrast, more male students than females have been encouraged to develop implicit dispositions and mastery orientations that channel failures into opportunities for learning and growth. Moreover, this greater female vulnerability or sensitivity to failure will be most apparent in those novel situations in which success is uncertain and in which they are exposed to the possibility of performance

assessments and ability attributions for their outcomes. From middle school to university, mathematics and related subjects are characterized by ever new and difficult material, a shrinking ratio of females to males, and an increasing emphasis on ability. When faced with such situations, females are apparently more likely than males to expect less success, to avoid the situation if possible, and persevere less strongly in the face of difficulties. Most disturbingly, Dweck's analysis suggests that such motivational factors are strongest, and most maladaptive, for the brightest girls—those who have had a string of early and consistent successes. Dweck (1999) argues that, to counteract such outcomes, "an emphasis on challenge, effort, and strategy is absolutely essential for girls. . . . They should be taught that challenges are exciting and should be praised for taking on challenges and sticking with them. They must learn that the hallmark of intelligence is not immediate perfection, but rather the habit of embracing new tasks that stretch your skills and build your knowledge." (p. 125).

The school environment may provide females with socialization toward powerlessness not only through messages about academic success and failure, but also through messages about relationships and sexuality. One survey of more than 1,000 university science students showed that 17 per cent of the females and 2 per cent of the males reported that they had been sexually harassed by an instructor (McCormack, 1985). Other studies have found similarly high percentages of female harassment victims among college students (Adams et al., 1983; Bailey and Richards, 1985), and a *Seventeen* magazine survey that prompted responses from 4200 young women in North America revealed that 39% said they experienced sexual harassment *every day* in school (Mann, 1993). When the harassers are peers, teachers often stand by and do nothing (Stein, 1995), but even more un-nerving may be the situations where the harassment is carried out *by* teachers. A young woman being sexually harassed by her teacher or professor is made to feel powerless in several ways; she feels that she has little control over the relationship; she feels that her achievement-oriented behaviors will make little or no difference to the academic outcomes that are controlled by the harasser; she is aware that she is not being taken seriously as a whole person, but is being related to mainly in terms of her sexuality. Since sexual harassment of female students is not a rare event, but rather seems to affect directly a significant proportion of female high school and college students (and indirectly, through observation and discussion, many more), it must be regarded as part of the process through which females absorb the message of powerlessness in school situations.

Peers

What parents, teachers, and school systems illustrate by example and leadership, children are quick to model and reproduce. Children and adolescents apparently collude with adults in the socialization of females and males into different roles and styles when it comes to power. Clearly there are strong, cognitive categorizing and social identity forces at work: children use the cultural information that surrounds them to construct gender stereotypes (Maccoby, 1998), and also to enforce them (Fagot, 1984; Harris, 1995). Messages about appropriate behavior for males and females are absorbed from parents, teachers and other socializing agents, encoded and then reenacted in a multitude of contexts.

Children join actively in the process of socializing one another into gender-appropriate patterns of mastery and influence. Even among toddlers, girls paired off with male playmates behave more passively than boys or than girls paired with other girls (Jacklin and Maccoby, 1978). As preschoolers, boys make more attempts than girls to influence their peers—mainly by making direct requests and giving orders (Serbin et al., 1982). As boys move from the ages of 3 to 5 years, they become increasingly likely to use direct modes of influence; orders ("give me that"), announcements ("you have to give me that") or assigning roles ("pretend you're the doctor"). During the same time period, girls are becoming more likely to use *indirect* influence styles: implying rather than clearly stating the request ("I need that toy"), or bracketing requests in polite, deferential phrases ("May I please have that toy?"). Between the ages of 3 and 5, boys become increasingly impervious to influence attempts by their peers, while girls' responsiveness to influence remains stable. It is possible that boys' decreasing responsiveness is related to the high number of influence attempts directed at them by parents and teachers.

When girls do use direct influence strategies, they are more effective with other girls than boys. This experience, researchers suggest, helps to perpetuate both the high levels of same-gender play found in pre-school and elementary school classrooms and the development of verbal influence styles that are increasingly gender-differentiated (Maccoby, 1998; Powlishta and Maccoby, 1990). These researchers note that boys, because of their higher use of power assertion and physical power, tend to get more than their share of a scarce resource in a mixed-gender, competitive situation. This disparity is attenuated in the presence of adults, because boys do not try so hard to dominate girls when adults are present. It appears that girls learn early that they are ineffective influencers with respect to boys and that they retreat to the influence styles (indirect, polite) and contexts (other females, adults) that *are* effective for them.

For girls who do not retreat into accepted styles, there may be problems ahead. One study of first and second graders suggests that reactions to power holders may differ in female and male groups. Boys who were the most dominant members of their groups tended to be liked and accepted by their same-gender peers; dominant girls, on the other hand, were targets of dislike and rejection by other group members (Jones, 1983). Girls in elementary school report more positive attitudes toward girls who act in communal, connection-oriented ways than toward girls who behave in agentic, status-oriented ways, and say that they would encourage other girls to use communal rather than agentic styles (Hibbard & Buhrmester, 1998). Whereas aggressive male adolescents are rated by their peers as sociable, aggressive females are not; to be described as sociable by her peers, a female adolescent must display facilitative and problem-solving behavior (Hops, Alpert, & Davis, 1997). An awareness of the interpersonal dangers of abandoning the communal style apparently reverberates in young adulthood: young women in college express more worry than men do that, if they hold powerful roles, they will have difficulties with relationships (Lips, 2000; In press b).

Extensive (self-chosen) segregation between girls and boys in elementary schools provides gender-differentiated contexts for learning the processes of power and influence. Boys obtain considerable practice in interactions that are competitive and dominance-oriented (Maccoby, 1990; 1998) and they experience the shared excitement and bonding that accompanies public transgression of rules (Thorne and

Luria, 1986). Girls, on the other hand, practice interactions that are facilitative and supportive, form friendships through self-disclosure, and construct a shared identity based partly on being 'good' (Ullian, 1984). Research in both the United States and Brazil shows that female adolescents rate support from peers and siblings higher than boys do (Van Horn & Marques, 2000). These different patterns of socialization lay the groundwork for future gender differences in power when the two groups must finally work and live together as adolescents or adults. A woman, used to a facilitative style of relating, is bound, in many contexts, to find herself at a power disadvantage when interacting with a man who has been socialized toward a more dominant, competitive interaction style (Maccoby, 1998).

Children's conversations reflect and strengthen gender differences in approaches to power. Studying children from a sample of largely white, working- and middle-class families, researchers have noted that boys are more likely than girls to 'take charge' of conversations (Austin, Salehi and Leffler, 1987). In preschool, third and sixth grades, boys were more likely than girls to initiate various conversations and to use various devices, from tapping another child insistently on the arm to shouting 'Look at me', for getting attention. Girls, by contrast, were more likely than boys to try to facilitate an ongoing conversation and to use reinforcers (nodding, 'um-hm') to acknowledge a partner's speech or behavior.

Gender differences in interaction patterns are similar among African American children. A study of African American children from urban, low-income family backgrounds revealed that boys and girls differed most in their behavior when in same-gender groups. In same-gender groups, boys were more likely than girls to use controlling acts and domineering exchanges; however, both boys and girls were less likely to use such behaviors when interacting with girls (Leaper, Tenenbaum, & Shaffer, 1999). For both African American and European American boys, it appears that relationships with same-gender peers provide an important arena for the childhood socialization of dominance orientation.

Such childhood socialization has implications for later mixed-gender peer relations. Among university students, women receive more supportive responses and fewer negative responses from female friends than male friends when making decisions together (Leaper, 1998). One study that compared the social interactions of African American and European American adolescents in same-race mixed-gender groups showed a similar tendency for males to provide fewer supportive responses than females, although there was greater gender equality in the conversations of the African Americans (Filardo, 1996). In the European American groups, but not in the African American groups, a higher percentage of the girls' than of the boys' speech attempts were interrupted and never completed. Also, the tendency for males to make more influence attempts than females was found only in the European American groups. On the whole, the European American girls showed speech patterns that were more conciliatory, polite, tentative and less powerful than any of the other gender-race categories. African American girls were more assertive, and this assertiveness, rather than any accommodating behavior from African American boys, led to greater gender equality in social interactions. In fact, African American girls had to work extremely hard to have their say: African American boys had the highest percentage of speech that expressed commands or lack of consideration for the viewpoint of others than any of the four groups. In both racial groups,

girls worked harder than boys at listening to others and maintaining conversations. These patterns in childhood and adolescence are the precursors of the frequently observed patterns of greater effort at conversational maintenance by females and conversational dominance by males and among adults (for example, Spender, 1989; Tannen, 1990). Such dominance is not always limited to the conversational arena. There is evidence that men's domineering conversational behavior toward women, but not toward other men, is correlated with a personality profile labeled "hostile masculinity" and with self-reported sexual aggression against women (Malamuth & Thornhill, 1995).

Female adolescents' perceptions of opportunity for themselves is predicted by the amount of support they perceive from peers, family and teachers, whereas boys seem most sensitive to family support (Wall, Covell, & MacIntyre, 1999). The importance of peer and teacher support for education and career aspirations can backfire on girls. Female students, after being exposed for years to schooling conditions and interactions with teachers that tend to make them sensitive to negative feedback and failure, may have to face the barrage of such negative feedback from peers if they choose, in high school or university, to pursue academic goals in areas stereotyped as masculine. Up to and including the university level, male students are more likely than females to stereotype mathematics, science, engineering and computing as male domains (Hyde et al., 1990; Lips, 1989, 1992; Temple and Lips, 1989). Such findings suggest that, like their younger counterparts, women in college mathematics, computing and science classrooms may face a more negative social context in the form of peer judgements than do men. Peer reactions are likely to be especially important among college-age students because students in college have the leeway to adjust their programs of study if they sense peer disapproval.

Prepared for Powerlessness

By adolescence, females are showing a pattern of lowered self-confidence and readiness to accept the notion that they are not capable of mastering certain situations. In late adolescence, both African American and European American girls show a more external locus of control than boys (Wade, 1996). Female adolescents underrate their competence in a number of life skill areas (Lips, 1998; Poole and Evans, 1989). Female high school students rate themselves as significantly more powerless than do their male counterparts (Calabrese and Seldin, 1985/86). At the ages of 4, 9, and 14 years, boys control more decision outcomes than do girls; by the age of 14, girls are less likely than their male counterparts to perceive themselves as decision controllers (Lind and Connole, 1985). One study of young African American adolescents showed that, although females listed more successful experiences, males self-reported higher confidence (Alderman and Doverspike, 1988). A large study sponsored by the American Association of University Women documents a disturbing drop in self-esteem among girls as they move from childhood to adolescence (AAUW, 1991). At the age of 9 years, 60–70 per cent of girls and boys responded positively to questions designed to measure their confidence and self-esteem. However, among the 15-year-olds sampled, the percentage of positive responses was dramatically lower for girls (29 per cent) than for boys (46 per cent). The pattern is still apparent in college, where female students describe the holding of powerful roles

in the future as less possible for themselves and less positive than do their male counterparts (Lips, 2000).

Clearly, children are socialized into, and also construct, using the information that surrounds them, gender-differentiated perceptions of their own possibilities for power. Such socialization bears a seamless relation to what the two gender groups can expect in later life: gender-segregation into occupations in which women experience lower status and a lower sense of control than men do (Ross & Wright, 1998) and mixed-gender relationships in which, regardless of income or occupational status, women often hold less power than men simply because of their gender (Tichennor, 1999). What is being absorbed and reproduced is far less innocuous than 'pink for girls; blue for boys' or 'boys play football; girls do aerobics.' For girls, it is an abiding path of acquiescence, of relative silence in the face of uncertainty, conflict or the throes of daily testing. What is absorbed is a habit of self-doubt in the face of confusion or competition, a hesitancy that can affect a young woman's later decisions in situations ranging from speaking up with a good answer, to entering a male-dominated contest, to choosing career options, to asserting her rights strongly and publically when faced with discrimination, sexual harassment, or abuse.

In the context of current gender power relations, an implementation of alternatives to women's well-nurtured habits of silence or self-doubt is extremely difficult. Whatever the difficulties, though, this gender difference is not inevitable. If the difference in preparedness for power is fundamentally a micro-accumulation of broadly supported interaction patterns, then different patterns may be envisioned, modelled and implemented. And if non-linear dynamics are truly at play in these situations, then it is not unreasonable to expect that the un-clipped wings of a growing few can set in motion improvements in the climate for many. The changes implied by such a simple statement are far-reaching and demanding, but they begin and continue whenever women, using their own strength and the support of others, refuse, in small or large ways, to accept, for themselves or for their daughters, a silent or powerless stance.

References

Adams, J., Kottke, J., & Padgitt, J. (1983). Sexual harassment of university students, *Journal of College Student Personnel, 24*: 484–90.

Alderman, M. K., & Doverspike, J. E. (1988). Perceived competence, self- description, expectation, and successful experience differences among students in grades seven, eight, and nine, *Journal of Early Adolescence, 8(2)*: 119–31.

American Association of University Women (1991). *Shortchanging girls, shortchanging America: A call to action.* Washington, DC: Author.

Austin, A. M., Salehi, M., & Leffler, A. (1987). Gender and developmental differences in children's conversations, *Sex Roles, 16(9/10)*: 497–510.

Austin, A. M., Summers, M., & Leffler, A. (1987). Fathers' and mothers' involvement in sibling communication, *Early Childhood Research Quarterly, 2(4)*: 359–65.

Bailey, N., & Richards, M. (1985). Sexual harassment in graduate training programs in psychology, paper presented at the American Psychological Association Conference, Los Angeles.

Baker, D. P., & Entwisle, D. R. (1987). The influence of mothers on the academic expectations of young children: a longitudinal study of how gender differences arise, *Social Forces, 65(3)*: 670–94.

Becker, B. J. (1981). Differential treatment of males and females in mathematics classes, *Journal for Research in Mathematics Education, 12*: 40–53.

BenTsvi-Mayer, S., Hertz-Lazarowitz, R., & Safir, M. P. (1989). Teachers' selection of boys and girls as prominent pupils, *Sex Roles, 21*: 231–45.

Block, J. H. (1984). Psychological development of female children and adolescence, in J. H. Block, *Sex Role Identity and Ego Development.* San Francisco: Jossey Bass, pp. 126–42.

Branchfield-Child, S., Simpson, T., & Izenson, N. (1988). Mothers' and fathers' speech to infants in a teaching situation, *Infant Mental Health Journal, 9(2)*: 173–80.

Briere, J., & Runtz, M. (1986). Suicidal thoughts and behaviors in former sexual abuse victims, *Canadian Journal of Behavioral Science, 18(4)*: 413–23.

Bronstein, P. (1984). Differences in mothers' and fathers' behavior toward children: a cross-cultural comparison, *Developmental Psychology, 20(6)*: 995–1003.

Brophy, J. (1985). Interactions of male and female students with male and female teachers, in L. C. Wilkinson & C. B. Marrett (Eds), *Gender Influences in Classroom Interaction.* Orlando, Fla: Academic Press, pp. 115–42.

Calabrese, R. L., & Seldin, C. A. (1985/86). Adolescent alienation: an analysis of the female response to the secondary school environment, *High School Journal, 69(2)*: 120–5.

Chen, P. (1988). Empirical and theoretical evidence of economic chaos, *System Dynamics Review, 4*: 81–108.

Constantinople, A., Cornelius, R., & Gray, J. (1988). The chilly climate: fact or artifact? *Journal of Higher Education, 59*: 527–50.

Crandall, V. C. (1969). Sex differences in expectancy of intellectual and academic reinforcement, in C. P. Smith (Ed.), *Achievement-related Motives in Children.* New York: Russell Sage Foundation pp. 11–45.

Crawford, M., & MacLeod, M. (1990). Gender in the college classroom: An assessment of the "chilly climate" for women, *Sex Roles, 23*: 101–22.

Crouter, A. C., Manke, B. A., & McHale, S. M. (1995). The family context of gender intensification in early adolescence. *Child Development, 66(2)*, 317–329.

Deslandes, R., Bouchard, P., & St-Amant, J. (1998). Family variables as predictors of school achievement: Sex differences in Quebec adolescents. *Canadian Journal of Education, 23(4)*, 390–404.

Diener, E., Bugge, I., & Diener, C. (1975). Children's preparedness to learn high magnitude responses, *Journal of Social Psychology, 96*: 99–107.

Dweck, C. S. (1986). Motivational processes affecting learning, *American Psychologist, 41*: 1040–8.

Dweck, C. S. (1999). *Self-theories: Their role in motivation, personality, and development.* Philadelphia, PA: Psychology Press.

Dweck, C. S., Davidson, W., Nelson, S., & Enna, B. (1978). Sex differences in learned helplessness: II. The contingencies of evaluative feedback in the classroom. III. An experimental analysis, *Developmental Psychology, 14:* 268–76.

Dweck, C. S., Geotz, T. E., & Strauss, N. L. (1980). Sex differences in learned helplessness: IV. An experimental and naturalistic study of failure generalization and its mediators, *Journal of Personality and Social Psychology, 38:* 441–52.

Dweck, C. S., & Leggett, E. L. (1988). A social-cognitive approach to motivation and personality, *Psychological Review, 95:* 256–73.

Dweck, C. S., & Licht, B. G. (1980). Learned helplessness and academic achievement, in J. Garber & M. Selgman (Eds), *Human Helplessness: Theory and Application.* New York: Academic Press.

Ebbeck, M. (1984). Equity issues for boys and girls: some important issues, *Early Child Development and Care, 18(1/2):* 119–31.

Eccles, J. S., Wigfield, A., Flanagan, C. A., Miller, C., Reuman, D. A., & Yee, D. (1989). Self-concepts, domain values, and self-esteem: relations and changes at early adolescence, *Journal of Personality, 57:* 283–310.

Edwards, P. W. and Donaldson, M. A. (1989). Assessment of symptoms in adult survivors of incest: a factor analytic study of the Responses to Childhood Incest Questionnaire, *Child Abuse and Neglect, 13(1):* 101–10.

Eisenberg, A. R. (1999). Emotion talk among Mexican American and Anglo American mothers and children from two social classes. *Merrill-Palmer Quarterly, 45(2),* 267–284.

Eisenmann, B. (1997). Gender differences in early mother-child interactions: Talking about an imminent event. *Discourse Processes, 24,* 309–335.

Elliott, E. S., & Dweck, C. S. (1988). Goals: an approach to motivation and achievement, *Journal of Personality and Social Psychology, 54:* 5–12.

Entwisle, D. R., Alexander, K. L., Pallas, A. M., & Cadigan, D. (1987). The emergent academic self-image of first graders: its response to social structure, *Child Development, 58:* 1190–206.

Fagot, B. (1984). Teacher and peer reactions to boys' and girls's play styles, *Sex Roles, 11:* 691–702.

Falbo, T., & Peplau, L. A. (1980). Power strategies in intimate relationships. *Journal of Personality and Social Psychology, 38,* 618–628.

Feldlaufer, H., Midgley, C., & Eccles, J. S. (1988). Student, teacher, and observer perceptions of the classroom environment before and after the transition to junior high school, *The Journal of Early Adolescence, 8:* 133–56.

Filardo, E. K. (1996). Gender patterns in African American and White adolescents' social interactions in same-race, mixed-gender groups. *Journal of Personality and Social Psychology, 71*(1), 71–81.

Finkelhor, D. (1994). Current information on the scope and nature of child sexual abuse. *The future of children, Sexual Abuse of Children, 4*(2), 31–53.

Fivush, R. (1993). Emotional content of parent-child conversations about the past. In C. A. Nelson (Ed.), *The Minnesota Symposium on Child Psychology: Memory and affect in development* (pp. 39–77). Hillsdale, NJ: Erlbaum.

Fivush, R., Brotman, M. A., Buckner, J. P., & Goodman, S. H. (2000). Gender differences in parent-child emotion narratives. *Sex Roles, 42*(3/4), 2000.

Frankel, M. T., & Rollins, H. A., Jr (1983). Does mother know best? Mothers and fathers interacting with preschool sons and daughters, *Developmental Psychology, 19(5):* 694–702.

Gibbons, J. L., Lynn, M., & Stiles, D. A. (1997). Cross-national differences in adolescents' preferences for free-time activities. *Cross-Cultural Research: The Journal of Comparative Social Science, 31*(1), 55–69.

Giuliano, T. A., Popp, K. E., & Knight, J. L. (2000). Football versus barbies: Childhood play activities as predictors of sport participation by women. *Sex Roles, 42*(3/4), 159–181.

Gold, D., Crombie, G., & Noble, S. (1987). Relations between teachers' judgments of girls' and boys' compliance and intellectual competence, *Sex Roles, 16(7/8):* 351–8.

Golub, S. (1983). Menarche: the beginning of menstrual life, *Women and Health, 8(2/3):* 17–36.

Grebogi, C., Otto, E., & Yorke, J. A. (1987). Chaos, strange attractors, and fractal basin boundaries in nonlinear dynamics, *Science, 238:* 632–8.

Guastello, S. J. (1988). Catastrophe modelling of the ancient process: organizational subunit size, *Psychological Bulletin, 103:* 246–55.

Harris, J. R. (1995). Where is the child's environment? A group socialization theory of development. *Psychological Review, 102*(3), 458–489.

Hibbard, D. R., & Buhrmester, D. (1998). The role of peers in the socialization of gender-related social interaction styles. *Sex Roles, 39*(3/4), 185–202.

Holloway, J. B., Beuter, A., & Duda, J. L. (1988). Self-efficacy and training for strength in adolescent girls, *Journal of Applied Social Psychology, 18(8):* 699–719.

Hops, H., Alpert, A., & Davis, B. (1997). The development of same- and opposite-sex social relations among adolescents: An analogue study. *Social Development,* 6(2), 165–183.

Hyde, J. S., Fennema, E., Ryan, M., Frost, L. A., & Hopp, C. (1990). Gender comparisons of mathematics attitudes and affect: A meta-analysis, *Psychology of Women Quarterly, 14:* 299–324.

Irvine, J. (1986). Teacher-student interactions: effects of student race, sex, and grade level, *Journal of Educational Psychology, 78(1):* 14–21.

Jacklin, C. N., & Maccoby, E. E. (1978). Social behavior at thirty-three months in same-sex and mixed-sex dyads, *Child Development, 49:* 557–69.

Jones, D. C., (1983). Power structures and perceptions of power holders in same-sex groups of young children, *Women and Politics, 3:* 147–64.

Katz, P. A. (1986). Gender identity: development and consequences, in R. D. Ashmore and F. K. Del Boca (Eds), *The Social Psychology of Female-Male Relation* (pp. 21–67). Orlando, Fla: Academic Press.

Kimball, M. (1989). A new perspective on women's math achievement, *Psychological Bulletin, 195(2):* 198–214.

Koehler, M. C. S. (1986). Effective mathematics teaching and sex-related differences in algebra one classes. Unpublished PhD dissertation, University of Wisconsin.

Leaper, C. (1998). Decision-making processes between friends: Speaker and partner gender effects. *Sex Roles,* 39(1–2), 125–133.

Leaper, C. (2000). The social construction and socialization of gender during development, in P. H. Miller & E. K. Scholnick (Eds.), *Toward a feminist developmental psychology* (pp. 127–152). London: Routledge.

Leaper, C., Tenenbaum, H. R., & Shaffer, T. G. (1999). Communication patterns of African American girls and boys from low-income, urban backgrounds. *Child Development,* 70(6), 1489–1503.

Lenny, E. (1977). Women's self-confidence in achievement settings, *Psychological Bulletin, 84:* 1–13.

Licht, B. G., Stader, S. R., & Swenson, C. C. (1989). Children's achievement-related beliefs: effects of academic research area, sex, and achievement level, *Journal of Educational Research, 82:* 253–60.

Lind, P., & Connole, H. (1985). Sex differences in behavioral and cognitive aspects of decision control, *Sex Roles, 12(7/8):* 813–23.

Lips, H. M. (1989). The role of gender, self- and task perceptions in mathematics and science participation among college students, ERIC Document ED 297 945, ERIC Clearinghouse for Science, Mathematics and Environmental Education.

Lips, H. M. (1991). *Women, Men, and Power.* Mountain View, CA: Mayfield.

Lips, H. M. (1992). Gender and science-related activities as predictors of college students' academic choices, *Journal of Vocational Behavior, 40:* 62–81.

Lips, H. M. (1993). Bifurcation of a common path: Gender splitting on the road to engineering and physical science careers. *Initiatives,* 55(3), 13–22.

Lips, H. M. (1995). Through the lens of mathematical/scientific self-schemas: Images of students' current and possible selves. *Journal of Applied Social Psychology,* 25(19), 1671–1699.

Lips, H. M. (1998, June). *Gendered possibilities: Young women's and men's visions of their future power and competence.* Invited plenary address, Canadian Psychological Association convention, Edmonton, Alberta.

Lips, H. M. (2000). College students' visions of power and possibility as mediated by gender. *Psychology of Women Quarterly,* 24, 37–41.

Lips, H. M. (In press, a). Power: Personal and social dimensions. *Encyclopedia of Gender,* Academic Press.

Lips, H. M. (In press, b). Envisioning position of leadership: The expectation of university students in Virginia and Puerto Rico. *Journal of Social Issues,* special issue on "Gender, Hierarchy, and Leadership."

Lowery, M. (1987). Adult survivors of childhood incest, *Journal of Psychosocial Nursing and Mental Health Services, 25(1):* 27–31.

Lytton, H., & Romney, D. M. (1991). Parents differential socialization of boys and girls: a meta-analysis, *Psychological Bulletin, 109(2):* 267–96.

Maccoby, E. E. (1998). *The two sexes: Growing up apart, coming together.* London, England: Belnap/Harvard University Press.

Maccoby, E. E. (1990). Gender and relationships: a developmental account, *American Psychologist, 45(4):* 513–20.

Magolda, M. B. (1990). Gender differences in epistemological development, *Journal of College Student Development, 31(6):* 555–61.

Malamuth, N. M., & Thornhill, N. W. (1995). Hostile masculinity, sexual aggression, and gender-biased domineeringness in conversations. *Aggressive Behavior, 20*(3), 185–193.

Mann, J. (1993, June 23). What's harassment? Ask a girl. *Washington Post*, p. C20.

Marshall, S. P., & Smith, J. D. (1987). Sex differences in learning mathematics: a longitudinal study with item and error analysis, *Journal of Educational Psychology, 79:* 372–83.

McCormack, A. (1985). The sexual harassment of students by teachers: the case of students in science, *Sex Roles, 13(1/2):* 21–32.

Mende, W., Herzel, H., & Wermke, K. (1990). Bifurcations and chaos in newborn infant cries, *Physics Letters A, 145:* 418–24.

Miller, C. M. (1987). Qualitative differences among gender-stereotyped toys: implications for cognitive and social development in girls and boys, *Sex Roles, 16(9/10):* 473–87.

Miller, J. L., & Levy, G. D. Gender role conflict, gender-typed characteristics, self-concepts, and sport socialization in female athletes and nonathletes. *Sex Roles, 35(1/2),* 111–122.

Nelson-LeGall, S. (1990). Academic achievement orientation and help-seeking behavior in early adolescent girls. *Journal of Early Adolescence, 10,* 176–190.

Nolen-Hoeksema, S. (1987). Sex differences in unipolar depression: Evidence and theory. *Psychological Bulletin, 101,* 259–282.

O'Hagan, F. T., Sale, D. G., MacDougall, J. D., & Garner, S. H. (1995). Response to resistance training in young women and men. *International Journal of Sports Medicine, 16,* 314–321.

Orenstein, P. (1994). *Schoolgirls: Young women, self-esteem, and the confidence gap.* New York: Doubleday.

Parsons, J., & Ruble, D. (1977). The development of achievement-related expectancies, *Child Development, 48:* 1075–9.

Pearson, J. C., & West, R. (1991). An initial investigation of the effects of gender on student questions in the classroom: Developing a descriptive base. *Communication Education, 40*(1), 22–32.

Poole, M. E., & Evans, G. T. (1989). Adolescents' self-perceptions of competence in life skill areas, *Journal of Youth and Adolescence, 18(2):* 147–73.

Powlishta, K. K., & Maccoby, E. E. (1990). Resource utilization in mixed-sex dyads: the influence of adult presence and task type, *Sex Roles, 23(5/6):* 223–40.

Rheingold, H., & Cook, K. (1975). The contents of boys' and girls' rooms as an index of parents' behaviors, *Child Development, 46:* 459–63.

Richards, Dianna (1990). Is strategic decision-making chaotic?, *Behavioral Science, 35:* 219–32.

Robinson, T., & Ward, J. V. (1991). A belief in self far greater than anyone's disbelief: Cultivating resistance among African American female adolescents, in C. Gilligan, A. G. Rogers, & L. Tolman (Eds.), *Women, girls, and psychotherapy: Reframing resistance* (pp. 87–103). New York: Haworth Press.

Ross, C. E., & Wright, M. P. (1998). Women's work, men's work, and the sense of control. *Work & Occupations, 25*(3), 333–355.

Rubin, J., Provenzano, F. J., & Luria, Z. (1974). The eye of the beholder: Parents' views on sex of newborns, *American Journal of Orthopsychiatry, 44:* 512–19.

Sadker, M., & Sadker, D. (1985). Sexism in the schoolroom of the '80s, *Psychology Today, 19:* 54–7.

Schnellman, J., & Gibbons, J. L. (1984). *The perception by women and minorities of trivial discriminatory actions in the classroom,* Paper presented at the American Psychological Association Conference, Toronto.

Serbin, L., & O'Leary, K. (1975). How nursery schools teach girls to shut up, *Psychology Today, 9(7):* 56–8, 102–3.

Spender, D. (1989). *The Writing or the Sex.* New York: Pergamon.

Stein, N. (1995). Sexual harassment in schools: The public performance of gendered violence. *Harvard Educational Review, 65*(2), 145–162.

Sterman, John D. (1988). Deterministic chaos in models of human behavior: methodological issues and experimental results, *Systems Dynamics Review, 4:* 148–78.

Tannen, D. (1990). *You just don't understand: Women and men in conversation.* New York: Morrow.

Tapasak, R. C. (1990). Differences in expectancy-attribution patterns of cognitive components in male and female math performance, *Contemporary Educational Psychology, 15:* 284–98.

Temple, L., & Lips, H. M. (1989). Gender differences and similarities in attitudes toward computers, *Computers and Human Behavior, 5:* 215–26.

Thorne, B., & Luria, Z. (1986). Sexuality and gender in children's daily worlds, *Social Problems, 33(3):* 176–90.

Tichenor, V. J. (1999). Status and income as gendered resources: The case of marital power. *Journal of Marriage and the Family, 61,* 638–650.

Ullian, D. (1984). Why girls are good: a constructivist view, *Sex Roles, 11(3/4):* 241–56.

Updegraff, K. A., McHale, S. M., & Crouter, A. C. (1994). Gender roles in marriage: What do they mean for girls' and boys' school achievement?, *Journal of Youth and Adolescence, 25,* 73–88.

Van Horn, K. R., & Marques, J. C. (2000). Interpersonal relationships in Brazilian adolescents. *International Journal of Behavioral Development, 24*(2), 199–203.

Vaselakos, W. D. (1999). *The effects of women's self—protection training on the belief of perceived control.* Unpublished doctoral dissertation, Adler School of Professional Psychology.

Wade, T. J. (1996). An examination of locus of control/fatalism for Blacks, Whites, boys and girls over a two year period of adolescence. *Social Behavior and Personality, 24*(3), 239–248.

Wall, J., Covell, K., & MacIntyre, P. D. (1999). Implications of social supports for adolescents' education and career aspirations. *Canadian Journal of Behavioral Science, 31*(2), 63–71.

Way, N. (1995). Can't you see the courage, the strength that I have?: Listening to urban adolescent girls speak about their relationships. *Psychology of Women Quarterly, 19*(1), 107–128.

Wichstrøm, L. (1999). The emergence of gender difference in depressed mood during adolescence: The role of intensified gender socialization. *Developmental Psychology, 35*(1), 232–245.

Yarrow, L. J., MacTurk, R. H., Vietze, P. M., McCarthy, M. E., Klein, R. P., & McQuiston, S. (1984). Developmental course of parental stimulation and its relationship to mastery motivation during infancy, *Developmental Psychology, 20*(3): 492–503.

Yee, D. K., & Eccles, J. S. (1988). Parent perceptions and attributions for children's math achievement, *Sex Roles, 19:* 317–33.

4

Masculinity and Gender Roles Among Puerto Rican Men: Machismo on the U.S. Mainland

José B. Torres

According to Torres, the literature on Puerto Rican men in the United States is lacking in two major ways: It provides persistent negative images of Puerto Rican men based on misconceptions of the machismo construct and it gives scant attention to the experiences and needs of Puerto Rican men as they confront contradictory cultural expectations for masculinity **(defined norm),** social and economic discrimination, and gender role transitions of Puerto Rican women **(gender role effects).** In response to these shortcomings in the literature, Torres presents a reconceptualization of masculinity and machismo rooted in their historical, socioeconomic and cultural contexts **(cultural diversity).** He claims that a better understanding of how machismo operates within the traditional Puerto Rican family systems—including its positive expressions—will enhance the ability of mental health practitioners to help Puerto Rican men adapt to their changing environment and respond effectively to discrimination. He also highlights systemic changes that are necessary for successful adaptation.

Questions to Consider:

1. According to Torres, how do traditional Puerto Rican conceptions of masculinity differ from Anglo conceptions? How does he account for these differences? What challenges do these differences present to Puerto Rican males living in the US?
2. According to Torres, how are the relationship dynamics between Puerto Rican men and women in the US

changing? What accounts for these changes, and what challenges and opportunities do they present for Puerto Rican males?

3. Imagine that you are a counselor working with a Puerto Rican male who is having difficulties bridging his traditional conception of masculinity with the Anglo conception. Based on the information that Torres has provided you concerning the role of machismo in the traditional Puerto Rican family system, and the cultural values of respeto and dignidad, how might you assist your client in making a healthy personal adjustment to life in the US?

4. According to Torres, what changes need to be made beyond individual ones, to help Puerto Rican males adapt effectively to mainland US culture? How can Puerto Rican women be allies while undergoing their own gender role transitions?

5. How might the experiences of Puerto Rican men described in this reading apply to the men of your culture? If you are Puerto Rican, does your experience agree with what you have read? Explain.

My father was a gentle man. His mestizo face lovingly carved by joys, sorrows, and warm sunny rays. His greenish, greyish eyes always squinting like lips with half smiles. I remember watching him sitting in the backyard, his mind, spirit, and body in quiet harmony. He was a man of sayings: "It all comes out in the mirror" and "Words are like oil." My favorite has become my definition for coalitions: *"juntos pero no revueltos"* (together but not scrambled).

When he talked to us, my brother, my mother, and me, he spoke about truth, integrity, and love. He did sit at the head of the table, and demanded our deference. He loved and treated my mother as a partner, a lover, a mother, and a wife. You see, my father was a macho . . . and I loved him. Machismo in my cultural dictionary is *hombria*, manhood. A macho is not the oiled, tan, muscular guy with a woman hanging from his left shoulder in a shaving cream commercial. He is not the woman hater or the wife beater. He is not the enemy in the battle of the sexes, or the tough man with a distorted view of his manhood. He is who he is and not who he is made to be. So machismo—it's okay with me.

—Gladys Benavides
(Unpublished writing)

As a result of changing socioeconomic and labor market conditions in the United States, conflict has developed for Puerto Rican men in their marital relationships and in certain gender-role characteristics. Much of the conflict stems from their desire to retain traditional ideals of masculinity that may no longer be attainable. Today's urban environment is characterized by rapidly changing sociopolitical conditions, gender-role ambiguities, and contradictory cultural expectations and values. A central source of conflict can be found in the cultural form of masculinity known as machismo that is observed among Puerto Ricans on the U.S. mainland. Machismo may be defined as the complex interaction of social, cultural, and behavioral components forming male gender-role identity in the sociopolitical context of the Latino society (*De La Cancela, 1986; Deyoung & Zigler, 1994*).

Traditionally, researchers have focused on such negative connotations of machismo as male dominance, aggression, patriarchy, authoritarianism, and oppressive behavior toward women and children. They have often failed, however, to recognize that machismo can have positive expression,

such as emphasis on self-respect and on responsibility for protecting and providing for
the family. They have also failed to consider
the sociopolitical realities for Puerto Rican
men, and the "ideal" of masculinity and
gender roles held by Puerto Rican women.
Studies of these factors might result in less
emphasis on the sexual and aggressive aspects of machismo, and more on such traits
as patience, sensitivity, artistic appreciation,
and open verbal communication that exist
within Puerto Rican culture.

Although machismo is popularly
viewed as the major factor in Latino men's
masculine identity, research on the topic,
particularly with Puerto Rican men, is limited compared to research with socioeco-
nomically advantaged white Americans of
European ancestry *(Levant & Pollack, 1995)*.
Kimmel and Messner *(1992)* have argued
that "the meaning of masculinity varies
from culture to culture" *(p. 9)*, and that,
consequently, masculinity is reflected in
many different forms. This oversight in the
literature has left Puerto Rican men, and
Latinos in general, burdened with stereotyped characteristics that have negative implications for their emotional, social, and
physical well-being. Among these implications are anxiety, confusion, depression,
hostility, isolation, loneliness, panic, tension, sexual dysfunction, and a sense of
emasculation *(De La Cancela, 1988)*.

Puerto Rican men are often told that
their culture, attitudes, and behavior are ir-
redeemably sexist *(De La Cancela, 1986;
Ramírez, 1993)*. In truth, this perspective is
secondary to the fact that the dominant culture does not permit them to explore adaptive options. They are not, for example, given
access to economic opportunities equal to
those of the women in their culture; the result is a reversal of traditional gender roles in
which Puerto Rican women become the primary source of income and achieve greater
levels of economic self-sufficiency than the

men. It is hardly surprising that, challenged
at the very core of their traditional masculinity, many Puerto Rican men feel vulnerable
and off balance, expressing dissatisfaction,
discontent, and confusion, while struggling
for emotional survival.

In this context, it is a matter of concern whether Puerto Rican men will be able
to tolerate, accept, or survive the new active
role of Puerto Rican women. To do so, they
must relinquish some kinds of traditional
behavior in order to explore the potential
benefits of a more egalitarian relationship
with their partners. A dilemma for the
Puerto Rican community on the U.S. mainland is the tendency of educated Puerto
Rican women to marry white Americans of
European background (Anglos), possibly to
bypass the threat presented to some Puerto
Rican men by the women's changing roles
(Comas-Díaz, 1989). Others are choosing to
leave unhealthy or unsatisfying relationships with Puerto Rican men through separation or divorce; still others are remaining
single female heads of households.

To help Puerto Rican men and their
families deal effectively with this changing
environment, a more thorough understanding of how machismo operates within traditional family systems is necessary. The intent
of this article is to identify common conceptions and misconceptions about machismo,
describe the adaptive role machismo has traditionally played within the Puerto Rican
family system, and discuss ways of enhancing the ability of Puerto Rican men to adapt
more effectively to shifts in gender and role
identities among Puerto Rican women.

Machismo: Characteristics and Misconceptions

Historically, the male gender-socialization
process and popular perspective on mas-

culinity for Anglos in the United States has emphasized such traits as assertiveness; obsession with achievement and success; individualism; status; aggression, toughness, and winning; restricted emotionality and affectionate behavior, concerns about power, control, and competition; and homophobia *(Levant, 1992; Levant & Pollack, 1995; O'Neil, 1982)*. The Puerto Rican male gender-socialization process and view of masculinity has historically emphasized bravery, strength, male dominance, honor, virility, aggression, and autonomy.

Although the mental health literature depicts machismo as one of the major forces in the ethos of Latino males *(Gonzalez, 1982; Mirandé, 1988; Ramírez, 1993)*, it has defined it in inconsistent, contradictory, superficial, and negatively stereotypic ways that are as ambiguous and misunderstood as any other aspect of the Latino culture. Among the stereotyped characteristics are physical aggression, sexual promiscuity, insecurity, alcohol abuse, spousal violence (i.e., emotional and physical abuse of women and children), and other oppressions of women *(Ramírez, 1993; Valdéz, Barón, & Ponce, 1987)*. Other such characterizations have focused on irresponsible behavior, immaturity, feelings of inferiority, latent homosexuality, narcissistic personality, ambivalence toward women, and sexual anxiety *(Aramoni, 1972; Ramírez, 1993; Ruiz, 1981)*. While these traits might be important dimensions of the machismo construct, they reflect only a narrow perspective on gender-role identity of Puerto Rican men.

In contrast, De La Cancela *(1991)* and Mayo *(1993)* have suggested that machismo is characterized by other important and positive, though less culturally profiled, elements. These include: forcefulness of personality, strength of will, daring, self-assertiveness, and self-confidence, in conjunction with softer and more emotional aspects such as affection, caring, tenderness,

love, respect for self and others, and protectiveness toward women, children, and less fortunate members of society; provision for and protection of the family, strength in adverse situations, uncompromising positions on matters of great personal importance, pride, respect, dignity, and honor. De La Cancela *(1986)* further included stoicism; varying levels of intimacy among men, leading to attachments in certain contexts and disengagement in others; attempts to avoid shame and gain *respeto* (respect) and *dignidad* (dignity) for self and family; the displacement of stress related to economic and social factors onto the interpersonal and familial sphere; and patterns of assertiveness and dominance like those caricatured in the literature.

Among Puerto Ricans, the concept of *respeto* governs all positive reciprocal interpersonal relations *(Diaz-Royo, 1976)*; it particularly dictates appropriate deferential behavior toward others—especially older people, parents, and relatives—on the basis of age, socioeconomic position, and authority. Often associated with *respeto, dignidad* refers to a strong belief in the worth and value of each individual as a human being, whatever his or her social standing. This aspect of machismo primarily refers to how Latino males carry out their functions within the family, the community, and the culture at large.

Regardless of the origin or construction of machismo and the variants of macho or *machista* (exaggerated manliness), Latino men's adherence to and tolerance of its negative attitudinal and behavioral characteristics not only make life difficult, emotionally and physically, for their female partners and families, but are also dangerous. Alcoholism, infidelity, domestic and other forms of violence, minimal involvement with child rearing, and abandonment of partners and families are only a few of the dysfunctional and destructive consequences for family life when machismo is exercised as an exaggerated masculinity.

In general, Latino men have been socialized to perceive themselves as dominant of women, with rights and privileges that can be asserted legitimately by force. Puerto Rican men are not given *respeto* and *dignidad* in the traditional way on the U.S. mainland, where male *machismo* and female *marianismo* are deprecated *(Ghali, 1977)*.

Marianismo, based on the cult of the Virgin Mary, serves as the counterpoint to machismo; it stipulates that women are morally and spiritually superior to men and, therefore, better able to endure suffering *(Stevens, 1973)*. Women are, however, expected to accept male authority *(Ramos-McKay, Comas-Díaz, & Rivera, 1988; Stevens, 1973)*. Implicit in their socialization process is the expectation of self-sacrifice in favor of their children and husbands, repression or sublimation of sexual drives and consideration of sex as an obligation to their husband, chastity until marriage, and conformity to husbands' *macho* (male) behavior *(Comas-Díaz, 1988)*. Gil and Vazquez *(1996)* stressed that, like *machismo, marianismo* has a positive and lighter side, including loyalty, compassion, and generosity, and that accessing and harnessing these qualities can fuel women's empowerment and provide healthy support to those around them *(p. 6)*.

Adjustment to changing gender roles in the Puerto Rican family demands sensitivity to changing *marianismo* and *machismo* constructs, and to the people most affected by different levels of acculturation. Adaptive acculturation may be expected to influence the emergence of *la nueva marianisma* (the new Latina), manifested as a competent, assertive, self-assured, and empowered Latina *(Gil & Vazquez, 1996, p. 15)*.

In their effort to integrate the demands of their Latino heritage into the accepted male gender role on the mainland, Puerto Rican men may persist in maintaining a sense of autonomy and independence and a show of manliness. How these are expressed is influenced by such factors as level of education, generational shifts, acculturation patterns, ethnic identity, responsibility to the extended family, and socioeconomic status. Redefinition and reconstruction of the Puerto Rican male gender-role identity demands attention both to the male role and to the interface of machismo with other individuals and systems within the mainland culture. It must also identify valid and constructive aspects of the traditional Puerto Rican male code and target obsolete and dysfunctional aspects for change *(Levant & Pollack, 1995)*.

In view of the historically fragmented aspects of machismo, ongoing investigations would best be served by viewing Puerto Rican male gender role and machismo as a dynamic set of both positive and negative traits; by identifying the prevalence of and distinctions between positive and negative forms *(Mirandé, 1988)*; and by recognizing that its behavioral manifestations occur on a continuum from negative to positive.

Male-to-Male Behavior

While macho behavior has often been discussed in terms of male-female relationships, machismo has rarely been considered in relationships among males. Early studies focusing on male relationships *(Landy, 1959)* noted that Puerto Rican males constantly try to form relationships *de confianza* (of confidence, trust, intimacy) with other males, while at the same time fearing the possibility of being exploited by them. As Landy *(1959)* stated:

> The more he seeks a close relationship with other males, the less the young man is apt to find it. When relationships are

established, they are brittle and easily fragmented. Thus, the male's poignant desires find little permanent gratification, and repeated short-lived relationships lead to distrust of others. At the same time however, he longs for nothing so much as to be able to trust the relationship of other men. And so he looks continually for trust, or confianza relationships. But he looks within a lonely crowd in which confianza relationships are rare because while the demand is great, supply is short. *(p. 246)*

De La Cancela *(1991)* and Mayo *(1993)* have suggested that similar patterns of behavior still persist, although more flexible and adaptive roles are developing with the advent of greater education and acculturation.

In the past, relationships among Puerto Rican men, and between men and women, have been structurally and culturally defined according to specific values, such as *afecto* (affection), *personalismo* (the need to relate to people and not to institutions), *respeto, dignidad,* and *confianza.* Any man, whatever his situation in life, is thought to be worthy of *respeto.* In modern Puerto Rico, men still treat each other with more formality than one finds on the U.S. mainland. Any *falta de respeto* (lack of respect) toward a man violates his dignity and contributes to a stressful situation. Other behavioral patterns observed among Puerto Rican males are a) a tendency to be more open than men in general in expressing emotion, particularly extremes of joy and anger; and b) casual, routine, and unembarrassed expression of affection toward other males by handshaking, an embrace on meeting, and frequent touching during conversation *(Padilla & Ruiz, 1973).*

Given the paucity of serious analytic and qualifying data on machismo in the literature, the preceding observations must be viewed with caution and as an attempt to open up the multidimensional aspects of the construct. Whether machismo is perceived as a negative behavioral pattern or as a cultural norm with both negative and positive attributes, it must be understood, when used for descriptive purposes, as reflecting a complex interaction of cultural, sociopolitical, economic, psychological, and behavioral components of personality *(De La Cancela, 1986).*

Machismo in a Changing Environment

With the exception of Mexican Americans, Puerto Ricans are the largest Latino group on the U.S. mainland. Although they share with other Latino groups a language and cultural traits and values reflecting their Spanish heritage (e.g., religion, *familism*), there are demographic, historical, political, and socioeconomic indicators that distinguish Puerto Ricans and contribute significantly to their oppressed socioeconomic condition *(De La Cancela, 1986).*

Consistent with previous demographic and socioeconomic data profiles, recent census reports on Puerto Ricans reflect both positive and negative socioeconomic indicators of well-being. During the past decade, they have achieved some socioeconomic progress (e.g., increased average household income). However, they continue to lag far behind other Latino groups on several socioeconomic dimensions, and behind the majority population on virtually all of them. According to the U.S. Bureau of the Census *(1994)*, while the employed portion of the Latino male labor force ranged from 63% to 83% as of March 1994, that of Puerto Rican men was 66%. Like other Latino males, Puerto Rican men were more likely to be employed as operators, fabricators, and nonskilled laborers, and in service occupations. During the period 1982–1994, Latino unemployment rates were consistently higher than those of non-Latinos. While the March 1994 unemployment rate among all Latinos was nearly twice that of non-Latino whites (11.1% and 5.7%, respectively), the rate among Latinos ranged from 6.8% for Cubans to 14.2% for Puerto Ricans. Of the Latino male unemployment figures, Puerto Rican men represented the highest rate at 15.9% *(Institute for Puerto Rican Policy, 1995)*.

The mainland's societal criteria for "manhood" intensify for Puerto Rican men the psychological stress and role strains stemming from immigration, acculturation, racism, and poverty. The inability to find employment and be good providers for their families adds to this stress, causing many of these men to experience guilt, feelings of inadequacy, and a form of psychological emasculation stemming from fear of not being able to live up to the male role *(Doyle, 1983)*.

The symptomatic behavioral reactions of many Puerto Rican men to such personal crises tend to be aggressive rather than depressive, and aimed at protecting personal vulnerability. Drinking, gambling, fighting, and promiscuity are common reported manifestations of attempts to maintain *hombria* (manhood). Baca-Zinn *(1982)* observed:

> Perhaps manhood takes on greater importance for those who do not have access to socially valued roles. Being male is one sure way to acquire status when other roles are systematically denied by the workings of society. *(p. 39)*

Such reactions can also be seen as attempts to salvage their pride in terms of *dignidad* and *respeto*. They have also been found to create panic, confusion, marital discord, and breakdown of family ties *(De La Cancela, 1991)*. A different self-concept and better

self-esteem may be experienced by Puerto Rican men who have better access to resources and the ability to regulate their behavior in conformity with the prescribed male and female norms of the majority culture *(Bem, 1985)*.

Clinical Recommendations

The preceding discussion on gender roles and the construct of machismo among mainland Puerto Rican men holds several implications for the development and delivery of mental health services to this population.

Ethnic or Cultural Biases

It is necessary that practitioners working with Puerto Rican men commit themselves to a process of self-exploration designed to overcome personal biases, prejudices, and racism, and to develop their own integrative ethnic identity. This self-exploration should disclose any preconceptions they may have regarding Puerto Rican men, their communication and relationship patterns with both sexes, and their particular cultural values and norms. Practitioners must also become aware of the impact of culture, history, socioeconomic and political conditions, religion, and racism on these men and their families. They must then reach an understanding of their own level of comfort with personal flexibility and appropriate self-disclosure when this is therapeutically necessary.

Mental health practitioners must exercise caution in using traditional Anglo models of psychological counseling (e.g., psychodynamic theory) with Puerto Rican clients, who are likely to resist such treatment approaches, since they reflect several assumptions that are inconsistent with

Puerto Rican values, particularly among those who are bicultural or of low acculturation levels. Among these is the view that it is appropriate and beneficial to discuss personally sensitive issues, and the belief that achieving an intellectual understanding of a problem is likely to reveal a course of action that can rectify it. Puerto Rican men, in particular, are usually reluctant to participate in an activity that involves revelation of personal information, sharing of deep feelings, and submission to a situation in which they perceive themselves as helpless and weak.

Cultural Importance of Family

For non-Puerto Rican practitioners, knowledge of the role played by Puerto Rican men in the family is of utmost importance. Appreciation of male and female gender roles and the impact of machismo and marianismo at all levels of Puerto Rican family life requires familiarity with specific cultural values, including *dignidad, respeto, personalismo,* and *familismo* or *familism.* Counseling with Puerto Rican men also requires constant and acute sensitivity to the difficulties encountered by them as they strive to achieve success within the dominant sociocultural context. In a society where success is often associated with economic wealth, reconciling cultural, masculine, and gender-role identities with economic and social obstacles is critical for Puerto Rican and other men of color *(Lazur & Majors, 1995).*

Much of the literature has reported the significance of *la familia* (the family) as a primary source of emotional and economic support among Latino families. This is particularly true in the Puerto Rican community, where the extended family system is its "heart and soul" *(Canino & Canino, 1980).* Bearing this in mind, practitioners should display understanding and appreciation of the cultural dictates, roles, structure, values, and complex relationships that comprise the interactive, mutually supportive, and strong family orientation in the Puerto Rican community. It is within this family and community that Puerto Rican men draw on their culture of machismo to define their male gender role in the face of the demands of the dominant culture.

Adapting the Concept of Machismo

To understand better the multidimensional and dynamic components of Puerto Rican men's individual identity and thus maximize their openness to counseling, practitioners must be prepared to expand their own clinical conceptualization of male gender role and machismo beyond an exclusive intrapsychic or sociocultural view *(De La Cancela, 1991).* This requires enough flexibility to reach out from an individualistic to a collective or systemic perception of intervention so as to permit an integration of individual treatment with family dynamics that is consistent with Puerto Rican culture.

Culturally sensitive assessment and treatment planning can be attained through an ecosystemic orientation that takes into account the elements of cultural, linguistic, educational, economic, gender, political, and environmental context. Diagnostic assessment must include not only presenting concerns and personal history, but an exploration of the individual's level of acculturation, period of migration, education, adherence to traditional cultural role expectations, and experiences with racism. Also important are the client's understanding of his own symptomatology, evaluation of motivation, capacity for change, and available opportunities in his community.

Overall, the therapeutic intervention must encourage empowerment of the individual through his acknowledgment of responsibility for his role of *respeto* within his family and community. The socioeconomic and political forces obstructing fulfillment of this role must also be considered. Confrontation of the client's resistance must itself be respectful, and attentive to his wounded self-esteem.

With practitioners' help, Puerto Rican men may learn not to respond to changes in Puerto Rican women by entrenching themselves in or attempting to regain their former male prerogatives. Instead, they may learn to redefine the concept of masculinity so as to encompass greater egalitarianism, achieving a better balance between individuality, gender, and culture, whatever their present level of machismo. Only through such a process can these men survive, flourish, and ultimately attain a healthy personal self apart from a world predicated on men's power over women *(Rodríguez, 1996)*.

Change often involves loss, and the integration of loss requires mourning. Therefore, it is of the utmost importance that any therapeutic intervention with Puerto Rican men be designed to help them to bear, and gain perspective on, their sense of loss as they let go their traditional forms of masculinity and patriarchal privilege, a loss none the smaller for being politically unacceptable or personally dysfunctional *(Pollack & Levant, 1995)*. The reconstruction of masculinity in more functional form could produce many benefits for Puerto Rican men, as well as women *(Brooks & Silverstein, 1995)*. Clinical help in working through the mourning process and moving on to a richer, more empowered level of gender-role identity may be necessary, depending on the form or level of machismo involved, which in turn reflects stages of acculturation and development.

Contradictory Aspects of Machismo

Therapeutic work with Puerto Rican male clients requires attention to the contradictory aspects of machismo and to any tendency by the practitioner to minimize the client's personal responsibilities. According to De La Cancela *(1991)*, this task is notable for the attention needed to:

> The danger of displacing employment-related conflicts onto his mate; the utilization of the family, sex and substance abuse as a refuge from the world; the distinction between protection of the family and paternalism; how social institutions like welfare and schools encourage displacing the Puerto Rican man; and the oppression of women. *(p. 200)*

Of course, not all Puerto Rican men adhere to the traditional negative perspectives of machismo. In fact, some Puerto Ricans, men and women, reject the negative construct of machismo outright.

Behavioral Manifestations of Machismo

The approach to clinical interventions with Puerto Rican men must, then, be both micro- and macrosystemic, taking into consideration the behavioral manifestations of male gender role and machismo as they fall on a continuum from negative to positive *(Martinez, 1994)*, or the degree to which maladaptive behavior is rendered functional by modification to the cultural context. Ability to reframe culturally maladaptive behavior without diminishing either the client's self-esteem on the one hand, or the behavior's potential for destructive consequences on the other may further increase the possibility of engaging Puerto Rican men in counseling.

Practitioners will also find De La Cancela's *(1991)* dialectical perspective on machismo useful: he sees it as both progressive and reactionary, and as intimately related to the socioeconomic and historical forces maintaining the colonization of Puerto Ricans; he suggests that "the Puerto Rican male role is neither a Latino malady that must be eliminated nor a healthy cultural value that must be reinforced" *(p. 198)*.

Use by clinicians of such key cultural dimensions as dignity, integrity, honor, and pride will also be conducive to establishing trust in the therapeutic relationship.

Practitioners who view macho behavior only in terms of physical aggression, sexual promiscuity, dominance over women, and excessive use of alcohol, and who pathologize these kinds of behavior without understanding their other cultural aspects, will significantly limit opportunities for engaging Puerto Rican men and their families in a counseling relationship. Development of culturally competent clinical skills should take into consideration the positive elements of machismo, the Puerto Rican male gender role, and other cultural values such as *respeto* and *dignidad*.

Psychological Empowerment

Emphasis on empowering Puerto Rican male clients—by increasing their sense of personal control over their lives, helping them feel good about themselves, and supporting their assumption of personal responsibility for change—should also further continuation of their engagement in counseling *(Goldstein, 1995)*. Reframing the client's concerns about treatment, addressing his strong sense of obligation and responsibility for himself and his family, and

appealing to his sense of honor may also be in keeping with his own gender-role expectations. Attention to the individual as a whole—psychological, social, and physical health—also implies openness by practitioners to collaborative work with medical and other health-care-related professionals *(Casas, Wagenheim, Banchero, & Mendoza-Romero, 1994)*.

Facilitative Approaches

The positive qualities of the male gender role (e.g., respect, loyalty, fairness, responsibility, and family centrality) can be used as bridges instead of barriers in the process of therapeutic engagement. In addition to promoting and nurturing personal change, such a focus can help the client reach a level of empowerment from which he can more effectively advocate for himself and contribute to collective efforts for change in the community and larger society.

Other potentially facilitative approaches include psychoeducational groups; same-gender consciousness-raising groups; group-oriented work focused on discovering a different understanding of masculinity; and a combination of individual, marital, and family therapy approaches.

Practitioners must be vigilant about the contradictory and inconsistent behavioral patterns presented among Puerto Rican men. While some are readily making satisfactory adaptations to the dominant culture and socioeconomic situation, others remain oblivious and resistant to the need to reevaluate certain dysfunctional characteristics (e.g., aggression and emotional inhibition) that can provoke negative psychological or physical consequences for themselves and others. Instead of dwelling on these negative aspects, or on clients' limitations or deficits, practitioners should consider exploring their strengths, competence, resilience, and resourcefulness. Validation and strengthening of ethnic identity may need to be fostered as part of their quest for a healthy personal adjustment. Also, hope for good results from behavioral changes should be encouraged.

Overall, competent practice requires cultural awareness and sensitivity, as well as excellent diagnostic and treatment skills that can accurately distinguish culturally related conflicts and issues from problems of psychopathology and daily life. In general, treatment should be active, structured, time-limited, and goal-oriented; it may also require a degree of self-disclosure on the part of practitioners; regardless of which culturally sensitive intervention approach is used, the practitioner's authentic presentation of self will remain his or her most valuable therapeutic tool.

Systemic Change

Mental health practitioners must recognize and acknowledge that not all Puerto Rican men, and certainly not all females, subscribe to the machismo perspective, and may be actively seeking a profound revision of the man-woman relationship. They must, however, bear in mind that many individuals of both genders are more affected by machismo than they themselves realize, often through the social system at large. Change and transformation are necessary not only in individuals, but also in social, political, and legal institutions that affect work, marriage, and family life and are the architects of the dominant cultural society. Attitudes, values, and expected behavior within these structures must change if there is to be large-scale, collective, and systematic modification that will have an impact on culturally defined gender roles.

Role of Puerto Rican Women

The liberation of Puerto Rican women could also have a liberalizing effect on the traditional confining attitudes and behavior of Puerto Rican men. Some men may resist the gender-role reversals associated with the pressures of economic survival, or other changes perceived as challenging their role as providers and protectors of the family. Others, however, may welcome the opportunity to reduce the stress of maintaining sole responsibility for their traditional family role as provider.

The changing position of Puerto Rican women has been reported as detrimental to some Puerto Rican men *(Comas-Diaz, 1989; Torres-Matrullo, 1976)*, but it may also contribute to men's personal growth. By codifying the attitudes and behavior associated with machismo, women may help to liberate men from the oppressive and constricting aspects of their traditionally defined roles. This could lead to men's better self-integration and balance, and have beneficial effects on gender and family interactions (e.g., increased communication, cohesiveness, and stable relationships).

For these changes to occur, Puerto Rican women, like their sisters world-wide, must pursue efforts to establish cultural and social norms that allow a wider range of human expression and endeavor. As the sociocultural role of Puerto Rican women changes and thereby broadens their personal choices (i.e., greater independence without loss of interdependence, responsibility, and maturity), the role of Puerto Rican men need not be diminished but may be expanded, empowered, and enriched.

Social Services

To improve their economic status and thus let them fulfill their expected role as a family provider, Puerto Rican men need adequate opportunities for education and training. Assumption of a proper status as equal partner or titular family head would benefit personal relationships, families, and community.

Social and psychological services for Puerto Ricans on the U.S. mainland need to be tailored to meet their characteristics and needs. Policy makers and program developers share the responsibility to address Puerto Ricans more adequately as a unique ethnic group. Acknowledgment and respect for the cultural elements that distinguish Puerto Ricans from other ethnic populations may enable development of more comprehensive programs for improved social and mental health services for this population.

Implications for Research

Because of the lack of literature about the distinct cultural values and behavior of different Latino subgroups in the U.S., the ways in which men from these groups form their gender-role identity are misunderstood and unappreciated. This very lack of information, however, suggests some interesting avenues for further research. How do men from different ethnic groups in the U.S. view traditional norms of masculinity? Are there variations of machismo between Puerto Ricans and other Latino groups on the mainland? Are there significant differences in how machismo is perceived by mainland and island Puerto Ricans? Are there differences in how men and women view machismo across and within each of the Latino groups? What, specifically, are the functional versus dysfunctional attitudinal and behavioral manifestations of the construct of machismo in the Latino culture and within each individual Latino group?

Rigorous research to answer these questions could help diffuse some of the unrealistic stereotypes that exist for Latino men on the U.S. mainland, as well as differentiate variations of machismo among Latino subgroups. Investigations of Puerto Rican patterns of adaptation and acculturation to their new environments on the mainland should, by focusing on culture-specific behavior, reveal different levels of help-seeking and the different engagement skills needed by practitioners to be consistent with the culture. Such research would help practitioners increase their understanding of how male gender role and the construct of machismo operate within a Latino multicultural society and how they can more effectively provide mental health services to Puerto Rican men and their families.

Conclusion

The preceding discussion on masculinity and gender roles among Puerto Rican men is a response to the persistent negative stereotyping of Latino men by what is popularly referred to as machismo, and the paucity of available literature addressing the needs of this large Latino group in the United States. A contributing factor to the lack of understanding of Puerto Ricans, their distressing socioeconomic problems, and their lack of visibility has been the tendency to lump them together with other Latino groups.

The discussion has noted the prevalent use, misuse, and abuse of the highly volatile concept of machismo in its association with Latino men. Too often given a narrow interpretation by Anglos and some Latinos as self-aggrandizement and exaggerated masculinity, machismo and male gender role have been presented here as distinct aspects of Puerto Rican men's lives. Specifically, machismo has been considered as a significant component of the broader Latino male gender role construct that needs to be understood in its historical, sociopolitical, and cultural context.

Although numerous behavioral traits associated with machismo have certainly been evidenced among the diverse Latino groups, the discussion has noted the critical need for further serious dialogue and in-depth study of machismo. Other, less prominent, elements of the broader male gender role norm have been presented that contrast with the machismo aspect.

Finally, this analysis should encourage clinical practitioners to facilitate Puerto Rican men's gender-role transitions by exploring their restricted traditional masculine identity and helping adapt it to healthier roles in their personal and social lives.

References

Aramoni, A. (1972). Machismo. *Psychology Today, 5,* 69–72.

Baca-Zinn, M. (1982). Chicano men and masculinity. *Journal of Ethnic Studies, 10,* 20–44.

Bem, S. L. (1985). Gender schema theory: a cognitive account of sex typing. *Psychological Review, 88,* 354–364.

Brooks, G. R., & Silverstein, L. B. (1995). In R. F. Levant & W. S. Pollack (Eds.), *A new psychology of men* (pp. 280–333). New York: Basic Books.

Canino, I., & Canino, G. (1980). Impact of stress on the Puerto Rican family: Treatment considerations. *American Journal of Orthopsychiatry, 50,* 535–541.

Casas, J. M., Wagenheim, B. R., Banchero, R., & Mendoza-Romero, J. (1994). Hispanic masculinity: Myth or psychological schema meriting clinical considerations. *Hispanic Journal of Behavioral Sciences, 16,* 315–331.

Comas-Díaz, L. (1989). Culturally relevant issues and treatment implications for Hispanics. In D. R. Koslow, & E. Salet (Eds.), *Crossing cultures in mental health* (pp. 31–48). Washington, D.C.: Society for International Education Training and Research.

De La Cancela, V. (1986). A critical analysis of Puerto Rican machismo: Implications for clinical practice. *Psychotherapy, 23,* 291–296.

De La Cancela, V. (1988). Labor pains: Puerto Rican males in transition. *Centro de Estudios Puertorriqueños Bulletin, 2,* 40–55.

De La Cancela, V. (1991). Working affirmatively with Puerto Rican men: Professional and personal reflections. In M. Bograd (Ed.), *Feminist approaches for men in family therapy* (pp. 195–211). New York: Hawthorn Press.

Deyoung, Y., & Zigler, E. F. (1994). Machismo in two cultures: Relation to punitive child-rearing practices. *American Journal of Orthopsychiatry, 64,* 386–395.

Diaz-Royo, A. (1976). *Dignidad y respeto. Dos temas centrales en la cultura puertorriqueña tradicional* [Dignity and respect: Two central themes in the traditional Puerto Rican culture]. Unpublished manuscript, Department of Psychology, University of Puerto Rico, Rio Piedras, Puerto Rico.

Doyle, J. A. (1983). *The male experience.* Dubuque, IA; William C. Brown.

Ghali, S. B. (1977). Cultural sensitivity and the Puerto Rican Client. *Social Case work, 58,* 459–468.

Gil, R. M., & Vazquez, C. A. (1996). *The Maria paradox: How Latina women can merge old world traditions with new world self-esteem.* New York: Putnam.

Goldstein, E. G. (1995). *Ego psychology and social work practice* (2nd ed.). New York: Free Press.

Gonzalez, A. (1982). Sex roles of the traditional Mexican American family: A comparison of Chicano and Anglo students' attitudes. *Journal of Cross-Cultural Psychology, 13,* 330–339.

Institute for Puerto Rican Policy. (1995, August). *IPR datanote on the Puerto Rican community.* New York: Author.

Kimmel, M. S., & Messner, M. A. (Eds.). (1992). *Men's lives.* New York: Macmillian.

Landy, D. (1959). *Tropical childhood: Cultural transmission and learning in a rural Puerto Rican village.* Chapel Hill: University Press of North Carolina.

Lazur, R. F., & Majors, R. (1995). Men of color: Ethnocultural variations of male gender role strain. In R. F. Levant & W. S. Pollack (Eds.), *A new psychology of men.* New York: Basic Books.

Levant, R. F. (1992). Toward the reconstruction of masculinity. *Journal of Family Psychology, 5,* 379–402.

Levant, R. F., & Pollack, W. S. (1995). *A new psychology of men.* New York: Basic Books.

Martinez, K. J. (1994). Cultural sensitivity in family therapy gone awry. *Hispanic Journal of Behavioral Sciences, 16,* 75–89.

Mayo, Y. (1993). *The utilization of mental health services, acculturation, and machismo among Puerto Rican men.* Unpublished doctoral dissertation, School of Social Work, Adelphi University, Garden City, NY.

Mirandé, A. (1988). Qué gacho es ser macho: It's a drag to be a macho man. *Aztlan, 17,* 63–69.

O'Neil, J. M. (1982). Gender-role conflict and strain in men's lives. In K. Solomon & N. Levy (Eds.), *Men in transition: Theory and therapy* (pp. 5–44). New York: Plenum.

Padilla, A. M., & Ruiz, R. A. (1973). *Latino mental health. A review of literature.* Washington, DC: Government Printing Office.

Ramírez, R. L. (1993). *Dime capitán: Reflexiones sobre la masculinidad* [Tell me: Reflections on masculinity]. Rio Piedras, PR: Ediciones Huracán.

Ramos-MacKay, J. M., Comas-Diaz, L., & Rivera, L. A. (1988). Puerto Ricans. In L. Comas-Diaz & E. E. E. Griffith (Eds.), *Clinical guidelines in cross-cultural mental health* (pp. 204–232). New York: Wiley.

Rodríguez, L. J. (1996). On macho. In R. González (Ed.), *Muy macho: Latino men confront their manhood* (pp. 187–201). New York: Anchor Books.

Ruiz, R. A. (1981). Cultural and historical perspective in counseling Hispanics. In D. W. Sue (Ed.), *Counseling the culturally different: Theory and practice* (pp. 186–216). New York: Wiley.

Stevens, E. (1972). Machismo and marianismo. *Transaction–Society, 10,* 57–63.

Torres-Matrullo, C. (1976). Acculturation and psychopathology among Puerto Rican women in mainland United States. *American Journal of Orthopsychiatry, 46,* 710–719.

U.S. Bureau of the Census. (1994). *Hispanics-Latinos: Diverse people in a multicultural society. A Special Report. Population characteristics, Current Population Reports, 1995.* Washington, DC: National Association of Hispanic Publications.

Valdéz, L., Barón, A., & Ponce, F. (1987). Counseling Hispanic men. In M. Scher, M. Stevens, G. Good, & Eichennfield (Eds.), *Handbook of counseling & psychotherapy with men* (pp. 203–217). Newbury Park, CA: Sage.

*Chapter 2: Putting It All Together*_____

1. How might the experience of female powerlessness affect Puerto Rican girls and women?

2. Lips defines power as "the capacity to have an impact or produce an effect," and describes two major areas of powerlessness for females—mastery over tasks and influence over people. How might machismo help or hinder Puerto Rican men to experience power in these areas?

3. In what areas of your life do you feel powerful? In what areas do you feel powerless? How might your experience of power and powerlessness be related to your gender?

4. Torres argues that "the changing position of Puerto Rican women has been reported as detrimental to some Puerto Rican men . . . but may also contribute to men's personal growth." How might men and boys benefit if girls and women are encouraged to become more powerful? Be specific.

3

Alike or Different?
The Relationship of Gender
to Academic Performance
and Communication

It is often assumed that males and females have different abilities, either because there are innate differences between the sexes, or because males and females are taught different skills. The authors of the readings in this chapter argue that behaviors that appear to be the result of innate or learned gender differences are, in fact, the temporary result of situational factors. For example, the first reading describes research which demonstrates that female deficiencies in math performance may be due to the situation of "stereotype threat," rather than due to innate abilities or internalized cultural messages. When the situation of stereotype threat is eliminated, women perform as well as men. The second reading takes a critical look at research on gender differences in interaction. The author argues that the popular belief that males and females have different styles of interaction which are consistently displayed is incorrect. Instead, it is the situational context, and social factors such as stereotyped expectations, status differences, and social roles which cause an individual to display masculine or feminine behavior in a particular interaction.

5

Stereotype Threat and Women's Math Performance

Steven J. Spencer, Claude M. Steele, and Diane M. Quinn

It is a stereotype that women have less ability in math than men. When women perform math, they risk being judged by this stereotype and seen as deficient, an experience known as "stereotype threat" **(defined norm).** Spenser, Steele, and Quinn hypothesize that the experience of stereotype threat may negatively impact on women's math performance. In this reading, they report the results of two studies* which support this hypothesis. The first study replicates research demonstrating that women perform as well as men on easy tests of math ability, but do less well on advanced tests. In the second study, all participants were given the same difficult math exam, but stereotype threat was manipulated by telling half of the participants that the test had demonstrated gender differences in the past (thus evoking stereotype threat), and the other half that the test had never shown gender differences (thus making the stereotype irrelevant). It was found that women performed as well as men when they were told that the test showed no gender differences (i.e., when there was no stereotype threat). Interestingly, the reverse held true for men. They performed slightly worse when they were told there were no gender differences, compared to their performance in the gender difference condition. In their discussion of this research, Spenser, Steele, and Quinn make the point that gender differences in math performance may be the result of situations where women experience stereotype threat, rather than the result of innate abilities or internalized cultural messages about math ability **(more alike than different).** If this is so, then women's math performance can be improved, simply by developing strategies for removing stereotype threat.

---

*A third study which investigates mediating factors in stereotype threat is reported in the original article, but has not been included here.

Questions to Consider:

1. According to Spenser, Steele, and Quinn, why does stereotype threat affect women's math performance?
2. Give an example of a time you experienced stereotype threat. How did it affect your performance?
3. If you were to conduct a study to follow-up the studies described here, what variables would you examine?
4. What strategies would you suggest to reduce stereotype threat?
5. What are some implications of Steele's findings for gender differences in other abilities?

This paper was based on a doctoral dissertation completed by Steven J. Spenser under the direction of Claude M. Steele. This research was supported by a National Institute of Mental Health predoctoral fellowship to Steven J. Spenser and grants from the National Institute of Mental Health (MH45889) and the Russell Sage Foundation (879.304) to Claude M. Steele. The authors thank Jennifer Crocker, Lenard Eron, Hazel Markus, David Myers, Richard Nisbett, William Von Hippel, and several anonymous reviewers for their helpful advice and comments on earlier drafts of the manuscript. They also thank Latasha Nash, Sabrina Voelpel, and Nancy Faulk for their help in running experimental sessions.

There was an enormous body of masculine opinion to the effect that nothing could be expected of women intellectually. Even if her father did not read out loud these opinions, any girl could read them for herself; and the reading, even in the nineteenth century, must have lowered her vitality, and told profoundly upon her work. There would always have been that assertion—you cannot do this, you are incapable of doing that—to protest against, to overcome.

Virginia Woolf (*A room of one's own*)

No other science has been more concerned with the nature of prejudice and stereotyping than social psychology. Since its inception, the field has surveyed the content of stereotypes (e.g., Katz & Braly, 1933), examined their effect on social perception and behavior (e.g., Brewer, 1979; Devine, 1989; Duncan, 1976; Sagar & Schofield, 1980; Gaertner & Dovidio, 1986; Hamilton, 1979; Rothbart, 1981), explored the processes through which they are formed (Hamilton, 1979; Rothbart, 1981; Smith & Zarate, 1992), examined motivational bases of prejudice (e.g., Rokeach & Mezei, 1966; Tajfel, 1978), and, along with personality psychologists, examined the origins of prejudice in human character (e.g., Adorno, Frenkel-Brunswick, Levinson, & Sanford, 1950; Ehrlich, 1973; Jordan, 1968). It is surprising, then, that there has been no corresponding attention to the experience of being the target of prejudice and stereotypes. Of all the topics covered in Gordon Allport's (1954) classic *The nature of prejudice*, this one has been among the least explored in subsequent research. Happily now, this situation has begun to change (e.g., Swim & Stangor, 1998, and this issue), at least in the sense of there having emerged a greater interest in the effects of and reactions to societal devaluation. For the most part, this work has focused on stigmatization, the experience of bearing in the words of Goffman (1963), "a spoiled identity"—some characteristic that, in the eyes of society, causes one to be broadly devalued (Crocker & Major, 1989; Frable, 1989; Jones, Farina, Hastorf, Markus, Miller, & Scott, 1984; S. Steele, 1990).

The present research extends this focus by examining the experience of being in a situation where one faces judgment based on societal stereotypes about one's group, an experience we refer to as "stereotype threat." This experience begins with the fact that most devaluing group stereotypes are widely known throughout a society. For example, in a sample of participants who varied widely in prejudice toward African–Americans, Devine (1989) found that all participants knew the stereotypes about this group. Possibly because communicative processes play such a central role in the acquisition of stereotypes (Ashmore & Del Boca, 1981)—that is, public and private discourse, the media, school curricula, artistic canons, and the like—knowledge of them is widely disseminated throughout a society, even among those who do not find them believable. This means that people who are the targets of these stereotypes are likely to know them too. And herein lies the threat. In situations where the stereotype applies, they face the implication that anything they do or any feature they have that fits the stereotype makes it more plausible that they will be evaluated based on the stereotype. As in the opening quote by Woolf, there is always that assertion "to protest against, to overcome." This predicament we argue is experienced as a self-threat. Consider the aging grandfather who has misplaced his keys. Prevailing stereotypes about the elderly—their reputed memory deficits, for example—establish a context where his actions that fit the group stereotype, such as losing keys, make it a plausible explanation of his actions. Stereotype threat, it is important to stress, is conceptualized as a situational predicament—felt in situations where one can be judged by, treated in terms of, or self-fulfill negative stereotypes about one's group. It is not, we assume, peculiar to the internal psychology of particular groups. It can be experienced by the members of any group

about whom negative stereotypes exist—generation "X," the elderly, white males, etc. And we stress that it is situationally specific—experienced in situations where the critical negative stereotype applies, but not necessarily in others. In this way, it differs from the more cross-situational devaluation of "marking" that, for example, stigma is thought to be (e.g., Jones et al., 1984).

In the present research, our central proposition is this: when a stereotype about one's group indicts an important ability, one's performance in situations where that ability can be judged comes under an extra pressure—that of possibly being judged by or self-fulfilling the stereotype—and this extra pressure may interfere with performance. We test this proposition in relation to women's math performance, both as a test of the theory and as a means of understanding the processes that depress women's performance and participation in math-related areas. Consider their predicament. Widely known stereotypes in this society impute to women less ability in mathematics and related domains (Eccles, Jacobs, & Harold, 1990; Fennema & Sherman, 1977; Jacobs & Eccles, 1985; Swim, 1994). Thus in situations where math skills are exposed to judgment—be it a formal test, classroom participation, or simply computing the waiter's tip—women bear the extra burden of having a stereotype that alleges a sex-based inability. This is a predicament that others, not stereotyped in this way, do not bear. The present research tests whether this predicament significantly influences women's performance on standardized math tests.

We believe, however, that these processes may also contribute to gender differences in other forms of math achievement as well as test performance (and to achievement deficits in other groups that face stereotype threat, e.g., Steele & Aronson,

1995). For example, the stereotype threat that women experience in math-related domains may cause them to feel that they do not belong in math classes. Consequently they may "disidentify" with math as an important domain, that is, avoid or drop the domain as an identity or basis of self-esteem—all to avoid the evaluative threat they might feel in that domain (Major, Spenser, Schmader, Wolfe, & Crocker, 1998; Steele, 1992, 1997). Such a process, then, originating with stereotype threat, may influence women's participation in math-related curricula and professions, as well as their test performance. But for now, we turn to the question of gender differences in math test performance.[1]

In this literature, although such differences are not common (Hyde, Fennema, & Lamon, 1990; Kimball, 1989; Steinkamp & Maehr, 1983), a general pattern has begun to emerge: women perform roughly the same as men except when the test material is quite advanced; then, often, they do worse. Benbow and Stanley (1980, 1983) found, for example, that among talented junior high school math students, boys outperformed girls on the quantitative SAT, a test that was obviously advanced for this age group. Similarly, Hyde, Fennema, and Lamon (1990) in an extensive review of the literature found that males did not outperform females in computational ability or understanding of mathematics concepts, but did outperform them in advanced problem solving at the high school and college levels. Kimball (1989) found virtually no gender differences in math course work except for college level calculus and analytical geometry courses, where males did better.

Finally, several national surveys (Armstrong, 1981; Ethington & Wolfe, 1984; Fennema & Sherman, 1977, 1978; Levine & Ornstein, 1983; Sherman & Fennema, 1977) reached the general conclusion that gender differences are more likely to emerge as students take more difficult course work in high school and college.

Explanations of these differences have tended to fall into two camps. Benbow and Stanley (1980, 1983) have argued that they reflect genetically rooted sex differences in math ability. Others (e.g., Eccles, 1987; Fennema & Sherman, 1978; Levine & Ornstein, 1983; Meece, Eccles, Kaczala, Goff, & Futterman, 1982) argue that these differences reflect gender-role socialization, such that males, far more than females, are encouraged to participate in math and the sciences and that the cumulative effects of this differential socialization are most evident on difficult material.

While acknowledging the contribution of socialization, we suggest that these differences might also reflect the influence of stereotype threat, another process that may be most rife when the material is advanced for the performer's skills. It is important to stress that a test need not be difficult for stereotype threat to occur. Simply being in a situation where one can confirm a negative stereotype about one's group—the women simply sitting down to the math test, for example, could be enough to cause this self-evaluative threat. But for several reasons, it should be most likely to interfere with test performance when the test is difficult. If the test is less than difficult, a woman's successful experience with it will counter the threat the stereotype might otherwise have

---

[1]In this paper we will use the terms gender and gender difference when we are referring to a difference that we believe has a psychological cause. We will use the term sex when dividing men and women into categories and when we refer to a difference that is purported to be based on biological differences between men and women.

caused. Also, easier material is simply less likely to be interfered with by the pressure that stereotype threat is likely to pose. When the test is difficult, however, any difficulty in solving the problems poses the stereotype as a possible explanation for one's performance. Thus for women stereotype threat should be highest on difficult tests.

Study 1

As a first step in our research we sought to replicate the pattern found in the literature—that women underperform in comparison to men on difficult tests, but perform equally with men on easy tests—in a sample of highly qualified equally prepared men and women. The men and women were selected to have a very strong math background.

In the experiment we varied the difficulty of the math test that was given. The difficult test was taken from the advanced GRE exam in mathematics. Most of the questions involved advanced calculus, although some required knowledge of abstract algebra and real variable theory (Educational Testing Service, 1987b). The easier test was taken from the quantitative section of the GRE general exam. It assumes knowledge of advanced algebra, trigonometry, and geometry, but not calculus (Educational Testing Service, 1987a). For the well-trained participants used in this research, this latter exam should be more within the limits of their skills.

The experiment was administered on a computer. This enabled us to measure the amount of time participants spent on the test and thereby to assess the extent to which differences in performance might be related to differences in participants' effort.

Method

Participants and Design.   Twenty-eight men and 28 women were selected from the introductory psychology pool at the University of Michigan. All participants were required to have completed at least one semester (but not more than a year) of calculus and to have received a grade of "B" or better. They also were required to have scored above the 85th percentile on the math subsection of the SAT (Scholastic Aptitude Test) or the ACT (American College Test). Further, on 11-point scales anchored by strongly agree and strongly disagree, participants had to strongly agree (by responding between 1 and 3) with both of the following statements: (1) I am good at math and (2) It is important to me that I am good at math. Markus (1977) has used these items to measure whether a person is self-schematic in a domain. The experiment took the form of a 2 (male and female) × 2 (easier and difficult math test) design. The primary dependent variables were performance on the math test and the time participants spent working on the test.

Materials and Apparatus.   The tests were administered on a microcomputer. On each question participants had the options of answering the question, leaving the question blank, or skipping the question, which allowed them to answer it later. The computer recorded participants' responses and how long they worked on each problem. The test was scored using the standard formula for scoring the GRE, which yields a percentage score corrected so as to disadvantage guessing. Correct items got 1 point, items left blank got no points or deductions, and incorrect items got a deduction of 1 point divided by the number of response options for that item (usually 4 or 5)—the correction factor for guessing.

Procedure. Participants reported to the laboratory in mixed, male and female groups of three to six. They were told. "We are developing some new tests that we are evaluating across a large group of University of Michigan students. Today you will be taking a math test." The first screen of the test contained instructions that were common to both tests. These instructions explained how to use the computer and how the test would be scored. Participants were also informed that they would have 30 min to complete the test and that they would receive their score at the end of the test. All subsequent instructions were taken directly from the GRE exam itself. These instructions provided definitions for certain terms and symbols, explained the range of items on the test, and included a sample item. The experimenter typed into the computer a randomly assigned code word that determined the participant's test difficulty condition. This enabled the experimenter to remain blind to participants' condition assignments. The single experimenter was male. After participants completed the test they were thoroughly debriefed and thanked for their participation.

Results and Discussion

This experiment tested whether the pattern observed in the literature—that women underperform on difficult tests but perform just as well on easier test—holds true with the highly selected participants used in this research. As the means in Fig. 1 show, this pattern did emerge. A two-way ANOVA (Sex × Test Difficulty) revealed a significant main effect for sex, $F(1, 52) = 3.99$, $p = .05$, and a main effect for test difficulty. $F(1, 52) = 137.27$, $p < .001$, that were both qualified by the significant interaction between gender and test difficulty, $F(1, 52) = 5.34$, $p < .05$.[2] Student–Newman–Keuls posthoc comparisons of all possible pairs of means showed that women taking the difficult math test did worse than each of the other groups and that men taking the difficult math test did worse than men or women taking the easier test ($p < .05$).

On average, women taking the difficult test worked 1497 s; men taking the difficult test worked 1539 s; women taking the easy test worked 1738 s; and men taking the easy test worked 1599 s. A two-way (Sex × Test Difficulty) ANOVA of this measure revealed only a marginally significant main effect for test difficulty, with participants spending slightly more time on the easier test, $F(1, 52) = 3.151$, $p < .10$. No other effects obtained significance.

These results show that the differences observed in the literature can be replicated with a highly selected and identified group of participants. Women underperformed in

---

[2]Throughout the paper we report the results using ANOVA and posthoc comparisons. We also analyzed the results testing planned comparisons based on our predictions. All of these planned comparisons were highly significant, $p < .01$. We present the ANOVA and posthoc comparisons, however, because these more conservative tests show that the results are significant even without the added assumptions that are required for a planned comparison. In addition, for each of the analyses of participant's scores reported in the paper we also conducted analyses of covariance using standardized test scores, previous grades, number of semesters of calculus, and importance of math as covariates. These analyses produced results which were essentially the same as those reported. Also, we do not report participants' performance in terms of an accuracy index, that is, the percentage of problems correct of the number they attempted. Because of the small number of items on the test, almost all participants attempted almost all of the items. Therefore, it is not surprising that analyses of this index yielded results that were virtually identical to those reported in the text.

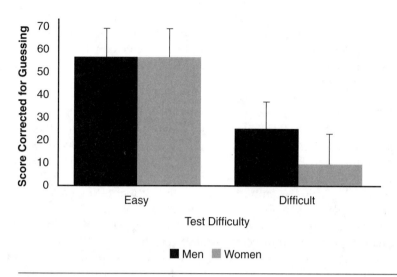

FIGURE 3.1   *Performance on a math test as a function of sex of subject and test difficulty.*

comparison to men on the difficult test, but did just as well as men on the easy test.

Study 2

The results of Study 1 mirror the results observed in the literature, but the question still remains about what causes these differences. Our position is that women experience stereotype threat—the possibility of being stereotyped—when taking math tests, and this stereotype threat is especially likely to undermine performance on difficult tests. But alternative interpretations remain. Perhaps women equaled men on the easier math exam in Study 1 not because stereotype threat had less effect when women

took this exam, but because only advanced material is sensitive to real ability differences between men and women.

In the present study we tested the effects of stereotype threat directly by giving all participants a difficult math exam—similar to the one used in Study 1—but varied whether the gender stereotype was relevant to their performance. We manipulated the relevance of the stereotype by varying how the test was represented. In the relevance condition participants were told that the test had shown gender differences in the past—a characterization that explicitly evoked the stereotype about women's math ability.[3] In the condition where the stereotype was to be irrelevant, participants were told that the test had never shown gender differences in the past. It is important to

[3]We assumed that telling participants that there were gender differences would lead them to believe that men did better than women. Of course, this conclusion is not inevitable, but all participants in this condition when asked informally reported this to be their interpretation.

stress that this last instruction did not attack the validity of the stereotype itself. It merely represented the test in such a way as to make the stereotype irrelevant to interpreting women's performance on this *particular* math test—it being a test on which women do as well as men.

If women underperformed on the difficult test in Studies 1 because of stereotype threat—the possibility that one's performance could be judged stereotypically then making the stereotype irrelevant to interpreting their performance should eliminate this underperformance. That is, representing the test as insensitive to gender differences, and thus as a test for which the gender stereotype is unrelated to their performance difficulty, should prevent performance decrements due to stereotype threat. But if this underperformance is due to an ability difference between men and women that is detectable only with difficult math items, women should underperform regardless of how relevant the stereotype is to their performance. In this way, this study provides a direct test of our theory—that it is a stereotype-guided interpretation of performance difficulty that causes women's underperformance on the difficult math tests in these experiments.

Method

Participants and Design. Thirty women and twenty-four men were selected from the introductory psychology participant pool at the University of Michigan using the same criteria as in Study 1. The experiment took the form of a 2 × 2 mixed model design with one between-participants factor (sex) and one within-participants factor (test characterization). The primary dependent variables were performance on the math test and the time participants spent working on the test.

Materials and Apparatus. The tests were administered on computers using the same format as described in Study 1. The difficult test used in Study 1 was divided into two halves, and participants were given 15 min to complete each half. The first six questions from this earlier test comprised the first test and the next five questions comprised the second test. Half of the participants were told that the first test was one on which there were gender differences and that the second test was one on which there were no gender differences. The other half were told the opposite, that the first test was one for which there were no gender differences and that the second test was one on which there were gender differences. Participants were randomly assigned to these order conditions.

Procedure. The directions and procedure were basically the same as those of Study 1, except that participants were told that they would be working on two tests and would have 15 min to complete each test. Participants read: "As you may know there has been some controversy about whether there are gender differences in math ability. Previous research has sometimes shown gender differences and sometimes shown no gender differences. Yet little of this research has been carried out with women and men who are very good in math. You were selected for this experiment because of your strong background in mathematics." The instructions went on to report that the first test had been shown to produce gender differences and that the second test had been shown not to produce such differences, or vice versa, depending on the order condition. The single experimenter was again male.

Results and Discussion

The two halves of the test did not prove to be equally difficult. In fact, the mean for both men and women on the second test was not different from 0, creating a floor effect for that test. To circumvent this problem, we used performance on the first test, the half that did not produce a floor effect, as the dependent variable in this experiment. Test characterization was then treated as a between-participants factor such that people who were told that the first test did yield gender differences made up one level of this factor and people who were told that it did not yield gender differences made up the other level of this factor. A two-way ANOVA (Sex × Test Characterization) of participants' scores on the test confirmed our predictions. When participants were explicitly told that the test yielded gender dif-

ferences, women greatly underperformed in relation to men. But when the test was purported not to yield gender differences, women performed at the same level as equally qualified men. This happened, of course, even though the test in these two conditions was the same. The condition means are reported in Fig. 2. There was a main effect for sex, $F(1, 50) = 5.66$, $p < .05$, but it was qualified by a significant sex-by-test characterization interaction, $F(1, 50) = 4.18$, $p < .05$. Student–Newman–Keuls post-hoc comparisons of all possible pairs of means revealed that the mean for women in the gender-differences condition was significantly lower than each of the other means and that no other means differed from each other ($p < .05$).

We analyzed the time spent on each item only for the first test participants, that is, the half for which there was no floor effect. Women in the gender-differences condition spent an average of 609 s on the test; men in the gender-differences condition

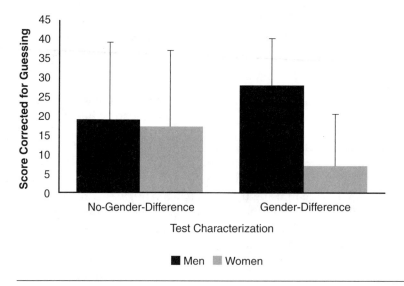

FIGURE 3.2 *Performance on a difficult math test as a function of sex of subject and test characterization.*

spent an average of 817 s; women in the no-gender-differences characterization condition spent an average of 659 s; while men in the no-gender-differences condition spent an average of 697 s. A two-way (Sex × Test Characterization) ANOVA of this measure revealed a near-significant main effect for sex, $F(1, 50) = 2.76$, $p = .10$, with men tending to spend more time on these test items than women. No other effects reached significance.

Characterizing the test as insensitive to gender differences was enough to totally eliminate women's underperformance in this experiment. Yet when the same test was characterized as sensitive to gender differences, women significantly underperformed in relation to equally qualified men. We believe that by presenting the test as one on which gender differences do not occur, we made the stereotype of women's math inability irrelevant to interpreting their performance on the test—this particular test. It allowed these women to be as unconcerned with the gender-based stereotype as equally qualified men, which, in turn, allowed them to perform as well as these men. These findings provide strong evidence that women's underperformance on these difficult math tests results from stereotype threat, rather than from sex-linked ability differences that are detectable only on advanced math material. If women were just unable to do math at the most advanced levels as measured on these tests, their performance would not have improved when we told them that there were no gender differences on the test they were taking. That women did improve demonstrates that it was something about the test taking situation rather then something about their ability that accounted for the difference in their performance.

We should also note that men did slightly worse when they were told that there were no gender differences on the test than when they were told that there were gender differences. This difference did not obtain significance and therefore should be interpreted with caution. However, it might suggest that characterizing the test as producing gender differences benefited men or that characterizing the test as not producing gender differences interfered with men's performance. . . .

General Discussion

Being the potential target of a negative group stereotype, we have argued, creates a specific predicament: in any situation where the stereotype applies, behaviors and features of the individual that fit the stereotype make it plausible as a explanation of one's performance. We call this predicament stereotype threat. The crux of our argument is that collectively held stereotypes in our society establish this kind of threat for women in settings that involve math performance, especially advanced math performance. The aim of the present research has been to show that this threat can quite substantially interfere with women's math performance, especially performance that is at the limits of their skills, and that factors that remove this threat can improve that performance.

The experiments reported here provide strong and consistent support for this reasoning. Study 1 replicated the finding in the literature that women underperform on advanced tests but not on tests more within their skills. Study 2 attempted to directly manipulate stereotype threat by varying how the test was characterized—as one that generally found gender differences or as one that did not. Representing test performance as unaffected by gender, we reasoned, would make the gender stereotype irrelevant as an interpretation of test performance, preclude stereotype threat, and thereby allow women to match the performance of equally qualified men. This is precisely what happened in this condition, while in the condition where the same test was represented as affected by gender, women again underperformed in relation to men.

These findings also speak to the generality of stereotype threat's negative effect on standardized test performance. Other research (Steele & Aronson, 1995; Croizet & Claire, 1998) has shown that stereotype threat can interfere with the performance of African-American and low socioeconomic students on difficult standardized tests. Thus, by showing a comparable effect among women test takers, the present findings help to establish the generality across groups of stereotype threat's impairment of standardized test performance.

This is not to say that there are no important differences in the way that stereotype threat affects different groups. We believe that such important differences do exist. For example, the nature of the stereotype about women's math ability is different than the stereotype about African-Americans' ability in school. The stereotype about women is relatively confined—pertaining mainly to math and science—whereas the stereotype about African-Americans is relatively broad, impugning almost all academic areas, which may lend to important differences in the way stereotype threat affects women and African-Americans. When women face stereotype threat in a math class, for instance, they can avoid it by dropping math and picking up most other classes. African-Americans, however, face a much more difficult problem when they face stereotype threat in school. For them it will be much more difficult to avoid. Women can still maintain a

view of themselves as smart and capable, but just not good in math, if they disidentify with math. African-Americans, however, are likely to find it much more difficult to maintain a view of themselves as smart and capable, but just not able to cut it at school, if they disidentify with school. This reasoning suggests that stereotype threat may lead women to disidentify with math more readily than it leads African-Americans to disidentify with school. . . .

Stereotype Threat and the Genetic Interpretation of Gender Differences in Math Ability

Our research also has implications for the lingering controversy over the role of biology versus the environment in determining the few sex differences that persist in mathematics performance. In its most recent incarnation, this issue has centered on the claims of Benbow and Stanley (1980, 1983). This much-cited research studied a group of seventh and eighth grade boys and girls, exceptionally talented in math, who scored above 700 on the quantitative section of the SAT. Boys were overrepresented in this group by a factor of 10 to 1. And since these boys and girls all had the same prior course work in math, the authors took this fact to indicate a sex difference in biological capacity for math.

There have been several important critiques of this research and its conclusion (e.g., Eccles & Jacobs, 1986; Fennema, 1981; Jacobs & Eccles, 1985). A principal one is that being in the same classes does not mean that boys and girls have the same environment. Considerable research shows, for example, that boys and girls are treated very differently in the same classrooms (Constantinople, Cornelius, & Gray, 1988; Leinhardt, Seewald, & Engel, 1979). Over time, this argument goes, these differences in treatment, as well as differences in the larger societal socialization of women, could produce the findings that Benbow and Stanley report. While endorsing these arguments, we suggest that the present findings take them a step farther. The experience of the testing situation itself may be dramatically different for women and men. As the present research shows, stereotype threat as a feature of this situation can undermine women's performance, precisely when the test is difficult. The seventh and eighth grade boys and girls in the Benbow and Stanley research, who are matched in eighth grade math ability, but given what for them is a very advanced math test (the quantitative SAT exam), are essentially in the same position as the participants in the high stereotype threat conditions in the present research. As this threat was able to dramatically depress the performance of talented women math students in the present experiments, it may well have depressed the performance of the talented girls in the Benbow and Stanley research. Thus we may not need to look to the earlier experience of these girls or to their biology to explain their performance. The critical factor may be the stereotype threat of the immediate test-taking situation.[10]

Finally, in the interest of careful generalization, we note several important parameters of the stereotype threat effect. It assumes that the test taker construes the test as a fairly valid assessment of math ability, that they still care about this ability at least somewhat, and that the test be difficult. Stereotype threat effects should be less likely if the test is either too easy or too difficult (either in item content or time allotted) to be seen as validly reflecting ability. Also, if the test taker has already disidentified with math, in the sense of not caring about their performance, stereotype threat is not likely to drive their performance lower than their lack of motivation would. Thus, it is only when the test reflects on ability and is difficult and the test takers care about this ability that the stereotype becomes relevant and disturbing as a potential self-characterization. For this reason, stereotype threat probably has its most disruptive real-life effects on women as they encounter new math material at the limits of their skills—for example, new work units or a new curriculum level.

---

[10]If stereotype threat depresses women's performance on standardized math tests relative to that of men, one might ask whether it is appropriate to use the SAT as a means of equating men and women for skill level in these experiments? Several considerations are relevant. The first bears on the strong math students selected for these experiments. As the results of Study I show, performance-depressing stereotype threat emerged in these studies only when the test was at the limits of their skills. Thus it is very unlikely that stereotype threat hampered women's performance on the SAT exam they had taken just a few years earlier. It too was well within their skills, as indicated by their high scores. Over the full range of women taking the quantitative SAT, the performance of some, if not many, is likely to be depressed by stereotype threat and this may well contribute to the mean differences between men and women on this test. But because of the strong skills of the women used in our experiments, stereotype threat is considerably less likely to have affected their SAT performance. Second, even if it did depress their SAT performance, it would mean that the women in our studies actually have stronger math ability than the men with whom they were matched. This would only make it more difficult to detect a performance-depressing effect of stereotype threat; women in these conditions would have to underperform in relation to men who actually have weaker skills than they do. Thus, while acknowledging that stereotype threat almost certainly influences the SAT performance in the general population of test takers, we do not believe that this fact undermines our interpretation of these experimental results.

This process may also contribute to women's high attrition from quantitative fields, especially math, engineering, and the physical sciences, where their college attrition rate is 2 ½ times that of men (Hewitt & Seymour, 1991). At some point, continuously facing stereotype threat in these domains, women may disidentify with them and seek other domains on which to base their identity and esteem. While other factors surely contribute to this process gender-role orientation (Eccles, 1984; Eccles et al., 1990; Yee & Eccles, 1988), lack of role models (Douvan, 1976; Huckett, Esposito, & O'Halloran, 1989), and differential treatment of males and females in school (Constantinople et al., 1988; Peterson & Fennema, 1985)—we suggest that stereotype threat may be an underappreciated source of these patterns.

Embedded in our analysis is a certain hopefulness: the underperformance of women in quantitative fields may be more tractable than has been assumed. It attempts to understand the math performance of women not in terms of internal characteristics (e.g., abilities or internalized cultural orientations) but in terms of the interaction between the individual and a threatening predicament posed by societal stereotypes. Predicaments are circumstantial and thus should be easier to change than internalized characteristics. And though our experimental manipulations have yet to establish broadly generalizable strategies for changing this predicament, they do show that it can be changed.

References

Adorno, T. W., Frenkel-Brunswick, E., Levinson, D. J., & Sanford, R. N. (1950). *The authoritarian personality.* New York: Harper.

Allport, G. W. (1954). *The nature of prejudice.* Cambridge, MA: Addison-Wesley.

Armstrong, J. M. (1981). Achievement and participation of women in mathematics: Results from two national surveys. *Journal of Research in Mathematics Education, 12,* 356–372.

Ashmore, R. D., & Del Boca, F. K. (1981). Conceptual approaches to stereotypes and stereotyping. In D. L. Hamilton (Ed.), *Cognitive process in stereotyping and intergroup behavior* (pp. 1–35). Hillsdale, NJ: Erlbaum.

Bandura, A. (1977). *Social learning theory.* Englewood Cliffs, NJ: Prentice Hall.

Bandura, A. (1986). *Social foundations of thought and action: A social cognitive theory.* Englewood Cliffs, NJ: Prentice Hall.

Baron, R. M., & Kenny, D. A. (1986). The moderator-mediator variable distinction in social psychological research: Conceptual, strategic, and statistical considerations. *Journal of Personality and Social Psychology, 51,* 1173–1182.

Baumeister, R. F., & Showers, C. J. (1986). A review of paradoxical performance effects: Choking under pressure in sports and mental tests. *European Journal of Social Psychology, 16,* 361–383.

Benbow, C. P., & Stanley, J. C. (1980). Sex differences in mathematical ability: Fact or artifact? *Science, 210,* 1262–1264.

Benbow, C. P., & Stanley, J. C. (1983). Sex differences in mathematical reasoning ability: More facts. *Science, 222,* 1029–1031.

Brewer, M. B. (1979). In-group bias in the minimal intergroup situation: A cognitive-motivational analysis. *Psychological Bulletin, 86,* 307–324.

Constantinople, A., Cornelius, R., & Gray, J. (1988). The chilly climate: Fact or artifact? *Journal of Higher Education, 59,* 527–550.

Crandall, (1969). Sex differences in expectancy of intellectual and academic reinforcement. In C. P. Smith (Ed.), *Achievement-related behaviors in children.* New York: Russell Sage Found.

Crocker, J., & Major, B. (1989). Social stigma and self-esteem: The self-protective properties of stigma. *Psychological Review, 96,* 608–630.

Croizet, J. C., & Claire, T. (1998). Extending the concept of stereotype threat to social class: The intellectual underperformance of students from low socioeconomic backgrounds. *Personality and Social Psychology Bulletin, 24,* 588–594.

Devine, P. (1989). Stereotypes and prejudice: Their automatic and controlled components. *Journal of Personality and Social Psychology, 56,* 5–18.

Douvan, E. (1976). The role of models in women's professional development. *Psychology of Women Quarterly, 1,* 5–20.

Duncan, B. L. (1976). Differential social perception and attribution of intergroup violence: Testing the lower limits of stereotyping of blacks. *Journal of Personality and Social Psychology, 34,* 590–598.

Dweck, C. S., & Bush, E. (1976). Sex differences in learned helplessness: I. Differential debilitation with peer and adult evaluations. *Developmental Psychology, 12,* 147–156.

Dweck, C. S., & Gilliard, D. (1975). Expectancy statements as determinants of reactions to failure: Sex differences in persistence and expectancy change. *Journal of Personality and Social Psychology, 32,* 1077–1084.

Eccles, J. S. (1984). Sex differences in achievement patterns. In Sonderegger (Ed.), *Nebraska symposium on motivation* (Vol. 32). Lincoln, NE: Univ. of Nebraska Press.

Eccles, J. S. (1987). Gender roles and women's achievement-related decisions. *Psychology of Women Quarterly, 11,* 135–172.

Eccles, J. S., & Jacobs, J. E. (1986). Social forces shape math attitudes and performance. *Signs: Journal of Women in Culture and Society, 11,* 367–380.

Eccles, J. S., Jacobs, J. E., & Harold, R. E. (1990). Gender role stereotypes, expectancy effects, and parents' socialization of gender differences. *Journal of Social Issues, 46,* 183–201.

Eccles Parsons, J. S., Adler, T. F., Futterman, R., Goff, S. B., Kaczala, C. M., Meece, J. L., & Midgley, C. (1983). Expectations values, and academic behaviors. In J. T. Spence (Ed.), *Achievement and achievement motivation* (pp. 75–146). New York: Freeman.

Eccles Parsons, J. S., & Ruble, D. N. (1977). The development of achievement-related expectancies. *Child Development, 48,* 1075–1079.

Educational Testing Service (1987a). *Practicing to take the GRE General Exam.* Princeton, NJ: Educational Testing Service.

Educational Testing Service (1987b). *Practicing to take the GRE Mathematics Test.* Princeton, NJ: Educational Testing Service.

Ehrlich, H. J. (1973). *The social psychology of prejudice: A systematic theoretical review and propositional inventory of the American social psychological study of prejudice.* New York: Wiley.

Ethington, C. A., & Wolfe, L. M. (1984). Sex differences in a causal model of mathematics achievement. *Journal for Research in Mathematics Education, 15,* 361–377.

Fennema, E. H. (1981). Women and mathematics: Does research matter? *Journal for Research in Mathematics Education, 12,* 380–385.

Fennema, E. H., & Sherman, J. A. (1977). Sex-related differences in mathematics achievement, spatial visualization, and sociocultural factors. *American Educational Research Journal, 14,* 51–71.

Fennema, E. H., & Sherman, J. A. (1978). Sex-related differences in mathematics achievement and related factors: A further study. *Journal for Research in Mathematics Education, 9,* 189–203.

Frable, D. E. (1989). Marginal and mindful: Deviants in social interaction. *Journal of Personality and Social Psychology, 59,* 140–149.

Gaertner, S. L., & Dovidio, J. F. (1986). The aversive form of racism. In J. F. Dovidio, & S. L. Gaertner (Eds.), *Prejudice, discrimination, and racism* (pp. 61–90). New York: Academic Press.

Geen, R. G. (1991). Social motivation. *Annual Review of Psychology, 42,* 377–399.

Goffman, E. (1963). *Stigma: Notes on the management of spoiled identity.* New York: Touchstone.

Hamilton, D. L. (1979). A cognitive-attributional analysis of stereotyping. In L. Berkowitz (Ed.), *Advances in experimental social psychology* (Vol. 12, pp. 53–84). New York: Academic Press.

Hackett, G., Esposito, D., & O'Halloran, M. S. (1989). The relationship of role model influence to the career salience and educational and career plans of college women. *Journal of Vocational Behavior, 35,* 164–180.

Hewitt, N. M., & Seymour, E. (1991). *Factors contributing to high attrition rates among science and engineering undergraduate majors.* Report to the Alfred P. Sloan Foundation.

Hilton, T. L., & Lee, V. E. (1988). Student interest and persistence in science: Changes in the educational pipeline in the last decade. *Journal of Higher Education, 59,* 510–526.

Hyde, J. S., Fennema, E. H., & Lamon, S. J. (1990). Gender differences in mathematics performance: A meta-analysis. *Psychological Bulletin, 107,* 139–155.

Jacobs, J. E., & Eccles, J. S. (1985). Gender differences in math ability: The impact of media reports on parents. *Educational Researcher, 14,* 20–25.

Jones, E. E., Farina, A., Hastorf, A. H., Markus, H., Miller, D. T., & Scott, R. A. (1984). *Social Stigma.* New York: Freeman.

Jordan (1968). *White over black: American attitudes toward the Negro.* Chapel Hill, NC: Univ. of North Carolina Press.

Katz, D., & Braly, K. W. (1933). Racial stereotypes of 100 college students. *Journal of Abnormal and Social Psychology, 28,* 28–290.

Kimball, M. M. (1989). A new perspective on women's math achievement. *Psychological Bulletin, 105,* 198–214.

Leinhardt, G., Seewald, A., & Engel, M. (1979). Learning what's taught: Sex differences in instruction. *Journal of Educational Psychology, 71,* 432–439.

Levine, D. U., & Ornstein, A. C. (1983). Sex differences in ability and achievement. *Journal of Research and Development in Education, 16,* 62–72.

Major, B., Spencer, S. J., Schmader, T., Wolfe, C., & Crocker, J. (1998). Coping with negative stereotypes about intellectual performance: The role of psychological disengagement. *Personality and Social Psychology Bulletin, 24,* 34–50.

Markus, H. (1977). Self-schemata and processing information about the self. *Journal of Personality and Social Psychology, 35.*

Meece, J. L., Eccles, J. S., Kaczala, C. M., Goff, S. B., & Futterman, R. (1982). Sex differences in math achievement: Towards a model of academic choice. *Psychological Bulletin, 91,* 324–348.

Peterson, P. L., & Fennema, E. (1985). Effective teaching, student engagement in classroom activities, and sex-related differences in learning mathematics. *American Educational Research Journal, 22,* 309–335.

Rokeach, M., & Mezei, L. (1966). Race and shared beliefs as factors in social choice. *Science, 151,* 167–172.

Rothbart, M. (1981). Memory processes and social beliefs. In D. L. Hamilton (Ed.), *Cognitive processes in stereotyping and intergroup behavior.* Hillsdale, NJ: Erlbaum.

Sagar, H. A., & Schofield, J. W. (1980). Racial and behavioral cues in black and white children's perceptions of ambiguously aggressive cues. *Journal of Personality and Social Psychology, 39,* 590–598.

Sarason, I. G. (1972). Experimental approaches to test anxiety: Attention and the uses of information. In Spielberger, C. D. (Ed.), *Anxiety: Current trends in theory and research* (Vol. 2). New York: Academic Press.

Schlenker, B. R., & Leary, M. R. (1982). Social anxiety and self-presentation: A conceptualization and model. *Psychological Bulletin, 92,* 641–669.

Sherman, J. A., & Fennema, E. H. (1977). The study of mathematics by high school girls and boys: Related variables. *American Educational Research Journal, 14,* 159–168.

Smith, E. R., & Zarate, M. A. (1992). Exemplar-based model of social judgment. *Psychological Review, 99,* 3–21.

Spielberger, C. D., Gorsuch, R. L., & Lushene, R. E. (1970). *Manual for the State-Trait Anxiety Inventory.* Palo Alto, CA: Consulting Psychologist Press.

Steele, C. M. (1992). Race and the schooling of Black Americans, *Atlantic Monthly,* April, 68–78.

Steele, C. M. (1997). A threat in the air: How stereotypes shape intellectual identity and performance. *American Psychologist, 52,* 613–629.

Steele, C. M., & Aronson, J. (1995). Contending with a stereotype: African-American intellectual test performance and stereotype threat. *Journal of Personality and Social Psychology, 69,* 797–811.

Steele, S. (1990). *The content of our character: A new vision of race in America.* New York: St. Martin's Press.

Steinkamp, M. W., & Maehr, M. L. (1983). Affect, ability, and science achievement: A quantitative synthesis of correlation research. *Review of Educational Research, 53,* 369–396.

Swim, J. K. (1994). Perceived versus meta-analytic effect sizes: An assessment of the accuracy of gender stereotypes. *Journal of Personality and Social Psychology, 66,* 21–36.

Swim, J. K., & Stangor, C. (1998). *Prejudice: The target's perspective.* New York: Academic Press.

Tajfel, H. (Ed.). (1978). *Differentiation between social groups.* New York: Academic Press.

Wigfield, A., & Eccles, J. S. (1989). Test anxiety in elementary and secondary school students. *Educational Psychologist, 24,* 159–183.

Wigfield, A., & Meece, J. (1988). Math anxiety in elementary and secondary school students. *Journal of Educational Psychology, 80,* 210–216.

Wine, J. (1971). Test anxiety and direction of attention. *Psychological Bulletin, 76,* 92–104.

Yee, D. K., & Eccles, J. S. (1988). Parent perceptions and attributions for children's math achievement. *Sex Roles, 19,* 317–333.

6

Gender Differences in Interaction: A Reexamination

Elizabeth Aries

Research has consistently demonstrated that men and women have different styles of interaction. In this reading, Aries questions this well-established finding. She describes how differences in male and female behavior are frequently small (even though they may be statistically significant) and have been inaccurately presented as mutually exclusive **(more alike than different).** She points out that most of the research has relied on white, middle class samples and has failed to examine how communication styles may be affected by race, ethnicity, class, and sexual orientation **(cultural diversity).** In addition, gender differences in interaction are not consistent across all situations. Aries argues that it is inaccurate to say that masculine or feminine interaction styles reside within the individual. Instead, gendered behavior is evoked by situational factors outside of the individual, such as stereotyped expectations, status differences, and social roles.

Questions to Consider:

1. According to Aries, why is it important to look beyond statistical significance in order to understand gender differences in interaction?
2. How can stereotypes affect our interpretations of male and female behavior in interactions? Give specific examples.
3. Why have researchers focused on finding gender differences in interaction?
4. In what situations are you more likely to show gendered behavior in your interactions?

The study of gender differences in interaction has drawn the attention of numerous researchers from the disciplines of psychology, sociology, linguistics, communication, women's studies, and organizational behavior. Across a wide variety of subject popula-

Reprinted from D. J. Cananry & K. Dindia, eds., *Sex Differences and Similarities in Communication: Critical Essays and Empirical Investigations of Sex and Gender in Interaction.* By permission of Lawrence Erlbaum Associates, Inc.

tions, interaction settings, and research methodologies, researchers typically report that men are more likely than women to emerge as leaders, to be directive and hierarchical, to dominate in groups by talking more and interrupting more, and to be oriented toward solving problems. In contrast, women are found to be more expressive, supportive, facilitative, egalitarian, and cooperative than men, and to focus more on relationships and share more personally with others (Aries, 1987, 1996).

By taking a different perspective on these data, however, these well-established truths about men and women in interaction may be called into question. The prevailing picture that has emerged is based on the fact that we have not paid careful attention to five important questions:

1. Do our stereotypes describe most men and women or only selected samples of men and women?
2. What is the magnitude of the differences we have found?
3. To what extent does the appearance of gender differences depend on the situational context?
4. Are the gender differences we have found attributable to other variables that co-vary with gender like status and social roles?
5. To what extent are gender differences in conversation due to stereotype effects?

If we reframe our thinking around these five questions, we come to see that knowledge of a person's gender gives us little ability to make an accurate prediction about how a person will behave and that variables that co-vary with gender may be responsible for many of the gender differences observed.

Reliance on White Middle-Class Samples

Research findings regarding sex differences in interaction are based primarily on White middle-class samples. What we have taken to be the characteristics of men and women in interaction may pertain only to the selected samples we have studied. Neither men nor women form homogenous groups. Members of the same sex differ from one another in age, race, ethnicity, social class, sexual orientation, variables that affect self-definition, and patterns of interaction. Because we have based our findings on men and women who are White and middle class, we have exaggerated the coherence within male and female styles of communication and failed to appreciate the extent to which members of the same sex differ, thereby making comparisons between men and women problematic.

The extension of research to diverse subject populations has already begun to challenge the accuracy of traditional gender stereotypes. Sex role prescriptions that hold for mainstream Americans may not be identical for minority groups (De Leon, 1995). African-American subjects report masculine characteristics (e.g., assertiveness, independence, self-reliance) to be as desirable for women as for men (Harris, 1994). Black women attribute more masculine traits to themselves than do White women (Binion, 1990; De Leon, 1995). Black women, in their capacity as wives, mothers, providers, and heads of households, have had to exhibit more masculine qualities to be successful in the performance of their multiple roles (De Leon, 1995). When describing the communication style that characterized their friendships with people of their own race, Black friends used terms like *quick-tempered* and *confrontive*, whereas White participants' terms included *nonconfrontive, tactful,* and *withdrawn* (McCullough, 1987; cited in Kramarae, 1990).

As we begin to pay attention to the differences that exist in communication styles among members of the same sex who differ in race, ethnicity, class, or sexual orientation, the clarity of our conception of gender differences diminishes. What we see instead is that there may be multiple sex role systems that differ in their prescriptions for the behavior of men and women.

The Magnitude of Gender Differences

One criterion that has been widely used to determine whether men and women differ is statistical significance. Several limitations exist to the use of statistical significance as the sole criterion for the interpretation of research evidence. A statistically significant difference may not be a large or substantial difference. When sample sizes are large, a small mean difference can be statistically significant (at $p < .05$).

To take a research example from the literature on role differentiation in mixed sex groups, Anderson and Blanchard (1982) examined the extent to which men and women differed in their focus on task behavior and the socioemotional aspects of interaction. They assessed the magnitude of the differences found in studies of gender and role differentiation and found that men on average were eight percentage points higher than women on the use of task behavior and women were eight percentage points higher than men on the use of positive socioemotional behavior. These differ-

ences were statistically significant yet small in magnitude. We describe men as task-oriented and women as socioemotional in orientation when in fact both devote the majority of their behavior to the task and the difference in their behavior is not even moderate. We have tended to overlook the considerable overlap between the behavior of men and women and to misrepresent small differences as mutually exclusive.

Researchers have begun to look to other criteria to assess research findings, such as the percentage of variance in behavior that can be accounted for or explained by knowledge of a person's sex. Sex generally accounts for less than 10% of the variance in social behavior and typically less than 5% (Canary & Hause, 1993; Eagly, 1987; Hyde & Linn, 1986). For example, in a study of interruptions, Natale, Entin, and Jaffe (1979) found that in dyads the speaking time of the conversational partner predicted 63% of the variance in interruptions, whereas the sex of the speaker accounted for only 7% of the variance. Thus, to make an accurate prediction of how frequently a person will interrupt, knowledge of the speaker's sex has relatively little predictive value in comparison with other variables. As Unger (1990) argued, sex is not "particularly important in comparison to all the independent variables that influence any particular human behavior" (p. 115).

A related piece of information that can be used to assess research findings is the magnitude of the difference or the effect size (i.e., the degree to which gender differences are manifested). Effect size can be conceptualized in terms of how much overlap there is between the distributions for men and women: The smaller the overlap between the distributions for men and women, the larger the effect size. An effect size of 0, as measured by Cohen's *d* (Cohen, 1977), reflects a 100% overlap between the distributions of men and women. Cohen considers an effect of *d* = .20 to be small (with an 85% overlap between the distributions for men and women), an effect of *d* = .50 to be moderate (with a 67% overlap), and an effect of *d* = .80 to be large (with a 53% overlap). A small effect accounts for 1% of the variance in behavior, a medium effect for 6% of the variance, and a large effect 14% of the variance.

Effect sizes can be used to assess the results of single studies as well as whole domains of research through a statistical technique called *meta-analysis*. Meta-analysis enables researchers to combine effect sizes found in individual studies to assess the overall magnitude of effect size across all studies in a given area.

Let us review some of the effect sizes that have been found for meta-analyses carried out in the area of gender and communication. Dindia and Allen (1992) did a meta-analysis of self-disclosure covering 205 published studies and 51 dissertations. They found women to be more disclosing than men but the effect size to be small (*d* = .18). They concluded that, "Whether the magnitude of sex differences in self-disclosure is theoretically meaningful and practically important is debatable. . . . It's time to stop perpetuating the myth that there are large differences in men's and women's self-disclosure" (p. 118).

Two meta-analyses have been carried out in the area of gender and leadership behavior. Eagly and Johnson (1990) carried out a meta-analysis of 162 studies of gender differences in leadership style. Male leaders did not differ from female leaders on task orientation (*d* = .00), nor did female leaders show more of an interpersonal orientation

than male leaders (*d* = .04). Women showed a more democratic style than did men (*d* = .22) but the effect size was small. In this meta-analysis, gender differences were found in the laboratory studies but not the field studies. Eagly and Johnson concluded that the criteria used by organizations to select and socialize managers into their roles minimizes any tendencies that men and women might bring to lead or manage with distinctly different styles. Eagly and Karau conducted a meta-analysis of 58 studies of leadership emergence in mixed-sex, initially leaderless, task-oriented groups (Eagly & Karau, 1991). Men emerged more frequently than women when task leadership was assessed (*d* = .41) and women emerged more as leaders when social leadership was assessed (*d* = −.18).

Although there are numerous narrative reviews of the literature on gender differences in language, the magnitude of these differences has not been assessed. Initial analyses from a meta-analysis of gender and language, which aggregated results from studies using different language forms, revealed no consistent gender differences in language use (Smythe & Schlueter, 1989).

Thus, effect sizes found for gender differences in communication style range from *very small* to *moderate*, accounting for less than 6% of the variance in behavior at best and generally less than 1% of the variance in communication behavior. Canary and House's (1993) review of meta-analyses on sex differences in communication activities suggests that only 1% of variance is accounted for by sex. When we look beyond statistical significance and attend to effect size or percent of variance explained, the data suggest that the overlap in the behavior of men and women is considerable and that polarized depictions of interaction styles are not warranted.

The Situational Context of Interaction

Gender differences are not manifested in all situational contexts. As Deaux and Major (1987) argued,

> Because perceivers, individual selves, and situations all vary in the content and salience of gender-linked expectations, we expect a wide range in observed female and male behaviors, from virtual identity of the sexes in some circumstances to striking differences in others. (p. 382)

A review of the literature on gender differences in interaction reveals that the appearance of gender differences is inconsistent from one study to the next. In a review of the literature on interruptions, James and Clarke (1993) reported that in the majority of studies no significant sex differences were found. In an analysis of 64 data sets looking at power and prestige in mixed-sex task groups, Lockheed (1985) found that 70% showed more male activity, influence, or leadership; 17% showed no gender difference; and 12.5% favored women. In a review of sex differences in amount of talk, James and Drakich (1993) found men to talk more in 43% of the studies, no gender differences in 28.6% of the studies, 27% of the studies to have equivocal results, and women to talk more than men in 3.6% of studies. In a review of 28 studies of task behavior, Wheelan and Verdi (1992) found men to be more task-oriented than women in 19 studies, whereas 9 studies showed no sex difference. In their review of 20 studies of socioemotional behavior, Wheelan and Verdi also found that 16 reported women to be higher than men and 4 reported no sex difference.

Although many studies find gender differences that fit the stereotypes, numerous studies report no gender differences and some report findings in the opposite direction. We may not even be aware of all the findings of no gender difference for two reasons. Findings of no difference are often considered to be unworthy of publication. In addition, in studies that use multiple dependent variables, the lack of gender differences on many of those variables is rarely cited by later reviewers while only the few significant differences are highlighted.

We must look to the situational context of the interaction in each study to explain why it is that gender differences are manifested in some studies but not in others. How people behave depends on such moderating variables as the demands of the task, the length of the interaction, the sex composition of the group, and the relationship between the participants—variables that may affect the salience of gender-linked expectations for behavior.

Task

If tasks draw on roles, interests, or expertise assumed to be more typically acquired by men, men are more likely to show higher levels of task activity than women in groups (Aries, 1996). For instance, when the task was taken into consideration in Eagly and Karau's (1991) meta-analysis of gender and leadership emergence, men were found to be much more likely to emerge as leaders in initially leaderless task groups when tasks were masculine ($d = .79$) than when tasks were feminine ($d = .26$) or when tasks required greater social complexity (e.g., interpersonal problem solving, extensive sharing of ideas, negotiation; $d = .23$).

Women are found to be more self-disclosing to same-sex partners than are men

(Dindia & Allen, 1992; Hill & Stull, 1987). However, whether men are disclosing depends on the context. When men and women were asked to bring a same-sex best friend to the laboratory to have an intimate conversation and reveal thoughts and feelings, no gender differences were found in self-disclosure (Reis, Senchak, & Solomon, 1985). Thus, when self-disclosure was legitimized between men, their behavior was similar to that of women.

Length of the Interaction

Gender differences tend to be greater in groups that are engaged in brief or one-time encounters than in groups that meet over time. As members get to know the relative task-relevant competencies and attributes of other members, sex becomes less important as a determinant of behavior. Because so many of our studies involve short encounters, the tendency for men to emerge as leaders has been exaggerated. The meta-analysis of gender and leadership emergence by Eagly and Karau (1991) shows that men were more likely to emerge as leaders when groups lasted less than 20 minutes ($d = .58$) than when interaction lasted more than a single session ($d = .09$). In their review of the literature on gender and role differentiation, Wheelan and Verdi (1992) found few studies of groups that met for extended periods. In their own study of a 4-day group relations conference, Wheelan and Verdi found that gender differences emerged initially in expressive and goal-directed activity but these differences disappeared over time.

Sex Composition of the Speakers

Another factor that affects the expression of gender differences is the sex composition of the speakers. In many cases, gender differ-

ences have been found to be greater in single-sex than in mixed-sex interaction (Aries, 1996). The sex of one's conversational partner has been found to affect the amount a person is willing to disclose. The highest levels of self-disclosure are found to occur between women and the lowest between men, whereas cross-sex disclosure falls between the two. Meta-analytic findings reveal gender differences in self-disclosure to be greater in single-sex ($d = .31$) than in mixed-sex interaction ($d = .08$; Dindia & Allen, 1992). Men's lower level of disclosure to other men does not mean that men cannot be self-disclosing; rather, men may be more likely to choose women as the target for their disclosures. Indeed, Dindia and Allen found equal disclosure to men by men and women ($d = 0.00$).

When comparisons are made of all-male and all-female groups, men are found to place a greater emphasis on displays of dominance (Aries, 1976; Ellis, 1982; Miller, 1985). However, men are found to place less emphasis on dominance in their interactions with women than with other men (Aries, 1976; McCarrick, Manderscheid, & Silbergeld, 1981).

The sex composition of the group has been found to affect leadership behavior. In studies of dominance and leadership behavior involving interaction with strangers, women who are high in dominance assumed leadership over women low in dominance but not over men low in dominance (Carbonell, 1984; Davis & Gilbert, 1989; Megargee, 1969; Nyquist & Spence, 1986). Leadership is associated with masculinity and women are aware of gender-linked expectations for their behavior, making them reluctant to assume overt leadership over men. Some evidence suggests that women use more qualifications of speech in mixed-sex task groups than in single-sex groups (Carli, 1990; McMillan, Clifton, McGrath, &

Gale, 1977). Carli found that women in mixed-sex dyads who prefaced remarks with such phrases as, "I'm no expert, I may be wrong," frequently had greater influence over their male partners. Thus, women may adopt stereotypic deferent behavior with men to be effective.

It can be seen from these studies that men and women do not display a single style of interaction; interaction style varies with the social context. Situations place different pressures on individuals to display gender-stereotypic behavior (Deaux & Major, 1987). Contextual variables play an important role in determining the magnitude of gender differences found in our studies.

Status and Social Roles

For decades, feminists have argued that the differences attributed to gender can be accounted for by differences in social roles and social status (Henley, 1973–1974, 1977; Kramarae, 1981; Spender, 1980; Thorne & Henley, 1975; Unger, 1976, 1979). Despite the profound social change that has occurred in American society in the past 25 years, men and women are still positioned differently in society: Men hold more power and status than women. Women have indeed entered the labor force in greater numbers, but they are still paid less for the same work and on average hold jobs with lower status than men.

A great deal of evidence demonstrates that the dominance and leadership attributed to men is displayed more often by high-status than low-status individuals; when status is controlled for, sex differences are diminished. For example, in a study of dominance displayed at work, dominance was predicted by participants' social roles. Less dominance was displayed toward

coworkers and supervisors than toward people being supervised (Moskowitz, Jung Suh, & Desaulniers, 1994). However, dominance was not predicted by the sex of the participant. High-status and powerful individuals have been found to interrupt more than low-status, less powerful individuals (Eakins & Eakins, 1983; Greif, 1980; Kollock, Blumstein, & Schwartz, 1985; West & Zimmerman, 1977; Woods, 1988). In discussions among intimate heterosexual couples, speaking time was related to the amount of power each person held in the relationship in decision making. The more powerful person spoke more in discussions. When men and women enjoy equal power, men do not speak significantly more than their female partners in discussions (Kollock et al., 1985). When men and women are placed in equal status positions, sex differences are reduced. When dominance and leadership are legitimized for women in organizational settings, the behavior of male and female leaders is quite similar (Eagly & Johnson, 1990).

Similarly, many of the characteristics attributed to women—interpersonal sensitivity, politeness, use of "women's language" (e.g., tag questions, qualifications of speech), and so on—are found more often in low-status than in high-status individuals. In two studies of interaction in dyads in which one person was the leader and the other the follower, subordinates showed more sensitivity to the way the leader felt about them than the leader showed to the subordinate's feeling; but there were no gender differences (Snodgrass, 1985, 1992). People who hold power show less politeness than do those with low power (McLachlan, 1991). People mitigate their requests when speaking to superiors (Baxter, 1984; P. Johnson, 1976; Sagrestano, 1992; Steil & Hillman, 1993). "Women's language" appears to be used more frequently by people who are unemployed, housewives, or hold lower status jobs than by well-educated and professional people (O'Barr & Atkins, 1980). Subordinates have shown higher rates of speech associated with women than managers (C. Johnson, 1994). Risman (1987) found that the behavior of men who were single fathers and had primary responsibility for the care of young children was more similar to the behavior of working or single mothers than it was to married fathers. Men are capable of providing nurturance and do so when placed in the traditionally female role.

We have not always given sufficient attention to the importance of social, political, and economic contexts in examining gender differences. The gender differences we observe are produced in a context in which men hold positions of power over women. Many have argued that gender is not simply a matter of difference but must be understood as a matter of power and dominance (Henley, 1977; Kramarae, 1981; Spender, 1980; Thorne & Henley, 1975; Torres, 1992). Our reliance on laboratory studies masks the effect of these variables by taking people out of their current roles and context. When status and social roles are built into our studies as independent variables along with gender, gender differences are mitigated.

Stereotype Effects and Self-Fulfilling Prophecies

In interaction, we immediately recognize the sex of our conversational partners based on discernable visible cues. To the extent that we hold stereotyped beliefs about men and women, these beliefs can lead us to differential expectations about how people will behave based on their sex and can

cause us to perceive gender differences even when they are not present (Aries, 1996).

Broad consensus has existed about the characteristics presumed to be typical of each sex. Men are described as leaders—as dominant, aggressive, independent, and competitive. Women are described as emotional, subjective, and aware of the feelings of others (Broverman, Vogel, Broverman, Clarkson, & Rosenkrantz, 1972). These stereotypes have remained relatively stable over the past 20 years (Bergen & Williams, 1991; Werner & LaRussa, 1985). Male speakers are believed to be louder, more forceful, dominating, and aggressive, whereas female speakers are believed to be more friendly, open, self-revealing, emotional, and polite, and to show more concern for the listener (Kramer, 1977). Women (vs. men) are thought to use more indirect influence strategies (Johnson, 1976) and more tag questions (Siegler & Siegler, 1976), whereas men are thought to interrupt more than women (Hawkins, 1988).

Stereotypes are probably not always accurate depictions of group members. Research shows that Black American and Puerto-Rican women attribute more masculine characteristics to themselves than do White women, and the former do not fit traditional stereotypes of femininity (Binion, 1990; De Leon, 1995). In a similar manner, men are perceived as leaders. Yet in a test of the accuracy of people's beliefs, Swim (1994) found the perceived effect size for leadership emergence by men to be quite large ($d = 1.04$), whereas actual meta-analytic findings were much smaller ($d = .49$). Women are believed to use tag questions more than men do, but women have not consistently been found to do so (Aries, 1996).

Studies show that even when men and women behave in an identical manner they may be perceived differently. Listeners bend their perceptions in the direction of expectation. When participants heard tape recordings of conversations in which male and female speakers used tag questions and qualifiers equally, women were perceived to use these speech forms more frequently than were men (Newcombe & Arnkoff, 1979). When participants read transcripts of speech believed to be spoken by a woman, speech was rated higher on aesthetic quality (pleasing, nice, sweet, and beautiful); when speech was believed to be spoken by a man, it was rated higher on dynamism (strong, active, aggressive, and loud; Mulac, Incontro, & James, 1985). This occurred regardless of whether the actual speaker from whom the transcript was based was male or female or whether there were actual speech differences. In a follow-up study, when participants believed a speaker to be male they rated speakers higher on dynamism than if the speaker was believed to be female, but the effect held for only two out of four conversations (Lawrence, Stucky, & Hopper, 1990). Thus, stereotype effects, like gender differences, may be evoked to different degrees depending on specific speakers or specific conversational contexts.

Male and female speakers may not only be perceived differently, but they may be evaluated differently when displaying identical behavior. Bradley (1981) observed 24 experimental groups with a male or female confederate in each who posed as a subject. The confederates were instructed to argue a position contrary to the other group members. Half the confederates advanced their cases without proof while the other half advanced arguments by giving evidence and factual data. Half the confederates in each condition used tag questions and disclaimers and half did not. Women who advanced arguments without support were evaluated as less intelligent, knowl-

edgeable, and influential than men who argued without support. Women who used tag questions and disclaimers were rated as less intelligent and knowledgeable than men who used these speech forms. Whether men used tag questions or disclaimers hardly affected their ratings, whereas women were perceived as less intelligent and knowledgeable when they used tag questions and disclaimers. Thus, the sex of the speaker contributes to the impression the speaker makes beyond actual behavior differences, if any. Similarly, women who used forceful language in job interviews were seen as more aggressive than men who used similar language (Wiley & Eskilson, 1985).

In a meta-analysis of 61 studies of gender and the evaluation of leaders, Eagly, Makhijani, and Klonsky (1992) found a small tendency for female leaders to be evaluated less favorably than male leaders ($d = .05$), but the effect was more pronounced for leaders using an autocratic style ($d = .30$). The further women departed from sex role expectations the more negatively they were evaluated. Women are caught in a double bind: When they use behavior associated with women, they are perceived as lacking in instrumental competency; when they use behavior associated with men, they are seen as aggressive.

Two theories put forth to account for gender differences in interaction emphasize the importance of stereotypes in shaping these differences. The theory of status characteristics and expectation states holds that when direct information about the relative competency of group members is not available, members will rely on external status to form expectations (Berger, Cohen, & Zelditch, 1972; Berger, Fisek, Norman, & Zelditch, 1977). Higher expectations will be formed for men because of their higher status in society and these expectations will become self-fulfilling prophecies for behavior. Men will be given more opportunities to participate and their contributions will be more highly valued. Research shows that when no expectations are given about the competency of group members, men are believed to be more competent than women. These gender differences are reduced when women are believed to possess more task-related competency than men (Pugh & Wahrman, 1983, 1985; Wood & Karten, 1986).

Social role theory contends that because men and women are assigned to different roles in work and in the family, men and women will be expected to possess different characteristics that suit them for those roles. Men will be expected to be more agentic and task-oriented, women to be more communal and emotionally expressive in accordance with their social roles (Eagly, 1987). These expectations furnish guidelines for how men and women should behave; people are expected to behave in a manner consistent with their roles.

Thus, gender stereotypes have both a descriptive and a prescriptive component. They indicate what group members are like, but also what group members *should* be like—that is, what behavior is appropriate for members of the group. People do not necessarily perform gender-related behaviors because they are internalized in personality. Eagly (1987) contended that,

> People often conform to gender-role norms that are *not* internalized, because of the considerable power that groups and individuals supportive of these norms have to influence others' behavior through rewards and punishments of both subtle (e.g., nonverbal cues) or more obvious (e.g., monetary incentive, sexually harassing behavior) varieties. (p. 19)

As both expectations states theory and social role theory predict, gender stereotypes have the power to become self-fulfill-

ing prophecies for behavior. In a study of West Point cadets, Rice, Bender, and Vitters (1980) demonstrated that the attitudes that group members held about women's roles could affect the behavior of women leaders. In all-male groups where members held liberal attitudes toward women, women leaders initiated more structure and played a more important role than they did in groups where men held traditional attitudes toward women's roles. Thus, men's attitudes toward women were reflected in their behavior toward women, which in turn affected the ability of those women to be effective leaders.

In summary, research shows that gender stereotypes play an important role in setting expectations for our own behavior and that of others. Stereotypes dictate what we notice. They may cause us to see gender differences even when they are not present and to respond differently to individuals on the basis of sex. Gender stereotypes also have the power to become self-fulfilling prophecies for behavior. However, it is important to note that stereotype effects are evoked to a different degree depending on the situational context and are most pronounced when gender is a salient issue in an interaction (Aries, 1996). Gender stereotypes have a larger impact in shaping the expectations and perceptions of speakers in initial encounters when more personal information about participants is not yet available. The magnitude of gender stereotypes has not been assessed. Like gender effects, it is likely that stereotype effects are statistically significant but not large.

Conclusions

A review of the research on conversational interaction reveals many gender differences. A polarized depiction of men and women has emerged from these findings that has been widely popularized by best sellers such as Tannen's (1990) *You Just Don't Understand: Women and Men in Conversation* and Gray's (1992) *Men Are From Mars, Women Are From Venus.* Gray went so far as to claim, "Not only do men and women communicate differently but they think, feel, perceive, react, respond, love, need, and appreciate differently. They almost seem to be from different planets, speaking different languages" (p. 5).

The research evidence, however, permits multiple interpretations. We have tended to focus on men and women as groups, overlooking individual differences between members of the same sex. The findings for samples that are not White and not middle-class do not always support popular stereotypes. We have tended to polarize differences misrepresenting small differences as mutually exclusive. We have failed to pay sufficient attention to situational variability in behavior—to the fact that gender differences do not appear consistently across situational contexts and are not found in many studies. We have overlooked the importance of social roles, status, and gender stereotypes as alternative explanations for gender differences.

Those who take an essentialist position have argued that the differential socialization of men and women leads to the development of contrasting styles of communication. Women learn to be polite and expressive and to assume an interpersonal orientation, whereas men learn to be assertive and direct. These differences need not be biologically based, but they are assumed to reside within the individual. However, the data reviewed in this chapter suggest that we must move beyond the essentialist model to explain why there is so much within-gender variability, why the appearance of gender differences in interaction is situationally variable, why no gender differences are found in many contexts, and why people use

behaviors associated with the opposite sex in certain roles and contexts. We can only begin to make an accurate prediction of the particular behaviors speakers will choose if we know something about their role and status, the type of conversation in which they are engaged, their conversational partners, and the goals they are trying to achieve. Knowledge of the speaker's sex will give us little predictive power.

Many researchers are beginning to move toward an understanding of gender as something that people do in social interaction (West & Zimmerman, 1987). West and Zimmerman argued that, "A person's gender is not simply an aspect of what one is, but, more fundamentally, it is something that one *does,* and does recurrently, in interaction with others" (p. 140). The display of feminine or masculine behavior depends on the situational context. As Bohan (1993) contended, "Thus, none of us is feminine or is masculine or fails to be either of those. In particular contexts, people do feminine; in others, they do masculine" (p. 13).

We need to move beyond the conception that the interaction styles of men and women reside within individuals. We should return gender to its larger social context, taking into consideration other social forces that shape the expression of gendered behavior. We must weigh carefully how we choose to understand the gender differences we have found as well as how much importance we choose to give to these gender differences. Our construction of polarized conceptions of men and women in interaction helps sustain current realities and keep inequalities in place.

References

Anderson, L. R., & Blanchard, P. N. (1982). Sex differences in task and social-emotional behavior. *Basic and Applied Social Psychology, 3*(2), 109–139.

Aries, E. (1976). Interaction patterns and themes of male, female, and mixed groups. *Small Group Behavior, 7*(1), 7–18.

Aries, E. (1987). Gender and communication. In P. Shaver & C. Hendrick (Eds.), *Sex and gender* (pp. 149–176). Newbury Park, CA: Sage.

Aries, E. (1996). *Men and women in interaction: Reconsidering the differences.* New York: Oxford University Press.

Baxter, L. A. (1984). An investigation of compliance-gaining as politeness. *Human Communication Research, 10*(3), 427–456.

Bergen, D. J., & Williams, J. E. (1991). Sex stereotypes in the United States revisited: 1972–1988. *Sex Roles, 24*(7/8), 413–423.

Berger, J., Cohen, B. P., & Zelditch, M. (1972). Status characteristics and social interaction. *American Sociological Review, 37,* 241–255.

Berger, J., Fisek, M. H., Norman, R. Z., & Zelditch, M. (1977). *Status characteristics and social interaction.* New York: Elsevier.

Binion, V. J. (1990). Psychological androgyny: A Black female perspective. *Sex Roles, 22*(7/8), 487–507.

Bohan, J. S. (1993). Regarding gender: Essentialism, constructionism, and feminist psychology. *Psychology of Women Quarterly, 17,* 5–21.

Bradley, P. H. (1981). The folk-linguistics of women's speech: An empirical examination. *Communication Monographs, 48,* 73–90.

Broverman, I. K., Vogel, S. R., Broverman, D. M., Clarkson, F. E., & Rosenkrantz, P. S. (1972). Sex-role stereotypes: A current appraisal. *Journal of Social Issues, 28,* 59–78.

Canary, D. J., & Hause, K. S. (1993). Is there any reason to research sex differences in communication? *Communication Quarterly, 41*(2), 129–144.

Carbonell, J. L. (1984). Sex roles and leadership revisited. *Journal of Applied Psychology, 69,* 44–49.

Carli, L. (1990). Gender, language, and influence. *Journal of Personality and Social Psychology, 59*(5), 941–951.

Cohen, J. (1977). *Statistical power analysis for the behavioral sciences.* New York: Academic Press.

Davis, B. M., & Gilbert, L. A. (1989). Effect of dispositional and situational influences on women's dominance expression in mixed-sex dyads. *Journal of Personality and Social Psychology, 57*(2), 294–300.

Deaux, K., & Major, B. (1987). Putting gender into context: An interactive model of gender-related behavior. *Psychological Bulletin, 94,* 369–389.

De Leon, B. (1995). Sex role identity among college students: A cross-cultural analysis. In A. M. Padilła (Ed.), *Hispanic psychology: Critical issues in theory and research* (pp. 245–256). Thousand Oaks, CA: Sage.

Dindia, K., & Allen, M. (1992). Sex differences in self-disclosure: A meta-analysis. *Psychological Bulletin, 112*(1), 106–124.

Eagly, A. H. (1987). *Sex differences in social behavior: A social-role interpretation.* Hillsdale, NJ: Lawrence Erlbaum Associates.

Eagly, A. H., & Johnson, B. T. (1990). Gender and leadership style: A meta-analysis. *Psychological Bulletin, 108*(2), 233–256.

Eagly, A. H., & Karau, S. J. (1991). Gender and the emergence of leaders: A meta-analysis. *Journal of Personality and Social Psychology, 60*(5), 685–710.

Eagly, A. H., Makhijani, M. G., & Klonsky, B. G. (1992). Gender and the evaluation of leaders: A meta-analysis. *Psychological Bulletin, 111*(1), 3–22.

Eakins, B., & Eakins, R. G. (1983). Verbal turn-taking and exchanges in faculty dialogue. In B. L. Dubois & I. Crouch (Eds.), *Proceedings of the conference on the Sociology of the Languages of American Women* (pp. 53–62). San Antonio, TX: Trinity University Press.

Ellis, D. G. (1982). Relational stability and change in women's consciousness-raising groups. *Women's Studies in Communication, 3,* 77–87.

Gray, J. (1992). *Men are from Mars, women are from Venus: A practical guide to improving communication and getting what you want in your relationships.* New York: HarperCollins.

Greif, E. B. (1980). Sex differences in parent–child conversations. *Women's Studies International Quarterly, 3,* 253–258.

Harris, A. C. (1994). Ethnicity as a determinant of sex role identity: A replication study of item selection for the Bem Sex Role Inventory. *Sex Roles, 31*(3/4), 241–273.

Hawkins, K. (1988). Interruptions in task-oriented conversations: Effects of violations of expectations by males and females. *Women's Studies in Communication, 11*(2), 1–20.

Henley, N. (1973–1974). Power, sex, and nonverbal communication. *Berkeley Journal of Sociology, 18,* 1–26. Reprinted in B. Thorne & N. Henley (Eds.). (1975). *Language and sex: Difference and dominance* (pp. 184–203). Rowley, MA: Newbury House.

Henley, N. M. (1977). *Body politics: Power, sex and non-*

verbal communication. Englewood Cliffs, NJ: Prentice-Hall.

Hill, C. T., & Stull, D. E. (1987). Gender and self-disclosure: Strategies for exploring the issues. In V. J. Derlega & J. H. Berg (Eds.), *Self-disclosure: Theory, research, and therapy* (pp. 81–100). New York: Plenum.

Hyde, J. S., & Linn, M. C. (Eds.). (1986). *The psychology of gender: Advances through meta-analysis*. Baltimore: Johns Hopkins University Press.

James, D., & Clarke, S. (1993). Women, men, and interruptions: A critical review. In D. Tannen (Ed.), *Gender and conversational interaction* (pp. 231–280). New York: Oxford University Press.

James, D., & Drakich, J. (1993). Understanding gender differences in amount of talk: A critical review. In D. Tannen (Ed.), *Gender and conversational interaction* (pp. 281–312). New York: Oxford University Press.

Johnson, C. (1994). Gender, legitimate authority, and leader-subordinate conversations. *American Sociological Review, 59*, 122–135.

Johnson, P. (1976). Women and power: Toward a theory of effectiveness. *Journal of Social Issues, 32*, 99–110.

Kollock, P., Blumstein, P., & Schwartz, P. (1985). Sex and power in interaction: Conversational privileges and duties. *American Sociological Review, 50*, 34–46.

Kramarae, C. (1981). *Men and women speaking*. Rowley, MA: Newbury House.

Kramarae, C. (1990). Changing the complexion of gender in language research. In H. Giles & W. P. Robinson (Eds.), *Handbook of language and social psychology* (pp. 345–361). Chichester, England: Wiley.

Kramer, C. (1977). Perceptions of female and male speech. *Language and Speech, 20*, 151–161.

Lawrence, S. G., Stucky, N. P., & Hopper, R. (1990). The effects of sex dialects and sex stereotypes on speech evaluations. *Journal of Language and Social Psychology, 9*(3), 209–224.

Lockheed, M. E. (1985). Sex and social influence: A meta-analysis guided by theory. In J. Berger & M. Zelditch (Eds.), *Status, rewards and influence* (pp. 406–429). San Francisco: Jossey-Bass.

McCarrick, A. K., Manderscheid, R. W., & Silbergeld, S. (1981). Gender differences in competition and dominance during married-couples group therapy. *Social Psychology Quarterly, 44*(3), 164–177.

McLachlan, A. (1991). The effects of agreement, disagreement, gender and familiarity on patterns of dyadic interaction. *Journal of Language and Social Psychology, 10*(3), 205–212.

McMillan, J. R., Clifton, A. K., McGrath, D., & Gale, W. S. (1977). Women's language: Uncertainty or interpersonal sensitivity and emotionality. *Sex Roles, 3*(6), 545–559.

Megargee, E. I. (1969). Influence of sex roles on the manifestation of leadership. *Journal of Applied Psychology, 53*(5), 377–382.

Miller, J. B. (1985). Patterns of control in same-sex conversations: Differences between women and men. *Women's Studies in Communication, 8*, 62–69.

Moskowitz, D. S., Jung Suh, E., & Detaulniers, J. (1994). Situational influences on gender differences in agency and communion. *Journal of Personality and Social Psychology, 66*(4), 753–761.

Mulac, A., Incontro, C. R., & James, M. R. (1985). Comparison of the gender-linked language effect and sex role stereotypes. *Journal of Personality and Social Psychology, 49*(4), 1098–1109.

Natale, M., Entin, E., & Jaffe, J. (1979). Vocal interruptions in dyadic communication as a function of speech and social anxiety. *Journal of Personality and Social Psychology, 37*(6), 865–878.

Newcombe, N., & Arnkoff, D. B. (1979). Effects of speech style and sex of speaker on person perception. *Journal of Personality and Social Psychology, 37*(8), 1293–1303.

Nyquist, L., & Spence, J. T. (1986). Effects of dispositional dominance and sex role expectations on leadership behaviors. *Journal of Personality and Social Psychology, 50*(1), 87–93.

O'Barr, W., & Atkins, B. (1980). "Women's language" or "powerless language"? In S. McConnell-Ginet, R. Borker, & N. Furman (Eds.), *Women and language in literature and society* (pp. 93–110). New York: Praeger.

Pugh, M. D., & Wahrman, R. (1983). Neutralizing sexism in mixed-sex groups: Do women have to be better than men? *American Journal of Sociology, 88*(4), 746–762.

Pugh, M. D., & Wahrman, R. (1985). Inequality of influence in mixed-sex groups. In J. Berger & M. Zelditch (Eds.), *Status, rewards, and influence* (pp. 142–162). San Francisco: Jossey-Bass.

Reis, H. T., Senchak, M., & Solomon, B. (1985). Sex differences in the intimacy of social interaction: Further examination of potential explanations. *Journal of Personality and Social Psychology, 48*(5), 1204–1217.

Rice, R. W., Bender, L. R., & Vitters, A. G. (1980). Leader sex, follower attitudes toward women, and leadership effectiveness: A laboratory experiment. *Organizational Behavior and Human Performance, 25,* 46–78.

Risman, B. J. (1987). Intimate relationships from a micro-structural perspective: Men who mother. *Gender and Society, 1,* 6–32.

Sagrestano, L. (1992). Power strategies in interpersonal relationships. *Psychology of Women Quarterly, 16,* 481–495.

Siegler, D. M., & Siegler, R. S. (1976). Stereotypes of males' and females' speech. *Psychological Reports, 39,* 167–170.

Smythe, M., & Schlueter, D. W. (1989). Can we talk? A meta-analytic review of the sex differences in language literature. In C. M. Lont & S. A. Friedley (Eds.), *Beyond boundaries: Sex and gender diversity in communication* (pp. 31–48). Fairfax, VA: George Mason University Press.

Snodgrass, S. E. (1985). Women's intuition: The effect of subordinate role on interpersonal sensitivity. *Journal of Personality and Social Psychology, 49*(1), 146–155.

Snodgrass, S. E. (1992). Further effects of role versus gender on interpersonal sensitivity. *Journal of Personality and Social Psychology, 62*(1), 154–158.

Spender, D. (1980). *Man made language.* London: Routledge & Kegan Paul.

Steil, J. M., & Hillman, J. L. (1993). The perceived value of direct and indirect influence strategies: A cross-cultural comparison. *Psychology of Women Quarterly, 17,* 457–462.

Swim, J. K. (1994). Perceived versus meta-analytic effect sizes: An assessment of the accuracy of gender stereotypes. *Journal of Personality and Social Psychology, 66*(1), 21–36.

Tannen, D. (1990). *You just don't understand: Women and men in conversation.* New York: William Morrow.

Thorne, B., & Henley, N. (1975). Difference and dominance: An overview of language, gender and society. In B. Thorne & N. Henley (Eds.), *Language and sex: Difference and dominance* (pp. 5–42). Rowley, MA: Newbury House.

Torres, L. (1992). Women and language: From sex differences to power dynamics. In C. Kramarae & D. Spender (Eds.), *The knowledge explosion: Generations of feminist scholarship* (pp. 281–290). New York: Teacher's College Press.

Unger, R. K. (1976). Male is greater than female: The sociialization of status inequality. *Counseling Psychologist, 6*(2), 2–9.

Unger, R. K. (1979). *Female and male: Psychological perspectives.* New York: Harper & Row.

Unger, R. K. (1990). Imperfect reflections of reality: Psychology constructs gender. In R. T. Hare-Mustin & J. Marecek (Eds.), *Making a difference: Psychology and the construction of gender* (pp. 102–149). New Haven, CT: Yale University Press.

Werner, P. D., & LaRussa, G. W. (1985). Persistence and change in sex role stereotypes. *Sex Roles, 12,* 1089–1100.

West, C., & Zimmerman, D. H. (1977). Women's place in everyday talk: Reflections on parent–child interaction. *Social Problems, 24,* 521–529.

West, C., & Zimmerman, D. H. (1987). Doing gender. *Gender and Society, 1*(2), 125–151.

Wheelan, S. A., & Verdi, A. F. (1992). Differences in male and female patterns of communication in groups: A methodological artifact? *Sex Roles, 27*(1/2), 1–15.

Wiley, M. G., & Eskilson, A. (1985). Speech style, gender stereotypes and corporate success: What if women talk more like men? *Sex Roles, 12*(9/10), 993–1007.

Wood, W., & Karten, S. J. (1986). Sex differences in interaction style as a product of perceived sex differences in competence. *Journal of Personality and Social Psychology, 50*(2), 341–347.

Woods, N. (1988). Talking shop: Sex and status as determinants of floor apportionment in a work setting. In J. Coates & D. Cameron (Eds.), *Women in their speech communities: New perspectives on language and sex* (pp. 141–157). New York: Longman.

*Chapter 3: Putting It All Together*_____

1. These readings demonstrate that although stereotypes about gender may be inaccurate, they can have a powerful effect. Explain.
2. Based on what you have learned from these readings, are women and men more alike or different? Justify your answer.
3. What suggestions do you have for combating the effects of stereotypes in academic performance and communication?

4

Gender and Mental Health

The readings in this chapter examine the ways that gender role restrictions can affect mental health. The first reading explores the connection between depression and gender. While "pure depression" occurs at similar rates in males and females, "anxious somatic depression" is more likely experienced by females. The authors link this type of depression to sexism experienced by daughters whose mothers modeled gender related limitations and whose fathers expressed attitudes of male superiority. The second reading looks at the impact that absent fathers can have on their abandoned sons. A male gender role that discourages men from active parenting may contribute to the high numbers of absent fathers in our society. This loss may impact negatively on a son's self-esteem and affect his ability to achieve effective intimate relationships. The third reading describes how African-American women have higher self-esteem and a more positive body image than do Caucasian women. This may be because of cultural differences in gender role expectations which lead African-American women to see themselves as higher in masculine personality differences and to believe that African-American men prefer heavier women.

7

Gender Differences in Depression: The Role Played by Paternal Attitudes of Male Superiority and Maternal Modeling of Gender-Related Limitations

Brett Silverstein and Arthur D. Lynch

Studies of the relationship between gender and depression consistently reveal that females, beginning at adolescence, are at least twice as likely as males to experience depression. Silverstein and Lynch however, distinguish between two types of depression—"anxious somatic depression" and "pure depression"—and provide evidence that gender differences in depression are explained by the "anxious somatic" type only. They define "anxious somatic depression" as a type of depression accompanied by sleep and appetite disturbances, fatigue and anxiety, while "pure depression" is unaccompanied by these symptoms. Furthermore, their research links the higher prevalence of anxious somatic depression among women to sexism. Specifically, female respondents who perceived that their academic and career achievement had been limited by negative responses to their gender were more likely than other respondents to report symptoms of anxious somatic depression. Also, daughters of mothers who reported that their own opportunities have been limited by their gender were more likely to report these symptoms. Finally, the new data presented by Silverstein and Lynch directly links women's depression to attitudes of male superiority reported by their fathers. It appears, therefore, that anxious somatic

Reprinted by permission of Kluwer Academic/Plenum Publishers. From B. Silverstein & A. D. Lynch (1998). "Gender Differences in Depression: The Role Played by Paternal attitudes of Male Superiority and Maternal Modeling of Gender-Related Limitations," *Sex Roles, 38,* (7/8), 539–555.

depression is a form of powerlessness that is linked to the psychological internalization of sexist beliefs about women **(gender role effects).**

Questions to Consider:

1. In the reading, Silverstein and Lynch claim that many females appear to view their mothers as role models and to be strongly influenced by the opinions of their fathers. In their view, how does this contribute to the development of anxious somatic depression?

2. How well do the findings reported by Silverstein and Lynch concerning anxious somatic depression fit with your experiences of depression and/or your observations of depressed females? Explain.

3. This study makes use of archival data, so that the youngest women in the sample were born in 1950–1959. Do you think these findings are generalizable to current generations of young women? Have parental attitudes of male superiority changed significantly? Explain.

4. What actions can you take to help overcome the devaluation of women that is experienced by females of all ages? Be specific.

5. How might sons be affected by fathers who have attitudes of male superiority and mothers who report that their opportunities had been limited by gender?

6. How might this research be incorporated into a dialectical model of gender and depression?

The gender difference in depressive symptomatology has received a great deal of attention (Culbertson, 1997; McGrath, Keita, Strickland, & Russo, 1990). Recent evidence suggests that the higher prevalence of clinical and subclinical depression among females results because one subtype of depression rooted in limitations placed upon women is much more prevalent among females. Another subtype of depression, however, appears to be uninfluenced by such forces and is equally prevalent among females and males. The first type, which has been termed "anxious somatic depression," involves depression accompanied by anxiety and somatic symptomatology such as sleep and appetite disturbance as well as fatigue. The second type, termed "pure depression," involves depression unaccompanied to any great extent by these other symptoms and may possibly be heavily rooted in genetic factors.

Two bodies of evidence are consonant with the hypotheses that the gender difference in depression results from a difference in a subtype of depression involving anxiety and somatic symptoms and that this subtype is rooted in limitations placed upon women. The first body of evidence involves studies that measure the individual symptoms of anxious somatic depression but that do not combine them into a measure of a single syndrome. For example, many studies of depressive symptomatology, including several studies of large epidemiologic samples, have found large gender differences in the prevalence of anxiety, fatigue, sleep, and appetite disturbance but little or no gender differences in the prevalence of the other symptoms of depression in samples of depressed patients as well as in the general

The research reported here was based on the data set entitled *A Longitudinal Study of Generations and Mental Health.* These data were collected by Vern L. Bengston and donated to the archive of the Henry A. Murray Research Center of Radcliffe College, Cambridge, Massachusetts (Producer and Distributor).

community (Weissman, Bruce, Leaf, Florio, & Holzer, 1991; Young, Fogg, Scheftner, Keller, & Fawcett, 1990; Young, Scheftner, Fawcett, & Klerman, 1990. For citation of other studies, see Silverstein, Caceres, Perdue, & Cimarolli, 1995). Furthermore, many studies have found relationships between the individual symptoms of anxious somatic depression and women's reports of having been exposed to gender bias. Landrine, Klonoff, Gibbs, Manning and Lurid (1995) found that the degree to which women reported having experienced gender discrimination significantly predicted scores on self-report inventories of depression, anxiety, and somatization. Martz, Handley and Eisler (1995, p. 506) found that appetite disturbance was particularly common among women who scored high on a scale measuring the extent of perceptions of "the negative aspects of the feminine role." Depression, anxiety, and somatization, including appetite disturbance, have also been found in women who have been subjected to sexual harassment (Koss et al., 1994), sexual assault (Winfield, George, Swartz, & Blazer, 1990), and incest (Pribor & Dinwiddie, 1992).

The second body of evidence in support of the hypotheses examines the symptoms of anxious somatic depression in combination with one another. Many studies have reported high intercorrelation or comorbidity between depression, anxiety, somatization, and appetite disturbance, particularly among females (e.g., Maser & Cloninger, 1990; Swartz, Blazer, Woodbury, George, & Landerman, 1986; Wilson & Eldredge, 1991). A series of studies used self-report inventories, such as the Center for Epidemiologic Studies Depression Scale, to divide respondents into those reporting low levels of depression, those reporting the combined symptoms of anxious somatic depression, and those reporting pure depression. These studies found females to exhibit

a higher level of anxious somatic depression than males but not a higher level of pure depression in both a high school sample (Silverstein, Caceres et al., 1995) and a college sample (Silverstein, Clauson, Perdue, Carpman, & Cimarolli, 1998).

In addition, measures of social-psychological variables related to limitations placed on female achievement were found in these studies to be highly related to female respondents' reports of anxious somatic depression, but unrelated to reports of pure depression. These variables include the beliefs reported by females in a sample of high school students and an independent sample of college students that their opportunities had been limited by social reactions to their gender (sample item: "More people would pay attention to my ideas if I were male") (Silverstein, Caceres et al., 1995); female high school and college students' beliefs that their mothers' opportunities had been limited by reactions to their mothers' gender (sample item: "When you were growing up, how much did your mother feel limited because she was female?") (Silverstein, Caceres et al., 1995; Silverstein et al., 1998; Silverstein, Perlick, Clauson, & McKoy, 1993); and female high school and college students' beliefs that their fathers would have preferred them to be male (sample item: "When you were growing up, how much did you have the sense that your father would have been prouder of you if you were not a girl?") (Silverstein et al., 1993; Silverstein et al., 1998). In a recent study of female high school students and their mothers, mothers' self-reports of having been limited by reactions to their gender (sample item: "When your daughter was growing up, how much did you feel limited by being female?") were found to predict their daughters' reports of anxious somatic depression, but not daughters' reports of pure depression (Silverstein & Blumenthal, 1997). Mothers' self-reported depression was found to be unrelated to their daughters' reports of anxious somatic depression but related to daughters' reports of pure depression, suggesting the possibility that pure depression may be influenced by genetic factors.

Additional evidence that anxious somatic depression may be influenced by social psychological forces comes from a series of studies that have found that several indices of the prevalence of anxious somatic depression among females share similar variation across birth cohorts. These indices include the gender difference in the prevalence of depression (Silverstein & Perlick, 1991), the gender difference in the prevalence of somatic symptomatology (Silverstein & Perlick, 1995), the incidence of anorexia among teenage females (Silverstein & Perlick, 1995 derived from Lucas, Beard, O'Fallon, & Kurland, 1991), and the extent of the relationship among females between self-reported depression and somatic symptomatology (Silverstein, Clauson, McKoy, Perdue, & Raban, 1995). All of these studies include measures demonstrating that the shared covariation is due not to the age of respondents but to the year in which they were born. In other words, these indices of anxious somatic depression were found to be similarly related to the period when respondents were born, which is further suggestive of a syndrome rooted in social-psychological factors that exhibit short-term historical change rather than genetic factors that do not.

The mechanisms wherein limitations placed upon women may eventuate in the development of anxious somatic depression have been discussed in detail elsewhere (Silverstein & Perlick, 1995). Briefly, many bright, ambitious girls develop identities and senses of self-worth based upon their intelligence and their competence in school. But some of these girls find limitations placed on their achievements or on the respect they receive for their achievements because they are female, particularly after they reach adolescence. The message that living up to their aspirations and obtaining the respect for their achievements that they desire may be rendered more difficult by social responses to their gender can be communicated to these girls through several channels. They may receive less support, both financial and psychological, than boys for attending college. They may come up against gender biases in hiring and promotion practices that limit their career opportunities. Thus, we might expect anxious somatic depression to be particularly prevalent among women who were unable to attend college or to achieve respected careers. They may find that people whose opinions matter to them, such as their fathers, do not accord them as much respect for their achievements as they would if they were male. Thus, we might expect anxious somatic depression to be particularly prevalent among women whose fathers hold attitudes of male superiority. And by modelling themselves upon, and identifying with, mothers who themselves may have been unable to live up to their aspirations, some girls may come to associate being female with facing limitations on their possibilities of achievement. Thus, we might expect anxious somatic depression to be particularly prevalent among women whose mothers failed to live up to their aspirations for career success. The sense of failure many of these women may come to feel may result in depressed mood. The fear they may develop that they will never be allowed to live the lives they desired may result in anxiety. The combination of depression and anxiety may result in somatic symptoms.

The study reported here reanalyzes data from a study (Bengtson & Dunham,

1986) in which the Center for Epidemiologic Studies Depression Scale (CES-D) was distributed to a large multi-generational sample of families. This database allows several further tests of the hypothesis that the gender difference in depression results because females are more likely than males to report a type of depression accompanied by anxiety and somatic symptomatology rooted in factors related to limitations placed on female achievement, but not more likely to exhibit a type of depression unaccompanied by these other symptoms, possibly rooted more heavily in genetic factors. First, included in the study are many pairs of mothers and daughters, allowing replication of the finding that daughters' reports of anxious somatic depression are correlated with mothers' reports of limitations placed on their own achievement. Second, the inclusion in the study of many father-daughter pairs allows the first direct examination of the relationship between daughters' reports of anxious somatic depression and fathers' reports of attitudes regarding male superiority. This extends the previous finding that young women who believe that their fathers exhibited a preference for males are particularly likely to report anxious somatic depression. Third, the gender difference in anxious somatic depression but not pure depression and the relationship between anxious somatic depression and indices of limitations placed on females have previously been reported for several samples of high school and college students. This study reports similar analyses of a large multi-generational sample of adults. Fourth, although the study does not include controls that allow the effects of birth cohort to be disentangled from the effects of age, it does allow preliminary tests of the hypothesis that the prevalence of a social-psychologically rooted syndrome of anxious somatic depression should vary

among different birth cohorts while the prevalence of a genetically rooted pure depression should not vary among people born during different time periods.

Method

Sample

The study reported here was a reanalysis of data from a longitudinal study of generations and mental health done by Bengtson (Bengtson et al., 1986). In the original wave of the study, in 1971–72, data were collected from 2045 predominantly Caucasian subjects. The participants in the study were recruited through the first-generation male subjects, who were members of a large metropolitan health maintenance organization in southern California. Twelve percent of the men who were above age 55 and who had at least one dependent that were enrolled in the plan were sent a screening questionnaire. Five hundred and fifteen of these men were selected because they were members of multi-generation families and were willing to participate. These men and the members of their families (totalling 3,184 individuals) were mailed lengthy questionnaires. In 1985, the families were contacted for a second time. 2612 members of the original Time 1 pool were identified and sent questionnaires. Sixty two percent of the questionnaires were returned. The surveys mailed to these respondents in the second wave of the study, from which the data analyzed here were taken, included the CES-D, the depression inventory used in previously-published studies of anxious somatic depression. Fifty eight percent of the Time 2 respondents were females and 74% of the respondents were married. The 221 respondents belonging to the first generation (the original members of the HMO and their spouses) had a mean age at Time 2 of 78. The 556 respondents belonging to the second generation of the study (the daughters and sons of the first generation and their spouses) had a mean age of 57. The 554 third generation respondents had a mean age of 33.

Measures

The CES-D is one of the self-report depression inventories most frequently used in epidemiologic research. It consists of 20 questions regarding symptomatology experienced during the previous week. Possible scores range from 0 through 60. In utilizing a self-report inventory to compare two types of depression, it is necessary to use a cutoff to define high levels of depression. Previous studies of non-adolescent groups have used the cutoff of 16 or greater recommended by the developers of the scale (Radloff & Locke, 1986) for measuring moderately-high levels of depression, but this cutoff results in high estimates of depression prevalence (Silverstein et al., 1997). This is the first study of anxious somatic depression in which the sample size of adult respondents is large enough to use the cutoff of 28 or greater on the CES-D that is suggested by the developers of the scale for defining clinical depression because it results in prevalence estimates similar to the prevalence of major depression found in studies that have used research interviews. Other symptoms used to create an operational definition of anxious somatic depression that is as close as possible to that used in other studies were measured using individual items from the CES-D. This inventory asks respondents to indicate using a four-point scale ranging from "Rarely or none of the time" to "Most of the time" how often during the previous week they experienced each of a number of symptoms. Sleep

disturbance was measured with the item "My sleep was restless." Appetite disturbance was measured with the item "I did not feel like eating: my appetite was poor." Fatigue was measured with the item "I could not get 'going'." Anxiety was measured with the item "I felt fearful." Respondents who reported experiencing these problems "occasionally" or "most of the time" were categorized as scoring high on these items.

The double use of items from a single questionnaire results because the currently accepted definition of depression does not distinguish between two subtypes of anxious somatic and pure depression and so includes somatic symptoms such as sleep and appetite disturbance and fatigue. As a result, the research instruments that are widely-used and well-validated include such symptoms as possible criteria in their definition of depression. At present, it is not possible to create operational definitions of any type of depression based on validated instruments that do not include these symptoms. But because all research measures also allow depression to be defined or diagnosed in the absence of these symptoms, it is possible to use such measures to define two subtypes of depression with and without much anxiety and somatic symptomatology.

Categorizing Pure vs. Anxious Somatic Depression. Respondents were categorized as exhibiting anxious somatic depression if they scored above cutoff on the total CES-D and also reported at least two of the other four symptoms: sleep disturbance, appetite disturbance, fatigue, and anxiety. Respondents were categorized as exhibiting pure depression if they scored above cutoff on the CES-D but reported only zero or one of the other symptoms. (This operational definition of pure depression receives further attention in the discussion.) Respondents were categorized as exhibiting low depression if they scored below cutoff on the CES-D.

Other Measures. Limitations possibly associated with gender were measured using items regarding respondents' education and their attitudes regarding jobs. Respondents answered the question "Do you feel the job you do is respected by others?" using a five-point scale ranging from "1 = never" to "5 = very often." Respondents who answered "fairly often" or "very often" were categorized as feeling that their jobs were respected. Respondents were asked to rank order the importance of nine "values in life" (e.g., patriotism, personal freedom, a world at peace). Those who ranked "achieving success in your job or profession" in the top five were categorized as placing emphasis on career success.

Two items measuring attitudes about gender roles were included in the survey. Both were measured on four-point agree-disagree scales in which 1 = "strongly agree" and 2 = "somewhat agree." One item was "Some equality in marriage is a good thing, but by and large the husband ought to have the main say in family matters." The other item was "It goes against nature to place women in positions of authority over men." Respondents who agreed with either of these statements were categorized as exhibiting belief in male superiority.

For the cohort analyses, respondents were divided by their decade of birth (pre-1920, 1920–29, 1930–39, 1940–49, 1950–59. The 203 respondents born prior to 1920 were combined into one cohort in order to obtain an adequate number of respondents for the earliest cohort.) Because the measure of symptomatology was only administered to this sample at one point in time, it is not possible to disentangle birth cohort effects from age effects as has been done in previously published studies of co-hort differences in the symptoms of anxious somatic depression.

Results

Perhaps the most intriguing findings reported here deal with the relationship between daughters' symptomatology and parental attitudes. In order to avoid confounds with the cohort effects reported below, examination of the relationships between the symptomatology reported by women and the attitudes of their parents were limited to daughters in one generation and their parents. Symptomatology reported by women in the third generation (the last generation of adults reported in the study), which was born after World War II, was related to attitudes reported by their parents.

Mothers were divided into those who did not place emphasis on career success, those who placed emphasis on career success and felt that their jobs were respected and those who placed emphasis on career success but did not feel that their jobs were respected. Although the number of mother-daughter pairs (141) included in the analysis was not small, given the relatively low prevalence of the two subtypes of depression and the relatively low percentage (13% n = 19) of mothers who placed emphasis on careers but did not feel that their jobs were respected (it appears that some women without jobs did not respond to this item), a 3 (mothers' attitudes toward jobs) by 3 (daughters' depression category) analysis could not be validly performed due to small cell sizes. But by collapsing cells, it was possible to perform an analysis comparing the prevalence (21% = 4/19) of anxious somatic depression reported by daughters of mothers who placed high emphasis on jobs and did not feel that their jobs were respected with the prevalence (7% = 8/122) of anxious somatic depression reported by daughters of other mothers (Fishers exact test $p = .05$). (The daughters of the mothers in the two groups that were collapsed into the "other" group in this analysis exhibited 6.3% and 6.7% prevalence of anxious somatic depression.) It appears that mothers who place importance on, but do not attain, career success have daughters who are particularly likely to report anxious somatic depression. A similar analysis relating daughters' anxious somatic depression to fathers' attitudes toward jobs did not even approach significance (Fishers exact test $p = .15$), but this finding is difficult to interpret given that only 9% of fathers (n = 13) reported placing emphasis on career success but feeling that their own jobs were not respected.

On the other hand, 60% (n = 88) of the 143 fathers for whom data regarding their daughters' symptomatology was available agreed with at least one of the two attitude items regarding male superiority. Whereas 11% of the daughters of these men reported anxious somatic depression, none of the daughters of the 57 fathers who did not agree with either of these two items reported anxious somatic depression (Fishers exact test two-tail $p = .01$). Of the mothers in this sample for whom daughter data was available, 42% agreed with at least

one of the two items measuring beliefs in male dominance. In contrast with the analysis of the father-daughter data, however, the daughters of mothers who agreed that males should be dominant actually exhibited slightly (nonsignificantly) lower prevalence of anxious somatic depression (8%) than the daughters of mothers who did not agree with either of the two male-dominance items (11%). It appears that fathers, but not mothers, who believe in male superiority have daughters who exhibit anxious somatic depression.

The importance of this subtype of depression that is associated with these parental attitudes is exhibited in the comparison of depression prevalence among females and males. In this sample, females were twice as likely as males to score 28 or greater on the CES-D (12% vs. 6%, $\chi^2(1,1232) = 13.64, p < .001$). But, as shown in Table I, this (6%) gender difference in self-reported depression is due primarily to the (5%) difference in prevalence of anxious somatic depression (females—9%, males 4%), not to the small (1%) gender difference in prevalence of pure depression (overall $\chi^2(2,1231) = 13.71, p < .002$).

As in earlier studies of high school and college students, in this sample of adults, psychosocial variables were related to reports of anxious somatic depression. The proportion of respondents reporting anxious somatic depression was almost twice as

TABLE I.   *Male and Female Respondents Reporting Low Depression, Pure Depression, or Anxious Somatic Depression*[a]

	Low Depression	Pure Depression	Anxious Somatic Depression
Males	485 (94%)	9 (2%)	20 (4%)
Females	634 (88%)	24 (3%)	61 (9%)

[a]Numbers in parentheses indicate the percentage of respondents in each row exhibiting each type of symptomatology.

high among those who had not attended college (9%) as among those who had attended college (5%) and almost three times as high (11%) among respondents who reported feeling that their jobs were unrespected as among those who reported feeling that their jobs were respected (4%).

The effects of both of these limitations are most apparent in Table II, in which the female and male respondents were separately categorized into those who did not attend college, those who attended college but felt their jobs were unrespected, and those who attended college and felt their jobs were respected. Both a practical and a theoretical rationale existed for not dividing the respondents who did not attend college into two groups based on how respected

TABLE II. *Female and Male Respondents Categorized Separately According to College Attendance and Feeling Unrespected in Their Jobs Who Report Low Depression, Pure Depression, or Anxious Somatic Depression[a]*

	Women			
	Low Depression	*Pure Depression*	*Anxious Somatic Depression*	*Total*
No college	271 (86%)	12 (4%)	12 (10%)	115 (52% of women)
Attended college but felt job was unrespected	73 (83%)	3 (3%)	12 (14%)	88 (14% of women)
Attended college and felt job was respected	188 (91%)	9 (4%)	9 (4%)	206 (34% of women)

	Men			
	Low Depression	*Pure Depression*	*Anxious Somatic Depression*	*Total*
No college	141 (50%)	5 (3%)	17 (7%)	157 (35% of men)
Attended college but felt job was unrespected	38 (91%)	2 (3%)	4 (6%)	64 (14% of men)
Attended college and felt job was respected	221 (97%)	2 (1%)	4 (2%)	227 (50% of men)

[a]Numbers in parentheses in first three columns indicate the percentage of respondents in each row exhibiting each type of symptomatology. Numbers in parentheses in fourth column indicates the percentage of female or male respondents in each college/job category.

they felt their jobs were. The practical ratio- nale was the need to maximize cell sizes. The theoretical rationale was that for many years, not being allowed to attend college has been a major limitation placed upon women. Even some women who have eventually attained success have reported feeling distress over not having been able to pursue higher education (Silverstein & Perlick, 1995).

The prevalence of anxious somatic de- pression reported by women who attended college and felt their jobs were respected (4%) was much lower than the prevalence reported by women who had not attended college (10%) or by women who had at- tended college but felt their jobs were unre- spected (14%). In fascinating contrast, very little difference in reported prevalence of pure depression was found between women who had attended college and felt their jobs were respected (4%), those who had not at- tended college (4%), and those who had at- tended college and felt their jobs were unrespected (3%) (overall $\chi^2(4,605) = 8.47$, $p < .08$). The non-significance of the analy- sis results from the lack of difference be- tween the three groups of women in the prevalence of pure depression. In order to study the relationship between the psy- chosocial measures and reports of anxious somatic depression, all women who did not meet criteria for anxious somatic depression were combined into one group. If the low depression and pure depression groups are collapsed into one group of women who do not exhibit anxious somatic depression, a 3 (college/job category) by 2 (respondents do or do not report anxious somatic depres- sion) χ^2 analysis results in a highly signifi- cant ($p < .02$) χ^2 of 8.41. This analysis indicates a strong relationship between women's reports of limitations in their edu- cational or occupational achievement and their reports of anxious somatic depression.

As depicted in the table, the lack of re- lationship between the college/job cate- gories and reports of pure depression exhibited by females is not so clear among males, but cell sizes are too small to allow a 3 × 3 analysis. When the male respondents who did not exhibit anxious somatic depres- sion are combined into one group, a signifi- cant ($\chi^2(2,448) = 7.03$, $p < .03$) relationship between college/job category and preva- lence of anxious somatic depression is found. It appears that the gender difference in anxious somatic depression, and thus the gender difference in depression, is due in part to the lower percentage of women (34%) than of men (51%) who belong to the group that attended college and felt that their jobs were respected that exhibits low prevalence of anxious somatic depression.

In the cohort analysis presented in Table III, whereas the prevalence of anxious somatic depression was over twice as high in one cohort as it was in another, the prevalence of pure depression varied little by cohort. Although the cohort analyses were based on over 1200 respondents, statistical tests of inter-cohort variance must use the number of cohorts. Notwithstanding the small number of co- horts (5) used in the analysis, the inter- cohort variance in prevalence of anxious so- matic depression (3.3) was significantly greater (over ten times as high) than the minuscule inter-cohort variance in preva- lence of pure depression (0.3, $t = 2.51$, df = 4, one-tailed $p < .05$). The cohort analyses had to be performed on the data of females and males combined because when the data of females and males were separately di- vided into five cohorts, the number of re- spondents reporting pure or anxious somatic depression in most cohorts was so small (in 9 of 20 cells, the n was less than four) as to render meaningless any compar- ison of prevalence between cohorts.

TABLE III. *Respondents in Each Birth Cohort Reporting Low Depression, Pure Depression, or Anxious Somatic Depression*[a]

Years of Birth	Low Depression	Pure Depression	Anxious Somatic Depression
Prior to 1920	190 (94%)	4 (2%)	9 (4%)
1920–1929	253 (93%)	5 (2%)	15 (6%)
1930–1939	177 (87%)	7 (3%)	19 (9%)
1940–1949	112 (92%)	3 (3%)	7 (6%)
1950–1959	367 (90%)	13 (3%)	26 (6%)

[a]Numbers in parentheses indicate the percentage of respondents in each row exhibiting each type of symptomatology.

Discussion

This is the third sample in which the gender difference in the prevalence of self-reported depression accompanied by anxiety and somatic symptomatology was found to be large but the difference in depression unaccompanied by these other symptoms was found to be small or nonexistent. Much higher prevalence among females compared to males of anxious somatic depression but not pure depression has now been found among high school students, college students, and adults. It should be noted that all of these studies have relied on self-report measures of depression.

This is the fourth sample in which issues related to achievement reported by females have been found to be correlated with self-reported prevalence of anxious somatic depression but not of pure depression. Previous studies designed to test these relationships found reports of anxious somatic depression but not pure depression to be related to respondents' reports of feeling that their opportunities had been limited by responses to their gender. Because the data reported here are based on reanalysis of a survey distributed by others, the explicit link made in previously-published studies

between achievement limitations and gender must be inferred here. We know that reported anxious somatic depression but not pure depression is high among women who did not attend college and among those who attended college but did not feel that their jobs were respected. The relationship between gender and both educational and occupational attainment must have been well known to most of the respondents in this study, two-thirds of whom were born prior to 1950. But using the data available from this survey, we cannot determine whether the high prevalence of anxious somatic depression reported by women who did not attend college or who felt their jobs were unrespected was explicitly related to connections they may have made between their gender and their opportunities for advancement, as found in previous studies. Furthermore, the items used here to measure perceived job respect, emphasis on career success, and attitudes of male superiority are of unknown validity and reliability.

The same limitations apply to the mother-daughter data. A previous study of high school students found daughters' reports of anxious somatic depression to be related to mothers' beliefs that their own opportunities had been limited by their gender (Silverstein et al., 1997). In the analysis reported here, mothers who place importance on career success but do not feel that their jobs are respected have daughters who are likely to report anxious somatic depression, but we cannot determine the importance of the links made by either the mothers or the daughters between the mothers' gender and the lack of the mothers' career success.

To our knowledge, this study is the first to directly link women's symptomatology to attitudes toward women reported by their fathers. Earlier studies reported a significant relationship between daughters' disordered eating and their beliefs that their fathers agreed that "a woman's place is in the home" (Silverstein, Perdue, Wolf, & Pizzolo, 1988) and a relationship between daughters anxious somatic depression and the daughters' perceptions that their fathers exhibited a preference for males (Silverstein et al., 1993; Silverstein et al., 1998), but none of these studies actually surveyed fathers. In the study reported here, fathers who agree that men should be dominant over women are more likely than fathers who do not agree to have daughters who exhibit anxious somatic depression.

The comparison of the mother-daughter and father-daughter analyses reported here resembles findings from other studies. Mussen and Rutherford (1963) found that the sex-role preferences exhibited by girls were related to the amount of acceptance of femininity reported by their fathers, and the level of self-acceptance reported by their mothers, but not to fathers' self-acceptance or mothers' attitudes toward femininity. Silverstein, Perdue, Wolf, & Pizzolo (1988) found the disordered eating reported by college women to be significantly related to the women's perceptions of what their mothers thought about their own careers and to

whether they felt that their fathers treated a boy as the most intelligent sibling in the family, but not to their perceptions of what their fathers thought of their own careers or whether they felt that their mothers treated a boy as the most intelligent sibling in the family. In the analyses reported here, the amount of anxious somatic depression exhibited by women was found to be significantly related to reports made by their mothers of emphasizing career success but not feeling respected in their jobs, but not comparable reports made by their fathers, and to their fathers' attitudes of male superiority but not to comparable attitudes of mothers. (The small number of parents who reported both placing emphasis on career success and also feeling that their jobs were not respected renders confidence in the first conclusion reported above less certain than confidence in the second conclusion.) Many women appear to treat their mothers as role models and sources with whom to identify and to treat their fathers as sources whose opinions are influential.

The analyses reported here, including the cohort analyses, add some support for the hypothesis that pure depression is not based in social-psychological factors. Much more work must be done before firm conclusions can be drawn regarding this conjecture. As mentioned above, because at the present time the distinction between pure and anxious somatic depression is not yet recognized in the fields of psychology and psychiatry, validated self-report and diagnostic measures of depression include the somatic symptoms of fatigue, appetite and sleep disturbance, making pure depression a residual category comprised of people who meet criteria for depression but not for anxious somatic depression. If research continues to support the distinction between pure and anxious somatic depression, it should eventually be possible to develop independent criteria for the two subtypes of depression, overlapping in only a few symptoms, such as dysphoria, but with mostly distinct symptoms. Much future research remains to be done to develop these two sets of criteria.

Future research must also compare females and males using research interview measures of depression. Furthermore, the paternal attitudes of male superiority measured here among fathers of baby boomers may now be somewhat dated. Nowadays, fewer fathers may straightforwardly assert that men should be dominant over women. But many fathers may continue to exhibit to their daughters more subtle versions of these attitudes of male superiority, such as believing that it is more important for men than for women to succeed in careers. Research is needed to relate these more subtle contemporary paternal attitudes to the prevalence of anxious somatic depression reported by daughters born after the baby boom years.

Beginning at adolescence, women exhibit higher prevalence than do men of several disorders, including depression, anxiety, disordered eating, headaches, and fatigue. We hypothesize that most of these differences, which now tend to be treated as independent, may result from a gender difference in prevalence of a single disorder—anxious somatic depression. Furthermore, the higher prevalence of this disorder among women results from limitations placed on the ability of many women to achieve successful careers and to be accorded the respect for these achievements that might be given to men.

In order to understand who is apt to suffer anxious somatic depression and why it is now so prevalent, we must focus on the psychology of how these limitations affect women. That is, the people most likely to feel inadequate are those who fail to live up to their standards for themselves. Women

who do not aspire to career success, for example, are less likely to feel limited by traditional gender roles than those who judge themselves, at least in part, on their ability to achieve in areas historically reserved for men. The past few decades have seen a great increase in the number of young women who grow up feeling that they have the ability to succeed in nondomestic roles, who develop identities centered in part around such success, and who do not view full time homemaking as being a complete success. The good news is that more women than ever before are now able to attain such success by attending college and achieving respected careers. The bad news is that the increase in the number of women who harbor these aspirations may have outpaced the increase in the number who have been allowed to live up to them.

That is, many of the contemporary young women who aspire to attain respect for achievements in such areas as politics, professions, sports, and business also receive messages and treatment that undercut their sense of having succeeded in living up to these standards. These may take the form of glass ceilings, pressure to take "mommy track" jobs, and gender biases in hiring and promotion. They may also take the form of more subtle psychological biases such as media depiction of women as more helpless than men, teachers' beliefs that boys are naturally better than girls at math and science, community attitudes that working women, even those in good jobs, are not truly successful if they rely on others for childcare, and the attitudes of many fathers that the career achievements of their daughters are in the end less important than those of their sons. We suggest that feelings of inadequacy, and the symptoms of anxious somatic depression, are particularly likely to afflict women who exhibit the following three characteristics: 1. They aspire to achieve outside of the home; 2. They are exposed to mothers who model the notion that being female has hindered them from feeling successful and respected; 3. They are exposed to several of the limitations placed on women attaining respect just described.

Very many contemporary women appear to exhibit these three characteristics, which we believe goes a long way to explaining why women exhibit much more depression, anxiety, disordered eating, and somatic symptomatology than men.

References

Bengtson, V. L., & Dunham, C. (1986). Conceptual and theoretical perspectives of generational relations. In N. Datan, A. Green, & H. Reef (Eds.), *Life span developmental psychology: Intergenerational networks.* Hillside, NJ: Erlbaum.

Culbertson, F. M. (1997). Depression and gender: An international review. *American Psychologist, 52,* 25–34.

Koss, M. P., Goodman, L. A., Browne, A., Fitzgerald, L. F., Keita, G. P., & Russo, N. F. (1994). *No safe haven: Male violence against women at home, at work, and in the community,* Washington, DC: American Psychological Association.

Landrine, H., Klonoff, E. A., Gibbs, J., Manning, V., & Lund, M. (1995). Physical and psychiatric correlates of gender discrimination: An application of the schedule of sexist events. *Psychology of Women Quarterly, 19,* 473–492.

Lucas, A. R., Beard, M., O'Fallon, W. M., & Kurland, L. T. (1991). 50-year trends in the incidence of anorexia nervosa in Rochester, Minn.: A population-based study. *American Journal of Psychiatry, 148,* 917–922.

Martz, D. M., Handley, K. B., & Eisler, R. M. (1995). The relationship between feminine gender role stress, body image, and eating disorders. *Psychology of Women Quarterly, 19,* 493–508.

Maser, J. D., & Cloninger, C. R. (1990). Comorbidity of anxiety and mood disorders: Introduction and overview. In J. D. Maser & C. R. Cloninger (Eds.), *Comorbidity of mood and anxiety disorders.* Washington, DC: American Psychiatric Press.

McGrath, E., Keita, G. P., Strickland, B. R., & Russo, N. P. (1990). *Women and depression: Risk factors and treatment issues.* Washington, DC: American Psychological Association.

Mussen, P., & Rutherford, E. (1963). Parent-child relations and parental personality in relation to young children's sex-role preferences. *Child Development, 34,* 589–607.

Prihor, E. F., & Dinwiddie, H. (1992). Psychiatric correlates of incest in childhood. *American Journal of Psychiatry, 149,* 52–56.

Radloff, L. S., & Locke, B. A. (1986). The Community Mental Health Assessment Survey and the CES-D Scale. In M. M. Weissman, J. K. Myers, & C. E. Ross (Eds.), *Community surveys of psychiatric disorders.* New Brunswick, NJ: Rutgers University Press.

Silverstein, B., & Blumenthal, E. (1997). Depression mixed with anxiety, somatization, and disordered eating: Relationship with gender-role-related limitations experienced by females. *Sex Roles, 36,* 709–724.

Silverstein, B., Caceres, J., Perdue, L., & Cimarolli, V. (1995). Gender differences in depressive symptomatology: The role played by "anxious somatic depression" associated with gender-related achievement concerns. *Sex Roles, 33,* 621–636.

Silverstein, B., Clauson, J., McKoy, E., Perdue, L., & Raban, J. (1995). The correlation between depression and headache: The role played by generational changes in female achievement. *Journal of Applied Social Psychology, 25,* 35–48.

Silverstein, B., Clauson, J., Perdue, L., Carpman, S., & Cimarolli, V. (1998). The association between female college students reports of depression and their perceptions of parental attitudes regarding gender. *Journal of Applied Social Psychology, 28,* 537–549.

Silverstein, B., Perdue, L., Wolf, C., & Pizzolo, C. (1988). Bingeing, purging, and estimates of parental attitudes regarding female achievement. *Sex Roles, 19,* 723–733.

Silverstein, B., & Perlick, D. (1991). Gender differences in depression: Historical changes. *Acta Psychiatrica Scandinavica, 84,* 327–331.

Silverstein, B., & Perlick, D. (1995). *The cost of competence.* New York: Oxford University Press.

Silverstein, B., Perlick, D., Ciauson, J., & McKoy, E. (1993). Depression combined with somatic symptomatology among adolescent females who report concerns regarding maternal achievement. *Sex Roles, 28,* 637–653.

Swartz, M., Blazer, D., Woodbury, M., George, L., & Landerman, R. (1986). Somatization disorder in a U.S. Southern community: Use of a new procedure for analysis of medical classification. *Psychological Medicine, 16,* 595–609.

Weissman, M. M., Bruce, M. L., Leaf, P. J., & Holzer, C., III (1991). Affective disorders. In L. N. Robins & D. A. Regier (Eds.), *Psychiatric disorders in America: The Epidemiologic Catchment Area Study.* New York: Free Press.

Wilson, G. T., & Eldredge, K. L. (1991). Frequency of binge eating in bulimic patients: Diagnostic validity. *International Journal of Eating Disorders, 10,* 557–561.

Winfield, I., George, L. K., Swartz, M., & Blazer, D. G. (1990). Sexual assault and psychiatric disorders among a community sample of women. *American Journal of Psychiatry, 147,* 335–341.

Young, M. A., Fogg, L. F., Scheftner, W. A., Keller, M. B., & Fawcett, J. A. (1990). Sex differences in the lifetime prevalence of depression: Does varying the diagnostic criteria reduce the female/male ratio. *Journal of Affective Disorders, 18,* 187–192.

Young, M. A., Scheftner, W. A., Fawcett, J., & Klerman, G. L. (1990). Gender differences in the clinical features of unipolar major depressive disorder. *Journal of Nervous and Mental Disease, 178,* 200–203.

8

Absent Fathers: Effects on Abandoned Sons

Dennis A. Balcom

A male gender role that requires men to be economic providers and discourages them from active parenting may contribute to the high numbers of absent fathers in our society **(gender role effects).** In this reading, Balcom describes how a father's absence in childhood can impact negatively on his adult son's self-esteem and capacity for intimate relationships. Frequently, a father's absence has not been adequately explained to a son, and this mystery contributes to these difficulties. Balcom proposes a model for treating the adult sons of absent fathers which reduces the mystery of the father's absence. This is accomplished through grieving the loss of the father and reuniting with the father. Balcom argues that this process enables abandoned sons to be more successful in their intimate relationships.

Questions to Consider:

1. According to Balcom, why does abandonment by a father affect a son's self-esteem?
2. Do you know someone who has been abandoned by their father? Does their experience match the experience of the abandoned sons Balcom describes? Explain.
3. Do you think abandoned daughters would be affected in the same ways? Why or why not?
4. What social factors contribute to high rates of absent fathers? What can be done to reduce the numbers of absent fathers?

Many adult sons abandoned by their fathers have difficulty developing and sustaining

Originally published in *The Journal of Men's Studies, 6,* (3), 283–296. Reprinted by permission of the Men's Studies Press.

The author wishes to acknowledge the thoughtful consideration of the following colleagues in helping him prepare this paper: Kendall Dudley, John Hubbell Richard Jacobs, Renda Mott, Jack Sternback, and this journal's anonymous reviewers.

self-esteem, forming lasting emotional attachments, recognizing their feelings, or being expressive with their adult partners and children. These men must turn their attention toward their absent fathers and resolve the mystery of their absence to ensure that their current intimate relationships can succeed. The reasons for the fathers' absence are paramount, as these dictate the effects on the sons.

This article, based on published research and the author's clinical and supervisory experiences, explores the experiences of men abandoned by their fathers, delineates the impact on the sons' feelings of worth and their intimate relationships, and highlights treatment issues central to this situation.

The prevalence of absent fathers across class and ethnic categories suggests that this social problem afflicts many families with profound emotional, developmental, educational, and legal consequences for the abandoned sons (Arendell, 1993; Blankenhorn, 1995; Ilarado, 1993; Kruk, 1992, 1994; Lamb, 1997; Phares, 1992; Sills, 1995).

Father Absence

Social Context

In the mid-nineteenth century fathers increasingly moved out of the home for economic reasons. Men came to spend less and less time in a parental role as they came to be seen primarily as economic providers for the family (Griswold, 1993). A major consequence of this shift, as described by Pleck (1987), was a change in role from being an active and present dominant influence in the family to being a physically absent and intermittent dominant influence. Fathers

lost the regular opportunity to parent, and children lost their fathers.

Luepnitz (1988) contends that the predominant American family structure is patriarchal and, paradoxically, father-absent. This pervasive construct represents the economic and gender inequities present in American society. Fathers, by virtue of being male, earn more money than mothers, which in turn gives them power (one patriarchal feature) over the rest of the family (Auerbach, 1996).

Fathers can be absent in a variety of ways, both physical and emotional. Many of the reasons fathers are absent from the lives of their sons are direct consequences of society's impact on the family. For example, Mott (1994) cites both historical and contemporary economic conditions that force men to work outside of the home for long hours in habitually dehumanizing environments.[1] The result is alienation in both directions—the father from the family and the family from the father.

The prevalence of divorce and single-parent families also contributes to this discouraging situation. With father absence a major fact of family structure, it's no surprise that we find a vast majority of single-parent families headed by mothers and the minority by fathers. The U.S. Department of Commerce (1994) reported an increase in mother-headed families from 4.4 million in 1960 to 11.9 million in 1993. The percentage of children living apart from their fathers more than doubled between 1960 and 1990, from 17.5% to 36.3% (Blankenhorn, 1995).

Social and economic institutions do not support fathers who, upon divorce or separation, seek to actively parent (Keshet, 1980). Fathers who have joint custody of their children after divorce work fewer hours, earn less money, and typically feel powerless. These disincentives block many fathers from continued involvement with their children after divorce, even those who were involved with their children while married. Of course, divorce does not automatically lead to emotional abandonment of the son and, ironically, some fathers spend more time with their children after divorce than when they lived full-time with them.

Keshet also reports that some attorneys counsel fathers away from seeking joint custody and that to win custody fathers have to prove the mother unfit. Other fathers are physically absent through divorce, yet dominate the family by breaking agreements regarding visitation or financial support. Fifty percent of divorced fathers have infrequent contact with their children, according to Bryant (1997). In cases of previous violence or threats, the family may still fear him, even thought he no longer has contact with them. He could be physically absent yet remain central to the family through myths (Daddy still loves you), secrets (Daddy has another family), or shame (Daddy was abusive to Mommy).

Family Dynamics

Absent fathers are those who, in the process of leaving the family, do not offer explanations to their children about the reasons for their departure. The other dominant attribute of this type of father is that he does not stay in contact with his children or, again, offer reasons for his continuing disconnection from them. The children thus abandoned feel their fathers are mysteriously, enigmatically, cryptically, or secretively absent.

Contrast this to the father in military service, who tells his children that he is leaving to perform his duty, maintains ongoing contact through letters and telephone calls, and informs them of his return date in advance, or the divorced father who remains in regular contact with his children and has an ongoing amicable relationship with their mother. These are both physically absent fathers but not emotionally or psychologically absent.

When a father abdicates responsibility in this way, the mother has to address the quandary he creates by his absence, and she frequently does this by attempting to portray the father as still loving his son. This process of the mother explaining the father to the child is problematic for both the son and his mother. A common anguished refrain by the son to his father is "Why did you leave me, too?" The mother, then, bears an unfair burden as she becomes the recurrent, if misplaced, target of her son's understandable rage at his father. The dominant culture reinforces the message of the silent man (Ackerman, 1993).

The absent father, by his lack of communication, conveys a powerful, constricting message to his son to hide his feelings and motives from others. "The inability of the communicator to send clear messages lays the ground-work for the cycle of ambiguity to begin" (Colgan, 1988, p. 76). This, in turn, frequently inhibits or damages the son-mother relationship.

Effects of Father Absence

Fathers abandon their sons for a variety of reasons: through divorce, death, absences due to employment or military service, addictions, incarceration, and chronic physical or mental illness. Society defines some as honorable, such as a father who is missing in action while in military service. Other reasons are felt as disgracing and stigmatizing, such as a father incarcerated for embezzlement, or a mentally disturbed one who commits suicide. An absent father may have a need for adventure or feel unable to meet the requirements of his role (Herzog & Sudia, 1971). The father may experience the son as a rival for the wife's affection and leave for this reason (Jacobsohn, 1976). Any one or any combination of these occurrences can have a powerful impact on the son.

Luepnitz (1988) contends that normal fathering in contemporary America includes some degree of abandonment, and that fathers are normally absent from family life and from emotional relationships with their sons. Yet not all sons suffer from this "normal" abandonment. Some men, with or without treatment, are successful in sustaining intimate relations with wives and children. The complicating factor that defines the sons presented in this article is the mystery of their fathers' absence, rather than the "normative" absence. The fathers' absence impairs the sons' ability to develop and sustain positive self-worth and to form lasting relationships with adult romantic partners. Men originating from this type of background often experience difficulties initiating (Bartholomew, 1990) and sustaining (Byng-Hall, 1991) intimate relationships. How can a boy, matured into adulthood, easily form intimate bonds with an adult spouse when he lacks any model from his absent father for emotional intimacy?

Paradoxically, abandoned sons often have intense feelings related to their absent fathers, typically in one of two variations. The first is emotional reactivity, characterized by the statement "I'll never be like him!" The emotion the son experiences is directly caused by his father's absence. The son's reaction leads him to reject the importance of his father. In so doing, he fetters

himself to a position of denial and unresolved grief. Until the son acknowledges his unfulfilled needs and longing for his father, he can remain in turmoil about himself and his intimate relationships.

The second possible form of emotional intensity is over-identification with the father. In this form, the abandoned son idealizes and worships the absent father. The son may base his worship on the actual father he experienced, or the fantasy father that he wishes or wished for, in spite of the father's apparent lack of contact, interest, commitment, or feelings for his son.

The son creates a fantasy image out of discontinuous pieces of information about him (Corneau, 1991).

Self-Esteem and Shame

Abandoned sons can have sustained damage to their sense of worthiness throughout their lives. The son may acquire "a sense of self as the kind of person who is abandoned and the son of a father who would abandon" (Herzog & Sudia, p. 30). The son acquires a profound distrust of the continuity and stability of relationships. The secrets about why the father left cause the son to question his value to others.

Abandonment can lead to experiences and feelings of shame and stigma. A shame-based identity prohibits men from accessing their needs or emotions and from communicating clearly to others (Schenk & Everingham, 1995). Shame, a feeling of worthlessness coupled with a core sense of inadequacy, can permeate all aspects of a person's life. Shame is a universally experienced affect that becomes problematic when internalized as the foundation of identity (Kaufman, 1985; Lansky, 1992). Men get "shame bound" due to some type of family intimacy dysfunction, such as secrecy perpetuated by or about their absent father.

Male gender socialization is fundamentally shaming around emotional expressiveness (Krugman, 1995). Boys learn to hide sadness and fear and to be overly expressive of anger through violence. Shame constrains a man's emotional expressiveness as he learns to perceive a part of himself as inferior and to believe it should remain hidden. Resocializing men to be aware and expressive of a fuller range of emotions can lead to greater emotional relatedness, both internally and with others.

Intimacy Struggles

For many abandoned sons the realization of intimacy is a mystery that eludes them. Abandoned men habitually have relationship difficulties with their parents, siblings, chosen partners, and their children. These men frequently enter treatment in response to obvious crises at family developmental transition points.

Engagement, planning for the wedding, and the pregnancy or birth of the first child (or subsequent children) are specific heterosexual milestones that activate anxiety in abandoned sons. At each developmental junction, there are increased intimacy demands. The man may be more likely to flee the relationship at the arousal of intense feelings. His partner may be increasingly anxious and angry at his lack of participation.

The first hurdle is the formation of an intimate premarital relationship (Lynch, 1990). The steady progression through successive stages, from initial attraction to dating to engagement, can be fraught with false starts, detours, and severe fighting. The basic question of boundary definition looms with great importance for both: "Are we a couple?" During this and subsequent phases, distance regulation frequently oscillates between intense closeness and intense distance.

Both members of the couple may be aware of the intimacy struggles. Once committed or married, abandoned sons can unwittingly replicate the roles enacted by their fathers by being emotionally or physically absent through excessive work, extramarital affairs, or by devaluing their partners. They may actually remain in the relationship physically but be emotionally absent.

Childbirth, especially that of the first son, is an especially intense transition for abandoned men. The new father, missing the model of a nurturing father himself, may become overwhelmed by the tasks of parenting. In addition, the man's own needs immediately become second to the infant's, a difficulty that the maturest of fathers have trouble managing at times. This is a time of great danger for these men and their families. The absence of nurturance from their fathers leaves some new fathers with a revulsion to nurture their own children. Unrealistic expectations of the child's capacities are often evident. It is sometimes painful for the new father to allow his son or daughter the freedom to explore the world, arousing as it does his own pain that emanates from the cryptic loss of his father.

For some men this becomes a time of (re)unification with their father. Caring for an infant son evokes the losses the abandoned men sustained. The dual tasks of mourning the father and bonding with the infant can arise. A desire not to repeat the pattern emerges as a motivation to overcome the loyalty binds and shame. Giving to his child what he didn't receive from his abandoning father sows unequal portions of pleasure and pain.

Treatment

Treatment for these abandoned sons seeks to reduce the mystery in order to enhance men's self-esteem and capacity for intimacy. Two types of treatment are possible. The first is with fathers who are available and willing to re-engage with their sons. The second is with sons whose fathers remain absent or wounding in extreme ways. Both treatment types have the potential for healing the wounds of the past and present.

Treatment of abandoned men originates largely from requests by the female partner for couples therapy, customarily when their relationship is in crisis. In heterosexual couples, female partners often complain about the men's emotional, psychological, and physical distance. The men express frustration but acknowledge that something deeper is missing in the relationship. These men willingly participate in treatment, with a stated desire for the relationship to improve and succeed.

I propose a three-tiered approach to treatment that begins by addressing the immediate crisis with marital therapy techniques (Dym, 1995). The first step is the cessation of the crisis. Next comes an in-depth focus on the abandoned son/absent father dyad. This phase consists of individual treatment of the adult son and includes deliberate grief work (Lazrove, 1996; Lee, 1995; Sprang & McNeil, 1995; Staudacher, 1991) and reunification with the absent father by following principals of intergenerational family therapy (Framo, 1976; Goldberg, 1995; Headley, 1977; McGoldrich, 1997; Schnitzer, 1993; Staudacher, 1991; Williamson, 1978). Treatment concludes with a return to couples therapy, which builds upon the changes developed in earlier phases.

Grief Work

Grief work is a central aspect of the treatment for abandoned sons. Investigating the son's relationship history will establish that a series of losses have occurred and how the mourning process has evolved or stopped. Helping an abandoned son grieve his actual and fantasy losses is perhaps the single greatest clinical challenge. The losses include the actual father, the ideal or fantasy father, aspects of childhood and adolescence, and other intimate relationships.

I invite the son in these initial individual meetings to introduce me vicariously to his father as he has experienced him. Inquiry into the nature of the father-son relationship will precipitate feelings of anger and sadness for most men. Asking how the son resembles or is different from his father usually evokes strong feelings. I ask sons to bring in photographs of their fathers, of the two of them together, or family portraits, and gifts the father has given to the son which bring practical and symbolic meaning into the therapy.

Open grieving goes against individual, family, and cultural imprinting for men. Grieving feels alien to men, especially allowing others (spouse, children, father, friends, or therapist) to see the tears, rage, and shame that are parts of their clandestine, disowned self.

Another aspect of grieving occurs while exploring the family-of-origin rules imposed on the son. These rules are part of the legacy that binds the son and inhibits him from being fully intimate. A typical rule in father-absent families is not to inquire or talk about the father. This mundane rule of silence further solidifies the societal message for boys not to be emotionally or verbally expressive. Silence within the family about the father may lead to the unspoken becoming unspeakable, which often evolves into, or coexists with, shame. Family rules in these types of situations protect the mysteriously absent father and harm his children and former partner.

One of the difficult aspects of these therapies is that by confronting and dispelling early family-of-origin rules, the abandoned son may flee both the treatment and his relationship. The creation of a positive therapeutic alliance is the foundation upon which the treatment can successfully proceed. The rage and shame that surface can get misdirected. Labeling these feelings as part of the absent father problem helps the son clarify and direct them toward the source. Wives, mothers, and children have too often born the brunt of men's misdirected anger. Containing the anger in the therapy gives the son an added perspective. The therapist can model and set limits regarding appropriate ways to express anger (Cullen & Freeman-Longo, 1995; Lee, 1993; Weisinger, 1985). The therapist can teach the son assertive methods to employ with his father and others. Repeated debriefings of the incidents that generate anger for the son reduce the intensity of his rage, an indication that he is ready to pursue (re)unification.

Preparation for (Re)unification

After a sufficient period of mourning, the next treatment goal is (re)unification between the abandoned son and his absent father. Depending upon the physical availability of the father, variations in treatment can take place. For adult sons who have had contact with their absent father, a focus on reunification is appropriate. For those sons without contact with their father, the goal of mourning will have to suffice.

Preparing the abandoned son to engage the absent father begins with clarifying the son's unspoken wishes. What did he always want to say to his father, to ask his fa-

ther, to share with his father? What were the impediments to asking or sharing?

Role playing these conversations, utilizing family sculpture, psychodramatic techniques, gestalt, or other active techniques assists the son in rehearsing what he wants to convey to his father.

Father-Son Therapy Sessions

Following the preparation, the son invites his father to participate in treatment. In my clinical experience, to date, each invited father has attended a family of origin meeting with his son, or participated in some type of son-father treatment. This speaks to the needs of the absent father as well as the needs of the son. These therapy sessions typically number between one and ten, often with as much as a month or more between sessions, during which specific relationship assignments are completed.

Headley (1977) offers excellent suggestions in how the therapist and client can work together to accomplish a successful invitation. This process focuses on understanding the needs of both generations, conveying in a letter the wish to reunite, and blocks aspects of blame that usually negate progress.

One principle in working with absent fathers is focus on what is within the son's power to relate in the ways that he prefers, regardless of the father's response. The therapeutic effort is not to change the father. The purpose of the treatment is to help the son relate to his absent father in different and preferred ways. The father is not the focus of change, although the father may change as well.

An abandoned man often says he could never ask his father to participate. Yet, the act of asking is often the climax of the treatment since the son now feels empowered.

Many fathers approach entering family therapy with apprehension or fear, particularly if they belong to a generation in which therapy implied severe mental illness. To their credit, they have embarked on a journey with their sons that often has wide-ranging impact on their own lives.

Based on an intergenerational premise, the needs of the absent father are viewed as identical to those of the abandoned son, that is, a need to increase his capacity for self-esteem and intimacy in his family, to initiate and respond to the needs of his partner and children, and to become more emotionally expressive. The father would need to grieve the loss of his father, (re)connect with his partner, and bond with his son.

Since the fathers share with their sons some degree of longing (usually unexpressed and often unacknowledged), the opportunity to "help" their son is an attractive offer. It reinforces their self-concept as a good father, even if the evidence is obviously contrary. For those fathers who know they have failed their sons in some way, it affords another chance.

Once the father has committed to the treatment, the task becomes to free the son from the earlier relationship constraints. To free himself, the son must talk to his father about the stored-up feelings, thoughts, and wishes from the past. Through this he takes on a realistic view of his father (past and present) that integrates the father's deficits and assets.

The son gains a new image of his father by the process of (re)unification. He has the benefit of watching his father struggle with a difficult relationship task. He hears his father discuss his side of their earlier relationship and whatever pains or dilemmas he experienced.

Unfortunately, some fathers rewound their sons. The father may not have changed his earlier abandoning or abusive behaviors. The possibility of greater wounding or disappointment is discussed during the preparation stage, before inviting the father to join the therapy. Rarely is an absent father all that a son wishes or hopes for. Some fathers lack interest, many are relationally incapable, and others abdicated their moral and family responsibilities decades earlier.

Adult Son/Adult Father Relationship

Some fathers and sons reconcile. The next task is employing the newfound intimacy generated in that relationship to help the son. This occurs through the active development of the adult-to-adult relationship and by the father's sharing of his own experiences.

The enhanced adult son/adult father relationship often requires the son to make the initial and subsequent moves towards (re)connection with his father.[2] Assessing the benefits to the son occurs in the context of the possible damage from rewounding. Therapies of all types assume a positive outcome. This is not always true for sons trying to form intimate relationships with their fathers.

The usefulness of the father's stated advice to his adult son is of secondary importance. The son need not accept or agree with the content. The effort by the father is his gift to his son. The danger in this stage is that the father will attempt to dominate or impose his beliefs onto his son. When the son can continue to assert himself with his father this stage is completed. If the father is unable to accept his son's adult decisions, or is invalidating to his son in other ways, this phase adjourns.

In the unhappy outcomes the fathers reveal their deficits or lack of interest, and the sons of necessity disconnect and say goodbye to them. A second round of grieving for the abandoned son ensues. The goal is once again to reduce the mystery of his absent father so the son can appropriately attach in his current intimate relationship.

At this point in the treatment, the abandoned son is in a better position to enhance his relationship with his intimate partner. Couples therapy resumes with the original complaints and goals being addressed.

Case Example

His marital therapist referred Mr. P., a 34-year-old businessman, for individual psychotherapy.[3] Married for five years, he and his wife separated soon after the birth of Daniel, Mr. P. felt "uneasy" about being a father. While continuing in marital therapy, he has not reunited with his family. He reported that he was worried about increased demands on his time, that he was catching up on things he had missed out on as a child, uncertain about how to be a father, and missing his wife, whose attention was more focused on their son. Mr. P. identified "unfinished business" with his father revolving around feelings of abandonment and anger.

Mr. P. is an only child. When he was six, his father divorced his mother, left without explanation, and has remained absent without any contact since then. His mother was the sole supporter of the family, often working two jobs. Mr. P. was "on his own" and economically self-supporting by age 14.

His initial goal in individual therapy was to understand why he left after his son was born. He also had a strong desire to reunite with his family. In a six-month course of treatment, Mr. P. explored his anger toward his father by talking with his mother, asking questions about his parents' marriage, his father's personality, and what trig-

gered the divorce. He reviewed photos of his father, noticing the physical similarities. He also began a journal of letters addressed to his father in which he was able to express his longing, his questions, his anger and frustration, most poignantly expressed in one letter as, "I'm not going to let your abandoning me ruin my future!"

As Mr. P. focused on family-of-origin work, he developed a wider range of emotional expression and was able to cry for the first time in his life for what he had missed and still missed. Sharing his grief with his wife helped him to distinguish between his life and his father's life. This separation of past and present allowed him to reconnect with his wife and to build a connection with his infant son.

Mr. P. searched for his father, based on the information that he received from his mother. He contacted his paternal aunt, who had remained in contact with his father. She agreed to help Mr. P. in contacting his father. Mr. P. and his father exchanged letters. Initially, these letters were short, chatty, and just reported the current news to each other. Letters progressed to telephone calls. After several calls, Mr. P. asked his father if he would like to meet in person. Encouraged by their contacts, he agreed to meet for lunch mid-way between their homes.

At follow-up contact three months after his last individual session. Mr. P. was reunited with his family and continuing to see his father. He persisted in couples therapy to help overcome the pains of marital separation and the loss of his father and to enrich his ability to be a father and husband.

Summary

The consequence of father absence reveals its damage when the son attempts to form and sustain an adult intimate relationship. At each developmental stage, the abandoned son typically experiences relationship difficulties that propel him into treatment, usually at the behest of his spouse. Treatment focuses on the reduction of mystery regarding his absent father. This process entails grieving and (re)unification with his father. Following the grieving and reduction of mystery, the son is in a more wholesome position to succeed in his intimate relationship.

References

Ackerman, R. (1993). *Silent sons: A book for and about men.* New York: Simon and Schuster.

Auerbach, C. (1996). Transforming patriarchal fathering: The role of shame and organizing metaphors. *SPSMM Bulletin, 2,* 9–11.

Arendell, T. (1993). After divorce: Investigations into father absence. *Gender and Society, 6,* 562–586.

Bartholomew, K. (1990). Avoidance of intimacy: An attachment perspective. *Journal of Social and Personal Relationships, 7,* 147–178.

Blankenhorn, D. (1995). *Fatherless America.* New York: Basic Books.

Bryant, M. (1997). *The prodigal father: Reuniting fathers and their children.* New York: Clarkson Potter.

Byng-Hall, J. (1991). The application of attachment theory to understanding and treatment in family therapy. In C. Parkes, J. Stevenson-Hinde, & P. Marris (Eds.), *Attachment across the life cycle* (pp. 199–215). New York: Routledge.

Corneau, G. (1991). *Absent fathers—lost sons.* New York: Shambhala Publications.

Colgan, P. (1988). Assessment of boundary inadequacy in chemically dependent individuals and families. In E. Coleman (Ed.), *Chemical dependency and intimacy dysfunction* (pp. 75–90). New York: Haworth Press.

Cullen, M., & Freeman-Longo, R. (1995). *Men and anger: A relapse prevention guide to understanding and managing your anger.* Brandon, VT: Safer Society Press.

Dym, B. (1995). *Readiness and change in couple therapy.* New York: Basic Books.

Framo, J. (1976). Family of origin as a therapeutic resource for adults in marital and family therapy: You can and should go home again. *Family Process, 15,* 193–210.

Goldberg, J. (1995). Reconnecting missing fathers to their children, *Family Therapy News, 26,* 18–29.

Griswold, R. (1993). *Fatherhood in America: A history.* New York: Basic Books.

Headley, L. (1977). *Adults and their parents in family therapy.* New York: Plenum Press.

Herzog, E., & Sudia, C. (1971). *Boys in fatherless families.* Washington, D.C.: U.S. Government Printing Office. DHEW Publication No. [OCD] 72–33.

Ilardo, J. (1993). *Father-son healing: An adult son's guide.* Oakland, CA: New Harbinger Publications.

Jacobson, A. (1976). The treatment of a type of chronically rejected child. In F. Turner (Ed.), *Differential diagnosis and treatment in social work* (pp. 140–21). New York: The Free Press.

Kaufman, G. (1985). *Shame: The power of caring.* Cambridge, MA: Schenkman Publishing.

Keshet, H. (1980). The visiting father. In C. Baden (Ed.), *Parenting after divorce* (pp. 21–26). Boston: Wheelock College Center for Parenting Studies.

Krugman, S. (1995). Male development and the transformation of shame. In R. Levant & W. Pollack (Eds.), *A new psychology of men* (Chapter 4). New York: Basic Books.

Kruk, E. (1994). The disengaged noncustodial father: Implications for social work practice with the divorced family. *Social Work, 39,* 15–25.

Kruk, E. (1992). Psychological and structural factors contributing to the disengagement of noncustodial fathers after divorce. *Family and Conciliation Courts Review, 29,* 81–101.

Lamb, M. (Ed.). (1997). *The role of the father in child development* (3rd ed.). New York: Wiley.

Lansky, M. (1992). *Fathers who fail: Shame and psychopathology in the family system.* Hillsdale, NJ: The Analytic Press.

Lazrove, S. (1996). The use of EMDR in complicated bereavement. Presented at EMDR Level II training, November, 1997, Orlando, FL.

Lee, J. (1993). *Facing the fire: Experiencing and expressing anger appropriately.* New York: Bantam Books.

Lee, J. (1995). *The wounded lover: A book for women raising sons and men coming to terms with their fathers.* Minneapolis: Ally Press.

Luepnitz, D. (1988). *The family interpreted.* New York: Basic Books.

Lynch, B. (1990). An anatomy of bonding in the dyadic system. *Journal of Couples Therapy, 1,* 127–145.

McGoldrich, M. (1997). *You can go home again: Reconnecting with your family.* New York: Norton.

Mitscherlich, A. (1974). *Society without the father.* New York: HarperPerennial.

Mott, F. (1994). Sons, daughters and fathers' absence: Differentials in father-leaving probabilities and in home environments. *Journal of Family Issues, 15,* 121–122.

Phares, V. (1992). Where's poppa? The relative lack of attention to the role of fathers in child and adolescent psychopathology. *American Psy-chologist, 47,* 656–664.

Pleck, J. (1987). American fathering in historical perspective. In M. Kimmel (Ed.), *Changing men: New directions in research on men and masculinity* (pp. 83–97). Beverly Hills: Sage.

Schenk, R., & Everingham, J. (Eds.). (1995). *Men healing shame: An anthology.* New York: Springer.

Schnitzer, P. (1993). Tales of the absent father: Applying the story metaphor in family therapy. *Family Process, 32,* 441–458.

Sills, A. (1995). Absent fathers, single mother: Clinical interpretation in political context. *Family Issues, Fall,* 33–34.

Sprang, G., & McNeil, J. (1995). *The many faces of bereavement: The nature and treatment of natural, traumatic, and stigmatized grief.* New York: Brunner/Mazel.

Staudacher, C. (1991). *Men and grief.* Oakland, CA: New Harbinger Publications.

United States Department of Commerce. (1994). *Statistical abstract of the United States* (114th Ed.). Washington, D.C.: U.S. Government Printing Office.

Weisinger, H. (1985). *Dr. Weisinger's anger workout book.* New York: Morrow.

Williamson, D. (1978). New life at the graveyard: A method of therapy for individuation from a dead former parent. *Journal of Marriage and Family Counseling, 4,* 93–100.

Notes

1. Changes in the American economy since 1940 have also forced mothers to work outside of the home in increasing numbers. Often this means that for single-parent (mother-headed) families, the children are without a parent in the home for much of their day.

2. Bryant (1997) offers a perspective for those interested in father-initiated reunifications.

3. Identifying information has been disguised to ensure confidentiality.

9

Body Image and Self-esteem: A Comparison of African-American and Caucasian Women

Beth L. Molloy and Sharon D. Herzberger

Cultural norms which demand that women be thin in order to be considered attractive can lead women to develop distorted body images and to diet in order to obtain the "ideal figure." In some cases, eating disorders may develop. In this reading, Molloy and Herzberger examine the ways that race/ethnicity and class may affect women's perceptions of themselves and their bodies **(cultural diversity).** They found that African-American women had higher self-esteem and a more positive body image than Caucasian women. This difference may be explained by the finding that African-American women also rated themselves as higher in masculinity personality characteristics (such as "assertive" and "strong") and believed that men preferred heavier women. These "protective factors" may shield African-American women from developing distorted body images and low self-esteem **(gender role effects).**

Questions to Consider:

1. How do Molloy and Herzberger explain the finding that there were no variations among African-American women in body image and self-esteem due to class and racial identity?
2. Based on their findings, Molloy and Herzberger make several suggestions for improving women's self-esteem and body image. How might you design a program to carry out their suggestions?
3. What do you see as the advantages and disadvantages to using self-reports of body size, weight, and physical condition in this study?

Reprinted with permission of Kluwer Academic/Plenum Publishers. From B. L. Molloy & S. D. Herzberger (1998). "Body Image and Self-Esteem: A Comparison of African-American and Caucasian Women," *Sex Roles, 38,* (7/8), 631–643.

4. In this study, women partly based their judgments of their bodies on what they believed men of their race desired. Do you think men are also affected in their judgments of their own bodies by what they think women of their own race desire? Why or why not?

As the American standard of beauty becomes more stringent, many women develop distorted body images and become frustrated at not being able to obtain the "ideal figure." Some women are so dissatisfied with their perceived body size that they are driven to become thin and maintain that thinness. According to Parker, Nichter, Nichter, Vuckovic, Sims, and Ritenbaugh (1995), some women diet in order to increase their self-confidence, establish affiliation with a group, or gain control over their lives. These dieting trends may reflect our cultural norms that say that women who eat less are considered to be more feminine (Chaiken and Pliner, 1987), and that women are more attractive if they are petite and delicate (Freedman, 1984).

These norms are constantly being reinforced by the media, especially with the prevalence of ultra-thin models, the multi-million dollar diet industry, and women's magazines that prey on female anxieties. As Polivy and Herman (1987) argued, these norms have become so pervasive that "normal" eating for American women is now synonymous with dieting. And some women who become obsessive about their body and weight may develop an eating disorder. The disorders mainly affect women; females comprise ninety five percent of anorexics and ninety percent of bulimics (Connor-Greene, 1988).

Women's eating habits and weights are best seen on a continuum, with anorexics and bulimics at one end and obese women at the other (Bowen, Tomoyasu, & Cauce, 1991). Exactly where an individual falls on this continuum may partly be determined by race or ethnicity, class, and gender role orientation. For example, Caucasian and African-American women hold significantly different definitions of beauty and perceptions of themselves. African-American women's perception of beauty is more flexible and fluid than Caucasian women's (Allan, Mayo, & Michel, 1993; Kumanyika, Wilson, & Guilford-Davenport, 1993; Parker et al., 1995). Research has found that African-American females are less concerned with weight, dieting, or being thin (Abrams, Allen, & Gray, 1993; Akan & Grilo, 1995; Rucker & Cash, 1992). When asked, sixty four percent stated that they would rather be "a little overweight" than "a little underweight." If they do diet, however, their attempts to lose weight are more realistic and less extreme than white women's attempts.

The differences in body image may translate into healthier behavior. While some research suggests that the gap is narrowing (Dacosta & Wilson, 1996; Hsu, 1987; LeGrange, Telch, & Agras, 1997), most research (e.g., Abrams et al., 1993; Akan & Grilo, 1995; Rucker & Cash, 1992; Pinkowish, 1995) acknowledges that eating disorders, especially anorexia and bulimia, are most prominently seen among white women.

There are various reasons for this difference between African-American and white women and for why African-American women as a cultural group seem

[1]The authors would like to thank Dr. Andrea Chapdelaine, Dr. James Fleming, Dr. David Reuman, and all of the community college students and professors who agreed to participate in this study.

to be better "protected" from body image distortions (Hsu, 1987; Root, 1990). First, both groups of women partially base their judgments of their bodies on what men of their race desire (Parker et al., 1995). Since African-American women believe that African-American males prefer larger women, they have less need to lose weight and, therefore, feel more attractive. White women, however, believe that white men prefer ultra-thin women. Research on men's preferences tend to support these perceptions (Cunningham, Roberts, Barbee, Druen, & Wu, 1995; Greenberg & Laporte, 1996; Powell & Kahn, 1995). While the perceptions in certain cases may be inaccurate, they still may cause white women to feel less attractive.

Another protective factor for African-American women is their gender role orientation. Harris (1994) found that African-American women are more likely to describe themselves with masculine or androgynous traits, while white women describe themselves as feminine or undifferentiated. Bem's (1981) gender schema theory proposes that gender-typed (masculine males and feminine females) individuals are more likely than non-gender-typed individuals to be responsive to appearance or appearance stereotypes. Further research has shown that masculine and androgynous individuals exhibit higher levels of self-esteem, have a more positive body image, and are more satisfied with their sexuality than those who are feminine or undifferentiated (Kimlicka, Cross, & Tarnai, 1983).

Of course, not all women within a racial/ethnic category are the same. Racial identity and identification with the dominant middle class culture may explain the variation within groups of African-American and white women. As Pyant and Yanico (1991) stated, racial identity attitudes can predict self-esteem, well-being, and depression in female African-Americans. To the extent that African-American women identify more with their racial/ethnic culture than with the dominant culture and to the extent that they interact mostly with other African-Americans, they may be "protected" from white norms regarding body styles.

Allan et al. (1993), for example, found that lower socioeconomic African-American women were heavier, and perceived heavier body styles as more attractive, than did higher socioeconomic black women and white women of all socioeconomic groups. Furthermore, the lower socioeconomic African-American women tended to be heavier than their white counterparts before identifying themselves as overweight. Women who interact with other heavy women may not denigrate their weight as much as those who tend to interact with women who are thinner (Bowen et al., 1991).

However, to the extent that African-American women identify more with the dominant white culture, they may be more vulnerable to body image distortions and eating disorders (Bowen et al., 1991). As African-American women experience greater social mobility, they may be especially at risk, due to the exposure to Caucasian preferences, attitudes, and ideals about beauty, weight, and food (Allan, et al., 1993; Iancu, Spivak, Ratzoni, Apter, & Weizman, 1994; Rosen, Anthony, Brown, Christian, Crews, Hollins, Privette, Reed, & Petty, 1991).

Most research on women's body image and self-esteem has involved adolescents or students at four year colleges and universities. Less is known about the body image of older women, and to our knowledge, no tests of racial/ethnic differences have been performed strictly on non-traditional or community college students. The purpose of this study, then, is to test past research findings on differences in body image and self-esteem with a more varied, representative sample of African-American and white women. By using community college students of varied ages, we hope to capture the nontraditional students who are too often overlooked by researchers and who may better represent people outside the residential college setting.

The present study was conducted to test the following hypotheses. First, we expect that African-American women will report a higher level of self-esteem and a more positive body image than Caucasian women. Second, we will test the generalizability of two explanations for the racial/ethnic differences. We predict that African-American women will be more likely to report that men find larger bodies attractive than will white women, and that African-American women will report more androgynous or masculine traits than will white women. Furthermore, masculinity, androgyny, and perceptions of men's preferences may protect women's body image and self-esteem. Third, we will try to understand variations among groups of African-American women, in their views of themselves and their bodies. African-American women who are more fully integrated into the dominant culture and less identified with their racial/ethnic group are predicted to report a more negative body image than their African-American counterparts.

Method

Subjects

A total of 134 female students from two community-technical colleges in Connecticut participated in a survey about their body image, self-esteem, gender role, race/ethnicity, class, and background. Due to the low numbers of Latina and Asian-American women, they were excluded from the analyses.

Of the remaining 114 participants, 45 were African-American and 69 were Caucasian. As Table I demonstrates, Caucasian women were significantly older than African-American women (by about three years), but they did not differ significantly in height or weight.

Procedure

At one college (CT$_1$), students in a Psychology 101 course were asked to participate in the study. The students received the surveys and cover letters and were given class time during which they could com-

TABLE I. *Demographic Characteristics of Sample*

Variable	African-American	Caucasian	t
Age (yrs.)	25.62 (6.82)	29.22 (9.88)	2.10[a]
Height	5′ 5″ (2.81)	5′ 5″ (2.85)	.52
Weight (lbs.)	154.26 (36.18)	142.67 (37.76)	1.57

[a]$p < .05$

plete the study materials. A total of 50 students participated, 41 African-Americans and 9 Caucasians. At the second college (CT₂), female students in Psychology 101 and Sociology 101 were chosen. Again, the students received the surveys and cover letters in class, but were asked to complete and return the survey by the next class meeting. A total of 64 students participated, 4 African-Americans and 60 Caucasians. The cover letters indicated that their participation was completely voluntary and their responses would be kept confidential. In addition, participants were asked not to include their names on the surveys, so all responses would be anonymous.

Measures

Participants were asked to report their age, race/ethnicity, social class (upper, middle, working, lower), and the racial/ethnic makeup of their hometown and high school. They were also asked to report their dieting habits (1 = had dieted in the past year, 2 = had not dieted in the past year) and their current and ideal height and weight. Four self-report measures were then administered.

Self-Esteem.   The Personal and Academic Self-Concept Inventory, PASCI, (Fleming and Whalen, 1990, adapted from Fleming and Courtney, 1984) consists of 45 questions regarding subjects' self-regard, social acceptance, physical appearance, and verbal, math, and physical ability. Participants were asked to rate each question on a scale of 1 (practically never/not at all) to 7 (very often/very). Each subscale on the PASCI has shown good internal consistency (*rs* = .72–.94) and test-retest reliability (*rs* = .81–.98).

Body-Esteem.   The Body-Esteem Scale (Franzoi and Shields, 1984) lists 32 parts of the body which subjects rate on a scale of 1 (have strong negative feelings) to 5 (have strong positive feelings). This measure examines women's sexual attractiveness, concern with weight, and physical condition. The Body-Esteem Scale has shown adequate internal consistency (alphas range from .78–.87) and moderately correlates with overall self-esteem (*rs* = .19–.51).

Body Image.   The Body Size Drawings Inventory (Silberstein, Striegel-Moore, Timko, and Rodin, 1988, as adapted from Stunkard, Sorenson, and Schulsinger, 1983) consists of 9 drawings of the male form and 9 drawings of the female form representing shapes from anorexic (coded as 1) to obese (coded as 9). These ratings are helpful in assessing body shape perception and dissatisfaction in men and women. Participants in this study were given the female forms to use in response to questions (taken from Cohn and Adler, 1992) about their perception of their actual body shape, their ideal body shape, and their perception of the body shape that men would find most attractive. The latter is referred to in the tables as "Men's Preferences." The difference between participants' ideal and actual body shape is referred to as "Id-Image."

Gender Role.   The Bem Sex Role Inventory (BSRI; Bem, 1974) consists of 60 personality characteristics. To rate how well each item describes themselves, participants used a scale ranging from 1 (never or almost never true) to 7 (always or almost always true). The Inventory was scored for masculinity, femininity, and androgyny (femininity score-masculinity score). Test-retest correlations for the BSRI on a one-month period are high (*rs* = .89–.93) and the sub-

TABLE II. *Correlations Among Dependent Measures and Between Dependent Measures and Protective Factors*

	PASCI	*ID-Image*	*Body-Esteem*	*Diet*	*Preferred Wt*
PASCI		−.41[c]	.54[c]	.33[c]	.20[a]
ID-Image			−.57[c]	−.41[c]	.13
Body-Esteem				.28[b]	.03
Diet					.05
Masculinity	.57[c]	−.28[b]	.46[c]	.15	.27[b]
Femininity	−.00	−.02	.10	−.06	.12
Androgyny	.51[c]	−.23[a]	.34[c]	.17	.16
Men's preferences	.18	−.08	.13	.02	.46[c]

[a]$p < .05$.

[b]$p < .01$.

[c]$p < .001$.

scales are internally consistent (alphas range from .75–.86).

Results

Relationship Between Self-Esteem and Body Image Measures

The top part of Table II shows the relationships among the various body image measures and their relationship with overall self-esteem, as measured by the PASCI. PASCI self-esteem correlates significantly with Body Self-Esteem, the tendency to diet, a lower preferred body weight, and a smaller difference between ideal and actual body image. As would be expected, the body image measures tend to intercorrelate, but show substantial independence as well.

Gender-Roles, Men's Preferences, and Self-Image

The previous literature has shown that masculinity and androgyny may protect women from society's pressures with regard to weight. As shown in the bottom section of

Table II, the present findings replicate these results: women who score as more masculine on the BSRI score higher on the PASCI and Body-Esteem measures and have a smaller discrepancy between their ideal and actual body images. More masculine women also have higher preferred body weights. Similar relationships are found between androgyny and the body image measures. BSRI Femininity does not correlate significantly with other measures.

Also as predicted, women's perceptions of men's preferences for female body size significantly correlate with women's preferred weight. None of the other correlations is significant, although men's perceived preferences tend to relate to overall self-esteem as measured by the PASCI, $r(109) = .18$, $p = .06$.

Comparisons of African-American and Caucasian Women's BSRI Scores and Perceptions of Men's Preferences

Table III shows mean BSRI scores and perceptions of men's preferences for women's body size among African-American and

TABLE III. *Differences Between African-American and Caucasian Women on Protective Factors*

Variable	African-American	Caucasian	t
BSRI Masculinity	100.80 (18.66)	90.88 (19.42)	2.71[a]
BSRI Femininity	105.44 (13.72)	101.58 (15.22)	1.38
BSRI Androgyny	−4.64 (20.45)	−10.69 (22.78)	1.44
Men's Preferences	4.07 (1.84)	3.04 (1.19)	3.56[b]

[a]$p < .01$

[b]$p < .001$

Caucasian women. As predicted by earlier literature, African-American women score significantly higher on the BSRI Masculinity scale than do Caucasian women. African-American and Caucasian women do not differ on BSRI-measured Femininity or Androgyny. Also as predicted, African-American women are significantly less likely to select thin, toned women's images as those that men would find attractive.

Regression Analyses

Next, a series of regression analyses was computed to assess the significance of race/ethnicity in understanding self-esteem and body image, as opposed to other factors. Table IV displays the results of these analyses. The top row of findings in Table IV lists the *F*-statistic associated with race/ethnicity for each dependent measure of interest, not controlling for other factors. As shown, African-Americans and Caucasians differ significantly on four of the five measures.

The remaining rows report the results of an analysis of covariance designed to determine whether race/ethnicity still significantly predicts self-esteem and body image when controlling for other demographic factors and the protective factors of BSRI Masculinity and Men's Preferences. Race/ethnicity no longer significantly predicts scores on any of the dependent measures after the effects of the other variables are partialled out. Only one interaction is significant, that predicting preferred body weight and between weight and race/ethnicity, but the interaction pales in comparison to the effect of body weight itself.

The importance of controlling for age, weight, and protective factors can be seen in Table V, which presents the uncontrolled mean differences between African-Americans and Caucasians and the adjusted mean differences, controlling for age, weight, masculinity, and perceived men's body preferences.

Influence of Culture on Body Image

Finally, we examined whether class and racial identity may have affected body image and self-esteem among African-Americans. We examined factors that may reinforce a woman's racial identity, such as reading magazines geared towards African-Americans and growing up in a home-town or graduating from a high school that was predominantly African-American in population. We also examined whether being a member of the upper/middle or lower/working class had an effect on self-image. Contrary to expectations, no measure of body image or self-esteem is

TABLE IV. *Summary of the Effect of Race/Ethnicity on Self-Esteem and Body Image Measures, Not Controlling and Controlling for Masculinity, Men's Preferences, Age, and Weight*

| | Dependent Measure | | | | |
Source	PASCI F	Id-Image F	Body-Esteem F	Diet F	Preferred Wt F
			Uncontrolled		
R/E	7.51[c]	5.69[b]	18.42[d]	1.76	11.48[d]
			Controlled		
R/E	.06	.42	2.50	.55	.02
BMAS	34.17[d]	10.69[c]	23.14[d]	.28	2.02
BMAS*R/E	.08	3.50	.70	2.42	1.89
Men's Pref	4.30[b]	1.10	3.15	.03	12.38[d]
Men's Pref*R/E	1.06	.01	.22	.06	.28
Age	4.01[b]	.44	1.01	3.71	.04
Age*R/E	.49	.04	1.52	.14	.00
Wt	.15	24.63[d]	20.59[d]	4.46[b]	58.11[d]
Wt*R/E	.01	.01	.78	.86	5.96[b]

[a]R/E = Race/Ethnicity, BMAS = Masculinity, Men's Pref. = perceived male preferences for body image, Wt = Self-reported weight.

[b]$p < .05$.

[c]$p < .01$.

[d]$p < .001$.

significantly affected by any of these factors.

Discussion

Race/ethnicity significantly relates to how women perceive themselves and their bodies. However, the present study suggests that the effects of race/ethnicity are largely attributable to racial/ethnic differences in masculinity and perceptions of the preferences for body size held by men. This study corroborates past research on younger women that shows that African-Americans are more likely to have certain protective factors that shield them from developing low self-esteem and distorted body images. Such factors allow them to be more satisfied with their body, regardless of its size or shape. This is, of course, correlated with high levels of self-esteem and well-being.

Research has shown a steady rise in eating disorders across all ages and these disorders develop as the result of distorted self-images (Harris, 1994; Hsu, 1987; Freedman, 1984; Rucker & Cash, 1992). Especially for white women, such feelings are reinforced by the dominant culture's rigid definition of beauty as ultrathin. If we socialize all young girls to have a fluid definition of beauty, our society may not be as

TABLE V. *Mean Differences Between African-Americans and Caucasians: Uncontrolled and Adjusted for Age, Weight, Masculinity, and Men's Preferences*

	Uncontrolled		Adjusted	
Variable	*African-American*	*Caucasians*	*African-American*	*Caucasians*
PASCI	208.77	190.43	200.26	198.45
Id-Image	1.47	2.03	1.45	1.79
Body-Esteem	102.04	86.16	100.15	90.55
Diet	29	41	25	36
Preferred Wt	136.60	127.20	133.16	129.40

plagued by anorexia, bulimia, or other eating disorders.

African-American women, however, may choose not to conform to the dominant culture's definition of beauty in part because of perceived and actual preferences of African-American men (Cunningham et al., 1995; Greenberg & Laporte, 1996; Powell & Kahn, 1995). Since men of their race may prefer larger women, African-American women are freer to maintain larger body structures. White women, however, lack this "protective factor."

Perceived differences in male body preferences suggests possible routes for intervention. First, to the extent that women's perceptions of male preferences correspond with reality, and research suggests that they do (Cunningham et al., 1995; Greenberg & Laporte, 1996; Powell & Kahn, 1995), interventions designed to reduce the rate of eating disorders need to be aimed just as much at men as women. Second, intervention attempts could be aimed at building self-esteem among girls and women and increasing independent judgments about their bodies.

A third route to intervention is suggested by the findings that masculinity protects women from lowered self-esteem and negative body-image. Caucasian girls and women, in particular, may feel more positive about their bodies if they perceive themselves as assertive or strong, rather than passive or gentle.

While we predicted that higher social class and integration with the dominant culture would explain variations in self-image among African-American women, we found no support for these ideas. Middle and upper class African-American subjects did not show a decrease in self-esteem and body image. In fact, an albeit nonsignificant trend indicated that upper/middle class African-American women have a better body image and higher self-esteem than lower/working class African-American women.

However, it may well be that few African-Americans are truly isolated from the dominant culture. The community college students attended institutions with a diverse student body, many of whom undoubtedly have differing definitions of physical beauty. In addition, minority students may be affected by the college itself, which may have white, middle class values and biases. Finally, they were inevitably exposed to media images of ultrathin, glamorous women who are portrayed as "the norm." Therefore, very few participants, regardless of class, have been shielded from the pressure to conform to the dominant culture's definition of beauty. African-American women's relatively enhanced security in their size is, then, particularly significant.

As LeGrange et al. (1997) note, similarities across racial/ethnic groups may suggest that interventions designed for one group may be effective with another. The present findings reinforce this notion by revealing similarities among African-American and Caucasian women's views. Perhaps this is best indicated by the measure of preferred body image. On a scale of 1 (smallest body size) to 9 (largest), African-American women averaged 4.40, while Caucasian women averaged 3.41. Both groups of women preferred body sizes on the small end. Therefore, while slight differences exist, they do not by themselves suggest a difference in orientation towards interventions with the two groups.

Before we conclude this, however, we should test whether similarities have the same etiological roots. For example, statistics from clinical populations reveal that, although African-American women may not suffer from the same rates of anorexia and bulimia as white women, they may be just as likely to engage in binge eating (Pinkowish, 1995). The latter may be due to the same causes in both groups (e.g., stress levels; Pinkowish, 1995). But it is also possible that different reasons exist for similar phenomenon (e.g., stress among African-American women, perceived male body preferences among whites). Longitudinal research that links body image, self-esteem, and behavior will be productive in addressing these questions.

Some limitations with the present study pertain to the accuracy of self-reports. Many of the questions required participants to report their weight or rate certain parts of their body, albeit anonymously. Some participants may have felt uncomfortable an-

swering such personal questions honestly. Future research that includes a validity check on reports of body size and weight might be beneficial. Finally, although this study used a wider sample by seeking out a community college population, efforts to obtain a more representative sample of African-American women should be undertaken. Just as earlier research showing racial differences in eating disorders has been criticized for being based on clinical samples, this study was restricted to a sample of women more educated than the norm. A better representative sample is needed to test for similarities and differences across racial/ethnic groups.

References

Abrams, K., Allen, L., & Gray, J. (1993). Disordered eating attitudes and behaviors, psychological adjustment, and ethnic identity: A comparison of black and white female college students. *International Journal of Eating Disorders, 14,* 49–57.

Akan, G., & Greilo, C. (1995). Sociocultural influences on eating attitudes and behaviors, body image, and psychological functioning: A comparison of African-American, Asian-American, and Caucasian college women. *International Journal of Eating Disorders, 18,* 181–187.

Allan, J., Mayo, K., & Michel, Y. (1993). Body size values of white and black women, *Research in Nursing and Health, 16,* 323–333.

Bem, S. (1974). The measurement of psychological androgyny. *Journal of Consulting and Clinical Psychology, 42,* 155–162.

Bem, S. (1981). Gender schema theory: a cognitive account of sex typing. *Psychological Review, 88,* 354–364.

Bowen, D., Tomoyasu, N., & Cauce, A. (1991). The triple threat: A discussion of gender, class, and race differences in weight. *Women and Health, 17,* 123–143.

Chaiken, S., & Pliner, P. (1987). Women, but not men, are what they eat: The effect of meal size and gender on perceived femininity and masculinity. *Personality and Social Psychology Bulletin, 13,* 166–176.

Cohn, L., & Adler, N. (1992). Female and male perceptions of ideal body shapes: Distorted views among Caucasian college students. *Psychology of Women Quarterly, 16,* 69–79.

Connor-Greene, P. (1988). Gender differences in body weight perception and weight loss strategies of college students. *Women and Health, 14,* 27–42.

Cunningham, M., Roberts, A., Barbee, A., Druen, P., & Wu, C. (1995). Their ideas of beauty are, on the whole, the same as ours: Consistency and variability in the cross-cultural perception of female attractiveness. *Journal of Personality and Social Psychology, 68,* 261–279.

Dacosta, K., & Wilson, J. (1996). Food preferences and eating attitudes in three generations of black and white women. *Appetite, 27,* 183–191.

Fleming, J., & Whalen, D. (1990). The personal and academic self-concept inventory: Factor structure and gender differences in high school and college sample. *Educational and Psychological Measurement, 50,* 957–967.

Franzoi, S., & Shields, S. (1984). The body self-esteem scale: Multidimensional structure and sex differences in a college population. *Journal of Personality Assessment, 48,* 173–178.

Freedman, R. (1984). Reflections on beauty as it relates to health in adolescent females. *Women and Health, 9,* 29–45.

Greenberg, D., & Laporte, D. (1996). Racial differences in body type preferences of men and women. *International Journal of Eating Disorders, 19,* 275–278.

Harris, S. (1994). Racial differences in predictors of college women's body image attitudes. *Women and Health, 21,* 89–104.

Hsu, L. (1987). Are the eating disorders becoming more common in blacks. *International Journal of Eating Disorders, 6,* 113–124.

Iancu, I., Spivak, B., Ratzoni, G., Apter, A., & Weizman, A. (1994). The sociocultural theory in the development of anorexia nervosa. *Psychopathology, 27,* 29–36.

Kimlicka, T., Cross, H., & Tarnai, J. (1983). A comparison of androgynous, feminine, masculine, and undifferentiated women on self-esteem, body satisfaction, and sexual satisfaction. *Psychology of Women Quarterly, 7,* 291–294.

Kumanyika, S., Wilson, J., & Guilford-Davenport, M. (1993). Weight-related attitudes and behaviors of black women. *Journal of the American Dietetic Association, 93,* 416–422.

Le Grange, D., Telch, C., & Agras, W. (1997). Eating and general psychopathology in a sample of Caucasian and ethnic minority subjects. *International Journal of Eating Disorders, 21,* 285–293.

Parker, S., Nichter, M., Nichter, N., Vuckovic, N., Sims, C., & Ritenbaugh, C. (1995). Body image and weight concerns among African-American and white adolescent females: Differences that make a difference. *Human Organization, 54,* 103–114.

Pinkowish, M. (1995). Eating disorders: No stereotypes need apply. *Patient Care, 29,* 13.

Polivy, J., & Herman, C. (1987). Diagnosis and treatment of normal eating. *Journal of Consulting and Clinical Psychology, 21,* 635–644.

Powell, A., & Kahn, A. (1995). Racial differences in women's desires to be thin. *International Journal of Eating Disorders, 17,* 191–195.

Pyant, C., & Yanico, B. (1991). Relationship of racial identity and gender role attitudes to black women's psychological well-being. *Journal of Counseling Psychology, 38,* 315–322.

Root, M. (1990). Disordered eating in women of color. *Sex Roles, 22,* 525–536.

Rosen, E., Anthony, D., Booker, K., Brown, T., Christian, E., Crews, R., Hollins, V., Privette, J., Reed, R., & Petty, L. (1991). A comparison of eating disorder scores among African-American and white college females. *Bulletin of the Psychonomic Society, 29,* 65–66.

Rucker, C., & Cash, T. (1992). Body images, body size perceptions and eating behaviors among African-American and white college women. *International Journal of Eating Disorders, 12,* 291–299.

Silberstein, L., Striegel-Moore, R., Timko, C., & Rodin, J. (1988). Behavioral and psychological implications of body dissatisfaction: Do women and men differ? *Sex Roles, 19,* 219–232.

*Chapter 4: Putting It All Together*_____

1. Both the Silverstein and Lynch reading and the Balcom reading argue that fathers play an important role in their children's mental health. Do you see this role as different or similar to the role that mothers play in their children's mental health? Explain.

2. Discuss how internalized oppression contributed to mental health problems for the women in the readings by Silverstein & Lynch and Molloy & Herzberger.

3. Based on what you have learned from these three readings, are changes in gender roles important to improving the mental health of men and women? Why or why not?

5

Gender and Physical Health

The readings in this chapter were chosen because they address health issues that affect all men and all women in the United States: male circumcision and menopause. It is important to note that these health issues are not necessarily concerns for men and women outside of the United States. This is because they are experiences that are strongly influenced by sociocultural processes. The first reading challenges the widespread practice of routine medical circumcision in the US, arguing that it serves cultural purposes (i.e., socialization into aggressive aspects of masculine gender identity) rather than health promotion. In fact, circumcision is actually a risk factor for physical and psychosexual health problems. The second article challenges the common tendency to attribute menopausal symptoms mainly to hormonal changes by exploring individual and cultural differences in the experience of menopause. The author concludes that menopausal symptoms are the result of not only physical factors, but also psychological and cultural influences.

10

Male Circumcision: A Gender Perspective

Joseph Zoske

In this reading, Zoske challenges the widespread acceptance in the US of the routine medical circumcision of newborn males, claiming that it serves cultural practices rather than health promotion. Differentiating medical circumcision from that which is religion-based, he frames medical circumcision as the first psychological and physical wounding of males, as a form of physical and sexual assault with potential lifelong consequences **(gender role effects).** To support this view, he cites research on the long-term psychological effects associated with the intense pain of circumcision, and on the associated risks of medical complications ranging from mild to severe. He traces the historical forces that gave rise to the practice in the mid-19th century (i.e., anti-sexual sentiment), and that led to its initial challenge in the mid-20th century after 100 years of common practice. He then outlines a half century of medical debate as to whether circumcision prevents disease or increases the risk of sexual, psychological, and health problems. Further, he traces the anti-circumcision activist movement that has accompanied this medical debate. Claiming a cultural denial of what is actually genital mutilation, Zoske concludes that routine neonatal circumcision is part of a larger socialization process that views power relationships, violence, and the denial of pain as central elements of masculine gender identity **(gender role effects).**

Questions to Consider:

1. According to Zoske, what are the scientific justifications for and against routine medical circumcision of newborn males? What is your position on the issue? Explain your thinking.
2. Why does Zoske refer to routine circumcision as a "fundamental men's issue?"

Originally published in *The Journal of Men's Studies, 6,* (2), 189–208. Reprinted by permission of the Men's Studies Press.

3. Do you agree with Zoske's comparison of female and male circumcision? Why or why not?
4. What, according to Zoske, are some of the cultural practices that sustain routine medical circumcision, and how do they undermine the well-being of males?
5. Draw a diagram that shows the relationship between the biological, psychological, and social aspects of circumcision.

Routine medical male circumcision, the surgical removal of a healthy male infant's foreskin, is "the most common surgical operation carried out in the United States" (Cendron, Elder, & Duckett, 1996, p. 2149). While a majority of men throughout the world remain uncircumcised (Wallerstein, 1985), annually circumcision is performed on more than one million American infants. Most authors, however, agree that the incidence of circumcision in the United States has fallen from a high of 80 to 90% during the 1980s to a low of nearly 65% at present. Inconsistent reports by hospitals and insurance companies leave national data unreliable and, in all probability, somewhat conservative (e.g., facilities often do not separate circumcision from the collective itemization of delivery services; see Graves, 1995). Regardless, circumcision will be a reality for a majority of male infants given a medical establishment that still condones it and a health insurance system that readily pays for it—estimated at $140 million in 1988 (Poland, 1990).

Circumcision is, however, more than a benign medical procedure. It is fundamentally an elective amputation of healthy genital tissue driven by the power of tradition and performed without a patient's consent, occurring when he is most vulnerable and completely dependent.

Broad medical, psychological, and ethical debates continue to surround this practice, displaying a perplexing lack of resolution. It continues to be readily authorized and infrequently questioned by parents or hospital personnel and not generally considered by the parties to be an act of violence. However, there are strong arguments that support viewing circumcision as a societal act of physical and sexual assault; an event that holds deep significance for men's psychosexual development, reinforces cultural attitudes of disregard for the well-being of men's bodies, and tacitly accepts violence as a part of men's lives. This article intertwines these ideas and presents routine neonatal circumcision as a fundamental men's issue. Framed within an historical context and an ongoing medical debate, circumcision should be seen as the first psychological and somatic wounding of men—a cultural act of gender betrayal and brutality. As questions surrounding this procedure are examined, a challenge is made to the continued acceptance of this widespread practice.

Technical Details

To avoid the discussion becoming lost in the abstract, it is important to understand the medical specifics of this surgery. Circumcision requires that a male infant be taken from his parents and placed on a restraint table with his extremities fastened or held down, while a variety of surgical instruments (probes, clamps, scalpel) are used to grasp the foreskin, separate it from the glans, slit it, stretch it, crush it, and amputate it (Cohen, 1992; Gelbaum, 1993). It has, also, most often been performed without anesthesia due to medical contraindications, or with the use of a painful local anesthetic injection (the dorsal nerve block). However, the latter "is not widely used due to concerns of sufficient safety, the additional time required to perform the block, and the continued belief that the pain of neonatal circumcision is insignificant" (Howard, Howard, & Weitman, 1994, p. 641). Numerous studies have clearly identified traumatic pain responses in infants, and specifically the severe and persistent pain of circumcision (Anand & Hickey, 1987; Stang, Gunner, Snellman, Condon, & Kesterbaum, 1988). While investigators are exploring the efficacy of topical anesthesia (Benini, Johnston, Faucher, & Aranda, 1993), there remains lasting impact from the pain experience of current practice. Taddio, Goldbach, Ipp, Stevens, and Koren (1995) found continuing pain response in baby boys at four to six months, and expressed concern for possible long-term effects of the intense pain of circumcision. Anand and Hickey (1987), concluding their review of more than 200 citations, spoke of the "memory of pain in neonates" and cautioned about circumcision's possible long-term psychological effects (p. 1325). Ritter (1992), an activist anti-circumcision physician, describes the procedure as a "great human and humane transgression" in which the baby's first perception of genital sensation is needless pain (p. 3–1).

Beyond pain, there are many other risks. "Although not technically difficult," Gluckman, Stoller, Jacobs, and Kogan report (1995), "it results in a large number of reported and unreported complications annually. . . . The potential for complications from circumcision is real and ranges from the insignificant to tragic" (p. 778). Among the complications noted we find: bleeding, infections (localized and systemic), excess foreskin removal, glans necrosis or amputation, removal of penile shaft skin, psychosocial problems in adulthood, erectile dysfunction, and death. "The fairly high rate (1.5% to 15%) reflects the fact that the procedure is often performed by an inexperienced individual without attention to basic surgical procedures" (p. 778).

History

> One might imagine that an intelligent species like man would leave them (the human genitals) alone. Sadly, this has never been the case. For thousands of years in many different cultures, the genitals have fallen victim to an amazing variety of mutilations and restrictions. For organs that are capable of giving us an immense amount of pleasure, they have been given an inordinate amount of pain. (Morris, 1985, p. 218)

Ritual circumcision (as differentiated from modern medical circumcision) has existed throughout history. Among the many 19th and 20th century authors who have studied its historical, religious, and cultural aspects, there is a consensus that its roots originated thousands of years ago, predating Judaism, with depictions of circumcision found even in Stone-Age cave drawings (Bitschai, 1956; Wallerstein, 1980; Wrana, 1939). Rites of initiation, fertility rituals, control of sexual drives, and tribal identification—for men and women—are considered the primary purposes for circumcision's many variations (Campbell, 1988; Zindler, 1990).

Male ritual circumcision involves various degrees of foreskin removal, while female circumcision ranges from clitoridectomy to vulvectomy to infibulation (known as Pharaonic circumcision—the most severe and mutilating form). However, whether past or present, ritual circumcision serves cultural purposes, as opposed to justification as a health promoting practice (Aldeeb Abu Sahlieh, 1994). As James DeMeo (1990) succinctly states, "The ritual [circumcision] has absolutely nothing whatsoever to do with medicine, health, or science in practically all cases" (p. 108). Regrettably, ritual circumcision of females, unlike males, is still extensively performed in many cultures throughout the world—especially within African and Arab-Islamic nations—where, for example, 80–90% of Somalian and Sudanese girls are infibulated by age seven or eight (Hicks, 1993; Hosken, 1982; Lightfoot-Klein, 1989; Van der Kwaak, 1992). Further cultural/religious discussion of ritual circumcision (male or female), however, is beyond the scope of this article. What is significant is the acknowledgment of the depths of circumcision's origins. It is a practice deeply imbedded within global consciousness—interwoven within centuries of cultural myths, values, and customs, all of which contribute to the resistance of 20th century thinking in releasing it from modern U.S. medical practice.

Routine medical circumcision is similarly rooted in neither science nor medicine. Instead, it grew out of the mid-19th century's hysteria and superstition about masturbation. Given the sexual mores of that time, child-rearing practices, and the lack of understanding of much disease etiology, masturbation was blamed for a litany of ills. Insanity, epilepsy, blindness, and even death were its feared results, with circumcision viewed as a "treatment" (Remondino, 1891/1974; Romberg, 1985). As a primary means of controlling masturbation in young children, circumcision peaked between 1850 and 1879 with even physicians recommending its use (deMausse, 1974, p. 49).

This was a time in American history when pervasive change was sweeping the nation: the Industrial Revolution, abolitionism, the Civil War and reconstruction, and the women's rights and labor movements, to cite a few. The practice of medicine itself was also changing. The emergence of the germ theory as the predominant scientific paradigm and the organization of professional medical societies—the American Medical Association was founded in 1847—signaled the profession's turn from its traditions in the healing arts (Coulter, 1994). The developing allopathic model of medical care took hold and began its evolution into a commodity of industrial capitalism (Brown, 1979). Within this cultural milieu the incidence of male circumcision steadily grew.

It took about 100 years for a different viewpoint, a more enlightened one, to grow within the medical community, stemming from the British physician Douglas Gardiner's (1949) critical article "The Fate of the Foreskin." For the first time, a direct challenge was made to the practice of routine circumcision. Physicians were encouraged to delay circumcision for 2–3 years, until its "minor advantages" could be better assessed. The message was heard within the structure of the British National Health Service. Together with its 1948 policy restrictions on elective surgery (Romberg, 1985) the circumcision rate in England—always less than the circumcision rate found in the United States—dropped dramatically (Wallerstein, 1985). In the United States, however, it would take another generation for alternative ideas to take hold.

Circumcision received a boost during World War II, with the justification that it helped minimize wartime "hygiene problems" (Gellis, 1978). Then, in the postwar years, another dynamic took hold—the growing class distinction in accessibility and utilization of health care. From the early 1940s to the late 1950s, "Educated middle-class parents almost always had their newborn sons circumcised," while, "the infant sons of poor parents were usually uncircumcised because their parents were unaware of the benefits [sic] and could not afford the cost" (Schoen, 1990, p. 1308). This rectified itself in the early 1960s with the rise of third-party reimbursement systems. While references to the contrary could be found in some medical texts of the time, for example, a standard urological medical text discrediting medical indications for circumcision (Campbell, 1963), by then, "circumcision became the American standard" (Schoen, 1990, p. 1309). A researcher from John Hopkins University made an acute cultural criticism of this interplay. "Linked to antisexual sentiment in the 19th century . . . currently, money-making interests in the U.S. lie behind this superfluous, often damaging, and sometimes lethal operation." (Money, 1989).

Though the *Journal of the American Medical Association* published a courageous editorial in 1965, written by Morgan and pointedly titled, "The Rape of the Phallus," it wasn't until the 1970s when formal medical organizations came out with official position statements opposing routine circumcision. The American Academy of Pediatrics (AAP, 1971) formed an Ad Hoc Task Force Committee on Circumcision that reported its objection and reiterated its stand once again in 1975: "There is no absolute medical indication for routine circumcision of the newborn" (Thompson, King, Knox, & Korones, 1975). The American College of Obstetricians and Gynecologists (ACOG, 1983) eventually concurred. Nevertheless, the incidence rate did not change. Instead, the 1980s brought more frequent opinions, studies, and debate in support of the practice. The AAP later reviewed existing data and changed its stance to a neutral position. While acknowledging issues of pain, contraindications of anesthesia, and the role of good hygiene, it concluded with the noncommittal statement that "newborn circumcision has potential medical benefits and advantages as well as disadvantages and risks" (AAP, 1989, p. 390).

With the repudiation of masturbation as an illness, physicians were now citing fears of infectious disease and cancer as justifications. Countless studies and articles were reporting on the protective effect of circumcision relative to: urinary tract infections (with a small projected 1.4% incidence rate), penile cancer (a serious albeit very rare malignancy occurring in 2/100,000 cases), HIV, cervical cancer in female sex partners, STDs, and minor inflammations and/or infections of the foreskin or urethral meatus (i.e., opening at the tip) (Wiswell, 1992, 1993). Further, adherence to tradition and custom were raised in arguments of "convenience" in personal hygiene and a need to "look like dad."

Consensus, however, remained illusive, and a consumer movement began adding its opposition voice to the debate. Organizations such as NOCIRC (the National Organization of Circumcision Resources Centers), the ISC (International Symposia on Circumcision), and INTACT (Infants Need To Avoid Circumcision Trauma) were founded in the mid-1980s. National networks of men's support groups also formed, for example, UNCIRC (Uncircumcising Information and Resources Center). More recently, medical professionals started taking radical stands in the face of conventional practice. Some nurses began courageously to identify themselves as "conscientious objectors," citing an ethical view that circumcision is an assault on the boy's sexuality and his right to an intact body. They offered testimony to their experience of having participated in too many "botched" procedures, leaving males with lifelong complications such as scarring, painful erections from excess foreskin removal, bowing and curvature, and hypospadia (Miya, 1994). Their ethical conflict is poignantly drawn in a letter from the nurses who founded Nurses for the Rights of the Child, "After years of strapping the babies down for this brutal procedure and listening to their screams, we couldn't take it any longer" (Sperlich & Conant, 1994). Physicians, too, organized, most notably by Dr. George C. Denniston's founding of the organization D.O.C. (Doctors Opposing Circumcision).

The Canadian Pediatric Society's Fetus and Newborn Committee, which officially agreed with the AAP in 1975, recently conducted an extensive reexamination of this issue. Reviewing 671 medical studies on circumcision's medical efficacy as a protective factor, and also performing a cost-benefit analysis, led them to a clear recommendation: "Circumcision of newborns should not be routinely performed" (CPS, 1996, p. 769). Yet, the debate continues.

Advocates speak of preventive medicine, while opponents call for an end to violence and the teaching of proper hygiene practices. The former group feels they are acting in the child's best interest, while the latter argues that the medical dictum "Primun Non Nocere" (First, do no harm) should guide this issue. Beyond the ongoing medical debate, however, there is a disturbing silence regarding such significant issues as foreskin physiology, the normalcy of the intact penis, loss and grief, and circumcision's impact upon a man's overall psychosexual development.

The Question of Normalcy

Medical warnings of potential problems for uncircumcised men persist, and parents continue to be approached for authorization for the permanent alteration of their newborn's healthy genitalia. Clearly, a sensitive understanding of the normalcy of penile foreskin and its functional purposes is needed. Indeed, even referring to it as "skin" dismisses its complex, specialized, biochemical nature. Fundamentally, the foreskin is a safety mechanism for the penis. It offers protection for the glans and shaft from external trauma, clothing abrasions, contact with potential infection sources (i.e., urine or feces), and thermal changes. Without the foreskin sheath, the glans becomes much more vulnerable. The American Academy of Pediatrics stated in a health education brochure, "Such problems virtually never occur in uncircumcised penises. The foreskin protects the glans throughout life" (AAP, 1984).

Such fundamental understanding, however, has gotten lost. A primary reason for this is the personal and professional experience of U.S. physicians themselves. "Because most males in the United States are circumcised" [including male physicians], writes Niku and his associates (1995), "there is little opportunity to observe the natural history of the uncircumcised penis; several errors have crept into American medical practice as a result" (p. 58). Most noteworthy, the unwarranted and forcible retraction of the foreskin, which creates the primary complications physicians use to justify circumcision.

Not naturally retractable at birth, the foreskin may take until adolescence until it is fully retracted. Niku (et al., 1995) elaborates, "Some physicians who have been denied the opportunity to observe the development of the uncircumcised penis are convinced that the prepuce must be retractable at an early age" (p. 58). That is unnecessary, and further perpetuates the myth and custom surrounding this practice. The opposing argument is that the intact penis is natural, in need of neither surgical improvement nor emotional fear. "It cannot be emphasized too strongly that no special care of the uncircumcised penis is required. The child should be encouraged to cleanse the area under his prepuce just as he is encouraged to wash behind his ears" (Niku et al., 1995, p. 58). Again, the British perspective is illustrative of the interplay between culture and clinical practice. Almost fifty years ago, Gardiner (1949) presented that foreskin development is normal in 99% of boys by the age of fifteen, and how only 15% of boys have a retractable foreskin by six months. More recent British researchers discuss how "Confusion over the term phimosis [i.e., the normal unretracted foreskin at birth versus the forcible retraction by a physician] continues, so that many children are thought to have a pathological condition when often there is none" (Williams, Chell, & Kapila, 1993, p. 29), and concludes with the point that physicians lack adequate understanding of this issue. Almost thirty years earlier, Morgan (1965) made the same arguments, though in a much more biting manner. Speaking candidly to his colleagues, "Why is the operation of circumcision practiced? One might as well attempt to explain the rites of voodoo! A nonretractable foreskin should not be used as pretext for lopping off an innocent and useful appendage. Appendicitis causes many more deaths every year in the United States than does cancer of the penis but nobody yet recommends routine appendectomy" (p. 123–124).

Sexuality

The foreskin also has an intricate role in sexual physiology. The 18th century masturbation-cure proponents knew that very well. Stimulation via the foreskin was a source of sexual pleasure that they were intent on reducing.

Nature intended for the glans of the unaroused penis to remain an internal organ (similar to the female clitoris shielded by its hood) with a lubricating mucous membrane as its outer surface, rather than becoming an external skin layer. During the arousal phase, the foreskin retracts gradually thereby allowing the glans to retain its highest tactile sensitivity until fully exposed during complete penile erection. The permanently exposed glans forms a dried, less sensitive skin layer called the corneum, as a somatic response to needing a protective replacement for the foreskin. The impact of circumcision upon the sexual nature of boys and men deserves consideration. A man's foreskin afterall is not an anachronistic error by nature, but an important functional aspect of masculine sexuality.

Rather than being solely a subject of disease and hygiene, the foreskin—together with the corona, glans—is an integral part of the "pleasure dynamics" of movement, sensation, and lubrication that occur during masturbation, foreplay, and intercourse. Current research has shown the foreskin has a high concentration of nerve endings that actually enhance the sensory function of the glans and shaft (Taylor, Lockwood, Taylor, 1996). However, as Taylor and his associates note, "Teaching on the anatomy of the prepuce (foreskin) has undergone little change since . . . the 15th century" (p. 294). Another physician-author succinctly challenges us to face the fact that, "Our foreskin, like our tonsils, does have a purpose in life . . . and . . . if new attitudes persist, the coming generation can revel in the new experience of having sex with a foreskin" (Purvis, 1992, p. 32). However, since male-affirmative messages regarding circumcision are not widely available to parents, and since most men and women have no experience with an intact penis—

many without even a visual image of one—a change in awareness and behavior will undoubtedly require considerable time.

In light of the knowledge society has gained about the complex interplay of psyche, soma, and sexuality, the continued medical practice of circumcision raises significant issues. When the natural state of male genitalia has been altered (i.e., a penis existing without an external, sliding, lubricating, stimulating sleeve of loose skin), how is a man's psychosexual experience changed? What of men whose skin on their shafts is too painful or desensitized during erection, from having had excess foreskin removed? Are there implications in sexual dysfunctions and difficulties of relationship formation? Beyond the individual, what affect does it have on sexual partners and what does it imply about our culture? As DeMeo (1990) has noted

> The fact that so many [Americans] are ready to defend the practice in the face of contrary epidemiological evidence is a certain give-away to hidden, unconscious motives and disturbed emotional feelings about the penis and sexual matters in general . . . before such painful and traumatic mutilations can be perceived as "good" . . . other antisexual and antichild social factors must be present and thriving. (p. 108)

Discussion of circumcision's negative impact upon a male's psychosexual development is limited, but Freud (1913) spoke to it. Regarding the trauma associated with the surgery, he wrote that a child's level of understanding of circumcision leads him to "equate it with castration" (p. 153, n1). Interestingly, a clinical-historian's review of Freud's other theoretical writings, letters, and dream accounts suggests that even Freud's own traumatic experience with the circumcision of his brother, Julius, provided the unconscious motivation for his conceptualization of the castration complex and its centrality to human development. Colman (1994) writes, "His [Freud's] writings are replete with emphasis on the importance of the penis and its destiny," and the argument is made that this significant circumcision event provides causal support to his "penis attention" (p. 603). Another psychoanalytic investigation into a 13-year-old boy's abnormal sadomasochistic sexual behavior attributed psychopathology to the overwhelming ego trauma of his circumcision (Kennedy, 1989). However, broad scope psychological research is lacking.

Relevant issues such as low self-esteem, sexual avoidance, trauma reactions, social interactional difficulties, and treatment considerations are more readily articulated about the female experience of circumcision (Bengston & Baldwin, 1993; Miller, 1992; Toubia, 1994). Psychotherapist Miller (1992) discusses the phenomena of women perpetuating the victimization of female circumcision to the next generation. "They were unable to defend themselves as young girls and were forced to repress their feelings. Today, as a result of their repression, they can justify the procedure as harmless and necessary (p. 74). Bengston and Baldwin (1993) specifically recommend counseling strategies for women similar to those used for a victim of sexual assault or for a woman grieving the loss of a female body part as in mastectomy. Toubia (1994), writing in the prestigious *New England Journal of Medicine*, speaks to circumcision's psychological effects on women often being subtle and buried in layers of denial and acceptance of social norms. Voicing the male counterpart to this surgical assault, however, has been much rarer. Psychologist Ronald Goldman (1997), after years of research, activism, and surveys of men regarding circumcision, contends that deep and lasting psychological damage does occur, and is directly contributory to certain emotional problems of men. This line of psychosexual inquiry begins with a specific premise. "All that takes place in the first days of life on the emotional level shape the pattern of all future reactions. How could a being so aggressed in this way, while totally helpless, develop into a relaxed, trusting person?" (Calderone, 1983, p. 10). Other psychotherapists, like Pharis and Eisler (1990), challenge clinicians to consider diagnostically the psychological reactions of children to genitourinary surgery. They recommend the incorporation of questions regarding circumcision and other genital surgeries into their clinical history-taking of men, so that the therapists "might evaluate and treat a variety of presenting complaints with a greater appreciation for the fears and body integrity issues which are likely to be common elements in such cases" (p. 473).

Loss

When a man is circumcised, a significant loss has occurred—one that represents a symbolic as well as a somatic amputation. While an individual's identification of and reaction to this will vary, many men do experience circumcision as a traumatic event. In numerous workshops led and attended by this author, where issues of circumcision have been examined, men have expressed intense loss and rage—feelings arising from deep within their mind-body memories that speak to this as "an act of assault, pain, and violation of innocence." Such personal accounts are also beginning to be found in print.

> I feel anger at the system that intimidated my parents to proceed with this senseless

and risky mutilation. I feel resentment for the collusion of physicians and my parents which made that decision for me, abusing my rights and destroying my birthright. (Green, 1991, p. 116; see also: Briggs, 1985).

Brietzke (1996) published survey accounts of men's personal reactions to their own circumcision. With numbers of men reporting unhappiness about the loss of their foreskins being equal to those who were content, the findings led to, "Our conclusion: every man has a profoundly different penis. For some, the foreskin is an impediment to pleasure; for others, it's the most erogenous area of their bodies" (p. 10).

A dramatic male response to this conceptualization of circumcision-as-loss has been the "restoration movement," that is, the growing popularity of surgical and non-surgical methods of foreskin reconstruction. There are various means of stretching penile shaft skin until it covers the glans. Though this new foreskin does not fully equate with a natural foreskin, many men report increased sensitivity and the return of a pleasurable gliding sensation during masturbation and intercourse (Bigelow, 1995; Griffen, 1991; Money, 1991). While it may require a considerable investment of time, discomfort, and money, it is a proactive response by some men who feel victimized by the unnecessary loss of their natural anatomical wholeness. In telling his personal account, Whipple (1987), with the added perspective as a public health medical investigator, writes,

> [C]hange is not so easy. While foreskin restoration has probably been with us since the first man's penis was forcibly altered, today's American medical professionals will test your masculinity, your personality, sanity and your financial resources before agreeing that you really want a pseudo-foreskin. (p. 113).

Activism on this issue has spawned sever-al self-help networks, including: BUFF (Brothers United for Future Foreskins), NORM (National Organization of Restoring Men), RECAP (RECover A Penis), and dozens of Internet Web sites and discussion groups (Rodrick, 1995).

The above statements and actions of men speak of circumcision in more graphic, personal, and political terms, providing a non-clinical framework in which to conceptualize this medical practice. This different language both broadens and confronts many prevailing cultural ideas regarding the surgery.

Cultural Denial

Through his linguistic studies, Mario Pei (1965) demonstrates language's cultural power in maintaining many ritualized activities over the centuries via its written, spoken, gestural, and symbolic forms. "Language," he writes, "is an all-pervasive conveyor, interpreter and shaper of humankind's social and scientific endeavors" (p. 29). When circumcision, then, is viewed by the culture as a "prophylactic surgical procedure performed by medical personnel as part of standard hospital practice," it creates a narrow framework in which to consider its implications upon the personal life of the boy and man. Boyd (1990) argues for the term "genital mutilation" when speaking about circumcision, as clinical words tend to trivialize and dismiss the depth of emotional and physical implications of foreskin removal. Such a term "is not only scientifically accurate, but also honors the feelings of those who feel they are victims of circumcision" (Boyd, 1990, p. 8). Directly speaking to men, Boyd further writes

> If what is routinely done to baby boys started being done to baby girls in the

U.S., there would be a great hue and cry and very legitimate charges of child abuse. But we've come to accept male circumcision as normal. The force of tradition has shut our cries at our own violation, our mutilation, and we've adapted to the silent denial. (p. 37)

Such language directly confronts cultural denial, that is, the forgetting that normal male genitalia has been intentionally altered, made unnatural not by the male's choice. This conceptualization is new for men, but not for women.

Illegal in the United Kingdom since the Prohibition of Female Circumcision Act of 1985, "female genital mutilation" became the preferred term at the U.K.'s First National Conference on Female Genital Mutilation in 1989 (Webb & Hartley, 1994). Also, at the International Conference on Population and Development held in Cairo in September, 1994, in response to World Health Organization estimates of more than 2 million circumcisions performed on girls and women each year, a uniform condemnation statement read, "Governments are urged to prohibit *female genital mutilation* wherever it exists." (International Conference on Population and Development, 1994). Both of these progressive international bodies, though, were silent on the same occurring to boys and men.

In 1984, invoking law and judicial case precedent, Brigman labeled "child mutilation through routine neonatal circumcision of males . . . as barbarous as female circumcision," and called for it to be acknowledged as the "most widespread form of child abuse in (U.S.) society" (p. 337). In exploring the constitutionality of parental decision-making rights and the child's rights to privacy and protection, he argues that neither physicians nor parents should be safe from government authority to prohibit non-medically warranted circumcision, and suggests a class-action civil rights suit as an effective societal response to "child mutilation." Farrell's (1986) words similarly confront our denial of the trauma of male circumcision by referring to it graphically as when "their penises are taken to the blade of a knife and cut," and underscores "the subconscious lack of caring about men that is displayed" (p. 231).

Re-framing circumcision into issues of abuse and rights is more than a conceptual shift. A generation ago, noted biologist and species analyst Desmond Morris (1973) called circumcision a form of "adult aggression" (p. 243). Today, however, more radical politicized anti-circumcision statements name it as "a crime" (K, 1995) and an act of "terrorism" (Worth, 1995), and consider it a core link to the perpetuation of fear, rage, and violence within men. It has also become the focus of citizen action. For example, the activist group NOHARMM (i.e., the National Organization to Halt the Abuse and Routine Mutilation of Males) was founded in 1992, and conducts national advocacy and information campaigns in defense of the child's right to an intact body, and in support of the empowerment of men.

The pro-feminist philosopher Mazis (1993), writing on the social construct of masculinity, looks at male experience with pain as the embodiment of masculine identity. Each successive pain violation upon the man is a further cutting, which continues to separate him from connection with the web of life. "Violence has become a haunting presence within the masculine psyche" (p. 36), an outgrowth of the hero model of masculinity and its insistence upon pain tolerance, the emotional armoring it fosters, and the cultural violence to self and others it perpetuates. The long-term impact of these cultural messages of masculinity upon male mortality and morbidity has been dev-

astating. Men continue to suffer disproportionate rates of disease, injury, crime victimization, disability, suicide, incarceration, and premature death (Farrell, 1993; Goldberg, 1976; Zoske, 1996). Men's health specialist Ken Goldberg (1993) calls "the notion that men are supposed to be bulletproof, to suffer through pain quietly and alone" (p. xxiii), a continuing male myth that still stands as a powerful barrier to gender well-being.

With sensitivity to the issue of male-as-perpetrator as well as male-as-victim, Mazis further writes, "hurting another, in violating their flesh or psyche, is actually very debilitating to the perpetrator" (p. 37). In the case of circumcision, it is the physician—most often male—who acts out the violence against the male baby. For physician-perpetrators, their choice extends from their history, their personal experience of penises, and their culture—including their elevated social status, and the economic and persuasive power they hold.

> In routine newborn circumcision, unlike most other surgical procedures, the newborn patient is obviously never able to consent or to be part of the decision making process. As such, parental cultural preferences and prejudices, presumed health benefits, and aesthetic choice of family, physicians and society play a large role in determining whether the procedure is done. Studies suggest that the single most important determinant is the physician's attitude. (Wilkes & Blum, 1990, p. 245)

A Gender Perspective

The implications of continued routine neonatal circumcision go to a depth that is personal, cultural, and beyond. Kipnis (1991) suggests that it is part of a larger socialization process affecting men's gender identity.

> At every stage of a man's development there is negative imprinting about the phallic aspect of maleness. Men are often taught that there is something wrong, nasty, or even evil about the penis. Often a little of it is cut off just after we're born" (Kipnis, 1991, p. 43)

Integrating male psychology and myth, Sam Keen (1991) goes further and defines circumcision's role as that of a "sacrament" in our culture, which initiates men into a life script that is based upon power relationships, violence, and warrior mentality. Keen goes on:

> Circumcision remains a mythic act whose real significance is stubbornly buried in the unconscious. That men and women who supposedly love their sons refuse to stop this barbaric practice strongly suggests that something powerfully strange is going on here. Feel the violation of your flesh, your being. What indelible message about the meaning of manhood [is] carved into your body? Masculinity requires a wounding of the body, a sacrifice of the natural endowment of sensuality and sexuality. A man is fashioned by a process of subtraction. We gain manhood by the willingness to bear mutilation. (pp. 30–31)

Newman (1991) concurs and discounts any relevance to circumcision's legacy as a legitimate rite of initiation. Preferring to call it a "false initiation," his integrative cultural-spiritual-political perspective describes circumcision as a ceremony of violence, a deconstruction of the male phallic image. "The ceremony itself and the rhetorical androgyny which embellishes the ceremony do not celebrate the male body, but use the violence of male dominant masculinity to

deny the existence of an inherent masculine sensuality." The results are simply pain and mutilation "for those of us who were cut before we even knew we had a body, before the world was anything but us" (p. 19).

A further bridge can be made between the modern and the ancient. In a Jungian study of phallos and its significance in identity formation and psychotherapy, Monick (1987) discusses how "men need to understand the psychological underpinnings of their gender and their sexuality better than they do," and that "to respect their sacred symbol" is a critical aspect (p. 9). With the existence of ancient images of phallus as an uncircumcised penis, found as far back as the 6th century B.C.E., the medical practice of circumcision leaves American men cut off not only from their foreskins, but from an inheritance of eons of universal male imagery. Monick argues that a connection is severed to an ancient identification of masculinity, leaving men damaged at an archetypal depth (p. 32).

Conclusion

In the face of a growing body of opposing scientific evidence and an increasingly vocal anti-circumcision movement by both consumers and professionals, the majority of newborn American males continue to experience non-consensual amputation of healthy genital tissue. Pro-circumcision empiricists pursue a search for scientific evidence that supports prophylactic benefits of surgery; however, their findings remain narrow and ambiguous. Their opponents submit that, as the United States holds a global minority stance on this medical custom, American males do not hold a distinction of being born in need of immediate surgical correction, and that simply good hygiene would allay concerns with medical risks, patient rights, and psychological trauma. Others take a middle ground and defer the issue to the process of informed consent between physician and parents. Finally, activists and victims speak about violence against innocent baby boys, urging that nature and justice prevail over social custom.

This article has attempted to show that beyond the biomedical aspects of routine medical circumcision lie complex societal issues that affect core elements of masculinity. Medical literature tends to avoid or obscure this via its more reductionistic clinical approach.

However, considering the massive scale upon which this elective neonatal surgery is performed, to one particular gender, an integrative cultural-based examination of this issue seems necessary. The broadest, most male-affirming statement found has been made by two female pioneering anti-circumcision advocates and nurses, Milos and Macris (1992b). They raise the debate about routine medical circumcision of U.S. boys to a global level, and speak to issues shared by both genders.

> Women have struggled to achieve rights of body ownership for themselves. It is imperative that mutual respect for these inalienable human rights be extended, not only to the women in Africa with whom we can identify, but also to men, male children, and male newborns. (p. 94S)

Boyd (1990) summarizes the issue concisely, "For over a hundred years, it has been a surgery in search of a justification" (p. 42). Unless health studies and men's studies combine, this search may continue in its circular fashion.

References

Aldeeb Abu Sahlieh, S. A. (1994). To mutilate in the name of Jehovah or Allah: Legitimation of male and female circumcision. *Medicine and Law, 13,* 575–622.

American Academy of Pediatrics (AAP), Committee on the fetus and newborn. (1971). *Standards and recommendations for hospital care of newborn infants* (5th ed.), 110, Evanston, IL: AAP.

American Academy of Pediatrics. (1984). *Care of the uncircumcised penis.* [Brochure].

American Academy of Pediatrics. (1989). Report of the ad hoc task force on circumcision. *Pediatrics, 84,* 388–391.

American College of Obstetricians & Gynecologists (ACOG). (1983). *Guidelines for perinatal care.* Washington, D.C.: Committee on Obstetrics, Maternal and Fetal Medicine.

Anand, K. J. S., & Hickey, P. R. (1987). Pain and its effects in the human neonate. *New England Journal of Medicine, 317,* 1321–1329.

Bengston, B., & Baldwin, C. (1993). The international student: Female circumcision issues. *Journal of Multicultural Counseling and Development, 21*(3), 168–173. [Special issue: Multicultural health issues].

Bigelow, J. (1992). *The joy of uncircumcising: Restore your birthright and maximize sexual pleasure.* Aptos, CA: Hourglass Book Publishing.

Benini, F., Johnston, C., Faucher, D., & Aranda, J. V. (1993, August 18). Topical anesthesia during circumcision in newborn infants. *Journal of the American Medical Association, 270,* 850–853.

Bitschai, J. (1956). *A history of urology in Egypt.* Cambridge, MA: Riverside Press.

Boyd, B. R. (1990). *Circumcision: What it does.* San Francisco: Taterhill Press.

Brietzke, C. E. (Ed.). (1996). Circumcision uncut. *Men's Confidential, 12*(3), 10–11.

Briggs, A. (1985). *Circumcision: What every parent should know.* Earlysville, VA: Birth & Parenting Publishers.

Brigman, W. (1985). Circumcision as child abuse: The legal and constitutional issues. *Journal of Family Law, 23*(3), 337–357.

Brown, E. R. (1979). *Rockefeller medicine men: Medicine and capitalism in America.* Berkeley: University of California Press.

Calderone, M. (1983, May-July). Fetal erection and its message to us. *SEICUS Report,* 9–10.

Campbell, J. (with B. Moyers). (1988). *The power of myth.* New York: Doubleday.

Campbell, M. (1963). *Urology* (2nd ed., Vol. 3). Philadelphia: Saunders.

Canadian Pediatric Society. (1996, March 15). Neonatal circumcision revisited. *Canadian Medical Association Journal, 154*(6), 769–780.

Cendron, M., Elder, J. S., & Duckett, J. W. (1996). Perinatal urology. In J. Y. Gillenwater, J. T. Grayhack, S. S. Howards, & J. W. Duckett (Eds.), *Adult & pediatric urology* (3rd ed., pp. 2149–2152). St. Louis: Mosley Yearbook.

Cohen, M. S. (1992). Circumcision. In J. F. Fowler (Ed.), *Urologic surgery* (pp. 422–428). Boston: Little, Brown.

Colman, W. (1994). The scenes themselves which lie at the bottom of the story: Julius, circumcision, and the castration complex. *Psychoanalytic Review, 81,* 603–625.

Coulter, H. (1994). *Divided legacy: A history of the schism in medical thought* (4 volume series). Washington, D.C.: Wehawken.

deMausse, L. (1974). *The history of childhood.* New York: Peter Bedrick Books.

DeMeo, J. (1990). Desertification and the origins of armoring: The Sahasasian connection. *Journal of Orgonomy, 24,* 99–110.

Farrell, W. (1986). *Why men are the way they are.* New York: McGraw-Hill.

Farrell, W. (1993). *The myth of male power: Why men are the disposable sex.* New York: Simon & Schuster.

Freud, S. (1913). Totem and taboo. *Standard Edition,* (13), 1–161.

Frost, N. (1992). Ethics, ethics everywhere. *Current Problems in Pediatrics, 22*(10), 422–423.

Gardiner, D. (1949). The fate of the foreskin: A study of circumcision. *British Medical Journal, 2,* 1433.

Gelbaum, I. (1993, Supplement. March/April). Circumcision: Refining a traditional technique. *Journal of Mid-Wifery, 38,* 18S–30S.

Gellis, S. S. (1978). Circumcision. *American Journal of Diseases of Childhood, 132,* 1168.

Gluckman, G. R., Stoller, M. I., Jacobs, M. M., & Kogan, B. A. (1995). Newborn penile glans amputation during circumcision and successful reattachment. *Journal of Urology, 153,* 778–779.

Goldberg, H. (1976). *The hazards of being male: Surviving the myth of masculine privilege.* New York: Signet Book.

Goldberg, K. (1993). *How men can live as long as women.* Fort Worth, TX: The Summit Group.

Goldman, R. F. (1997). *Circumcision: The hidden trauma.* Boston: Vanguard Publishing.

Goldman, R. F. (1997). *Questioning circumcision: A Jewish perspective* (2nd ed.). Boston: Vanguard Publishing.

Graves, E. J. (1995). Detailed diagnoses and procedures: National hospital discharge survey, 1993, from the National Center for Health Statistics, *Vital Health Statistics, 13,* 122–128.

Green, J. (1991). *The herbal male.* CITY: The Crossing Press.

Griffen, G. (1991). *Decircumcision: Foreskin restoration methods & circumcision practices.* Palm Springs, CA: Added Dimensions Publication.

Hicks, E. K. (1993). *Infibulation: Female mutilation in Islamic northeastern Africa.* New Brunswick, NJ: Transaction Publication.

Hosken, F. (1982). *The Hosken report: Genital and sexual mutilation of females* (Revised). Lexington, MA: Women's International Network News.

Howard, C. R., Howard, F. M., & Weitzman, M. L. (1994). Acetaminophen analgesia in neonatal circumcision: The effect on pain. *Pediatrics, 93,* 624–628.

International Conference on Population and Development. (1994, September 17). Knight-Ridder News Service.

K., A. (1995). [Letter to the editor]. *Mentor, 7*(1), 6.

Keen, S. (1991). *Fire in the belly.* New York: Bantam Books.

Kennedy, H. (1989). Sadomasochistic perversion in adolescence: A developmental-historical observation. *Journal of Psychoanalytic Theory and Practice, 4,* 348–360.

Kipnis, A. (1991). *Knights without armor.* New York: Perigee Books.

Lightfoot-Klein, H. (Ed). (1989). *Prisoners of ritual: An odyssey into female genital circumcision in Africa.* Binghamton, NY: Haworth Press.

Mazis, G. (1993). *The trickster, magician and grieving man: Reconnecting men with earth.* Santa FE, NM: Bear and Company.

Miller, A. (1991). *Breaking down the wall of silence.* New York: Dutton.

Milos, M., & Macri, D. (1992a, April 19). Body ownership rights of children: The circumcision question. [Speech at 22nd Annual Convention of American Atheists]. *American Atheist,* 50–59.

Milos, M., & Macri, D. (1992b, Supplement. March/April). Circumcision: A medical or a human rights issue? *Journal of Mid-Wifery, 37*(2), 87S–96S.

Miya, P. (1994). Botched circumcisions. [Ethical dilemmas column] *American Journal of Nursing, 94*(3), 56.

Money, J. (1989). Circumcision: Power and politics—2420 BC to 1989 AD. *Zeitschrift fur Sexualforschung, 2*(2), 171–176.

Money, J. (1991). Sexology, body image, foreskin restoration, and bisexual status. *Journal of Sex Research, 28*(1), 145–156.

Monick, E. (1987). *Phallos: Sacred images of the masculine.* Toronto: Inner City Books.

Morgan, W. (1965, July 19). The rape of the phallus [Commentary]. *Journal of the American Medical Association, 193*(3), 123–124.

Morris, D. (1973). *Intimate behavior.* New York: Bantam Books.

Morris, D. (1985). *Body watching.* New York: Crown.

Newman, R. (1991). Circumcision: The false initiation. *Changing Men, 23,* 19–21.

Niku, S. D., Stock, J. A., & Kaplan, G. W. (1995). Neonatal circumcision. *Urologic Clinics of North America, 22*(1), 57–65.

Pei, M. (1965). *The story of language.* New York: Lippincott.

Pharis, M., & Eisler, A. (1990). Psychological implications of childhood meatotomies. *Child & Adolescent Social Work, 7,* 461–474.

Poland, R. L. (1990). The question of routine neonatal circumcision. *New England Journal of Medicine, 322,* 1312.

Purvis, K. (1992). *The male sexual machine: An owner's manual.* New York: St. Martin's Press.

Remondino, P. C. (1974). *History of circumcision from the earliest times to the present.* New York: AMS Press. (Original work published 1891)

Ritter, T. (1992). *Say no to circumcision!* Aptos, CA: Hourglass Book Publishing.

Rodrick, S. (1995, May 29). Unkindest cut: Anti-circumcision and penile restoration activism. *The New Republic, 212.*

Romberg, R. (1985). *Circumcision: The painful dilemma.* South Hadley, MA: Bergen & Garvey Publishers.

Schoen, E. J. (1990). The status of circumcision of newborns. *New England Journal of Medicine, 322,* 1308–1312.

Sperlich, B. K., & Conant, M. (1994, June). Circumcision: Quality isn't the only dilemma [Letter to the editor]. *American Journal of Nursing, 94,* 16.

Stang, H. J., Gunner, M. R., Snellman, L., Condon, L. M., & Kesterbaum, R. (1988). Local anesthesia for neonatal circumcision: Effects on distress and cortisol response. *Journal of the American Medical Association, 259,* 1507–1511.

Taddio, A., Goldbach, M., Ipp, M., Stevens, B., & Koren, G. (1995, February 4). Effects of neonatal circumcision on pain responses during vaccination in boys. *Lancet, 345,* 291–292.

Taylor, J. R., Lockwood, A. P., & Taylor, A. J. (1996, February). The prepuce: Specialized mucosa of the penis and its loss to circumcision, *British Journal of Urology, 77,* 291–295.

Thompson, H. C., King, L. R., Knox, E., & Korones, S. B. (1975). Report of the ad hoc task force on circumcision. *Pediatrics, 56,* 610–611.

Toubia, N. (1994). Female circumcision as a public health issue. *New England Journal of Medicine, 331,* 712–716.

Van der Kwaak, A. (1992). Female circumcision and gender identity: A questionable alliance? *Social Science and Medicine, 35,* 777–787.

Wallerstein, E. (1980). *Circumcision: An American health fallacy.* New York: Springer Publishing Company.

Wallerstein, E. (1985). Circumcision: The uniquely American medial enigma. *Urology Clinics of North America, 12,* 123–132.

Webb, E., & Hartley, B. (1994). Female genital mutilation: A dilemma in child protection. *Archives of Disease in Childhood, 70,* 441–444.

Whipple, J. (1987). Circumcision: A conspiracy of silence. In F. Abbott (Ed.), *New men, new minds* (pp. 110–113) Freedom, CA: The Crossing Press.

Williams, N., Chell, J., & Kapila, L. (1993). Why are children referred for circumcision? *British Medical Journal, 306,* 28–30.

Wilkes, M. S., & Blum, S. (1990). Current trends in routine newborn male circumcision in New York State. *New York State Journal of Medicine, 90,* 243–246.

Wiswell, T. (1992). Circumcision: An update. *Current Problems in Pediatrics, 22,* 424–431.

Wiswell, T., & Hachey, D. O. (1993). Urinary tract infections and the uncircumcised state: An update. *Clinical Pediatrics, 32,* 130–134.

Worth, P. (1995, Fall). Beyond harm: The politics of circumcision. *Man, Alive!: Journal of Men's Wellness, 8*(3), 6–7.

Wrana, P. (1939). Historical review: Circumcision. *Archives of Pediatrics, 6,* 385–392.

Zindler, F. R. (1990, February). Circumcision: The stone age in the steel age. *American Atheist,* 34–40.

Zoske, J. (1996). Rethinking men's health and wellness. *Wellness Management, 12*(2), 1–6.

Appendix

Organizations Against
Male Circumcision

Doctors Opposing Circumcision, 2442 N. W. Market Street, Seattle, WA 98107.

National Organization of Circumcision Information Resource Centers, P.O. Box 2512, San Anselmo, CA 94979.

National Organization of Restoring Men, 3205 Northwood Drive, Suite 209 Concord, CA 94520-4506.

National Organization to Halt the Abuse and Routine Mutilation of Males, P.O. Box 460795, San Francisco, CA 94146.

Nurses for the Rights of the Child, 369 Montezuma, #354, Santa Fe, NM 87501.

11

Cross-Cultural Perspectives on Menopause

Gail Robinson

In this reading, Robinson reviews cross-cultural research to explore whether the physical and psychological symptoms that sometimes accompany menopause are caused mainly by hormonal changes, or by various psychological (e.g., role satisfaction) and sociocultural factors (e.g., cultural attitudes about aging women). She reasons that menopausal symptoms should be experienced by the majority of women, regardless of geographic location, if biological influences predominate. On the other hand, they should vary considerably within and between cultures if psychological and sociocultural influences predominate. While acknowledging the obstacles to conducting cross-cultural research on menopause (e.g., cultural differences in the definition of menopause), she reviews five important cross-cultural studies and draws several conclusions from them. First, she cautions us to keep in mind that most women experience menopause as a natural life event with few symptoms. However, for those women who experience many or more severe symptoms, the causes cannot be reduced to either biological or sociocultural influences. Instead, the wide variation in the experience of menopause reported by women within and across cultures (**cultural diversity**), results from a combination of hormonal changes, cultural influences, and individual perceptions and expectations. As with other gender-related issues, simplistic explanations of menopausal symptoms must be avoided if we are to separate myth from fact (**dialectical model**).

Questions to Consider:

1. Why is it important to conduct cross-cultural research on the experience of menopause? What are three obstacles to conducting good cross-cultural research on menopause?

Reprinted by permission of Lippincott, Williams, & Wilkins. G. Robinson (1996). Cross-Cultural Perspectives on Menopause. *Journal of Nervous and Mental Disease, 184,*(8), 453–458.

2. What are some of the cultural differences in the experience of menopause reported by Robinson? Refer to at least three of the five studies that she reviews.
3. Given the conclusions drawn from this review, how would you critique the popular tendency in this country to attribute menopausal symptoms such as hot flashes and depression mainly to hormonal changes? Be sure to give specific examples of some of the multiple influences.
4. How can this research be used to reduce menopausal symptoms for those women who experience them?

Numerous physical and psychological symptoms have been attributed to the hormonal changes that occur in women at midlife. Physical symptoms such as absent menses, hot flashes, and night sweats have been perceived to be an inevitable result of changing hormonal status. Although the idea of a specific involutional melancholia was abandoned in the early 1980s, many people still believe that menopause is frequently accompanied by depression, irritability, and loss of sexual interest. If these physiological and psychological symptoms are caused solely by the hormonal changes of menopause, they should occur in the majority of women in all cultures. If the emotional distress and physical symptoms experienced by women at midlife are more influenced by various psychological and sociocultural influences, however, the appearance of these symptoms should vary between societies.

Cross-cultural research allows anthropologists to study the relative importance of certain sociocultural variables by looking at the experiences of similar cohorts in a diversity of settings (Barnett, 1988). In this way, menopause, which occurs in all women, offers a wonderful opportunity to look at the effects of culture. It is important, however, to realize that identifying contrasts in middle age for women in different societies is simpler than proving that cultural variations actually affect women's experiences at menopause.

Cross-Cultural Research

In attempting to carry out cross-cultural research in the area of menopause, the first obstacle is often that of determining whether menopause has occurred. As menopause is officially defined as 1 year since the permanent cessation of menses resulting from loss of ovarian function (World Health Organization, 1981), this diagnosis can only be made retrospectively. In cultures in which women have multiple births and breastfeed for prolonged periods, women typically have long periods of amenorrhea (Beyene, 1986). Because women have babies late in life, the last period may, in fact, have predated a pregnancy and birth, and it is, therefore, often difficult to determine the onset of menopause. Furthermore, the definition of menopause varies in different cultures. In Japan (Lock, 1986a, 1991), menopause is part of a complex set of physiological changes related to aging. The cessation of periods, in itself, is not a sufficient reason for labelling one-self as being menopausal. Moreover, how women define their own status varies. For example, in Newfoundland, menopause is defined not only by the

Presented at the American Psychiatric Association Annual Meeting, Philadelphia, Pennsylvania, May 21–26, 1994.

woman's symptom experience but also by the menopausal status of women in her peer group, the occurrence of specific life events, changes in status and role, and her chronological age (Davis, 1983; Kaufert et al., 1986).

Cross-cultural research into menopause requires that the phenomena involved be studied over time using a large enough sample. It must incorporate factors such as diet, climate, ecology, patterns of menstrual fluctuation throughout a life cycle, and the woman's entire reproductive history (Kaufert et al., 1986). Women who use hormone replacement therapy or who are menopausal as a result of surgery or chemotherapy must be differentiated from those having natural menopause. Menopause must also be viewed in the wider context of illness behavior and symptom expression in another culture (Kaufert et al., 1986). For example, although in Western society women may admit to feelings of depression, in other cultures these feelings are often somatized. The use of instruments in determining the response to menopause in other cultures is problematic as well (Kaufert et al., 1986). It is not only a question of translating an instrument into another language—often there are no words in the other language for symptoms that we believe to be common. For example, in Japan, hot flashes are so infrequently reported that there is no word to describe them (Lock, 1986a, 1991).

Most importantly, researchers must rid themselves of Western biases and assumptions. For example, what may be a perceived increase in status in the Western world *e.g.,* that women are able to participate more freely in formerly male-dominated activities, may not equal a status gain for women in other cultures (Beyene, 1986).

Theories Related to Symptom Differences

The World Health Organization (1981) concluded that only vasomotor symptoms and vaginal dryness have been convincingly related to menopausal hormone changes. Cross-cultural comparisons, however, show that women in different societies even display different types and/or frequencies of physical symptoms. Whereas for Anglo-American women, hot flashes and night sweats are extremely common responses to menopause, with 65% to 70% women experiencing daily hot flashes (Wright, 1983), for Japanese (Lock, 1986a, 1991) and North American Navajo women (Wright, 1983), only 19.6% and 17%, respectively, experience hot flashes. Other authors have reported cultures in which symptoms are virtually absent: neither peasant Mayan Indians (Beyene, 1986) nor the Rajput of India (Flint and Samil, 1990) complain of any menopausal symptoms. Therefore, even if we look at frank physical symptoms that are theoretically caused by hormonal changes, we find differences in different cultures. The questions remain as to whether these are real differences or artifacts of research design and whether women in some cultures do not experience physical symptoms, or merely notice or complain about them less.

Women at midlife may experience a multitude of stressors including the meaning of the loss of fertility, redefining of roles, empty nest syndrome, loss of femininity, increased illness and disability, death of friends, financial insecurity, the burden of caring for elders, and changes of status. Variations among societies in the occurrence of these stressors have been used to explain the differences in symptoms reported by women in different cultures.

Empty Nest Syndrome

This syndrome explains menopausal symptoms as being caused by the difficulties that women encounter when their children leave home to go to college, gain employment, or get married (Parlee, 1976). It emphasizes the loss of the mothering role over any other losses faced by middle-aged women and assumes that it is this loss that makes women feel useless and devalued, thereby causing them to focus on physical symptoms and become depressed in midlife. This theory is related to earlier hypotheses, such as those of Benedek (1950), who believed that the relinquishment of maternal functions releases psychomotor energy which is either used in creative pursuits or leads to neurotic behavior and misery. Erikson (1950) spoke of the stage of "generativity versus stagnation." He believed that at midlife, when women lose the mothering role and feel unneeded, self-preoccupation may preclude further emotional growth, leading to stagnation and pathological self-absorbtion. This theory assumes that the loss of the mothering role coincides with the physiological experience of the menopause (Lock, 1986b). In current North American families, children have usually left the home at an early age and may, at this time, even be returning to live at home consequent to a divorce or an inability to obtain work. Other researchers have shown that many women, in fact, express relief about their children becoming independent and leaving home (Rubin, 1979).

Alternative Roles

It has been hypothesized that women who enjoy pursuits outside of mothering could avoid the empty nest syndrome and, therefore, decrease their risks of becoming symptomatic and depressed at midlife (Dennerstein and Burrows, 1978). Employment outside the home meant that the woman could gradually redirect her energies away from children as her maternal responsibilities lessened and, therefore, fare better. Studies, however, have found that this theory frequently holds for women in upper social classes with higher educations, but not for women in lower classes (Barnett, 1988).

Changes in Roles and Status

Women's menopausal symptomatology has been said to be a function of whether entering midlife is associated with decreased status or with increased rewards and an improvement in status (Bart, 1971; Maoz et al., 1977). In North America, with the emphasis on youth and attractiveness, menopause becomes a symbol of aging, and women may feel less wanted and valuable at midlife (Datan, 1990). In modern cultures, in which sex has been untied from procreation, the woman continues to be valued only as long as she is young and attractive, rather than as an older maternal figure (Bart, 1971). In contrast, in many nonindustrialized societies, women improve their status at midlife. The view of menstruation as a polluting and dangerous activity results in numerous taboos and restrictions concerning women during menses. After menopause, the women are freed from these restrictions, as well as from numerous reproductive burdens such as caring for children, doing household chores, and being under the protection of men (Barnett, 1988; Brown, 1985). In some cultures, different taboos come into place, which are to the women's advantage *e.g.*, in Peru, postmenopausal women are not allowed to touch detergent and, therefore, are freed from having to do any washing activities (Benedek, 1950). In many cultures, women of older age have the opportunity to assume new roles, such as midwives, healers, or singers, which garner a great deal of respect (Bart, 1971; Brown, 1985).

Bart (1971) discussed six variables, which she thought allowed women to maintain a valued status at the time of menopause by preventing the loss of the maternal role. These factors include: strong ties to the family of origin; an extended family system in which the mother continues to be the matriarch and has power and control; strong reciprocal ties between parents and children such that the mother retains a great deal of power; institutionalized grandmother roles; institutionalized mother-in-law roles in which the mother-in-law acquires a new daughter whom she must train; and the emphasis on procreative rather than free sex with the subsequent increased value of the maternal role.

Datan (1990) found that women can adjust to the status and expectation of either traditional or modern cultures but have difficulty if their culture is in transition.

Identity Continuity Theory

This theory suggests that a person who has found satisfaction in her principal life role, whatever it has been, continues to identify with that role despite any changes in role performance (Barnett, 1988). A low satisfaction with accomplishments in one's principle life role leads to a diminished view of oneself as successful after menopause. According to this theory, the empty nest only leads to depression if the woman, in contemplating her role as a parent, feels she has been unsuccessful. If women are satisfied with their children's accomplishments, their identity as mothers remains strong, and they are not distressed by their children's departure. Similarly, women who have had satisfying employment continue to feel good about themselves at menopause.

Case Studies

Israel.   Datan (Datan, 1990; Datan et al., 1981) studied five Israeli subcultures, including Israeli-born Muslim Arabs and immigrant Jews born in North Africa, Persia, Turkey, and Central Europe, using their ethnic identity as an approximate measure of degree of modernity. She started her studies working with Maoz, who believed that stress in mid-life is a function of modern, youth-oriented, European culture and is manifested in both the extreme response of involutional depression in some women and nonpathological distress in normal women (Maoz et al., 1977). Maoz felt that this overvaluation of youth led to the menopause being perceived as a transition to a devalued state (Maoz et al., 1977). Because modern women like active coping, menopause, which is an uncontrollable state, causes frustration. These theories stemmed from Deutsch's (1979) hypothesis that menopause means a "closing of the gates," loss of fertility, and an omen of aging and death. Further, Maoz (1977) postulated that, for women in traditional cultures who have more children and have had the fullest expression of their femininity, menopause brings relief rather than regret.

Datan came into this study with a different hypothesis. She believed that stress is a function of culture but would be less apparent in European women, who have roles other than child-rearing. She felt that because child-rearing had ended years before for these women, menopausal distress was not related to the end of fertility. Rather, she postulated that for traditional women, menopause meant the end of their only source of prestige. The conclusion of this study was that neither theory was upheld (Datan, 1990; Datan et al., 1981). Women across the five cultures welcomed menopause. There were cultural differences in the specific concerns each group had about menopause, with Muslim Arabs fearing a decline in marital relationships, Near Eastern groups worrying about failing physical health, and European women fearing loss of mental health. Overall, however, the women who were most distressed were those in transitional cultures *i.e.,* who had been socialized into traditional settings and transplanted into modern cultures. These women, she felt, had neither the stability of a traditional culture nor the freedom of a modern culture.

North America. Wright (1983) chose to study the effect of the empty nest syndrome, integration into kin networks, access to postmenopausal roles, and individual attitudes by comparing traditional and acculturated Navajo women with Anglo-Americans. She hypothesized that the Navajos would have fewer symptoms because they retained their child-bearing roles longer as a result of bearing children later in life and having extended families. In addition, these women were better integrated into their community and tended to have high status throughout their lives, which only increased after menopause, when they could assume the role of singers. She found, however, that the cultures differed in their symptoms only in the frequency with which they experienced hot flashes (17% of the Navajos experienced daily flashing versus 65% to 70% of the Anglo-Americans). Traditional Navajo women, however, tended to focus on positive changes related to the menopause and ignore other symptoms. Wright conclud-

ed that although hot flashes are probably biologically based, differences in interpretations and expectations can render menopause a very different experience in different cultures.

Mayans and Greeks. To isolate historical, cultural, and environmental factors relating to variations or similarities in response to menopause, Beyene (1986) compared Mayans in a small village of Yucatan and rural Greek women living on the island of Evia. She believed that the two cultures would be similar because both were non-Western in their views of women and aging and both shared similar cultural values with respect to beliefs and practices regarding menstruation, childbearing, and roles of women. In both cultures, older women were valued as mothers-in-law, healers, and carriers of traditions. For the Mayans, however, who had an average of seven pregnancies, menopause was welcomed and provided a sense of freedom. Because they had already produced many children, they did not feel they were losing anything by giving up their fertility. In addition, they were relieved from numerous restrictions and menstrual taboos. These women reported no physical or emotional menopausal symptoms other than the cessation of menses and did not have terminology for hot flashes. Healers there had never experienced women coming to them with menopausal complaints.

The Greek women, in contrast, had far fewer pregnancies and children. They tended to limit their childbearing as a result of the hard times that the community had experienced during the war years. As a result, they experienced better sex after menopause because there was no longer a risk of pregnancy. Despite the fact that older women could gain more status in the community, women associated menopause with aging, being less desirable, having less energy, and, generally, going downhill. Premenopausal women reported anxiety and a negative attitude toward menopause. Seventy-two percent of menopausal and postmenopausal women had experienced hot flashes and considered this a normal part of menopause. Thirty percent of them felt weak and sick during this time. Beyene concluded that because the great dissimilarities in symptoms were in marked contrast to the similarities in the cultures, the differences could not be attributed to culture alone. She did note that the two cultures had major differences in their diet, ecology, and fertility patterns and questioned the influence of these factors, as well as genetic differences, on the variation in menopausal symptoms.

Japan.   In studies by Lock (1986a, 1991), only 19.6% of Japanese women reported ever having hot flashes, compared with 64.6% of Canadian women. The main symptoms Japanese women experienced were headaches, shoulder stiffness, dizziness, and ringing in the ears. The Japanese described the whole process of *Konenki* as beginning at approximately 40 to 45 years of age. They saw this as a gradual change related to both hormonal shifts and autonomic instability. For them, menopause *i.e.,* the cessation of periods, was only the last part of this whole process. Few women reported symptoms of depression. Lock (1986a, 1991) hypothesized that both politics and history had an influence on Japanese women's experience of the menopause. Most Japanese women had mothers who had gone through extremely hard times during the war. Even though their own lives remained very difficult in comparison to Western standards, many Japanese women felt that, when compared with their mothers, their lives were very

fortunate. In addition, although there is an aging population, the Japanese government had been extremely reluctant to put money into facilities for old people. Japanese women, therefore, were expected to care for their aging parents. Menopause had been characterized as a "disease of modernity, a luxury disease affecting women with too much time on their hands who run to doctors with insignificant complaints" (Lock, 1986a, 1991). The message was that if women were occupied with looking after their relatives, they would not have time for complaints. Therefore, the good Japanese wife and daughter was discouraged from focusing on menstrual symptoms.

Peru.   In Barnett's study (1988) of women in a Peruvian village, she included both women who had roles essentially as mothers as well as those who had roles as laborers. She related the severity of menopausal symptoms to the women's principle role satisfaction. For women whose principle role had been mothers, she found the transition to the empty nest was only important because it triggered or coexisted with women's introspection on the success of their roles as mother. She believed that rather than merely reacting to the roles they are losing, women evaluate their children's accomplishments and decide whether they are satisfied with how they have performed as mothers. Barnett emphasized that it was important that children meet their mothers' expectations and not any outside standard. Similarly, with laborers, she found that it was not the work itself that was an important variable but rather their satisfaction with their role. She thought, therefore, that it is not just the external roles imposed by society but also internal roles that are significant in allowing women to continue to identify with their life's role despite any changes in role performance and, thereby, to attain satisfaction at this time of life. Barnett believed that women can be satisfied with their life role even if this role does not confer external status. The more control women have over their principal life roles, the greater their satisfaction.

Conclusions

In summary, a cross-cultural perspective on menopause gives us some interesting but often confusing information. Clearly, there are enormous differences in the experience of menopause among women in the same culture and among cultures. In interpreting these data, however, it is important to keep in mind a number of cautions. Most women pass through menopause with ease and see it as a natural life event (Avis and McKinlay, 1991; Kaufert et al., 1986). Perceptions of women's distress at this time are distorted because the women who come to menopause clinics do have elevated levels of distress (Stewart et al., 1992). For those women who do experience distress, we cannot assume that culture is the only variable. Diet, climate, ecology, genetics, and reproductive history might all contribute to differences. Studies that assume that certain events coincide with menopause *e.g.*, that menopause occurs at the same time children are leaving home, can lead to false correlations between life events and menopausal distress. Studies of other factors related to menopausal symptoms, such as education or employment, may have resulted in conflicting results by ignoring the issue of personal satisfaction. For example, research on the effects of unemployment may have included women who did not wish to work or for whom work has negative connotations. It is, therefore, not surprising that studies have often found that work has been a factor only for more edu-

cated women because they are more likely to have obtained work that is satisfying to them (Barnett, 1988).

We also have to be wary of our cultural biases. The value of work or the value of a change of status is often perceived from a very Western point of view and may not be relevant for women in other cultures. Similarly, we cannot make assumptions of how other cultures treat women and what status they are accorded based on our Western perspective. The key may not be whether women are better treated in other cultures but, rather, how individual women in that culture evaluate their lives at midlife. Thus, it seems that menopausal symptoms result from a combination of physical changes, cultural influences, and individual perceptions and expectations.

References

Avis, N. E., & McKinlay, S. M. (1991). A longitudinal analysis of women's attitudes toward the menopause: Results from the Massachusetts Women's Health Study. *Maturitas 13:65–79.*

Barnett, E. A. (1988). La edad critica: The positive experience of menopause in a small Peruvian town. In P. Whelehan, M. A. Bergin (Eds.), *Women and health: Cross-cultural perspectives* (pp. 40–54). Westport, CT: Bergin & Garvey.

Bart, P. (1971). Depression in middle-aged women, in V. Gornick, B. Moran (Eds.), *Women in sexist society.* New York: Basic Books.

Benedek, T. (1950). Climacterium: A developmental phase. *Psychoanal Q 21:1–27.*

Beyene, Y. (1986). Cultural significance and physiological manifestations of menopause: A biocultural analysis. *Culture Med Psychiatry 19:47–71.*

Brown, J. (1985). Introduction in J. Brown, V. Kerns (Eds.), *In her prime: A new view of middle-aged women.* Westport, CT: Bergin & Garvey.

Datan, N. (1990). Aging into transitions: Cross-cultural perspectives on women at midlife. In R. Formaner (Ed.), *The meanings of menopause: Historical, medical and clinical perspectives* (pp. 117–132). Hillsdale, NJ: Analytic.

Datan, N., Antonovsky, A., & Maoz, B. (1981). *A time to reap: The middle age of women in five Israeli sub-*

cultures. Baltimore: Johns Hopkins University Press.

Davis, D. L. (1983). *Blood and nerves: An ethnographic focus on menopause.* St. John's, Newfoundland, Canada: Memorial University of Newfoundland Institute of Social and Economic Research.

Dennerstein, L., & Burrows, G. D. (1978). A review of the studies of the psychological symptoms found at menopause. *Maturitas 1:*55–64.

Deutsch, H. (1979). *The psychology of women,* vol. 2. New York: Bantam.

Erikson, E. H. (1950). *Childhood and society.* New York: Norton.

Flint, M., & Samil, R. S. (1990). Cultural and subcultural meanings of the menopause. *Ann N Y Acad Sci 592:*134–148.

Kaufert, P., Lock, M., McKinlay, S., Beyenne, Y., Coope, J., Davis, D., Eliasson, M., Gognalons-Nicolet, M., Goodman, M., & Holte, A. (1986). Menopause research: The Korpilampi workshop. *Soc Sci Med 22:*1285–1289.

Lock, M. (1986a). Ambiguities of aging: Japanese experience and perceptions of menopause. *Culture Med Psychiatry 10:*23–46.

Lock, M. (1986b). Introduction. *Culture Med Psychiatry 10:*1–5.

Lock, M. (1991). Contested meanings of the menopause. *Lancet 337:*1270–72.

Maoz, B., Antonovsky, A., Apter, A., Wijsenbeek, H., & Datan, N. (1977). The perception of menopause in five ethnic groups in Israel. *Acta Obstet Gynecol Scand 65*(Suppl):35–40.

Parlee, M. (1976). Social factors in the psychology of menstruation, birth and menopause. *Primary Care 3:* 477–490.

Rubin, L. B. (1979). *Women of a certain age: The midlife search for sex.* New York: Harper and Row.

Stewart, D. E., Boydell, K., Derzko, C., & Marshall, V. (1992). Psychologic distress during the menopausal years in women attending a menopause clinic. *Int J Psychiatry Med 22:*213–220.

World Health Organization. (1981). Research on the menopause: Report of a WHO scientific group. *WHO Tech Rep Ser* Geneva: WHO.

Wright, A. L. (1983). A cross-cultural comparison of menopausal symptoms. *Med Anthropology 7:*20–35.

Chapter 5: Putting It All Together_____

1. Why is it important to consider the ways other cultures think about health-related issues such as male circumcision and menopause?
2. According to the readings, how do our cultural conceptions of masculinity and femininity contribute to the widespread practice of male circumcision and to the way menopause is experienced?
3. Did these articles change your thinking about male circumcision and menopause? Explain.

6

Gender and Intimate Relationships

It is in our intimate relationships that we should have the opportunity to truly be ourselves. Yet even here, gender role expectations can shape our behavior, attitudes, and experiences. The first reading in this chapter looks at male friendships and finds that even though men and women behave similarly in their friendships, men believe that male friendship differs from female friendship. To deal with this contradiction, men act and interpret their behaviors in ways that confirm their stereotypes about masculine friendship. In the second reading, the effect of gender roles on gay and lesbian relationships is explored. It is argued that unlike heterosexuals, gays and lesbians are freed from traditional gender roles in their romantic relationships and so can construct new ways of dividing power and responsibility. However, similar gender role socialization in gay and lesbian couples may lead to deficits in the components of a relationship that are generally handled by the other gender in heterosexual couples.

12

"I'm Not Friends the Way She's Friends": Ideological and Behavioral Constructions of Masculinity in Men's Friendships

Karen Walker

Cultural ideology concerning men's friendship behavior dictates that men do not share intimate thoughts and feelings with one another. Walker conducted in-depth interviews of middle and working class men (and women) to investigate how well actual friendship behaviors matched the cultural ideology. She showed that, overall, men and women behave similarly in their friendships **(more alike than different)**. However, in her study men attempted to maintain their ideology concerning gender differences in intimacy even when their behaviors contradicted it. They did this through reports of distinctively male patterns of telephone use, joking behavior, use of public space, and talking about what women are like. Walker also found some class differences in the construction of masculinity **(cultural diversity)** within friendship behavior, which she links to the different work lives of professional versus working class men.

Questions to Consider:

1. What matches did Walker find between the cultural ideology concerning male friendship behavior and the actual behaviors of her male participants? What contradictions between ideology and behavior did she find?
2. How closely do Walker's findings concerning intimacy between male friends match your experiences in male friendships and/or your observations of male friendships? Explain.

3. What evidence does Walker provide for the existence of masculinities in friendship behavior, and how does she explain these different constructions of masculinity? Do your experiences or observations support her explanation? Discuss.

4. In her conclusion, Walker claims that research focus on intimacy has limited our understanding of how men's friendships have been important and meaningful to them. What does she mean by this? Do you agree? Why or why not?

Contemporary ideologies about men's friendships suggest that men's capacity for intimacy is sharply restricted. In this view, men have trouble expressing their feelings with friends. Whether due to the development of the masculine psyche or cultural prescriptions, men are viewed as highly competitive with friends. Because of their competition, they are unlikely to talk about intimate matters such as feelings and relationships. The literature on gender differences in friendship suggests that the ideologies reflect actual behavior. Researchers have found that men limit verbal self-disclosure with friends, especially when compared to women (Aukett, Ritchie, & Mill, 1988; Caldwell & Peplau, 1982; Reid & Fine, 1992; Rubin, 1985; Sherrod, 1987 Swain, 1989). Men share activities with friends (Rubin, 1985; Swain, 1987). On the other hand, there are also suggestions that the degree of self disclosure among men may be underestimated (Hacker, 1981; Rawlins, 1992; Wright, 1982), particularly among men from

particular groups (Franklin, 1992). My research on friendship shows that men and women share the stereotypes about gender differences in friendship, but in specific friendships, men discuss their relationships and report relying on men friends for emotional support and intimacy (Walker, 1994). In addition, many activities of friendship—seeing friends for dinner, sharing ritual events, and visiting—are things both men and women do. Barry Wellman (1992) argues that there has been a widespread "domestication" of male friendship, with men seeing friends in their home in much the same way women do.

In much of the literature on gender differences in friendship, ideology has been mistaken for behavior. In part, researchers seem to have made this mistake because they have asked general, instead of specific, questions about friendship.[1] As a result, they have elicited good representations of what respondents *believe* their behavior is—beliefs that are shaped by the respondents' own ideologies. What they have sometimes failed to elicit is information about specific friendships in which variations from the ideologies may be substantial. Because researchers report what respondents tell them, it is easy to understand why researchers make this mistake. What becomes more difficult to understand is how the confusion between the ideology of friendship and friendship behavior comes to be constructed in everyday life. Why do men maintain their belief that men are less open than women in the face of considerable evidence that they do discuss their feelings with their friends? This is even more crucial

A version of this article was presented at the 1993 annual meetings of the American Sociological Association in Miami. The author gratefully acknowledges the comments of Robin Leidner and Vicki Smith.

1. Some researchers have made this mistake as part of a more general positive evaluation of women. Some of this literature is explicitly feminist and draws on literature which emphasizes and dichotomizes gender differences.

because the stereotype of intimate friendship that men believe characterizes women's friendship is currently highly valued. Feminist scholars and writers have successfully revalued women's intimate relationships to the detriment of earlier ideals that privileged male bonding. While not all respondents in this study positively evaluated the stereotype of women's openness with friends, many did, as evidenced by one professional man who said,

> I mean, we [men] talk about sports and politics sometimes, any kind of safe [topic], if you will. Not that any [every] kind of interaction needs to be intimate or this and that, but it's much different when you talk to women. Women catch on. I remember once seeing Robert Bly, and he said something that is really so in my experience, that women get to the heart of things and that they get there so quickly that it makes you, uh, it can put men into a rage because women are able to articulate these kinds of things that men can't.

Given the belief that being intimate and "getting to the heart of things" is good, and given the evidence that men are more intimate in practice than the ideology suggests, *why don't men challenge the ideology?*

There seem to be several answers to this question. First, when men do not conform to the masculine ideals about how they should act with their friends, they are occasionally censured. In the practice of masculine friendship, the positive evaluation of feminine intimacy disappears. Because of their friends' reactions, men come to see their behavior as anomalous and bad, and they do not reevaluate the extent to which the ideology of masculine friendship accurately reflects behavior.

Second, social class influences men's capacities for conforming to gender ideolo-

gies. Professional men are somewhat more likely than working-class men to conform to gendered norms with respect to intimate behavior (Franklin, 1992; Walker, 1994). Also, professional men's social class makes them—with other middle class men—the primary groups on which cultural stereotypes are based. Literature written specifically about men's friendships often relies on research of middle class men, particularly college-aged men (Caldwell and Peplau, 1982; Rawlins, 1992; Reid and Fine, 1992; Rubin, 1985; Swain, 1989). Very recently, some researchers have noted that men who are other than middle class or white may have different types of friendships from the ideology (Franklin, 1992; Hansen, 1992), but the knowledge of the existence of other forms of masculine friendship among working class African American and white men has not influenced the ideology of friendship.

Third, there *are* gender differences in behavior, and these differences reinforce stereotypes about gendered forms of friendship, even if the differences differ substantively from the substance of the ideology. For instance, male respondents in this study used the telephone somewhat differently from the ways women used it. Through their use of the telephone men constructed their masculinity, and in so doing they reinforced their notions that men are not open. As I will show, men claimed they called their friends for explicitly instrumental reasons—to make plans, get specific information, and so on—but not to find out how friends were, which they connected to women's telephone use. These practices generally supported the idea that women were better at maintaining friendships and talking to friends about feelings even though men's telephone conversations often included talk about personal matters. But a desire to talk to friends about personal matters was rarely the motive for phone calls.

In this article I examine the ways gender ideology about friendships is maintained through four behaviors and men's interpretations of those behaviors: telephone use, jokes, the use of public space, and how men talk about women. It is only when we understand how men behaviorally construct gender within friendship that we can begin to understand how men use these behavioral constructions to support ideological constructions of masculine friendship practices.

Method of Study

This paper relies on research from a study of men's and women's same-gender and cross-gender friendships. I interviewed 9 working-class and 10 professional men (as well as 18 working-class and 15 middle-class women). Within each class, I individually interviewed some men who were friends with other respondents in the study. Interviewing friends allowed me to gather information on group interaction that would have been unavailable had I interviewed isolated individuals. In addition, I was able to explore issues that were most salient to groups of friends. Finally, by interviewing friends I could examine the extent to which friends agree on what their interactions were like. This was particularly important when there was a discrepancy between behavior and ideology: Some men did not report on behavior that contradicted the masculine ideology of friendship either because they were unwilling to disclose that their behavior did not match the cultural ideal or because such behavior was somewhat meaningless to them, and they forgot it.

Respondents ranged in age from 27 to 48. Class location was determined by both life style and individuals' work. Thus, working class respondents tended to have high school educations or less, although one self-employed carpenter had a 4-year degree in accounting. Working-class men were in construction and some service occupations. Most working class men lived in densely populated urban neighborhoods in row houses or twins in Philadelphia. Professional respondents had graduate degrees, and they worked as academics, administrators, lawyers, and therapists. Professionals lived in the suburbs of Philadelphia or in urban apartments.

Interviews were semistructured, and respondents answered both global questions about their friendship patterns as well as questions about activities and topics of conversations in which they engaged with each friend they named. The use of in-depth interviews that included both global and specific questions allowed me to gather data indicating the frequent discrepancies between cultural ideologies of masculine friendships and actual behaviors. In addition, in-depth interviews allowed me to compare working class and professional respondents' experiences.

Recently, Christine Williams and Joel Heikes (1993) have observed that male nurses shaped responses to interview questions in ways that took into account the gender of the interviewer. In this study, my status as a woman interviewer appeared to have both positive and negative implications for data collection. On the one hand, being a woman made it more likely that men admitted behavior that contradicted gender ideology. Sociologists studying gender and friendship have consistently argued that men do not engage in self-disclosure with other men (Caldwell & Peplau, 1982; Reid &

Fine, 1992). Other research shows that men are likely to be more self-disclosing with women than with men (O'Meara, 1989; Rubin, 1985). While my research shows that men engaged in self-disclosure more frequently with friends than the literature suggests, they did so with men they considered close friends. Frequently, close friends were people they knew for a long time or people with whom they spent much time. Wright (1982) notes that long-time men friends engage in self-disclosure. I suspected that certain kinds of disclosures that men made during the interviews might have been more difficult to make to an unknown man instead of to me, an unknown woman.

On the other hand, respondents suggested that they more heavily edited their responses to questions about how they discussed women with their men friends than they did other questions. They frequently sprinkled their responses with comments recognizing my gender, "You don't have a gun in there, do you? (laugh)" or "I don't mean to be sexist here." I suspected that responses were much more benign than they would have been if I were a man. Thus, when I discuss men's talk about women below I believe that my data underestimate the extent to which men's talk about women constructs gender tensions.

Behavioral Construction of Masculinity

In recent years sociologists of gender have come to emphasize the active construction of gender. Gender is seen as an ongoing activity fundamental to all aspects of social life rather than a static category in which we place men or women (Connell, 1987; Leidner, 1991; West & Zimmerman, 1987). One advantage of a social constructionist perspective is that it allows researchers to explore both the ideological as well as the behavioral construction of gender. Gender is constructed *ideologically* when men and women believe that certain qualities, such as intimacy, characterize one gender rather than another. The way men and women interpret life and its meaning for them are deeply influenced by their ideological beliefs. Gender is constructed *behaviorally* in the activities men and women do and the way they do them.

Sometimes ideology and behavior match—such as when men talk about gender differences in telephone use and report behavior that differs from women's behavior. Sometimes ideology and behavior do not match. When there is a mismatch, the interesting problem of how ideology is sustained when behavior contradicts it emerges. I argue that, in the specific case of friendship, specific behaviors supported men's gendered ideologies. Men discounted or ignored altogether evidence that discredited a distinctly masculine model of friendship. This occurred because gender is a category culturally defined by multiple qualities. When men included themselves in the masculine gender category based on some behavior, they tended unreflectively to accept as given the cultural boundaries of the entire category *even if other of their behaviors contradicted those boundaries.*

Among respondents there were several ways masculinity was constructed in the activities of friendship. First, where men met, particularly working class men, became a mark of masculinity. Second, the way men used the telephone distinguished masculine from feminine behavior. Third, men used jokes in particular ways to establish masculinity and also to manage tensions between actual behavior and gender ideologies. Finally, men friends talked about women in ways that emphasized the differences and tensions between men and women.

There are class differences in the behaviors that form particular patterns of masculinity. Differential financial constraints, the social expectations of particular kinds of work, and lifestyle differences played roles in shaping particular forms of masculinity. The use of jokes was somewhat more elaborated among working class men than among professional men, but reports of jokes and joking behavior emerged in both groups. Professional men talked about wives and the strains of work and family differently from working class men; as I will discuss, this resulted from different work experiences.

Besides class differences, which I will address throughout the article, there were individual differences. All men did not engage in all the behaviors that I argue contribute to the construction of masculinity. One professional man said that while he talked "about what specific women are like," he did not talk about women in general and men who talked about what women are generally like "would not be my friends." Other men did not report the use of jokes and joking behavior in their friendships. Sociology frequently avoids discussion about individuals who do not participate in the behaviors that the sociologist argues shows the existence of meaningful social patterns. Unfortunately, doing so often reifies behavioral differences. This is a particular problem in the discussion of gender because there is currently (and happily for the existence of a lively, informed debate) a very close link between the results of social research on gender and broad social and political debates about men's and women's differences.

I wish, therefore, to give the reader a general indication of the individual variability in the gendered behaviors in which men engaged. In all the behaviors discussed below at least half, and frequently more, of the men participated in the behaviors whereas few women did. There were, however, individual exceptions to these behaviors, and those exceptions point to a flexibility in gendered behavior that, while not as expansive as many would wish, is broader than we frequently recognize. Current social theory about gender emphasizes the agentic nature of the construction of gender. It is a practice in which men and women have a considerable range of actions from which to choose. At given historical points, certain actions may be dictated more than others, and therefore individual men and women may frequently act in ways that conform to current ideology. But even when cultural ideology demands close adherence to particular practices, the practical nature of gender means that some individuals will not conform. Further, the multiplicity of practices that create gender enable individuals to maintain their positions within gender categories without much difficulty.

Men's Use of Public Space

The use of public space for informal and apparently unplanned socializing is much more common among men than among women, and it marks the gender boundaries between men and women. The frequent use of public space by working class men for informal socializing emerges in ethnographies of men's groups (Anderson, 1976; Komblum, 1974; Liebow, 1967; Whyte, 1981). Working-class men in this study met in public spaces such as local bars and playgrounds. There they talked about work and family, and they made informal connections with other men. Sometimes they picked up side work, sometimes they hung out. At the time of our interview, one working class man said that he spent some of his time at a local bar selling advertisements in a book to raise money for a large retirement dinner for a long-time coach of a community football team. He also spent time there drinking and talking to friends.

Working class men also met in semipublic spaces such as gyms or clubs. While membership in these spaces was frequently restricted, the spaces themselves functioned in similar ways to public spaces. Men met regularly and informally in public and semipublic spaces one or more times a week. Unlike women who made definite plans to meet friends occasionally in bars, the men assumed because of past practice that on particular nights of the week they would meet friends.

Wellman (1992) suggests that the use of public space for male socializing is diminishing, and men's friendships are becoming domesticated as their friendships move into the home and hence more like women's. This phenomenon of domestication was evident among professional respondents, most of whom reported socializing infrequently in public spaces. But it was not evident among the working class respondents in this study. All but one of the working class respondents had been brought up in the same communities in which they lived when I interviewed them. Among these men there were long-time, continuous patterns of public socializing. While Wellman's point is important, the domestication of male friendship seems to be influenced by circumstances in men's lives and is probably occurring unevenly. Further, barring significant structural changes in working class men's formal and informal work lives, the domestication of male friendships is unlikely to be complete.

Men's Telephone Use

Discussions of men's telephone use as a construction of gender make the most sense when contrasted with women's telephone use. Many men noted that their wives used the telephone very differently from them. A few, primarily working class men, stated that they disliked talking on the telephone, and they used it only for instrumental reasons (e.g., to make appointments or get specific information). Other men, both professional and working class, said their wives called friends just to see how they were doing and then talked for a long time, whereas men did not do so. Thus men ideologically constructed gender through their understandings of telephone practices. In addition, both men and women constructed gender behaviorally through using the telephone in different ways.

Telephone use differed slightly by class and work experiences, but even accounting for the effects of class and work, there were substantial gender differences. Men frequently reported that the purpose of their most recent telephone calls with friends were instrumental: lawyers discussed cases, men discussed upcoming social plans, and some working class men made plans to do side work together. Because of this instrumental motive for telephone calls to friends, many professional men reported that their frequent telephone contact was from their offices during working hours. Men rarely reported that they called friends just to say "hi" and find out how they were. One professional man, Mike,[2] reported differences between his wife and himself in being friends,

> I'm not friends the way she's friends. *How are you friends differently?* I don't work on

2. All names of the respondents have been changed.

them. I don't pick the phone up and call people and say, "How are you?"

While Mike reported that, in fact, he did call one friend to find out how he was doing at least once a year, most telephone contact was initiated when friends made plans to visit from out of town or he had business matters to discuss with friends. One result of this behavior was tremendous attrition in his friendship network over time. Mike was a gregarious man who reported many past and current friends, but he tended to lose touch with past friends once business reasons for keeping in touch with them diminished, even those who continued to live in Philadelphia. He only reported talking to two friends six or more times a year on the telephone. One of those friends was a man with whom he had professional ties, and they called one another when they did business. The other friend, Gene, was one of the few men who called friends for social conversations. The fairly frequent calls between Gene and Mike may have been initiated by Gene.

Gil, a working class man, usually spoke to friends on the phone to arrange meetings. Although he kept in touch with two friends largely through telephone use (he worked two jobs during the week and one of his friends worked on weekends— theirs was a telephone friendship), he said,

> I don't talk to them a long time because I'm not a phone person. I'd rather see them in person because I don't like holding the phone and talking because you really can't think of things to say too often on the phone, but when you're in person you can think of more things, cause I like prefer sitting and talk to a person face-to-face . . . I'll talk to people 10, 15 minutes sometimes, but I prefer not to if I can. But some you just can't get off the phone no matter what you do. And

you're like, "Uh, great, well, I'll talk to you a little bit later." And they go into another story. You know [my friend] Cindy will do that, Cindy is great for that. Now Joanne [my wife] can talk on the phone for two to three hours . . . And then the person she's with is not too far away so she could just walk over and talk, you know.

Peter, a young working class man, reported that he "avoided the phone as much as possible." He did not call friends to chat, and he only used the telephone for social chats with one friend, a woman:

> I'm not a phone person, but yeah, I do [talk to a specific friend] because she talks on the phone, she likes the phone so . . . She'll talk and I'll yes and no (laughs).

Peter did not do side jobs with other men, thus his reasons for using the telephone were sharply limited. Peter and Gil both reported that their telephone preferences were different from those of women they knew. Their general comment "I'm not a phone person" was a representation of their identity, and it was substantiated by their behavior that differs from women's behavior. Typically, working class men spoke on the telephone once or twice a week to those with whom they did side jobs. One man who ran a bookmaking business with a friend reported that they spoke several times a day about business. Men spoke much less frequently than that to friends for other reasons.

Although most men reported calling friends for instrumental reasons, many men reported that their telephone conversations were not limited to the reason for the call. During telephone calls men discussed their families or their work after they finished with their business. During telephone calls made to discuss social plans several men discussed infertility problems with their wives. Another complained to a friend about his marital problems during a phone call initiated to plan side work. One man called a friend to make plans for a birthday dinner for the caller's wife. During the conversation he told his friend how many feelings the interview I had with him had stirred up (the friend had referred me to him). These conversations, then, had several functions for men's friendships. The telephone was primarily considered a tool for business or to make social plans, but it was also used as means of communicating important personal information. Most men, however, deemphasized the telephone's function in the communication of personal information.

About one fourth of the men reported that they did call friends simply to find out how they were. Most of the time these men reported calling out-of-town friends with whom they lacked other regular means of contact, and most of the time their calls were infrequent—one to three times a year. In one exception, a professional man regularly called friends to see how they were (and sometimes became irritated and upset when the friends did not reciprocate by initiating some percentage of the telephone calls). He talked with one local friend once a week for no other reason than to keep in touch, but this pattern was unique. The friend he called had limited mobility, and the men rarely saw one another. The telephone was a primary vehicle for their friendship. In this instance, the two men's calls differed little from some women's calls.

There was tremendous variation in telephone use among men, but the variation does not erase the differences across genders. While only one quarter of the men in this study reported that they ever called friends to visit over the telephone and three quarters called for instrumental reasons, over four-fifths of the women reported that they called friends to visit. Also, men's reported frequency of telephoning friends was consistently lower than women's. Whereas two-thirds of all women reported that they spoke with at least one friend three or more times a week, less than one quarter of the men did so.

The finding that men use the telephone less than women and that women use it for social visiting has been noted by others (Fischer, 1992; Rakow, 1991). Fischer (1992) argues,

> research shows that, discounting their fewer opportunities for social contact, women are more socially adept and intimate than men, for whatever reasons—psychological constitution, social structure, childhood experiences or cultural norms. The telephone therefore fits the typical female style of personal interaction more closely than it does the typical male style (p. 235).

Fischer's comments may hold a clue about how ideologies of gender are maintained despite the evidence of intimate behaviors among men. Men and women both see the telephone as something women use more than men, and they see it as a way women are intimate. Men's telephone practices provided evidence to respondents that men are incapable of intimacy whereas women are very intimate with friends. Although women used the telephone more often for intimate conversation than men, men used opportunities at work and in public hangouts to talk intimately (one respondent reported that when they got together in the bar "we're worse than a bunch of girls when it comes to that [talking about their spouses]!"). Although telephone patterns are a poor measure of intimacy in friendship, men used them as such. Several men commented on hearing their wives call friends and talk about personal information. Doing so substantiated their impressions of women's friendships. Also, because the men focused on the reasons for their calls rather than on the contents of telephone calls, telephone use acted to provide confirmation that stereotypes about friendship are true.

Men's Jokes

Men's use of jokes is another way in which men construct their masculinity. In his ethnography, *America's Working Man*, David Halle (1984) points to several functions jokes serve among men: they reaffirm values of friendship and generosity, they ritually affirm heterosexuality among men whose social circumstances create a level of physical and emotional intimacy culturally regarded as unmasculine, and they mediate disputes. These functions were evident in the way working class men talked about jokes and humor in their friendships. They were less evident among the professional men, for reasons suggested by Halle.

Men friends, particularly working class men, used harsh teasing as a form of social control to reinforce certain behaviors. One working class man said that he and his friends were the worst "ball breakers" in the world. If a man did not show up at the bar or at some social event then my respondent said they heard about it from all their friends. Among these men the friendship group was highly valued, but also, like many contemporary friendships, somewhat fragile. Work and family responsibilities that kept men away from the friendship group might put a friend at risk of being teased.

Other men said that the failure to reciprocate favors, such as help with household projects, might be a basis for teasing friends. This was a particularly important way of defusing tension as well as reaffirming values of friendship for working-class

men. They frequently depended on friends to help them attain higher standards of living: friends provided craft services whose prices are high in the formal market and thus many working class people's material lives were somewhat improved through the help of friends. Failure to reciprocate had implications not only for friendship but also for family income. Jokes about a friend's failure to reciprocate became a public statement about his failure to conform to recognized norms, and they were a way for someone to handle his anger at his friend.

Another way jokes constructed masculinity was to highlight an activity that was outside the purview of men's activities that they nonetheless did. For instance, Greg and Chris were friends from law school who saw each other seven or eight times a year. One of those times was a yearly shopping trip to buy Christmas presents. Men generally claimed they did not shop—those who did usually said they went to hardware stores when they were doing a project with a friend. The shopping trip Greg and Chris went on was a traditional joke between them both. It began in law school when Greg asked Chris to go with him to buy a negligee for Greg's girlfriend. When they got to the store Chris ran away and Greg was left feeling terribly embarrassed. Ever since, they went shopping once a year, but both men downplayed the shopping aspect of the trips and highlighted the socializing. They said they did not accomplish very much on their trips. They also said they used the time to buy gag gifts for people instead of serious gifts. Turning the shopping spree into a joke subverted the meaning of shopping as something women do, and the trip became a ritual reaffirmation of masculinity.

Jokes were sometimes used as pseudoinstrumental reasons to call friends on the phone when men lacked instrumental reasons; they thus maintained the masculinity of men's telephone practices. Men called each other and told one another jokes and then moved into more personal topics. Gene, for instance, befriended Al's lover, Ken, before Al died of AIDS. During Al's illness Gene was an important source of support for both men, and he continued to keep in touch Ken after Al's death. They talked regularly on the telephone, but most of the conversations initiated by Ken began with jokes. After Ken and Gene had exchanged jokes the two men moved on to other topics, including their feelings for Al.

Finally, men used jokes to exaggerate gender differences and denigrate women. Gene considered himself sympathetic to women's issues. He said that he and his friends

> will tell in a joking way, tell jokes that are hostile towards feminism or hostile towards women. It's like there's two levels of it. One is, we think the joke is funny in and of itself or we think the joke is funny because it's so outrageously different from what's politically correct. You know, so we kind of laugh about it, and then we'll laugh that we even had the gall to tell it.

Not all men mentioned the importance of humor to friendship, the existence of jokes among friends, or the tendency to tease friends, but about half the respondents indicated that jokes and teasing were part of their friendship. Also, jokes and joking behavior were not limited solely to men. A few women also told jokes and engage in joking behavior with their friends, but men emphasized the behavior as part of their friendships, whereas women did not. Also, women reported using jokes in a much more restricted way than men. For men, jokes are an elaborated code with multiple meanings and functions.

Men Talk About Women

Finally, men constructed masculinity through their behavior with men friends through their talk about what women are like. While not every man reported that he engaged in discussions about women with his friends, most men did. Comments about women emphasized men's and women's differences. Men, for instance, discussed how their wives' had higher housekeeping standards than they, their wives' greater control over child rearing, and their greater propensity to spend money impulsively; they also discussed women's needs from relationships. These comments helped men interpret their relationships with their wives and served to reassure men that their experiences were not unusual.

> We would talk about like how long it would take them to get dressed . . . my wife took exceptionally long to get dressed, four or five hours in the bathroom. Um, but I mean, I don't think I talk a whole lot about women, when I did I guess I generalized and that kind of stuff, like how a wife expects a husband to kind of do everything for her. (Working class man)
>
> What we talked about was the differences, differences we have with our wives in terms of raising kids. . . . And how sometimes we feel, rightly or wrongly, we both agreed that we didn't have quite as much control over the situation or say in the situation as we might have liked . . . That's something that a lot of my friends who have younger kids, I've had that discussion with. I've talked to them about it in terms of something that I think mothers, in particular, have a different input into their child's lives than do fathers. (Professional man)

Through these sorts of discussions with men friends—some brief and jocular, some more sustained and serious—men defined who women are, and who they were, in contrast, as men. These discussions with friends frequently reinforced stereotypes about women and men.

Women were spendthrifts:

One individual may call me up and say, "Geez, my wife just went out and bought these rugs. I need that like a hole in the head. You know, this is great, I have these oriental rugs now, you know, I'm only going to spill coffee on it." (Professional man)

Women attempted to control men's free time:

[We might talk about] how much we're getting yelled at or in trouble or whatever, you know what I mean, for not doin' stuff around the house, or workin' over somebody else's house too much or staying out at the bars too late. (Working class man)

Women were manipulative:

Sometimes they seem, they don't know what they want, or what they want is something different than what they tell you they want. You know, tough to figure out, [we say] that they can be manipulative . . . Conniving. (Professional man)

Men evaluated women's behaviors and desires through such talk. They reported that such talk was a way of getting feedback on their marital experiences. Talking with friends frequently relieved the tensions men felt in their cross-gender relationships, and it did so without requiring men to change their behaviors vis-a-vis women. Men rarely reported that they accommodated themselves to their wives because their friends suggested that they should: in an unusual case, one working class man said his friend told him that women needed to be told, "I love you," all the time, and he thought his friend had been helpful in mitigating some strains in his marriage through their talk.

More frequently, men's jokes and comments about women—about their demands for more housekeeping help, their ways with money, and their desires to have men home more often—served to delegitimize women's demands. Men talked about women as unreasonable; as one man above said, "everybody needs time away." This tendency to delegitimize wives' demands was more apparent among working class men than among the professional men. Professionals reported that their jobs, not unreasonable wives, prevented them from greater involvement in child care, and they sometimes talked with friends about this as an inevitable part of professional life. The effect, however, was similar because talk among both professional and working class men friends supported the status quo. Instead of becoming a problem to be solved, professional men and their friends determined that professional life unfortunately, but inevitably, caused men to limit their family involvement. (One man who consistently seemed to play with the boundaries of masculinity had tried to solve the problem through scheduling his work flexibly along the lines that a friend had suggested. He reported that he still did not have enough time for his family.)

These four behaviors: using public spaces for friendship socializing, men's telephone practices, joking, and talking about women in particular ways are some ways that men construct masculinity in their friendships. There are many others. Discussions of sports, for instance, are one obvious other way men construct their masculinity, and such discussions were common among respondents. Like women's telephone use and ease with intimacy, men's talk about sports has become part of our cultural ideology about gendered friendships. Not all respondents, however, participated in such talk, and of those who did, some did not enjoy such talk but engaged in it because it was expected.

Cultural Ideology of Men and Friendship

When I began this article I asked not only how men construct masculinity through their behaviors but also why there was a discrepancy between the cultural ideology of men's friendships, which maintains that men do not share intimate thoughts and feelings with one another, and reports of specific behaviors that show that they do. It is in part by recognizing that the construction of gender is an ongoing activity that incorporates many disparate behaviors that this question becomes answerable. While one behavior in an interaction may violate the norms of gender ideology, other behaviors are simultaneously conforming to other ideologies of masculinity. When men reflect back on their behavior they emphasize those aspects of their behavior that give truth to their self-images as men. The other behavior may be reported, but, in this study, it did not discredit men's gender ideologies.

Second, as I noted earlier, masculinity is frequently reified, and behavior that does not conform does not affect the overall picture of masculinity. Men belong in the gender category to which they were assigned at birth, and their past in that category reassures them that they belong there. Occasionally respondents recognized that men do things that contradict gender ideol-

ogy. One man told me about a friend of his who "does thoughtful things for other men." When I asked what he did, and he said:

> Uh, remembers their birthdays. Will buy them gifts. Uh, and does it in a way that's real, I think, really, uh, I don't know, it's not uh, it's not uh, feminine in the sense of, feminine, maybe in the perjorative sense . . . I mean, I remember that John, uh, John's nurturing I saw, not that I was a recipient of it so much although I was in his company a lot and got to see him. Uh, I thought, boy, this guy's a, this guy's a real man, this guy. This guy's all right, you know.

Though my respondent identified his friend's behavior as different, almost feminine, he made sure to tell me that the man is a "real man." This seemed problematic for him, his language became particularly awkward, full of partial sentences. But in the end, the fact that his friend was a man and that my respondent liked and respected him enabled him to conclude, "this guy's a real man."

At other times, recognition that behavior contradicts gender ideology elicits censure instead of acceptance. When men censure one another for such behavior, they reinforce the idea that such behavior is anomalous and should not be expressed. For instance, Gene, who consciously worked at intimacy with his friends, told me about sitting and drinking with a friend of his one night when Gene was depressed. His friend asked him how things were going and Gene told him he was depressed because he was feeling financial pressures. Gene felt "house poor" and upset with himself for buying a house that would cause him to feel such pressures when he had determined that he would not do such a thing.

His friend's response was, "Oh, that's the last time I ask you how you're feeling." On an earlier occasion Gene called his gay friend in California on the telephone crying because he had just broken off with a woman he had been dating. His friend comforted him at the time, but later he said, "I didn't know you had it in you [to express yourself like that]." Gene believed that men had greater difficulties with self-disclosure than women, and these events acted as support for his beliefs instead of counterexamples. In both cases friends had let him know his self-disclosing behavior was either intolerable or unusual. His gay friend seemed to admire Gene's ability to call him up in tears by giving him a back-handed compliment, but this was a man who had rejected many norms of heterosexuality, and who saw Gene as participating in hegemonic masculinity (Connell, 1987) and teased him for it. Gene's interpretation of these events coincided with his friends: he was behaving in ways men normally did not.

In another case, Anna, a woman respondent, told me about her husband Tom's experience with his best friend. Anna had been diagnosed with a serious chronic illness that had profound consequences for her lifestyle, and Tom was depressed about it. One night he went out with two friends, Jim, Tom's best friend, and another man who was unhappy about his recent divorce. According to Anna, Jim commented that he wished he did not know either Tom or the other man at the time because they were both so depressed. From this, Anna said she and Tom concluded that men did not express their feelings and were not as intimate with one another as women were.

These sorts of events reinforce men's notions that men are emotionally distant. Self-disclosure and attempts to express one's feelings are seen as anomalous, even if desirable—desirable because the contempo-

rary evaluation on friendship as defined primarily by feminists is that women have better friendships than men. Women, by the way, also reported occasions when their friends were unsympathetic to their expressions of distress. The conclusions women and men drew about their unsympathetic friendship differed, however. Women concluded that particular friends lacked sympathy. Unlike men, they did not think their expressive behavior was inappropriate or unusual.

Conclusion

I have conceptualized gender as an ongoing social creation rather than a role individuals learn or a personality type they develop that causes differences in behavior. Individuals construct gender on an ideological and a behavioral level. On a behavioral level, many social acts contribute to the overall construction of masculinity. Men do not talk on the phone unless they have something specific they wish to find out or arrange. Men friends joke around together. Men hang out in bars. Men also talk about women and their wives in ways that distinguish women from men and define gender tensions and men's solutions to them. Some of these behaviors have become part of the cultural ideology of men's friendships. Respondents, for instance, talked generally about differences between men's and women's telephone use. Some also said that women stayed home with their friends whereas men went out. But the relationship between behavior and ideology is not so direct and simple that behaviors in which most men participate become part of the cultural ideology. To the extent that talking about women, for instance, is perceived as sharing personal information, then talking about women is something men do not recognize as characteristic of their friendships.

Because so many actions construct masculinity and gender is a practice over which individuals have some control, the failure to conform to the cultural ideology of masculine friendship does not necessarily threaten either the cultural ideology or the individual's position in the masculine gender category. This becomes particularly important in understanding why the many men who share personal information with friends continue to believe that men are inexpressive and find intimacy difficult. I have found that the exchange of intimate information, is something most respondents, men and women, engaged in, but most people also did it with selected friends. Furthermore, talking about personal matters or sharing feelings frequently constituted a small portion of all friendship interaction. Thus, for men whose identities included a notion that they, as men, were not open with friends, the times when they were open were insignificant. There were many other activities of friendship that men preferred to emphasize.

It is useful to expand the debate over gender differences in friendship to include behaviors other than intimacy that has dominated the recent literature on gender and friendship (Allan, 1989; Miller, 1983; Rawlins, 1992; Rubin, 1985; Sherrod, 1987; Swain, 1987). The narrowness of the debate has limited our understandings of why men's friendships have been meaningful and important to them. Working class men's reliance on friends for services and material support becomes invisible. The importance of joking behavior as a communicative style and its functions in maintaining stable relationships for both working class and professional men disappear. Finally, the narrow debate over intimacy obscures some implications of how men talk to one another

about women for gender relations and inequality.

References

Allan, G. (1989). *Friendship: Developing a sociological perspective.* Boulder, CO: Westview.

Anderson, E. (1976). *A place on the corner.* Chicago: University of Chicago Press.

Aukett R., Ritchie, J., & Mill, K. (1988). Gender differences in friendship patterns. *Sex Roles, 19,* 57–66.

Caldwell, M. A., & Peplau, L. A. (1982). Sex differences in same-sex friendships. *Sex Roles, 8,* 721–732.

Connell, R. W. (1987). *Gender and power.* Stanford, CA: Stanford University Press.

Fischer, C. (1992). *America calling: A social history of the telephone to 1940.* Berkeley: University of California Press.

Franklin, C. W. II (1992). Friendship among Black men. In P. Nardi (Ed.), *Men's Friendships* (pp. 201–214). Newbury Park, CA: Sage.

Hacker, H. M. (1981). Blabbermouths and clams: Sex differences in self-disclosure in same-sex and cross-sex friendship dyads. *Psychology of Women Quarterly, 5,* 385–401.

Halle, D. (1984). *America's working man: Work, home, and politics among blue-collar property owners.* Chicago: University of Chicago Press.

Hansen, K. V. (1992). Our eyes behold each other: masculinity and intimate friendship in antebellum New England. In P. Nardi (Ed.), *Men's friendships* (pp. 35–58). Newbury Park, CA: Sage.

Kornblum, W. (1974). *Blue collar community.* Chicago: University of Chicago Press.

Liebow, E. (1967). *Tally's corner: A study of Negro street-corner men.* Boston: Little, Brown.

Leidner, R. (1991). Serving hamburgers and selling insurance: gender, work, and identity in interactive service jobs. *Gender & Society, 5,* 154–177.

Miller, M. (1983). *Men and friendship.* Boston: Houghton Mifflin.

O'Meara, J. D. (1989). Cross-sex friendship: Four basic challenges of an ignored relationship. *Sex Roles, 21,* 525–543.

Rakow, L. F. (1991). *Gender on the line: Women, the telephone, and community life.* Urbana, IL: University of Illinois Press.

Rawlins, W. (1992). *Friendship matters: Communication, dialectics, and the life course.* New York: Aldine de Gruyter.

Reid, H. M., & Fine, G. A. (1992). Self-disclosure in men's friendships. In P. Nardi (Ed.), *Men's friendships* (pp. 132–152). Newbury Park, CA: Sage.

Rubin, L. (1985). *Just friends: The role of friendship in our lives.* New York: Harper & Row.

Sherrod, D. (1987). The bonds of men: Problems and possibilities in close male relationships. In H. Brod (Ed.), *The making of masculinities* (pp. 213–239). Boston: Allen and Unwin.

Swain, S. (1989). Covert intimacy: Closeness in men's friendships. In B. Risman & P. Schwartz (Eds.), *Gender and intimate relationships,* (pp. 71–86). Belmont, CA: Wadsworth.

Walker, K. (1994). Men, women and friendship: what they say; what they do. *Gender & Society, 8,* 246–265.

Wellman, B. (1992). Men in networks: private communities, domestic friendships. In P. Nardi (Ed.), *Men's friendships* (pp. 74–114). Newbury Park, CA: Sage.

West, C., & Zimmerman, D. (1987). Doing gender. *Gender & Society, 1,* 125–151.

Whyte, W. F. (1981). *Street corner society: The social structure of an Italian slum* (3rd ed.). Chicago: The University of Chicago Press.

Williams, C. L., & Heikes, E. J. (1993). The importance of researcher's gender in the in-depth interview: Evidence from two case studies of male nurses. *Gender & Society, 7,* 280–291.

Wright, P. (1982). Men's friendships, women's friendships and the alleged inferiority of the latter. *Sex Roles, 8,* 1–20.

13

Gendered Dynamics in the Romantic Relationships of Lesbians and Gay Men

Michelle Huston and Pepper Schwartz

Romantic relationships between heterosexual men and women are subject to gender role expectations which organize dating behavior, sexuality, communication, housework, childcare, and decision making. For example, men are expected to initiate dating and sex, while women are expected to be responsible for the childcare and housework **(gender role effects)**. Huston and Schwartz examine what happens in romantic relationships that cannot be organized by gender roles because the partners are of the same sex. They find that gay and lesbian couples are less constrained by gender roles than heterosexual couples, but face the challenge of creating their own patterns for dividing responsibilities and rights in a relationship **(cultural diversity)**. An added difficulty in gay and lesbian relationships is the fact that both members of the couple have been socialized into the same gender role, and so may lack certain relationship skills. For example, lesbians as women are

not raised with the idea that they should initiate dating, and so it may be difficult for them to begin a romantic relationship. It is necessary, then, for gay men and lesbians to find ways to overcome the shortcomings of their gender role socialization. Because gay men and lesbians create relationships outside of the conventional heterosexual model **(defined norm)**, and overcome their gender role socialization, Huston and Schwartz argue that they can serve as models for all of us who wish for more egalitarian relationships with less rigid gender roles.

Questions to Consider:

1. What do Huston and Schwartz mean when they argue that gender is "contextual?"
2. To what extent have your relationships been organized by conventional

gender roles? What changes in conventional gender roles seem the most challenging?

3. Huston and Schwartz make the point that there is a lack of research on gay and lesbian romantic relationships. If you were to do research in this area, what would you see as the most important issue to study? Justify your choice.

4. Imagine you are a marriage counselor working with either a gay male couple or a lesbian couple. Based on what you have learned from this reading, what unique issues might you have to address?

As children, many of us played "house" at one time or another. One of the first things to be decided when playing house was who would be the mommy and who would be the daddy. Once these roles were cast, the make-believe activities of "house" could run smoothly, with mommy staying home and cleaning and cooking, while daddy went to work and made money. But how would we have organized our "house" if we didn't have the preset social roles of mommy and daddy to play? Or what would we have done if there were two mommies or two daddies? This is a question many couples must answer, when "house" is no longer make-believe but instead the day-to-day reality of adulthood.

The interplay between gender and homosexuality is interesting, and it can be explored at several levels. A fair amount of research has looked at the gender (or gender orientation) of homosexuals on the individual level, while a much smaller body of literature has investigated the roles lesbians and gay men play within their relationships. The concept of "playing a role" is important, for it emphasizes the contextual nature of our behavior. That is, we often behave as our interpretation of the situation suggests we should, rather than out of some biological or psychological predetermination. From this perspective, "gender roles" are the behaviors and traits we think others expect of us as women or men. You can probably think of many things that our culture presumes men should or should not do or be: They shouldn't cry, they should work hard to support their families, and they should act as leaders. Conversely, women shouldn't be too aggressive, they should place the care of their children (and their husbands) ahead of their own careers, and they should be good at understanding other people. Notice that these roles help make the organization of heterosexual relationships more predictable and efficient. For example, women are expected to provide certain types of housework (cooking, laundry, and most child care), while men are expected to be responsible for other types (maintenance of the yard, cars, and plumbing). Between the two sets of roles, most (or all) tasks necessary for life are conveniently assigned to one partner or the other, with little need for negotiation.

When studying any couple, the question of gender involves both an individual's adherence to stereotypes the culture prescribes for his or her sex and the roles people play relative to one another. Gender dynamics are especially intriguing in the interaction of gay and lesbian couples. If Beth and Susan make a home together, who cares for the yard? If John and Steve are a couple, who cleans the bathroom? In traditional heterosexual relationships, these questions are not likely to arise. In homosexual couples, partners need to arrive at some solution so that the work gets done—but they can't rely on conventional notions of "women's work" or "men's work" to make that solution "obvious."

Traditional femininity and masculinity often shape heterosexual relationships in such a way that complementarity on a basic level is ensured. Gender roles assure that necessary tasks are taken care of in a two-partner, heterosexual partnership: Children are cared for primarily by the mother, while financial security is provided primarily by the father. Partners are also trained for separate spheres of responsibility for the relationship: She sees to its emotional needs by working hard at being a good listener, and a faithful reader of body language and other nonverbal cues, while he is responsible for sexual initiation and much of the large decision making (England & Farkas, 1986; Wood, 1994a). If there are disagreements, the male has the final say. In gay and lesbian relationships, however, this traditionally gendered division of labor cannot be assigned on the basis of the partners' sex(es).

There are also interesting dilemmas facing gay and lesbian couples because as women and men they are often socialized to lack (or have deficiencies in) certain components that are central to many relationships. If, for example, both women have internalized the norm that women should not be sexual initiators, and that an overt interest in sexual behavior is "wrong," then how do lesbians ever manage to have sex? If both men in a relationship have internalized the norm that men should not show emotions related to fear, unhappiness, and uncertainty, then how do gay men manage to communicate their apprehensions about love, work, family, and all the other issues that arise for modern adults? The lessons learned (sometimes subconsciously) by members of gay and lesbian relationships can teach us a great deal about all men and women and about the options available to them in their own lives. Becoming more sexually assertive, more emotionally revealing, and more communicative are goals that might benefit all individuals and, by exten-

sion, most couples. However, these goals revolve around the notion of gender and how individuals learn and relearn gender through the course of life.

The goal of this chapter is to introduce you to the many ways gays and lesbians organize their romantic relationships, and to point out how gender affects and is affected by this organization. Much of the data on gay and lesbian relationships are limited. Until the 1960s, the study of homosexuality focused on questions of etiology with an eye toward "curing" the wayward soul. Although researchers have moved away from this judgmental vein, it is still difficult to receive funding for large-scale, in-depth studies. Therefore, our work is restricted to either small samples for which statistical analyses would be impossible, or large samples for which we can collect only the most cursory data. While the HIV/AIDS crisis has focused public interest (and hence research dollars) on the intimate lives of gay men, research on lesbians is more rare.

We should also point out that sexuality is an often misunderstood component of our lives. While some people spend their whole lives as strictly homosexuals or heterosexuals, most people tend not to fit that description. Many people who identify themselves as lesbians have had sexual intercourse with men in their past and have sometimes married; some gay men marry women. People who identify themselves as homosexual today may in the future find they are attracted to a person of the opposite sex and act on that attraction. The converse is true of heterosexuals: Many will have some passing interest or even a sexual encounter with someone of their own sex, and may or may not continue to consider themselves strictly heterosexual. Even people who use a specific label for themselves may behave in ways that would seem to make that label inappropriate. The majority (although by no means all) of the research conducted about gays and lesbians uses self-identification as the primary determinant of who qualifies to participate in the study, yet self-identification does not always predict behavior or vice versa.

Gender in the Intimate Relationships of Homosexuals

We begin this section on relationships where the vast majority of modern American couples begin: dating and courtship. Although often a fun and exciting activity, finding a partner is rarely a completely pain-free process. The road to couplehood is often fraught with miscues, wrong turns, and dead-ends. Heterosexual men and women, however, have scripts that help make dating relationships a bit more predictable. For example, it is still the case that, in general, the man makes the "first move" by asking someone out, while it is up to the woman to turn him down or accept his offer. In general, it is still the man who attempts to increase the level of sexual intimacy with his sexual partner, and the woman who "puts on the brakes" (or not).

While some types of casual relationships are scripted in the world of gay dating, not all are, and not all aid the level of predictability in the situation, as we will soon see. The dating and courtship rituals of gay men and lesbians are, not surprisingly, affected by these "scripts," as well as by the gender identity of the individuals involved.

Although some stereotypes of gay men suggest otherwise, most lesbians and gay men report that they would like to "settle down" in a long-term relationship at some point in their life. However, the act of finding a permanent partner is not always easy. In isolated, rural areas (and some urban areas as well), gay and lesbian orga-

nizations and meeting places do not exist; hence, the most likely sources of finding others with similar sexual orientations and goals are not available. Furthermore, because homosexuals in isolated areas are more likely to be closeted because of the lack of any sort of gay community, even knowing who is gay and who is not is problematic. Even in those urban settings in which we find large gay populations, meeting potential partners is not always a simple process. A large number of people remain "in the closet," and finding partners in bars and gay-oriented meetings necessarily limits the population of potential partners to people who feel comfortable in such settings. Once a person decides to look for a partner, how does she or he do so, and is the process affected by gender?

The lesbian dating game can be tricky. Lesbian bars are not as common as gay bars, and hence women cannot always count on them as a way to meet potential partners. Furthermore, lesbian bars primarily serve as gathering places for already-established lesbian couples, and the norms governing the behavior that occurs within them generally favor socializing instead of overt, aggressive attempts to pick someone up. Because lesbians tend to go to bars in couples, finding unattached lesbians is unlikely. Therefore, lesbians tend to rely more on friendship circles, mutual acquaintances, and participation in lesbian and women's political groups for chances to meet prospective partners (Vetere, 1982).

Not surprisingly, gender has an impact on this process. For example, women who adhere to the traditional feminine role may find the thought of going to a lesbian bar very unattractive. They are required to go out at night, often to areas of the city that are not entirely safe for a lone woman (or even a group of women); furthermore, many people do not like the atmosphere of bars—they can be smoky, loud, and full of inebriated people. These women may also not feel comfortable in the realm of political activism, and thus may keep their distance from such organizations. Finally, the feminine gender role prohibits interest in same-sex behavior; in fact, norms surrounding female sexuality in general tend to put women in a reactionary role. In short, they are untrained and hence frequently uncomfortable making the first move toward a potential partner. This is one reason so many lesbian relationships develop from already existing friendships. It eliminates the necessity of straightforward romantic courting, although admitting and pursuing interest is no easy task even with a friend.

Although men may be socialized to handle the potentially ego-bruising chore of expressing interest (or at least more resigned to the task), and the culture of gay bars streamlines the process of finding a sexual partner, these two facts can also undermine long-term relationships. First, men are socialized to be the initiators, and taking the role of the one who is approached may seem foreign and undesirable to them—so much so that they may refrain from pursuing relationships in which they were the ones asked out. Furthermore, while the gay bar subculture has made finding a casual sexual partner relatively uncomplicated, it has also made finding a long-term companion rather difficult. Because male homosexuality has often included the endorsement of anonymous sex, the culture surrounding it has developed norms that tend to work against long-term relationships (Silverstein, 1981; Tuller, 1978). For example, most gay men pride themselves on their appearance, and tend to prefer partners who are also strikingly handsome (Deaux & Hanna, 1984). Although perhaps gratifying in the short-run, attractiveness is not a trait that ensures the durability of a relationship.

Until recently, even those gay men who managed to form long-term relationships were not well supported within their communities. Singlehood was, and in most places still is, the norm.

Maintaining Relationships

Once the rocky road of courtship is navigated, the work of maintaining a relationship begins. Although a great deal can be said about homosexual couples, we will explore only those aspects of relationships that are affected by or reflect the element of gender identity and roles.

Theoretically, homosexual couples have several options in organizing their relationships. For example, individuals can choose partners whose gender typing complements their own, which is usually referred to as "butch–femme" role playing. In this arrangement, a feminine woman and a masculine woman partner, and each plays the traditional role corresponding to her gender identity. This sorting by preexisting gender identities, although often found in stereotypes, is not common in real life. Many studies find that over 90% of the lesbians questioned desire egalitarian relationships, a quality difficult to maintain in butch–femme arrangements because the notion of "butch" is tied into elements of power and control, while "femme" is akin to dependency and submission. Nonetheless, there remain some lesbians who are happy with relationships organized in this way, most of whom grew up in the first half of this century before the widespread feminist critique of gender roles.

Even for those women of more recent generations who have reclaimed some aspects of the feminine role (so-called "lipstick lesbians"), gender typing does not run deep. In fact, even when we know the gender identity of an individual who identifies as homosexual, we cannot accurately predict his or her sex-role behavior within the relationship (Blumstein & Schwartz, 1983; Cardell, Finn, & Maracek, 1981). This suggests that gender is fluid and often contextually situated: The woman who wears the lipstick might also be the one to change the oil in the car or take out the trash.

We know even less about this type of relationship among gay men. However, we would suggest that again there may be a cohort effect, with much older men being more likely to arrange their lives in this manner. Some gay couples also display some elements of "butch–femme" in that an older, established man trades his wealth, experience, and leadership for the youth and attractiveness of a much younger partner, whereby the older man is seen as the provider for the couple and displays the younger man's attractiveness and youth as a "prize." Of course, this type of couple is also found among heterosexuals.

Another option is to create nongendered roles after the couple is established. In this case, once a couple is formed, they organize their home life and relationship around a division of labor in which each partner has a fixed set of chores and duties for which he or she alone is responsible. Although not as confining as heterosexual norms, this style of organization can still benefit one partner over the other if one person gets stuck doing all the "dirty work."

Another way homosexual couples can deal with their freedom from gendered relationship roles is by creating new divisions of labor, in which each partner does what she does best, with the unwanted chores shared evenly between the two. These relationships tend to be more egalitarian, at least when power is measured by who bears responsibility for what household tasks. However, when we look at specific examples of role sharing, we find that some attempts are more successful than others. We now turn to these concrete examples of effective communication, division of housework, and sexual relations.

Organization of Communication

Many people have suggested that men and women communicate differently: Women are taught to nurture conversation, to listen well, and to support their conversational partner, while men are taught that conversation is a way to display their own importance, to achieve status, or to arrive at definitive conclusions by following the rule "might makes right." Research on the communication styles of men and women in conversation with one another pinpoints different elements of conversation that can be defined as part of either a "masculine" or a "feminine" style of communicating. For example, men tend to interrupt their partner more (which is one way to retain the privilege of putting forth their own ideas), they tend to talk more, and they tend to fill lulls in the conversation with noncommittal "uh-huhs" (called minimal responses), which signal their disinterest in what the other person is saying. Women, on the other hand, tend to interrupt less, respond more to others, and use tag lines, which are questions at the end of their own statements that invite the other person to interject her or his own opinion.

Some theorists have suggested that different communication styles are a result of psychological differences between men and women, while others have pointed to the idea that men and women are raised in different cultures: one of power and privilege, another of powerlessness and servitude (Wood, 1994a). Other scholars have suggested that it may not be just gender that influences conversational style; it may be that power mediates the effects of gendered communication styles (Kollock, Blumstein, & Schwartz, 1985; Lakoff, 1990). In other words, it could simply be that men traditionally have more power in their relationships (both intimate and professional) than women, and this power allows them to communicate in a direct, confident way. One way to control for this factor is to study relationships in which power differentials occur, but in which sex (and by extension, gender to some degree) is held constant. Gay and lesbian relationships provide such an opportunity.

Women are often the caregivers in their relationships—they are taught to feel responsible for the well-being of those relationships (Wood, 1994b). Usually women develop skills that help them in this endeavor: They are good listeners, and they learn to "read" subtle communication cues that help them interpret and predict the needs of their companions. By and large, lesbians have learned these skills well, and their conversational style reflects this fact. They tend to avoid challenging one another (Clunis & Green, 1988; Tannen, 1990), they do not interrupt as often as other couples (Kollock et al., 1985), and the less powerful partner uses fewer tag questions.

However, because lesbians tend to use communication as a way to achieve emotional intimacy, this goal often supersedes other functions of conversation, such as solving problems or reaching agreements about disputed issues. Because confrontation and dominance tend to work against the main goal of augmenting intimacy, and because they are not emphasized in feminine speech cultures, lesbians sometimes suffer from an inability to deal constructively with problems (Becker, 1988; Clunis & Green, 1988). They find it difficult to express discontent or ask for change. Hence,

while lesbian communication tends to be warm and supportive, it may not always be effective for resolving painful differences of opinion or creating change. Partners may also feel suffocated if conversations return again and again to matters of emotional intimacy and to how each person feels about the relationship.

Communication between gay men is often influenced by the speech patterns common to most men, gay or straight. This is particularly true when the couple is trying to resolve a problem or talk over an issue about which the partners disagree. These "discussions" can take on great symbolic meaning, turning into a battlefield on which each partner tries to win the upper hand and assert or display his own dominance (Blumstein & Schwartz, 1983). If this is the case, winning is more important than resolution, and simple disagreements can evolve into serious arguments for which there seem to be no answers that satisfy both men's desire to dominate. One gender difference that remains even after controlling for power is that men resist others' attempts to interrupt them. Powerful gay men have a very low rate of successful interrupting, which suggests that their less powerful partners will not yield the floor even when the other person tries to take it by conversational force (Kollock et al., 1985). Consequently, gay men in couples have to work hard to build trust and intimacy because at least one of the traditional routes through which emotional closeness is formed (that is, communication) is problematic.

Power and the Organization of Housework and Decision Making

The vast majority of lesbians and gay men espouse an ideology of equality: They want their relationships to be based on an egalitarian model in which both partners have equal say in decision making, assume equal responsibilities for housework, and share the privileges and rights generated in the relationship. In most heterosexual relationships, power imbalances are an expected part of life: The man, by virtue of his greater earning power (and usually greater earnings) and also simply by convention, tends to have the "upper hand" in decision making, and is exempt from most of the responsibility for housework and child care. Gays and lesbians make concerted efforts to avoid such an imbalance; however, they are not always successful.

Lesbians are more likely to succeed at maintaining egalitarian relationships than gay men (Kurdek, 1993). In part, this could be due to the fact that women are not taught to measure their own worth by the amount of money they make, and do not apply that criteria to other women. It could also be related to the depressed, and hence more similar, earning power of women; in short, they are more likely than gay men to have incomes close to one another. Even when a large gap between incomes occurs, money is not correlated with power in lesbian relationships (Blumstein & Schwartz, 1983; Lynch & Reilly, 1985/86). Gay men, however, do measure power by income, and the partner who earns more tends to have more say in decision making and does less housework than his partner. This can become problematic when the partner making less money believes he should have as much influence as his partner in making decisions, or when he feels financially dependent on his partner. This is especially true when the more wealthy partner's income allows a luxurious lifestyle to which the poorer partner can contribute little.

In general, gay men and lesbians do not allocate household chores along the same lines as heterosexuals, that is, with the bulk of the work being assigned to one partner. Instead, gay men tend to divide the number of chores they do evenly between the two—carving out "separate but equal" domains based on preference and ability. Lesbians, on the other hand, are likely to share all the tasks relatively equitably—either taking turns or doing the chore together (Kurdek, 1993). For example, gay men might settle on an arrangement in which one is primarily responsible for preparing meals while the other cleans up afterward. Lesbians are more likely to cook the meal together and both clean up, or trade the jobs back and forth. Interestingly, while household labor is associated with elevated levels of psychological distress among married women, housework is negatively associated with distress for lesbians, perhaps because the context in which lesbians perform these duties is one in which they had some say and their partners also do housework. Wives, on the other hand, are traditionally expected to perform these chores with little or no recourse for change and with little, if any, help from partners (Hochschild with Machung, 1989; Kurdek, 1993).

In heterosexual relationships in which children are present, the mother is usually the primary caretaker of those children (despite the growing number of fathers who are trying to be more involved in their children's lives). The role of caretaker is extremely understudied in gay and lesbian relationships, probably because it was assumed for a long time that homosexuals did not have children. However, a large minority of lesbians are also parents, as are some gay men. For the most part, these children were conceived during heterosexual marriages, before the person "came out."

Very little is known about the way in which gay men and lesbians divide child-rearing tasks. Among lesbians, children—

and the chores that come with them—are often wanted by both partners. The biological mother in lesbian couples often has greater power than her partner when it comes to making large decisions and is less dependent on the relationship (Moore, Blumstein, & Schwartz, 1994). This element of the division of labor is ripe for study, and few (if any) researchers have explored the mechanisms by which child-care responsibilities are allocated.

Organization of Sex

While for some people sex can be a simple, uncomplicated act, most people discover that it is often bound tightly to emotions. What happens during sex can carry over into the rest of the relationship, or reflect the relationship's strengths and weaknesses in a microcosm. Furthermore, because men and women are usually raised with different understandings of the meanings and purpose of sex, gender has a profound impact on the organization of sex in the intimate relationships of lesbians and gay men.

In fact, we see the least amount of equality for lesbians in the organization of sex. Most lesbians espouse the ideal of equal right of initiation and refusal, usually because of their conscious rejection of "male" behaviors—including those associated with being sexually aggressive and passionate. However, few couples achieve this balance. Most couples tend to fall into patterns in which one person generally takes the role of sexual initiator, which can cause a variety of problems. Even the women comfortable in this role may grow to resent the responsibility of it, and wish their partners would shoulder some of the burden and risk of expressing interest. Conversely, the noninitiating partner may become dissatisfied with her role and with the obligation of having the final say about having sex (often hurt-

ing the initiator's feelings unintentionally). Interestingly, the more emotionally expressive partner (hence, by many tests, the more "feminine" one) tends to take responsibility for making sexual overtures (probably because lesbian sex usually starts with displays of affection), and it is usually the more powerful partner who refuses (Blumstein & Schwartz, 1983).

Gay men are not exempt from issues surrounding gender roles and sex, although their problems differ from those of lesbians. Men are trained to be initiators, but this leads to potential problems when both partners think that they should be the one to make the advance, and that by not making the advance they're somehow surrendering part of their masculinity. Furthermore, refusing sex can become a power play by which one partner tries to assert his own dominance of the situation (or the relationship). However, this is a less satisfying position to be in because refusing sex is not a sanctioned part of the male sexual role. If these issues are not resolved, sex can become a highly significant and symbolic battleground on which the partners spar for control, and more distantly, for the assertion of their own masculinity.

Specific sex acts can also take on symbolic meaning, although these meanings differ from one man to another. For example, some men who perform oral sex say it makes them feel powerful and in control, while other men say they feel most masculine and dominant while *receiving* oral sex. As with lesbians, reciprocity of oral sex is expected; if men do not rotate this responsibility, resentment can arise. Anal intercourse is a bit less ambiguous. Although there exists no evidence to suggest that sexual position (being the penetrator or penetratee) is related to overall gender identity, most men report that they feel differently, depending on the role they are taking during that moment of intercourse. Men report that they tend to feel more feminine and more passive when receiving anal sex, and more dominant and in control when they are the penetrators. Thus, power and masculinity can be implicated in sexual position and can have greater import than one might think (Blumstein & Schwartz, 1983).

Implicit in the discussion above is the notion that gender identity is influenced by context. For gay men, playing a given role during anal intercourse will connote certain feelings of maleness or femaleness that are not a part of their everyday routine. A similar phenomenon is found among lesbians. Rosenzweig and Lebow (1992) found that only a small part of their sample could be classified as "feminine" using a conventional measure of gender identity in a global context. However, when they used the same scale to measure gender identity within the specific context of sexual activity, nearly half the sample fell into the "feminine" category, and most of the rest were classified as "androgynous" (which means they scored above the mean for the measure of masculinity and the measure of femininity). The authors suggest that this migration toward femininity when it comes to matters of sex could be due to the restrictive and heavily sanctioned nature of the norms surrounding female sexual behavior. However, they have found evidence that a "feminine" style of sex (which emphasizes a caring, gentle, sensitive approach to lovemaking) is more rewarding and satisfying. More research is necessary in this area before any definitive conclusions can be made, however.

Conclusion

In conclusion, while gay men and lesbians are freed from many of the conventional ways of organizing relationships because sex does not automatically prescribe roles, they must also bear the responsibility of creating their own schemes for deciding how to divide responsibilities and rights within relationships. Often, they must also form ways of dealing with the deficits that socialization into one gender role produces. Although not impossible, this often presents challenges.

We can all learn from how these challenges are met. Those who wish to establish more egalitarian heterosexual relationships can use those models developed by gay men and lesbians, which demonstrate that equitable division of labor is not only rewarding, but also possible. Two gay men, both of whom work full time, still manage to keep their toilets clean and the dishes done. If they can do it, so can husbands and male partners of heterosexual women. Beyond applying the lessons learned from gay men and lesbians to relationships, we might learn something about the contextual nature of gender. While each individual's upbringing undoubtedly differs, we are all part of a culture that holds rather strict notions about what it means to be men and women. Many lesbians and gay men demonstrate that it is possible to overcome that socialization and to learn new ways of looking at ourselves, our relationships to intimate partners, and our relationship to the larger society. Women can learn to be independent, assertive, and self-confident without giving up their ability to nurture and feel empathy for others. Men, too, can maintain those traits valued most in the traditional masculine role while developing capacities to foster and express intimacy, compassion, and responsiveness. While we do not contend that these new models of relationships and gender would be satisfying for everyone, they nonetheless provide a place to start—and a glimmer of hope—for those who wish to change the current power imbalances prevalent in many heterosexual relationships.

References

Becker, C. S. (1988). *Unbroken ties: Lesbian ex-lovers.* Boston, MA: Alyson.

Blumstein, P., & Schwartz, P. (1983). *American couples.* New York: William Morrow.

Cardell, M., Finn, S., & Maracek, J. (1981). Sex-role identity, sex-role behavior, and satisfaction in heterosexual, lesbian, and gay male couples. *Psychology of Women Quarterly, 5*(3), 488–494.

Clunis, D. M., & Green, G. D. (1988). *Lesbian couples.* Seattle, WA: Seal Press.

Deaux, K., & Hanna, R. (1984). Courtship in the personals column: The influence of gender and sexual orientation. *Sex Roles, 11*(5/6), 363–375.

England, P., & Farkas, G. (1986). *Households, employment, and gender: A social, economic and demographic view.* Hawthorne, NY: Walter deGruyter.

Hochschild, A., with Machung, A. (1989). *The second shift.* New York: Avon Books.

Kollock, P., Blumstein, P., & Schwartz, P. (1985). Sex and power in interaction: Conversational privileges and duties. *American Sociological Review, 50*, 34–46.

Kurdek, L. A. (1993). The allocation of household labor in gay, lesbian, and heterosexual married couples. *Journal of Social Issues, 49*, 127–139.

Lakoff, R. (1990). *Talking power: The politics of language.* New York: Basic Books.

Lynch, J. M., & Reilly, M. E. (1985/86). Role relationships: Lesbian perspectives. *Journal of Homosexuality, 12*, 53–69.

Moore, M., Blumstein, P., & Schwartz, P. (submitted 1994). The power of motherhood: A contextual evaluation of family resources. Submitted to *Journal of Marriage and the Family.*

Rosenzweig, J., & Lebow, W. (1992). Femme on the streets, butch in the sheets? Lesbian sex-roles, dyadic adjustment, and sexual satisfaction. *Journal of Homosexuality, 23*(3), 1–20.

Silverstein, C. (1981). *Man to man: Gay couples in America.* New York: William Morrow.

Tannen, D. (1990). *You just don't understand: Women and men in conversation.* New York: Ballantine Books.

Tuller, N. R. (1978). Couples: The hidden segment of the gay world. *Journal of Homosexuality, 3*, 331–343.

Vetere, V. A. (1982). The role of friendships in the development and maintenance of lesbian love relationships. *Journal of Homosexuality, 8*, 51–65.

Wood, J. T. (1994a). *Gendered lives: Communication, gender, and culture.* Belmont, CA: Wadsworth.

Wood, J. T. (1994b). *Who cares: Women, care, and culture.* Carbondale, IL: Southern Illinois Press.

*Chapter 6: Putting It All Together*_____

1. What is the significance of the claims made in these readings that gender is "contextual" and "constructed?"

2. How do gender role expectations regarding masculine and feminine communication styles affect male friendship and gay and lesbian romantic relationships?

3. Is it possible to have intimate relationships that are not shaped by gender role expectations? Justify your answer using the material from these readings.

7

Gender and Sexuality

The two readings in this chapter describe how social constructions of gender and sexuality can affect individual sexual behavior. The first reading describes how the behavior of bisexual men is influenced by cultural, environmental, and contextual factors (such as homophobia, economic class, race, and conceptions of masculinity). The second reading examines the ways that beliefs about femininity can affect adolescent girls' acceptance of their sexuality, their sense of sexual agency, and their attitudes toward romance. Both readings offer new models for thinking about sexuality, and conclude by offering suggestions for helping individuals define sexuality on their own terms.

14

Toward an Understanding of Behaviorally Bisexual Men: The Influence of Context and Culture

Joseph P. Stokes, Robin L. Miller, and Rhonda Mundhenk

Sexual orientation is commonly divided into discreet categories of heterosexual, homosexual, and bisexual. A person's sexual orientation is assumed to be consistent over time and across the dimensions of sexual behavior, emotional attraction, and identity. Stokes, Miller, and Mundhenk offer an alternate model of bisexuality which sees attraction to men and attraction to women on two independent dimensions. People who are highly attracted to one gender, and not at all attracted to the other gender, would be considered to be fairly clear examples of heterosexuals or homosexuals. People who have some level of attraction (from low to high) for each gender are considered to be bisexual. According to their model, these attractions are determined by biological individual differences, but how the attractions are manifested in behavior and identity is determined by environmental and sociocultural factors **(dialectical model).** Stokes, Miller, and Mundhenk describe how con-

ceptions of masculinity, homophobia, socioeconomic status, and race and ethnicity influenced the bisexual behavior of men in their study **(gender role effects and cultural diversity).** In particular, they describe how these factors may affect the development of sexual orientation in African-American men, and conclude that models based on research with white gay men may not apply. They offer suggestions to health care professionals who work with bisexual men.

Questions to Consider:

1. What do you think of the two-dimensional model of sexual orientation offered by Stokes, Miller, and Mundhenk? Does it help clarify your thinking about sexual orientation? Why or why not?

This article was originally published in *The Canadian Journal of Human Sexuality,* 1998, 7(2), 101–114.

2. How has masculinity ideology affected your sexual behavior and/or the sexual behavior of your friends?
3. According to Stokes and Miller, why might a model of sexual orientation based on research with white gay men not apply to African-American men?
4. How might sociocultural conceptions of femininity affect the bisexual behaviors of women?

The increase in public attention to issues of sexual orientation in the past decade has been dramatic. Governments, corporations, and other institutions are adopting policies that prohibit discrimination based on sexual orientation, and benefits for same-sex domestic partners are increasingly being granted. Public attention has focused on the right of gay and lesbian citizens to marry and, in the United States, on the advisability of allowing openly gay men and lesbians to serve in the military.

The entertainment industry also is embracing homosexual themes and gay and lesbian characters. Contemporary movies, including some mainstream Hollywood products, have included gay and lesbian themes and characters, and, in some recent years, Broadway theatre goers must have wondered when an original show would open that did not feature homosexuality prominently. Even American network television, that most bland and conservative medium, has got into the act. A recent article in *The Advocate* (a magazine that targets gay men and lesbians) identified 22 recurring gay or lesbian characters in this season's network television programming (Frutkin, 1997). In addition, shows with no gay characters find scores of opportunities

for jokes or innuendo regarding sexual orientation.

Underlying much of the public attention to homosexuality is the implicit assumption that sexual orientation is dichotomous: One is either homosexual or heterosexual, gay or straight. Having two neat, non-overlapping categories is comfortable for most people. As Freud (1937/1964) said, "A man's heterosexuality will not put up with any homosexuality, and *vice versa*" (p. 244). Bisexuality is rarely considered in public debates or media presentations, although recent books (e.g., Firestein, 1996a; Garber, 1995) and articles (Fox, 1995; Leland, 1995) targeting both academic and general audiences have focused on bisexuality.

To the degree that people continue to operate with an implicit theory of sexual orientation as dichotomous, bisexuality is invisible. Even a survey of mostly gay-identified male readers of *The Advocate* revealed that about one-third of the respondents did not "believe in bisexuality" (Lever, 1994). Expanding the binary model for sexual orientation to include a third category for bisexuals, as many authorities have advocated (Firestein, 1996b; Fox, 1996), is a step in the right direction, but a more radical overhaul of how we think about sexual orientation may be needed. We recommend a different model later in this section, one that does not require rigid categories.

If sexual orientation were neatly packaged into two or three discreet categories that were constant over time, defining them would be easy. It is not. There are many dimensions on which to focus when defining homosexuality, heterosexuality, and bisexuality, including sexual behaviour, romantic

ACKNOWLEDGEMENTS: Support for our research with bisexual men has been provided through Cooperative Agreements Number U64/CCU506809, U64/CCU410874, and U62/CCU513631 with the Centers for Disease Control and Prevention.

and erotic fantasy, emotional and affectional attractions, and sexual orientation self identity (cf. Coleman, 1987; Klein, 1993; Taywaditep & Stokes, 1998). These various dimensions do not always correspond in ways that make for easy categorization (Gagnon, 1989; Lever, Kanouse, Rogers, Carson, & Hertz, 1992; McKirnan, Stokes, Doll, & Burzette, 1995). For example, we have talked with a number of men who self-identify as heterosexual, but who report having and enjoying sex with both men and women (or in some cases, only with men).[1]

Most of our research on bisexuality has been conducted to further our understanding of sexual behaviours as they relate to the transmission of HIV. In the past eight years or so, our various research groups have talked at length to more than 1,500 men who have sex with men, most of them men who have sex with both men and women, and most of them men of colour. This focus on HIV/AIDS has influenced our research in two ways. First, because the prevalence of HIV among men who have sex with men is relatively high and because unprotected anal intercourse is the most efficient sexual means of transmitting HIV, our research has focused on men. Second, because HIV is transmitted through behaviours, we have employed definitions of bisexuality that are based on behaviour (e.g., "having had penetrative sex with a man and a woman in the past six months"). In other situations with other purposes, another definition might be more satisfactory. We will not attempt to define bisexuality as a general term, but we emphasize the importance of researchers' making clear how they define the term, and of clinicians' exploring clients' understanding and use of "bisexual."

A Model of Bisexuality

Kinsey and his colleagues (Kinsey, Pomeroy, & Martin, 1948) recognized that sexual orientation was described better by a continuum than by discrete categories. Their well known 7-point scale was anchored on either end by exclusive heterosexuality and exclusive homosexuality, with the middle five points' representing some degree of bisexuality. We prefer to think of bisexuality using a model suggested by Storms (1978, 1980), where attraction to men (AttM) and attraction to women (AttW) are treated as separate, relatively independent dimensions. Unlike the unidimensional model where bisexuality lies somewhere between heterosexuality and homosexuality, in this two-dimensional model there is not necessarily a trade-off between AttM and AttW; as one becomes more attracted to men (or women), one does not have to lose attraction to women (or men). So bisexuality occurs where AttM and AttW are both above some minimal level.

To oversimplify for the sake of illustration, assume that everyone has quantities of AttM and AttW that range from a low of zero to a high of five. A person with a zero on one dimension and a five on the other would be extremely interested in sex/romance with one gender, and not at all in-

---

1. We've mentioned here only dimensions where partner's gender is primary. In its broadest sense, sexual orientation might include other aspects of partners one finds attractive. Some people are especially attracted to people with red hair, wealth, big muscles, quick minds, small feet, or a great sense of humor. For bisexual people, the gender of a potential partner is probably not so important or salient as it is for heterosexual or homosexual people.

terested in sex/romance with the other. Such people would constitute relatively clear examples of homosexuals or heterosexuals. Other combinations of AttM and AttW are associated with increased potential for various aspects of bisexuality. We think of AttM and AttW as being determined by genetic, hormonal, or other largely biological individual differences. How those attractions translate into behaviour, sexual orientation self identity, sexual fantasy, and even conscious awareness of attraction is determined by a variety of contextual, environmental, and sociocultural factors. How these more sociocultural factors influence behaviour and self identity is the topic of a later section of this paper.

An important implication of this model is that knowing that a man is attracted to women and has sex with women does not tell you much about his attraction to men or whether he has sex with men, and *vice versa*. The model, in combination with sociocultural influences, also helps explain the often noted lack of direct correspondence between attraction/desire, sexual behaviour, and self identity as heterosexual, bisexual, or homosexual.

Sociosexuality

One other individual difference variable that is important in understanding and predicting sexual behaviour is *sociosexuality*, the degree to which one is willing to engage in and comfortable engaging in sex in the absence of commitment or emotional closeness (Simpson & Gangestad, 1991; the term comes from Kinsey, Pomeroy, & Martin, 1948). Those with a restricted sociosexual orientation want emotional closeness and some level of commitment prior to having sex. An unrestricted sociosexual orientation suggests more interest in and comfort with

casual or anonymous sex, more sexual partners in a relatively short time period, and greater likelihood of having sex only once with a particular partner.

Simpson and Gangestad (1991) developed and validated a measure of sociosexuality that includes both attitudinal (e.g., "Sex without love is okay") and behavioural items (e.g., "With how many different partners have you had sex in the past year?"). Their measure was not correlated with sex drive, and only weakly associated with sexual satisfaction, anxiety, and guilt. Bailey, Gaulin, Agyei, and Gladue (1994) developed a measure of *Interest in Uncommitted Sex* that taps sociosexual orientation. Their measure includes only attitudes (e.g., "I could easily imagine myself enjoying one night of sex with someone I would never see again"). They avoided items that focused on behaviour, because such items confound opportunities for uncommitted sex with interest. Bailey et al. (1994) found that men were substantially higher than women in Interest in Uncommitted Sex (see also Buss & Schmitt, 1993, for other evidence supporting this finding and for an explanation in terms of evolutionary theory); they did not find differences between self-identified heterosexual and homosexual men or between heterosexual and homosexual women.

A Typology: Diversity Among Behaviourally Bisexual Men

As mentioned earlier, in our research we have defined bisexual in behavioural terms. There is enormous diversity among men who meet a behavioural definition of bisexual. We offer here a somewhat simplistic typology to illustrate that diversity. We emphasize the need to recognize the fluidity of sexual behaviour and orientation; this typology is heuristic and not a system of rigid categories. Our four types, which overlap with typologies described by other researchers (Beeker, Rose, & Ames, 1990; Boulton & Coxon, 1991; Gagnon, 1977; Hartfield, Smith, & Perdue, 1990), include men in transition, experimenters, opportunity-driven men, and men with dual involvement (see also Stokes & Damon, 1995).

Men in Transition

Some men who have sex with both men and women and who see themselves as bisexual will eventually self-identify as gay. About 40% of the mostly gay-identified men who responded to a survey in *The Advocate* (Lever, 1994) had at some point in their coming out process self-identified as bisexual. Given the stigma associated with homosexuality, adopting a bisexual identity and/or engaging in sex with women as well as with men may reduce the anxiety and sense of isolation many young men feel as they become aware of their attraction to other men. These "men in transition" are likely men whose AttM is high relative to their AttW, and whose AttW is below some threshold. Because homosexuality or bisexuality is relatively stigmatized, AttW is likely to be more influential than AttM in determining sexual behaviour and identity. If a man is above a certain level on AttW, he will probably have a female partner and is likely to think of himself (and be thought of by others) as heterosexual, even if his AttM is higher than his AttW.

Our previous longitudinal research with behaviourally bisexual men (Stokes, Damon, & McKirnan, 1997) supported this prediction. Over the course of one year, about one third of the sample moved toward the homosexual end of a bipolar scale of self-rated sexual orientation. This move-

ment was predicted by variables related to sexual experiences with female partners (number of female sexual partners and age of first heterosexual experience), but not by variables related to sexual experiences with men (number of male sexual partners and age of first homosexual experience). In other words, measures that reflected a relative lack of heterosexual experience, not indicators of homosexual experience, predicted who was "in transition."

Experimenters

Some men meet a behavioural definition of bisexuality because of isolated incidents of sexual behaviour. Men who identify as gay will sometimes have sex with women, usually women they know well. Men who see themselves as heterosexual may have engaged in sex with another man, often under the influence of alcohol or other substances. Some men who have open and accepting attitudes toward sexual diversity will experiment sexually in a conscious attempt to experience something different. These men are bisexual only in the rather narrow sense of having had sex with both a man and a woman.

Opportunity-Driven Men

We mentioned earlier Bailey et al.'s (1994) finding that men are on average more interested than women in sex without commitment or emotional attachment. If men are generally more interested in casual sex, then male partners would be easier to find; that is, there might be more opportunities to have sex with men. In fact, most cities have public places where men can have sexual encounters with other men. Therefore, men with a moderate level of AttM might have male sexual partners, even when their AttW is much higher than their

AttM. Similarly, some men who are mainly attracted to women might have sex with other men for pay. The opportunity to make money or find housing might drive these men's sexual behaviour with men.

Men might also have sex with men when they lack the opportunity to find female sexual partners. Some men have sex with men only in situations where women are not available (e.g., on ships at sea, in prisons). Opportunity-driven men, like experimenters, would usually score toward the unrestricted end of a sociosexuality measure.

Men With Dual Involvement

Dual involvement has two meanings: It refers to involvement at both emotional and sexual levels and to involvement with both men and women. Men in this group experience sexual attraction and emotional involvement with both men and women. Their AttM and AttW are both relatively high and multifaceted; they may or may not be interested in sex without commitment with men and/or women. Their sexual and romantic relationships with men and women may be concurrent or serial.

Sociocultural Influences on Bisexual Behaviour

Herdt and Boxer (1995) argued that consideration of cultural and historical factors is essential to understanding bisexuality. The meanings of bisexual behaviour and bisexual social identity have changed throughout history (see Fox, 1996, and Garber, 1995, for more discussion on bisexuality in a historical context), and in contemporary society their meanings are a function of specific contexts and cultures. Attitudes toward sexuality in general, and same-sex sexual be-

haviour in particular, vary according to cultural and socioeconomic contexts. These attitudes, especially when combined with racial discrimination and lack of economic opportunity, may form a system of oppressive social forces that influence bisexual men's conceptualization of their sexuality and the salience of issues of sexual orientation relative to other concerns. In this section we consider some of those sociocultural factors. Although the factors we discuss are by no means exhaustive, we believe they illustrate the complexity of bisexuality and the necessity of considering bisexuality within a broader sociocultural framework. Throughout the following discussion, we draw on insights we have gained from participants in our research, most of whom have been African American men.

Conceptions of Masculinity

In thinking about bisexuality, one must consider two independent influences on sexual behaviour and self-perception: gender preferences in sexual partners and conceptions of masculine role norms. Masculine ideology—the set of beliefs that an individual holds about what it means to be a man and how men should behave—shapes how men understand their own sexuality and influences their sexual behaviour. As Pleck, Sonnenstein, and Ku (1993) suggested, masculine ideology reflects an individual's internalization of cultural expectations for men independent of the degree to which an individual man actually possesses masculine traits or is strongly male-identified.

In North American society, mainstream descriptive norms for masculinity include achievement orientation, dominance, self-confidence, and aggressiveness (Thompson & Pleck, 1986). Pleck et al. (1993) suggested that the characteristics of the male role in our society can be organized along dimensions of status, toughness, and anti-femininity. Similarly, Herek (1986) defined three components of the stereotype of traditional men: success and status, toughness and independence, and aggressiveness and dominance. Herek also emphasized that heterosexual masculinity is defined by what it is not: It is not feminine, compliant, submissive, dependent, or gay.

Expectations that men should be dominant influence their sexual relationships. Research on gender roles has found that sex is of more importance to men than to women, and that men easily separate sex from intimacy (Bailey et al., 1994; Pleck et al., 1993). In Mosher and Sirkin's (1984) conception of a masculine or macho personality, key constructs include calloused attitudes toward sex and a belief that aggression and violence are manly. Men who hold more traditional masculine ideologies, compared to men with less traditional views, report more sexual partners and are more likely to view relationships with women as adversarial (Pleck et al., 1993). In general, then, men who have internalized mainstream masculine ideologies may place greater importance on sex, have multiple sexual partners, and maintain emotional distance from their partners.

At one level, we might assume that these conceptions of masculinity preclude men from engaging in sex with other men, and in some cultures that is probably true. On the other hand, adherence to a masculine ideology may be consistent with bisexual behaviour, as long as certain restrictions are in place. For example, one must not take a "feminine role" sexually, and the emphasis must be on physical pleasure to the exclusion of emotional intimacy. By being the insertive partner in sexual intercourse, men can engage in male-to-male sexual behaviour without raising concerns about their manhood. In fact, some men we have interviewed said that "taking another man" sexually is an especially satisfying way to show their power and dominance. Having sex with a man is acceptable, as long as the behaviour is "just sex," and not something more intimate and more threatening to the dominant role, like touching or kissing.[2]

The work with Latino men of Carrier and Magana (1992) and of Carballo-Dieguez (1995) showed the importance of the sexual role men take when having sex with other men. Men who take the insertive role are viewed as heterosexual and masculine, but men who take the receptive role are seen as homosexual and feminine. The latter are stigmatized, the former are not. The important cultural distinction is not the sex of one's sexual partner, but the role one takes in sexual intercourse. For these Latino men, bisexual behaviour in no way challenges their masculine, heterosexual identity. These assumptions about the relation of masculinity and same-sex sexual behaviour that are sometimes considered especially salient for Latino men also hold for many of the African American men we have interviewed. We consider further ethnic influences on masculinity and bisexual behaviour later in the section on racial and ethnic factors.

Homophobia

Homophobia, negative attitudes toward or fear of individuals who engage in same-sex behaviour, may have deleterious effects on

---

2. Note the inversion, relative to dominant cultural conceptions, of which physical behaviours are the most intimate. Intercourse is acceptable, but sexual touching and kissing are not.

people whose behaviours are not exclusively heterosexual. Men who engage in same-sex behaviour with other men may experience pervasive anxiety, shame, and guilt about their same-sex desires and encounters. Some men may have sex with women only to camouflage or counterbalance their homosexual feelings and activities (Peterson, 1992). Homophobia also may cause bisexual men to hide their behaviours from others. Stokes, McKirnan, Doll, and Burzette (1996) found that African American and white bisexual men who had high levels of internalized homophobia and who perceived that others around them were homophobic were less likely to disclose their bisexual behaviour to others. Homophobia, including internalized homophobia, may also limit the degree to which men self-identify as gay. Carballo-Dieguez and Donezal (1994) found that among Puerto Rican men who had sex with men, those who identified as bisexual or heterosexual were more homophobic than those who identified as gay. Stokes, Vanable, and McKirnan (1997) also reported that behaviourally bisexual men, compared to men who had only male sex partners, were more homophobic themselves and perceived others to be less accepting of their having sex with men.

Homophobia may also affect the type of male-to-male sexual contact that bisexual men pursue. If they have internalized society's homophobic beliefs, men who desire same-sex sexual contact may seek it only in anonymous, highly sexualized contexts, such as parks, cruise zones, adult bookstores, and bathhouses. Such furtive, anonymous encounters may increase some men's sense of shame and guilt. In addition, their sexual activities with men may be more likely to occur when they are using alcohol or other psychoactive substances, and this, in turn, might increase the likelihood that they will engage in behaviours that could put them at risk for sexually transmitted diseases, including HIV. Stokes and Peterson (1998) speculated about other ways that homophobia, through a negative impact on self-esteem, might lead to increased behaviours that put one at risk for HIV.

Socio-Economic Status

The difficulty of distinguishing the influences of socio-economic status (SES) and ethnicity has long plagued social scientists. Although in North American society ethnicity and SES are highly correlated, SES—a combination of educational attainment, employment status, and economic well-being—has a distinct influence on bisexuality.

Although people from middle and upper class backgrounds may experience greater freedom in sexual expression and may hold more accepting attitudes toward homosexual behaviour (Herek & Glunt, 1993; Marsiglio, 1993; Seltzer, 1992; West, 1977), men of lower socio-economic standing may have more opportunities for same-sex interaction. Men with fewer economic resources may have sex with men to attain money, drugs, housing, or other material goods. In a large study of male hustlers in New York City (Miller, Klotz, & Eckholdt, 1998), almost three-quarters of the male prostitutes self-identified as heterosexual or bisexual and reported both male and female sexual partners. Relative to other men frequenting the same settings, male prostitutes reported lower levels of formal education. In a cluster analysis of behaviourally bisexual men, Taywaditep and Stokes (1998) found one cluster of men characterized by low levels of education and income, high levels of unemployment, and high prevalence of sex for pay. Other researchers (e.g., Elifson, Boles, & Sweat, 1993; Pleak & Meyer-Bahlburg, 1990) have

found that high proportions of male prostitutes are behaviourally bisexual and do
not identify as gay. For some men, lack of
economic resources and opportunity may
lead to bisexual behaviour that has little to
do with their being sexually attracted to
men.

Poverty may also be associated with
gender segregated situations where the likelihood of male-to-male sexual behaviour is
increased. Two examples of such situations
are migrant labour camps and prisons.
Many migrant labour camps are segregated
by sex. Far away from family and friends,
men in migrant labour camps often live in
crowded, poorly maintained dormitories,
and they may spend up to 16 hours each
day at back-breaking labour. In labour
camps, men may engage in sex with other
male workers because women are not available. Similarly, men of lower SES are more
likely to be in prison than men who have
greater economic opportunity. Here, too,
male-to-male sex may be largely or entirely
attributable to the situation. Other all male
settings more commonly experienced by
men of lower SES include military life and
gang membership.

Researchers have suggested lack of
economic resources may be associated not
only with bisexual behaviour, but also with
self-identified sexual orientation. Carballo-
Dieguez and Donezal (1994) found that
among their sample of Puerto Rican men
who have sex with men, those who identified as heterosexual and bisexual were of
lower socio-economic status than those
who identified as gay. Rust (1996) argued
that because the working classes are less
likely to have been exposed to middle and
upper class values regarding tolerance of diversity in general, and of differences in sexual orientation in particular, they may hold
more negative views of homosexuality.
Others have found that negative attitudes

toward homosexuality decrease as education and other measure of socio-economic
status increase (Herek & Glunt, 1993). On
the other hand, working class men might be
less likely to subscribe to conventional middle class values about sex and may be less
concerned with what is appropriate or
proper sexual behaviour (Rust, 1996). This
combination of forces might lead to a situation where men from lower socio-eco-
nomics classes are more likely than other
men to engage in same-sex behaviour but
less likely to see themselves as gay.

Ethnic and Racial Factors

Because of the inherent difficulties of sampling a hidden population (Stokes,
Taywaditep, Vanable, & McKirnan, 1996),
estimating the prevalence of bisexuality
among various racial and ethnic communities is not an easy task. Some evidence,
however, suggests that bisexual behaviour
is more common among African American
and Latino men than among men in other
racial and ethnic groups (Doll & Beeker,
1996; Stokes, Vanable, & McKirnan, 1996).
Our most recent work has been with
African American men, and we focus on
them in this section.

If the prevalence of bisexual behaviour is relatively high among African
American and Latino men, one reason
might be the association between SES and
ethnicity. The previous section suggests several reasons why men from lower SES
groups might experience more sexual behaviour with other men. Although these
factors may lead to more bisexual behaviour, they are not likely to lead to a self-
identity other than heterosexual. Peterson
(1992) noted that many African American
men are behaviourally bisexual, but do not
identify as bisexual. The reason, he felt, is
quite simple: These behaviourally bisexual

men do not experience homosexual feelings, emotions, and attachments for other men during their same-sex encounters. These are the opportunity-driven men in our typology, and the opportunities for same-sex activities may be greater for men with lower SES.

One other important reason for the higher prevalence of bisexuality among African American men involves sociocultural factors that relate to what we have called "men in transition." We view these as men whose attraction to men (AttM) is high, both absolutely and relative to their attraction to women (AttW). For a variety of reasons that we will mention in this section, we think African American men, relative to white men with similar levels of AttM and AttW, are likely to remain "in transition" and never establish a gay identity. The African American men are more likely to marry or to maintain close, romantic relationships with women, less likely to disclose their same-sex sexual behaviour to others, and more likely to maintain a self-identity as bisexual throughout their lifetime. The extent to which some men go to maintain a self-identity as bisexual is illustrated by a respondent who said his friends see themselves as bisexual, despite their being sexually attracted only to men, because they talk to women in clubs and sometimes get their phone numbers. "If you would say that they're gay, they'd be like 'no, because I talk to girls.' But they're not having sex with girls."

Gender roles. The empirical literature on gender roles and notions of masculinity suggests that men of different SES and racial/ethnic backgrounds do not share a unified notion of what it means to be a man and what defines masculine behaviour. At its most simplistic level, racial group membership and SES may affect a man's ability to fulfil mainstream masculine ideals for achievement, so alternative constructions of manhood are developed to manage marginal social status. Social class and race/ethnicity may also provide men a set of cultural norms about masculinity that are different from European American cultural norms and expectations.

Researchers using a variety of empirical methods (Cazenave, 1984; Harris, 1994; Harris, Torres, & Allender, 1994; Hunter & Davis, 1992, 1994; Lewis, 1975) have suggested that gender role expectations for African Americans are different from those of the dominant European American culture. African American men and women are less likely to emphasize economic and status achievement as hallmarks of masculinity, and more likely to view expressive, nurturant, and communal behaviours as consistent with both masculinity and femininity. In general, African Americans are less likely than whites to link personal traits to gender, that is, to see characteristics as more appropriate to one gender than the other.

African American men, therefore, face the dilemma of having to manage European American expectations of masculine behaviour that differ from African American cultural expectations. If they follow African American values, they may not be seen as tough, hard, and dominating, all of which are part of mainstream expectations for masculinity. Moreover, racism limits their ability to succeed in terms of majority expectations for status and achievement. With their masculinity thus threatened on two fronts, the importance of behaving sexually "like a man" is increased, and sexual behaviour becomes an important arena for proving one's masculinity. Even if one is strongly attracted to men, maintaining some sort of sexual relationship with women is important.

Conceptions of sexuality.   At the same time as African American men seek to manage racial oppression and competing cultural notions of manhood, they must also manage African American conceptions of sexuality. Some theorists have argued that African Americans are more liberal and accepting of sex than are other racial groups (Weinberg & Williams, 1988). Lewis (1975) maintained that within a culture in which the same attributes are valued in both genders and where sexuality is normalized, sexual self-expression becomes the primary means by which one establishes a gender role. For women, sexual self-expression emphasizes procreation. For men, procreation is also important, but so is establishing one's masculinity by being very active sexually. These various cultural forces, especially when combined with limited economic resources, lead African American men to establish their masculinity through sexual interactions. Having sex with women and being dominant in sexual encounters are desirable, regardless of one's sexual attractions and desires.

Emphasis on family.   African American culture, relative to European American culture, emphasizes family and communality more than individual rights and desires (Jagers & Mock, 1993; Nobles, 1991), Rust (1996) has articulated the impact of this cultural difference for bisexual men and women. First, there is an increased obligation to marry and have children, regardless of one's same-sex attraction. There is also pressure to avoid self-identifying as gay or bisexual. "[T]o identify as bisexual, lesbian, or gay would be tantamount to rejecting not only one's gender role but also one's family and one's ethnicity" (Rust, 1996, p. 59). In addition, related to the emphasis on family is the idea that an individual's behaviour is a reflection on his or her family. Same-sex behaviour in this context brings shame to the entire family.

For men who are strongly attracted to women (i.e., those with high AttW), marrying and maintaining a heterosexual self-identity is not problematic. For men with high AttM and relatively low AttW, these pressures are stressful. Nonetheless, these men may avoid the "transition" to having sex only with men and to identifying as homosexual both to protect their families of origin, and to allow for having families of their own, assuming, of course, that they have at least some minimal AttW. For them, maintaining sexual relationships with women both provides cover for their same-sex behaviour and allows for procreation.

Culture of silence.   Despite our perception that talking about heterosexual sex is perhaps more common in African American culture than in European American culture, the African American cultural norm is not to mention homosexuality explicitly. Rust (1996) noted that in cultures where family is emphasized "often, the parents tacitly know that their child is bisexual, lesbian or gay, and both parents and child act under an unspoken agreement that the daughter or son—and often their same-sex partners—will be accepted as long as the subject is not discussed explicitly" (p. 59). One might think this a manifestation of homophobia in the African American community, and in some sense it is, but relative to European American culture, the "phobia" seems to reflect a reluctance to mention homosexuality, rather than a reflection of especially negative attitudes toward homosexuality. This reluctance extends to not disclosing one's same-sex attraction and behaviour to others, including female sexual partners, a phenomenon we have found to be more prevalent among African American than white men (Stokes, McKirnan, et al., 1996). The role of gay men in the African American church also illustrates this culture of silence around homosexuality. In private, almost everyone we have talked with who is knowledgeable about the African American church recognizes that gay men are heavily and probably disproportionately represented there (Zulu, 1996), and they are typically welcomed and loved. In public discourse at church, however, homosexuality is rarely mentioned except to condemn it. The tacit agreement is a variation of "don't ask, don't tell," and even men who are openly gay in other aspects of their lives are careful not to emphasize or even mention their sexual orientation in the church setting.

Double minority status. For African American men, the possible status as a gay or bisexual man must be viewed in the context of their status as an ethnic minority. For white gay and bisexual men, their status as a sexual minority is their only potential source of discrimination. Many have grown up with privilege and with faith in the political system. They believe they can mount political power to fight homophobia and heterosexism, thereby reestablishing their position of privilege and power.

As outsiders looking in, marginalized African American men may be less optimistic about their ability to muster political power. Their alienation from the political process is unlikely to change because they see themselves as bisexual or gay. The same forces that keep people of colour in general from "coming out" on Election Day also make coming out as bisexual or gay less attractive to African American men. Moreover, even if discrimination based on sexual orientation were to disappear magically, African Americans would still have to deal with racism directed at their very visible ethnic status.

As we have seen, family is an important source of support for African American men. Also, maintaining their ties with their ethnic community is highly desirable. Many of the African American men we have talked with feel that self-identifying as gay requires them to relinquish part of their identity as African American, and to do so publicly violates the culture of silence mentioned in the previous section. The two identities are sufficiently incompatible that fully embracing one requires downplaying the importance of the other.

Herdt and Boxer (1992) emphasized the importance of migration to gay ghettoes for the coming out process. For African Americans, migrating to a visible gay community means exposing oneself to potential racism and possibly losing their most important source of support, their extended family. Gay and bisexual African American men typically have no space comparable to mostly white gay neighbourhoods where they can develop and integrate their sexual and ethnic identities. Staying in the African American community, rather than the gay community, facilitates the development of their ethnic ties and identity, but may require subordinating their gay or bisexual identity; moving to areas with high concentrations of (white) gay and bisexual people fosters the opposite result. In the African American community, sexual orientation is relatively invisible, but in the gay community, ethnic identity is usually transparent. Moreover, having grown up in the African American community, bisexual men perceive support and have roots there. As a result, many African American men choose to live in their neighbourhoods of origin, downplaying their sexual orientation and finding their "gay community" where they can, often in underground bars and cruising areas.

Socialization.   One other relevant difference between African American and white men in contemporary society should be noted. As part of their socialization, many African American children learn to cope with a hostile, racist environment. In noting that Black Americans historically have needed strategies to deal with a hostile society, Peters (1985) quoted Richardson (1981): "It has been the responsibility and the task of black parents and the black community to prepare and condition black children for such a world" (p. 99). African American children learn that they are protected at home, but that they should be careful and suspicious outside of their communities of origin. This socialization predisposes African American men to do what is necessary to deal with and "get by" in a hostile environment. It also helps give men who are attracted to other men the coping skills necessary to deal with the hostility they may face as a result of their sexual orientation, and the ability to manage their self presentation depending on the context.

Implications for Health Care Professionals

We conclude with some suggestions for how health care professionals, especially counsellors and psychotherapists, can be most helpful to bisexual men.

Do not focus on categories or worry about determining whether a client is gay, bisexual, or heterosexual. Focus instead on the various aspects of his attraction to men and to women, including sexual behaviour, fantasy, and emotional or affectional intimacy. If the client uses categorical labels like "bisexual" or "gay," help him explore what they mean to him.

Where there is a need to know about sexual behaviour, and there may be in medical settings especially, ask about behaviour, not about labels or self-identification. A simple way to learn about behaviour is to start with a question like, "About how many different sexual partners have you had in the past year [or whatever time period is most relevant]?" and follow with, "Of those people, about how many were men and about how many were women?" These simple questions, asked in a non-judgmental manner, are relatively comfortable to answer and imply that having male and female partners is not unusual.

Help the client explore his sociosexual orientation, his comfort with and interest in casual sex with both men and women. Being non-judgmental is important, of course, as is being comfortable with hearing about multiple sexual partners and anonymous sexual encounters.

Explore with the client the nature and influence of his ethnic community's values about sexuality and masculinity. What is his perception of the intersection of sexuality or sexual orientation identity and cultural or ethnic identities?

Where relevant, talk with the client about what it means to "come out," both to himself and to others. Discuss not just when and to whom, but whether and how. Recognize that coming out as gay or bisexual is not necessarily the desired end point for everyone, and that failure to come out or adopt a gay identity may not be a reflection of shame and internalized homophobia. Given some of the sociocultural factors we have mentioned—the structure of gender roles, the emphasis on family and community as sources of support, the culture of silence around homosexuality, the need to manage multiple identities, the association of gay with white, the lack of faith in the political process, the ability to manage one's presentation depending on the context—delaying, perhaps permanently, the transition to a gay self-identity or to sexual behaviour exclusively with men may be a rational, adaptive, and psychologically healthy choice, especially for men of colour.

Educate the client, where necessary, about behaviours that put him and his future sexual partners at risk for HIV and AIDS. Issues of disclosing one's same-sex sexual behaviour become especially important and potentially problematic when high risk sexual behaviours are involved.

Recognize that not all issues a client has are related to his bisexual feelings or behaviours (Matteson, 1996). Do not let your own curiosity or fascination with bisexual issues trump every other concern.

Know thyself, especially in terms of your own feelings about sex, casual sex, anonymous sex, sex between men, and so on. Read widely and get supervision from providers who are more experienced than you are. When your comfort level or expertise are exceeded, be willing to refer clients to other providers.

References

Bailey, J. M., Gaulin, S., Agyci, Y., & Gladue, B. A. (1994). Effects of gender and sexual orientation on evolutionarily relevant aspects of human mating psychology. *Journal of Personality and Social Psychology, 66,* 1081–1093.

Beeker, C., Rose, D. T., & Ames, L. J. (1990, June). *Marginal men, mainstream risk* (Abstract FC711). Paper presented at the VIth International Conference on AIDS, San Francisco.

Boulton, M., & Coxon, T. (1991). Bisexuality in the United Kingdom. In R. Tielman, M. Carballo, & A. Hendriks (Eds.), *Bisexuality and HIV/AIDS* (pp. 65–72). Buffalo, NY: Prometheus Books.

Buss, D. M., & Schmitt, D. P. (1993). Sexual strategies theory: A contextual evolutionary analysis of human mating. *Psychological Review, 100,* 204–232.

Carballo-Dieguez, A. (1995). The sexual identity and behavior of Puerto Rican men who have sex with men. In G. Herek & B. Greene (Eds.), *AIDS, identity and community* (pp. 105–114). Newbury Park, CA: Sage.

Carballo-Dieguez, A., & Donezal, C. (1994). Contrasting types of Puerto Rican men who have sex with men (MSM). *Journal of Psychology and Human Sexuality, 6,* 41–67.

Carrior, J. M., & Magana, J. R. (1992). Use of ethnosexual data on men of Mexican origin for HIV/AIDS prevention programs. In G. Herdt & S. Lindenbaum (Eds.), *The time of AIDS: Social analysis, theory, and methods* (pp. 243–258). Newbury Park, CA: Sage Publications.

Cazenave, N. A. (1984). Race, socioeconomic status, and age: The social context of American masculinity. *Sex Roles, 11,* 639–656.

Coleman, E. (1987). Bisexuality: Challenging our understanding of human sexuality and sexual orientation. *Sexuality and Medicine, 1,* 225–242.

Doll, L., & Beeker, C. (1996). Male bisexual behavior and HIV risk in the United States: Synthesis of research with implications for behavioral interventions. *AIDS Education and Prevention, 8,* 205–225.

Elifson, K. W., Boles, J., & Sweat, M. (1993). Risk factors associated with HIV infection among male prostitutes. *American Journal of Public Health, 83,* 79–83.

Firestein, B. A. (Ed.). (1996a). *Bisexuality: The psychology and politics of an invisible minority.* Thousand Oaks, CA: Sage.

Firestein, B. A. (1996b). Bisexuality as a paradigm shift: Transforming our disciplines. In B. A. Firestein (Ed.), *Bisexuality: The psychology and politics of an invisible minority* (pp. 263–291). Thousand Oaks, CA: Sage.

Fox, R. C. (1995). Bisexual identities. In A. R. D'Augelli & C. J. Patterson (Eds.), *Lesbian, gay, and bisexual identities over the lifespan* (pp. 48–86). New York: Oxford University Press.

Fox, R. C. (1996). Bisexuality in perspective: A review of theory and research. In B. A. Firestein (Ed.), *Bisexuality: The psychology and politics of an invisible minority* (pp. 3–50). Thousand Oaks, CA: Sage.

Freud, S. (1937/1964). "Analysis terminable and interminable." *The Standard Edition of the Complete Psychological Works of Sigmund Freud,* vol. 23. James Strachey (translator). London: Hogarth.

Frutkin, A. (1997, February 8). "Television's 23 gay characters." *The Advocate, 727,* 30–31.

Gagnon, J. H. (1977). *Human sexualities.* Glenview IL: Scott, Foresman.

Gagnon, J. (1989). Disease and desire. *Daedalus, 118,* 46–77.

Garber, M. (1995). *Vice versa: Bisexuality and the eroticism of everyday life.* New York: Simon & Schuster.

Harris, A. C. (1994). Ethnicity as a determinant of sex role identity: A replication study of item selection for the Bem Sex Role Inventory. *Sex Roles, 31,* 241–273.

Harris, I., Torres, J. B., & Allender, D. (1994). The responses of African American men to dominant norms of masculinity within the United States. *Sex Roles, 31,* 703–719.

Hartfield, K., Smith, K., & Perdue, R. (1990, June). *Developing AIDS education interventions for nongay identified men having sex with other men* (Abstract THD 974). Paper presented at the VIth International Conference on AIDS, San Francisco.

Herdt, G., & Boxer, A. (1992). Introduction: Culture, history, and life course of gay men. In G. Herdt (Ed.), *Gay culture in America* (pp. 1–28). Boston: Beacon.

Herdt, G., & Boxer, A. (1995). Bisexuality: Toward a comparative theory of identities and culture. In R. G. Parker & J. H. Gagnon (Eds.), *Conceiving sexuality: Approaches to sex research in a postmodern world,* (pp. 69–83). New York: Routledge.

Herek, G. (1986). On heterosexual masculinity. *American Behavioral Scientist, 29,* 563–577.

Herek, G. M., & Glunt, E. K. (1993). Interpersonal contact and heterosexuals' attitudes toward gay men: Results from a national survey. *Journal of Sex Research, 30,* 239–244.

Hunter, A. G., & Davis, J. E. (1992). Constructing gender: An exploration of Afro-American men's conceptualization of manhood. *Gender & Society, 6,* 464–479.

Hunter, A. G., & Davis, J. E. (1994). Hidden voices of Black men: The meaning, structure, and complexity of manhood. *Journal of Black Studies, 25,* 20–40.

Jagers, R. J., & Mock, L. O. (1993). Culture and social outcomes among inner-city African American children: An Afrographic exploration. *Journal of Black Psychology, 19,* 391–405.

Kinsey, A., Pomeroy, W., & Martin, C. W. (1948). *Sexual behavior in the human male.* Philadelphia: W.B. Saunders.

Klein, F. (1993). *The bisexual option* (2nd Edition). New York: Haworth.

Leland, J. (1995, July 17). Bisexuality. *Newsweek,* 44–50.

Lever, J. (1994, August 23). Sexual revelations: The 1994 Advocate survey of sexuality and relationships: The men. *The Advocate, 661/662,* 16–24.

Lever, J., Kanouse, D. E., Rogers, W. H., Carson, S., & Hertz, R. (1992). Behavior patterns and sexual identity of bisexual males. *Journal of Sex Research, 29,* 141–167.

Lewis, D. K. (1975). The Black family: Socialization and sex roles. *Phylon, 36,* 221–237.

Marsiglio, W. (1993). Attitudes toward homosexual activity and gays as friends: A national study of heterosexual 15- to 19-year-old males. *Journal of Sex Research, 30,* 12–17.

Matteson, D. R. (1996). Counseling and psychotherapy with bisexual and exploring clients. In B. A. Firestein (Ed.), *Bisexuality: The psychology and politics of an invisible minority* (pp. 185–213). Newbury Park, CA: Sage.

McKirnan, D. J., Stokes, J. P., Doll, L., & Burzette, R. G. (1995). Bisexually active men: Social characteristics and sexual behavior. *Journal of Sex Research, 32,* 64–75.

Miller, R. L., Klotz, D., & Eckholdt, H. M. (1998). HIV prevention with males prostitutes and patrons of hustler bars: Replication of an HIV preventive intervention. *American Journal of Community Psychology, 26,* 97–131.

Mosher, D., & Sirkin, M. (1984). Measuring a macho personality constellation. *Journal of Research in Personality, 18,* 150–163.

Nobles, W. W. (1991). Extended self: Rethinking the so-called Negro self-concept. In R. Jones (Ed.), *Black Psychology* (3rd Ed.) (pp. 295–304). Berkeley, CA: Cobb and Henry.

Peters, M. F. (1985). Racial socialization of young black children. In H. P. McAdoo & J. L. McAdoo (Eds.), *Black children: Social, educational, and parental environments* (pp. 159–173). Beverly Hills, CA: Sage.

Peterson, J. L. (1992). Black men and their same sex desires and behaviors. In G. Herdt (Ed.), *Gay culture in America* (pp. 147–164). Boston: Beacon.

Pleak, R. R., & Meyer-Bahlburg, H. (1990). Sexual behavior and AIDS knowledge of young male prostitutes in Manhattan. *Journal of Sex Research, 27,* 557–587.

Pleck, J. H., Sonnenstein, F. L., & Ku, L. C. (1993). Masculinity ideology: Its impact on adolescent males' heterosexual relationships. *Journal of Social Issues, 49,* 11–29.

Richardson, B. B. (1981). *Racism and child-rearing: A study of Black mothers.* Dissertation Abstracts International, 42(01), 125A.

Rust, P. C. (1996). Managing multiple identities: Diversity among bisexual women and men. In B. A. Firestein (Ed.), *Bisexuality: The psychology and politics of an invisible minority* (pp. 53–83). Newbury Park, CA: Sage.

Seltzer, R. (1992). The social location of those holding antihomosexual attitudes. *Sex Roles, 26,* 391–398.

Simpson, J. A., & Gangestad, S. W. (1991). Individual differences in sociosexuality: Evidence for convergent and discriminant validity. *Journal of Personality and Social Psychology, 60,* 870–883.

Stokes, J. P., & Damon, W. (1995). Counseling and psychotherapy for bisexual men. *Directions in Clinical Psychology, 5* (lesson 10), 1–13.

Stokes, J. P., Damon, W., & McKirnan, D. J. (1997). Predictors of movement toward homosexuality: A longitudinal study of bisexual men. *Journal of Sex Research, 34,* 304–312.

Stokes, J. P., McKirnan, D. J., Doll, L., & Burzette, R. G. (1996). Female partners of bisexual men: What they don't know might hurt them. *Psychology of Women Quarterly, 20,* 267–284.

Stokes, J. P., & Peterson, J. L. (1998). Homophobia, self-esteem, and risk for HIV among African American men who have sex with men. *AIDS Education and Prevention, 10,* 278–292.

Stokes, J. P., Taywaditep, K., Vanable, P., & McKirnan, D. J. (1996). Bisexual men, sexual behavior, and HIV/AIDS. In B. A. Firestein (Ed.), *Bisexuality: The psychology and politics of an invisible minority* (pp. 149–168). Newbury Park, CA: Sage.

Stokes, J. P., Vanable, P. A., & McKirnan, D. J. (1996). Ethnic differences in sexual behavior, condom use, and psychosocial variables among black and white men who have sex with men. *Journal of Sex Research, 33,* 373–381.

Stokes, J. P., Vanable, P. A., & McKirnan, D. J. (1997). Comparing gay and bisexual men on sexual behavior, condom use, and psychosocial variables related to HIV/AIDS. *Archives of Sexual Behavior, 26,* 377–391.

Storms, M. D. (1978). Sexual orientation and self-perception. In P. Pliner, K. R. Blanstein, I. M. Spigel, T. Alloway, & L. Krames (Eds.), *Advances in the study of communication and affect: Vol. 5. Perception of emotion in self and others* (pp. 165–180). New York: Plenum.

Storms, M. D. (1980). Theories of sexual orientation. *Journal of Personality and Social Psychology, 38,* 783–792.

Taywaditep, K. J., & Stokes, J. P. (1998). Male bisexualities: A cluster analysis of men with bisexual experience. *Journal of Psychology and Human Sexuality, 10,* 15–41.

Thompson, E. H., & Pleck, J. H. (1986). The structure of male role norms. *American Behavioral Scientist, 29,* 531–543.

Weinberg, M. S., & Williams, C. J. (1988). Black sexuality: A test of two theories. *Journal of Sex Research, 25,* 197–218.

West, W. G. (1977). Public tolerance of homosexual behavior. *Cornell Journal of Social Relations, 12,* 25–36.

Zulu, N. S. (1996). Sex, race, and the stained-glass window. *Women and Therapy, 19,* 27–35.

15

Femininity as a Barrier to Positive Sexual Health for Adolescent Girls

Deborah L. Tolman

Early adolescence is a time in a girl's life when she begins to hold adult beliefs about gender and to develop adult sexuality. Tolman explores how girls' beliefs about femininity may be related to three elements of female adolescent sexual health: accepting one's sexuality, feeling entitled to positive sexual agency, and holding a critical perspective on conventions of romance. These three elements are part of a larger model Tolman has developed for thinking about female adolescent sexual health. This model goes beyond the physical consequences of sexuality to include: 1) the knowledge, attitudes, and self-concept of the individual girl; 2) her romantic and sexual relationships; 3) her social relationships; and 4) sociocultural and sociopolitical dimensions.

To explore the relationship between adolescent sexual health and beliefs about femininity, Tolman and her colleagues gave a survey to eighth-grade girls asking them about their sexual self-concept, sense of sexual agency, attitudes toward romance conventions, femininity ideology, and demographic background. They also interviewed a subsample of girls in depth about gender, relationships, and sexuality. It was found that girls who espoused more conventional beliefs about femininity also showed diminished positive sexual health **(gender role effects).** The results also indicate that ethnicity is a significant factor in the relationship between beliefs about femininity and sexual health **(cultural diversity).** Tolman suggests that offering adolescent girls a critical perspective on femininity may enable them to make healthy choices about sexuality and to have more positive sexual experiences.

Questions to Consider:

1. Is Tolman's model a dialectical model of sexual health? Why or why not?

D. L. Tolman (1999). Femininity as a barrier to positive sexual health for adolescent girls. *Journal of the American Medical Women's Association, 54* (3), 133–138. Copyright (c) 1999 American Medical Women's Association, Inc. All rights reserved. Reprinted with permission.

2. What differences did Tolman find in the responses of Latina and white girls? What is the significance of these differences?
3. Based on Tolman's findings, what would you want adolescent girls to learn in a sex education class?
4. How might beliefs about masculinity be related to the sexual health of adolescent boys?

Adolescence is a time of enormous change in girls' bodies, relationships, emotions, and experiences; changes that include the development of adult sexuality. Traditionally, the sexual health of adolescent girls has been evaluated in terms of their participation in heterosexual intercourse. Two primary questions have been regularly asked and answered: 1) Have adolescent girls ever had sexual intercourse or, alternately and more popular of late, have they been abstinent? 2) If they have had sexual intercourse, did they use effective contraception to protect against pregnancy, and in recent years, did they use condoms to protect as well against sexually transmitted diseases (STDs), specifically human immunodeficiency virus (HIV)?

This approach has a number of shortcomings. More often than not, these questions are asked of girls of color and girls living in poverty, with the not-so-subtle insinuation that only these girls are sexual. They maintain the invisibility of lesbian adolescents, as the only form of sexual behavior that they acknowledge is sexual intercourse. They reflect a model of adolescent sexuality in which "the discursive focus is on behavioral rates rather than an elaboration of the cultural logics of adolescent sexuality."[1] Yet these questions have defined what we know about adolescent sexuality. The most recent data suggest a trend of more abstinence and less unprotected sex: Pregnancy rates among all adolescents declined by 13% from 1991 to 1995,[2] more than half of girls have not begun to have sexual intercourse by the age of 18, and condom use among adolescents has increased 23% since 1991.[3] With the physically most risky sexual behavior on the decline, it is prudent to ask: Does this mean that all adolescent girls are sexually more healthy?

In 1995, the National Commission on Adolescent Sexual Health released a consensus statement, endorsed by 48 national organizations including the American Medical Association, declaring that becoming a sexually healthy adult is a key developmental task for adolescents.[4] This statement extended the conception of sexual health beyond pregnancy prevention and the avoidance of contracting STDs. The Commission incorporated into its conception of sexual health the ability "to develop and maintain meaningful interpersonal relationships" and to "express affection, love, and intimacy in ways consistent with one's own values" (p 4). To be considered healthy, they declared, sexual relationships and the expression of sexuality in behavior must be "consensual, nonexploitative, honest, pleasurable and protected against unintended pregnancies and STDs, if any type of intercourse occurs" (p 4). This statement represents a crucial step toward a positive conception of sexuality for adolescents, bypassing the notion that simply avoiding sexual intercourse or its negative consequences is good enough. Sexual health, then, goes beyond the physical consequences of sexuality and incorporates experiential, psychological, and relational dimensions as well.

Although a step forward, this statement is not sufficient, because it assumes an archetypal adolescent who does not exist in reality. It does not acknowledge the very real dimensions of gender, race, ethnicity, or class that organize adolescent sexuality in important ways. Feminist analysis has shown that sexuality is not gender neutral, because the meanings and realities associated with male and female sexuality are culturally constructed to be profoundly different and based on male privilege.[5-8] Feminists have also fleshed out the ways in which race, ethnicity, sexual orientation, and class create sexual hierarchies among women.[9-13] Despite the sexual revolution of the 1960s, society's conception of sexuality for adolescent girls who want to be considered good, normal, and acceptable remains constrained. Good girls are still supposed to "just say no," are not supposed to feel intense sexual desire, and remain responsible for the sexual desire of boys and for protecting themselves from harm. Good girls are still assumed to be white and middle class. Sexual violence, and the threat of violence, remain a real and pervasive feature of the terrain of female sexuality.[14] Girls are still expected to conform to the conventions of romance that organize and assume heterosexuality, including needing to have, please, and keep a boyfriend, and the media continue to incite and naturalize girls' desires for these trappings of heterosexuality.[15,16] Real, live adolescent girls must negotiate these constructions in working out their own conceptions of sexuality by and through which they express their own feelings, desires, and beliefs. The process by which girls create their sexual biographies is profoundly relational, carried out within the institutional and cultural spaces of their lived experience—in their schools, churches, synagogues, and mosques; in their neighborhoods, clinics, or doctors' offices; and within their racial and ethnic histories.

Feminist scholarship offers direction for the development of a model of positive sexual health for adolescent girls that recognizes how our society denies and diminishes female sexuality[7,8,17,18] and that incorporates forms of resistance that enable girls to become sexually healthy. If girls are not sup-

posed to acknowledge their own sexual desire or be assertive on behalf of their own wishes, and if they are supposed to comply with conventions of heterosexual romance, then it may be especially difficult for them to engage in sexual relationships that are "consensual, nonexploitative, pleasurable, honest and protected" from pregnancy and disease. To develop such relationships, both participants must have a sense of entitlement to say no and to say yes to forms of sexual expression, to know and have agency in relation to their own feelings, to acknowledge their own sexuality, and to be free from violence.

Feminist analysis has also suggested that sexual health is multidimensional. Together with my staff at the Adolescent Sexuality Project at the Center for Research on Women at Wellesley College, I am currently developing such a model of sexual health for female adolescents (see Diagram I), in which I identify four domains: 1) the individual girl, including her knowledge and attitudes, sense of entitlement to self-pleasure (ie, through masturbation, sexual fantasy) and sexual self-concept; 2) romantic/sexual relationships, including use of condoms and some forms of contraception, avoiding or leaving abusive partners when possible, and adopting a critical perspective on romance conventions; 3) social relationships, including having support to work through confusion and questions about sexuality, to communicate with others about sexuality, and to evaluate the quality of relationships; and 4) the sociopolitical dimensions of girls' sexuality, including access to and freedom to use reproductive health care, information and materials to sustain sexual health, and images of girls' sexuality as normal and acceptable.

Three elements of this model—accepting one's sexuality, feeling entitled to positive sexual agency, and holding a critical

SOCIOCULTURAL/SOCIOPOLITICAL
access to institutional resources such as educational, religious, community-based, elected, public service, and health-related organizations

SOCIAL RELATIONSHIPS
relationships with close friends, peers, older friends, teammates, siblings, parents, teachers, counselors, other adults, church members, etc. which offer emotional and social support:

DATING/ROMANTIC RELATIONSHIPS
feel entitled and be free to choose a partner, regardless of race, class, gender, ableness or sexual orientation

INDIVIDUAL
• feel own sexual feelings
• develop a sense of comfort with own sexuality
• resist objectifying sex and self
• feel entitled to explore sexual identity
• have knowledge about sexual activity and reproductive health
• differentiate between sexual desire and sexual behavior
• feel entitled to pleasure and sexual experiences without guilt, including self pleasure
• develop positive attitudes and sense of responsibility about protection from unwanted pregnancy and disease
• become aware of and have respect for own values about sexuality and relationships

recognize and employ a range of appropriate ways to express love, affection, intimacy and sexual desire consistent with one's own values

to work through confusion and questions about sexuality and relationships

access to violence-free home and relationships

to evaluate quality of relationships

identify limits of a girl's control and responsibility in situations that involve sexual violence

feel entitled and able to make active choices in consensual sexual and romantic contexts

prevent unwanted conception and STDs

for sharing information and getting advice about relationships

to get information about sexuality, contraception, and protection

access to images of girls' sexuality as normal and acceptable for all girls, regardless of race, ethnicity, class, ableness or sexual orientation

access to institutional support in making healthy and happy choices about sexuality and romantic sexual relationships

to develop and express critical perspectives on traditional beliefs about girls' sexuality

access to information about sexual expression besides sexual intercourse

feel entitled and able to communicate with partner about sexuality

be aware of and feel entitled to own needs and feelings in relationships, balanced by sensitivity to and respect for needs and feelings of partner

to identify and leave abusive relationships

develop a critical perspective on romantic conventions regulating heterosexual relationships

to make own choices about sexuality and relationships

to develop an understanding of one's own perspective on the values of one's culture regarding sexuality and relationships

to make safe choices about sexuality and relationships

access to information and materials to sustain sexual health (condoms, contraceptives, knowledge)

access to comprehensive sex education (school, other adults, parents, religious, institutions, community-based)

access and freedom to use reproductive health care

DIAGRAM 1   *A Model of Female Adolescent Health*

perspective on conventions of romance—have not yet been identified or investigated as possible key features of positive sexual health for adolescent girls. We began to assess this model by studying how these qualities help girls make healthy choices about their sexuality. We selected these constructs in part because they represent how individual girls negotiate the conceptions of sexuality available to them. Future analyses will evaluate the many other features of this model.

Holding conventional beliefs about femininity and endorsing or engaging in stereotypic feminine behaviors have been associated with health risks and outcomes in women, including eating problems, risk for HIV, smoking, and breast reduction or augmentation.[19-23] We investigated the ways in which early adolescent girls' beliefs about femininity might be associated with these three aspects of their sexual health in early adolescence. It is at early adolescence that girls first engage in romantic relationships and expressions of sexuality and develop the scripts that organize these experiences. It is also at early adolescence that beliefs about gender begin to intensify and to take their adult forms.[24,25] Because these processes occur simultaneously, an examination of the relationship between femininity and sexual health at this developmental moment is warranted.

Methods

We employed a universal sampling technique and studied all eighth-grade girls (n = 148) in one northeastern urban school district who are participating in a longitudinal study of gender ideology and its relationship to both risk of unintended pregnancy and sexual health. The response rate was very high (93% for the district).

The participants completed a survey that included demographic questions; questions about their sexual behavior, sexual health, and risk of unintended pregnancy; and standardized scales measuring their beliefs about femininity. Written permission was obtained from each child's parent or guardian, and the survey was available in Spanish, with a Spanish-speaking researcher present. A subset of 46 girls with high and low scores on measures of beliefs about femininity was selected and interviewed individually about their experiences with relationships, dating, and sexuality, using a clinical, semi-open interviewing technique designed to elicit narratives.

Beliefs about femininity were measured using two different scales. The *Femininity Ideology Scale* (FIS) is a 22-item scale using a 6-point response scale (strongly agree to strongly disagree) that measures the extent to which adolescent girls have internalized dominant cultural conventions of femininity associated with how they feel and act in relationships with others and how they relate to their own bodies.[26] It is comprised of the Self-in-Relationship (SIR) subscale and the Relationship-with-Body (RWB) subscale and was developed by our staff with diverse adolescent girls and incorporates the norms of femininity they perceive to regulate their behavior and identities as described by them in focus groups. High scores indicate internalization of a more conventional femininity ideology. The 12-item *Attitudes Toward Women Scale for Adolescents* (AWSA) was used to measure girls' beliefs about feminine gender roles.[27] Participants indicate their endorsement of more conventional and less traditional beliefs about how women should behave using a 4-point, Likert-type agree-disagree scale. High scores indicate less conventional attitudes toward women's roles and rights.

Girls' acceptance of their emerging sexuality was measured by the Sexual Self-Concept Scale (SSC), which contains 14 items answered on a 4-point Likert-type agreement scale.[28] Sexual self-concept is defined as an individual's evaluation of her own sexual feelings and actions. The scale was found to be internally consistent (standardized alpha coefficient = 0.90) for a college population and modified for our use with this early adolescent sample. In addition, our team developed two other measures of positive sexual health for this study. The Index of Romance Conventions includes 12 items answered on a 4-point, Likert-type scale, which demonstrated acceptable internal consistency (standardized alpha coefficient = .75). Based on research on girls' sexuality[29-31] and feminist analyses of romance'[30-33] these items reflect norms regulating heterosexual relationships and center on girls identifying and meeting boys' needs, including their sexual desires, and encouraging girls to seek and maintain these relationships at the expense of their own needs and desires. Finally, girls' perceptions of their sexual agency were measured by a composite of two single items: 1) "If I were uncomfortable I know I could refuse a sexual experience that my boyfriend/girlfriend wanted me to try" and "I'm sure I could ask someone I was having sex with to use protection (condoms or birth control)."

Our team performed correlation and simple regression analyses to evaluate the strength and statistical significance of possible associations between early adolescent girls' beliefs about femininity and their sexual health. In addition, we investigated the role of ethnicity in these associations. Class differences that may also be compelling in understanding these associations are not presented at this time. The multiracial subset was not included due to the difficulty in interpreting such analyses.

Results

The girls in the sample were 13 to 14 years old. Fifty-two percent were white, 20% Latina, and 17% bi- or multiracial. Fifty-two percent reported that their families had ever received public assistance, while 29% reported current assistance of some sort, including participation in a free lunch program. Only a third (36%) reported their mothers had college degrees or higher. These girls reported a range of sexual experiences: 82% had held hands, 68% had kissed on the mouth, 24% had touched someone under their clothes or with no clothes on, 28% had been touched under their clothes or with no clothes on, 7% had had sexual intercourse, and 14% reported other forms of sexual experience.

Accepting one's emerging sexuality, feeling entitled to positive sexual agency, and holding a critical perspective on conventions of romance correlated with various forms of beliefs about femininity (see table). We found statistically significant associations between early adolescent girls' espousal of more conventional beliefs about femininity and diminished positive sexual health. For the full sample, girls with higher scores on the Index of Romance Conventions had higher scores on the SIR subscale of the FIS (r = 0.24, p < 0.01), that is, tended to censor and compromise themselves in relationships, and had higher scores on the RWB subscale of the FIS (r = 0.41, p < 0.001), that is, tended to accept conventional norms of attractiveness and beauty and not to experience their own bodily feelings. Girls with lower scores on the sexual agency composite had somewhat higher scores on the SIR subscale of the FIS (r = −0.21, p < 0.01) and lower scores on the AWSA (r = .037, p < 0.001), that is, girls who felt less sexual agency tended to censor and compromise themselves in relationships and have more conventional beliefs about women's roles and rights. Finally, girls who scored lower on the Sexual Self-Concept Scale had lower scores on the AWSA ($r = 0.22$, $p < 0.01$), that is, girls who tended toward less acceptance of their sexuality had more conventional beliefs about women's roles and rights.

When we compared these associations for white girls and Latinas, different patterns emerged in the association between beliefs about femininity and sexual health (see table). There was a strong association between romance conventions and how girls relate to their bodies among white girls ($r = 0.53$, $p < 0.001$), and no significant correlation between these two variables for the Latina girls. We found a strong correlation between sexual self-concept and scores on the AWSA for Latina girls ($r = 0.50$, $p < 0.001$) and a moderate correlation be-

tween these two variables for white girls. In a simple regression analysis, the AWSA explained 9% of the variation in sexual self-concept for white girls [$F(1,75) = 6.99$, $p < 0.01$] and 25% of the variation for Latina girls [$F(1,27) = 9.01$, $p < 0.006$]).

Case Illustration

A subset of this sample (n = 46) was interviewed individually about their experiences with relationships and sexuality. I present here a 13-year-old Latina girl who has appropriated a male persona, calling herself "Will Smith." She was chosen because her stories illustrate how femininity ideology can organize, limit, and challenge girls' attempts at sexual health within a particularly traditional social context. Will Smith exem-

Estimated Correlations Between Adolescent Girls' Beliefs About Femininity and Sexual Health

Variable	Sexual Agency	Romance Conventions	Sexual Self-Concept	mean (sd)
Beliefs About Femininity				
FIS-Self-in-Relationship				
Full Sample (n = 148)	−0.21†	0.24†	0.01	3.27 (.73)
White Girls (n = 77)	−0.16	0.22	0.08	3.31 (.77)
Latina Girls (n = 29)	0.03	0.16	−0.22	3.40 (.75)
FIS-Relationship-with-Body				
Full Sample (n = 148)	−0.12	0.41‡	0.03	3.10 (.67)
White Girls (n = 76)	−0.18	0.53‡	0.08	3.15 (.72)
Latina Girls (n = 29)	−0.01	0.19	−0.04	3.23 (.69)
Attitudes Toward Women				
Full Sample (n = 148)	0.37‡	−0.22†	0.22†	3.45 (.44)
White Girls (n = 77)	0.13	−0.29*	0.29*	3.61 (.30)
Latina Girls (n = 29)	0.33	−0.11	0.50†	3.03 (.50)
mean(sd) Full Sample	3.55 (.67)	2.27 (.48)	3.29 (.54)	
mean(sd) White Girls	3.64 (.52)	2.30 (.47)	3.31 (.52)	
mean(sd) Latina Girls	3.21 (.90)	3.37 (.58)	3.21 (.57)	

*$p < 0.05$ †$p < 0.01$ ‡$p < 0.001$

plifies a pattern identified in these interviews. Girls who articulated a critical perspective on unequal gender arrangements and norms of femininity were better able to answer questions about how being a girl affected the choices they made in their relationships. She was interviewed by a Latina woman in both Spanish and English; the interviewer's questions are italicized.

When asked about how she's supposed to act or be in a relationship because she is a girl, she replied:

> The girl is down to like 5% and the boy is like 95%. Like the boy has the right to go out but the girl needs to stay home cleaning the house . . . I don't agree with that, cause like if I see my boyfriend talking to a girl and I get mad at him, he'll be saying, "Well, it's different, cause you're a girl and I'm a boy." I'll be like, "What's the difference?"
>
> *So if you don't behave the way you have just described you would* . . . I would be a so-called hoochie [a colloquialism for "whore"] . . . I think it's disgusting to tell you the truth . . . in the Dominican Republic, the thing is boys can have as many girls as they want. And you know that's not a problem . . . I was straight up with my boyfriend with that too. I was like, "If you think you're gonna be going on like from me to another girl and then another girl and stuff, you must be buggin, cause it ain't gonna be like that with me."

Will refuses to participate in the conventions of romance and femininity ideology that would have her put up with a double standard that enables boys to treat—and mistreat—girls as objects. She understands and is willing to live with the consequences of possibly losing her boyfriend by taking this stand.

She articulated her awareness of and resistance to being objectified:

> You need to worry what your breast size are. How your butt is formed. For a boy to like you you have to have like the features . . . First it's like the way you act around them [boys], then it's your body, and THEN comes like what's inside, you know what I mean. I don't like that.

Sensing that being objectified renders her agency, feelings, and desires irrelevant, Will demands that she be acknowledged and desired for "who I am." In refusing to be constructed as an object, she is less vulnerable to being used as an object.

Having asked her boyfriend out, Will was willing to be an active agent, taking the initiative in starting a relationship she wants, rather than waiting to be noticed by a boy, and defining its terms. In negotiating her relationship and her sexuality with her boyfriend, Will told him "straight out":

> If you want me because of sex you better be going opening the door and walking away cause it ain't gonna happen . . . I don't want to, nothing of that, not until I'm ready . . . The kissing is going to be done if I like it and if I don't like it, then it's off. And if you don't like that, well that's too bad, you're leaving.

Will feels empowered to include her own feelings in her decisions about sexual expression, as well as to demand that her boyfriend honor her decisions.

Will's stories offer a number of insights into how her femininity ideology shapes and, in her case, contributes to her sexual health. On the one hand, she has taken in the message that she has to fend her boyfriend off from doing sexual things to her, which creates a kind of negative sexual agency. However, she also voices a sense of entitlement to her own desire as an important ingredient in her sexual experiences. She also explicitly ties being used sexually and being sexually passive with more traditional ideas about both femininity and masculinity, ideas that she rejects. While Will is not risk free—she shows some signs of risk of unintended pregnancy, her self-esteem is low, and she is depressed—her ability to see, know, and understand how girls are positioned as sexually vulnerable by cultural norms about femininity constitutes a strength that needs to be recognized and built upon. Without support for this vision, she is at risk of losing what may be keeping her depression and low self-esteem from becoming diminished sexual health.

Discussion

Rather than simply striving to diminish and eliminate the risks associated with sexual intercourse, this work contributes to an expanding conception of sexual health for adolescent girls. Based on feminist scholarship and the obstacles facing girls and women in negotiating sexuality, we inquired about three components of positive sexual health for adolescent girls: accepting one's sexuality, having a sense of positive sexual agency, and rejecting romance conventions. Girls' beliefs about different aspects of femininity were associated with these three features of sexual health. How girls relate to their bodies was not pertinent to sexual agency, but their attitudes toward women and how they experienced themselves in relationships were. Only their attitudes toward women related to their sexual self-concept. Romance conventions emerged as pervasively related to girls' beliefs about femininity, correlating with all three measures. Some of these associations were stronger for the white or Latina girls in the sample.

While causality has not been established, and while all forms of femininity measured did not correlate strongly or significantly with all three aspects of sexual health, this correlational study does suggest that holding conventional beliefs regarding femininity is a barrier to positive sexual health for girls and needs further investigation. One interpretation of these results is that girls' beliefs about femininity extend into their sexual beliefs and practices, that is, that their femininity ideology incorporates cultural norms regulating their negotiation of sexuality. Because the girls in this study were early adolescents, many of whom have limited actual sexual experience, it will be important to see how their femininity ideology relates to their sexual health as they mature.[34]

These moderate correlations suggest that femininity ideology is only one factor that supports or undermines female adolescent sexual health and that ethnicity is an important factor in the relationship between girls' beliefs about femininity and their sexual health. This relationship needs to be investigated for African-American, Asian, Native-American, and biracial girls. The intersections and interplay between and among multiple identities, including race, ethnicity, socioeconomic class, religion, religiosity, abledness, and sexual orientation need to be explored; some will be addressed in future analyses by our team at the Adolescent Sexuality Project.

This study is the beginning of an empirical approach to female adolescent sexuality that connects sexual health with the multifaceted experiences of sexuality that may be part of female adolescence. The model of female adolescent sexual health from which this study is drawn identifies the various relationships and social contexts in which girls negotiate their sexuality. In so doing, our team hopes to shift away from a blaming—as well as "fixing"—the victim approach to girls' sexuality and toward examining and intervening in the relational and social circumstances of girls' lives in order to engender and sustain their sexual health.

This study suggests that conventional femininity ideology may function as a barrier—and, conversely, that critique of femininity ideology may offer a booster—to adolescent girls' sexual health. Girls are under pressure in their families, in their relationships, in their schools, from the media, and perhaps even from service and care providers to capitulate to conventions of femininity that may diminish their sexual health. These social institutions should be subject to the frequent and vocal scrutiny of adults who care for and about adolescent girls. Based on this and other studies in which girls have been interviewed about their lives, it is likely that many girls have never heard a critical perspective on femininity or on how society encourages them to think about their own sexuality. Equally important, girls who have had access to such critiques seem to be more likely to feel empowered and entitled to make healthy and safer choices and to have more positive experiences with sexuality.[17,29,31] Helping adolescent girls identify and question conventions of femininity and to consider that they are entitled to their own sexuality can offer the initial spark needed to begin a process of critical thinking about these aspects of their lives and identities.

References

1. Irvine, J. Cultural differences and adolescent sexualities. In: Irvine J., ed. *Sexual Cultures and the Construction of Adolescent Identities*. Philadelphia, Pa: Temple University Press: 1994: 3.

2. Kaufmann, R. B., Spitz, A. M., Strauss, L. T., et al. The decline in the U.S. teen pregnancy cases, 1990–1995. *Pediatrics*. 1998;102:1141–1147.

3. Centers for Disease Control and Prevention. Trends in sexual risk behaviors among high school students-United States, 1991–1997. *MMWR*. 1998;47:749–752.

4. Haffner, D., Ed. *Facing Facts: Sexual Health for America's Adolescents*. New York, NY: Sexuality Information and Education Council of the United States; 1995. The Report of the National Commission on Adolescent Sexual Health.

5. Hooks, B. *Ain't I a Woman*. Boston, MA: South End Press; 1981.

6. Koedt, A. *Radical Feminism*. New York, NY: Quadrangle; 1972.

7. Rich, A. Compulsory heterosexuality and lesbian existence. In: A. Snitow, C. Stansell, S. Thompson, Eds. *Powers of Desire*. New York, NY: Monthly Review Press; 1983.

8. Vance, C. S. Pleasure and danger: Toward a politics of sexuality, in: C. S. Vance, Ed. *Pleasure and Danger*. London: Pandora Press; 1989.

9. Collins, P. H. *Black Feminist Thought*. New York, NY: Routledge; 1990.

10. Wyatt, G. *Stolen Women*. New York, NY: Wiley; 1997.

11. Espin, O. *Women Crossing Boundaries*. New York, NY: Routledge; 1999.

12. Tolman, D. L. Adolescent girls' sexuality: Debunking the myth of the urban girl, in: B. Leadbeater, N. Way, Eds. *Urban Girls*. New York, NY: New York University Press; 1996: 255–271.

13. Walkerdine, V. *Daddy's Girl*. Cambridge, Mass: Harvard University Press; 1997.

14. Kelly, L. *Surviving Sexual Violence*. Cambridge, Mass: Polity; 1988.

15. Carpenter, L. From girls into women: Scripts for sexuality and romance in Seventeen magazine, 1974–1994. *J Sex Res*. 1998;35:158–168.

16. Durham, M. Dilemmas of desire: Representations of adolescent sexuality in two teen magazines. *Youth and Society*. 1998;29:369–389.

17. Fine, M. Sexuality, schooling, and adolescent females: The missing discourse of desire. *Harvard Educational Review*. 1988;58:29–53.

This research was supported by a grant from the Ford Foundation. The Adolescent Sexuality Project is currently staffed by Michelle Porche, Renee Spencer, Myra Rosen, Judy Chu, and Darce Costello. The author wishes to thank them for their assistance and contributions to this article as well as the three anonymous reviewers who offered thoughtful and helpful comments.

18. Tolman, D. L., Szalacha, L. A. Dimensions of desire: Bridging qualitative and quantitative methods in a study of female adolescent sexuality. *Psychology of Women Quarterly.* 1999;23: 7–39.

19. Birtchnell, S., Whitfield, P., Lacey, J. H. Motivational factors in women requesting augmentation and reduction mammaplasty. *J Psychosom Res.* 1990;34:509–514.

20. Brazelton, E. W., Greene, K. S., Gynther, M., O'Mell, J. Femininity, bulimia, and distress in college women. *Psychol Rep.* 1998;83:355–363.

21. Murnen, S. K., Smolak, L. Femininity, masculinity, and disordered eating: A meta-analytic review. *Int J Eat Disord.* 1997;22:231–242.

22. Hansel, N. K., Weeks, M. E., Ryan, J. G., Fowler G. C. The female role in the transmission of HIV infection. *Arch Fam Med.* 1993;2:870–873.

23. Waldron, I. Patterns and causes of gender differences in smoking. *Soc Sci Med.* 1991; 32:989–1005.

24. Katz, P., Ksansnak, K. Developmental aspects of gender role flexibility and traditionality in middle childhood and adolescence. *Dev Psychol.* 1994;30:272–282.

25. Galambos, N., Almeida, D., Petersen, A. Masculinity, femininity, and sex-role attitudes in early adolescence: Exploring gender intensification. *Child Dev.* 1990;61:1904–1914.

26. Tolman, D. L., Porche, M. V. *The Femininity Ideology Scale: Development and Validation of a New Measure for Adolescent Girls.* Wellesley, Mass: Center for Research on Women, Wellesley College; 1999.

27. Galambos, N., Petersen, A., Richards, M., Geitelson, I. The Attitudes Towards Women Scale for Adolescents: A study of reliability and validity. *Sex Roles.* 1985;13:343–356.

28. Winter, L: The role of sexual self-concept in the use of contraceptives. *Fam Plann Perspect:* 1988;20:123–127.

29. Tolman, D. L. Daring to desire. In: J. Irvine, ed. *Sexual Cultures and the Construction of Adolescent Identities.* Philadelphia, Pa: Temple University Press; 1994:250–284.

30. Lees, S. *Sugar and Spice: Sexuality and Adolescent Girls.* London: Penguin Books; 1993.

31. Thompson, S. *Going All the Way: Teenage Girls' Tales of Sex, Romance and Pregnancy.* New York, NY: Hill and Wang; 1995.

32. Christian-Smith, L. *Becoming a Woman Through Romance.* New York, NY: Routledge; 1990.

33. Radway, J. *Reading the Romance.* Chapel Hill, NC: University of North Carolina Press; 1984.

34. Brown, L. M., Gilligan, C. *Meeting at the Crossroads.* Cambridge, Mass: Harvard University Press; 1992.

*Chapter 7: Putting It All Together*_____

    1. Stokes and Miller discuss how cultural conceptions of masculinity affect the behavior of bisexual males, while Tolman describes how cultural conceptions of femininity affect the behavior of teenage girls. How do these two sets of conceptions fit together?

    2. Both readings offer new models for thinking about sexuality. Do you agree with the authors that there is a need for such models? Why or why not?

    3. What might sexual behavior look like if it was not shaped by cultural conceptions of gender?

8

Gender and Violence

The readings in this chapter explore the complex connections between gender and violence. The first reading describes how an understanding of the community context can enhance a feminist perspective on domestic violence. The feminist perspective, with its emphasis on the gendered nature of power and control, has made significant contributions to our understanding of domestic violence in Western cultures. This perspective may be limited however, when it comes to explaining domestic violence among American Indians. Although there is a tendency in the majority culture to view diverse American Indian societies as a homogeneous group, in fact, tribal differences exist in the rates, causes, and contexts of domestic violence. The author argues that it is necessary to integrate feminist and community approaches to understand this variation and effectively combat domestic violence in American Indian communities. The second reading describes how both feminist psychodynamic theory and socialization theory can be used to explain school violence. The authors make a connection between this violence and developmental processes which encourage boys to be autonomous and stoic, and to feel shame in weakness.

16

The Importance of Community in a Feminist Analysis of Domestic Violence among American Indians

Sherry L. Hamby

According to Hamby, domestic violence rates have risen sharply in many American Indian communities during the past 150 years. Hamby applies an ecological, feminist perspective to explain this sharp rise. This perspective is especially useful for three reasons. First, the same factors established as major contributors to domestic violence in the majority of Western cultures are examined as contributors in native societies: socioeconomic stress and three categories of male dominance (authority, disparagement of women, and restrictiveness). Second, the influence of White, colonial domination on current patriarchal relationships and socioeconomic stress is examined. Third, the cultural diversity of the over 500 native societies is acknowledged, thereby discouraging the tendency to view American Indians as a monolithic culture with a one-size-fits-all solution to social problems. After applying the ecological, feminist perspective, Hamby concludes that most of the factors linked to domestic violence in the majority Western cultures are also contributing factors in contemporary American Indian culture. These are poverty and two forms of male dominance: authority and restrictiveness **(defined norm).** However, disparagement of women—less common among American Indians—does not appear to be a contributing factor **(cultural diversity).** Hamby further concludes that White, colonial domination is largely responsible for socioeconomic stress and patriarchal relationships in many (but not all) native communities. She cautions, however, that levels of socioeconomic stress and male dominance vary widely across native communities, as do social organization (e.g.,

Reprinted by permission of Kluwer Academic/Plenum Publishers. S. L. Hamby (2000). "The Importance of Community in a Feminist Analysis of Domestic Violence Among American Indians. *American Journal of Community Psychology, 28* (5), 649–699.

matrilineal versus patrilineal) and the status of women **(cultural diversity).** These facts point to the importance of designing feminist solutions to domestic violence that take into account the cultural differences of American Indians, and that build on the strengths of each native society (such as the mutual respect between women and men found in several communities). The ecological, feminist model is viewed as an effective model for accomplishing these goals.

Questions to Consider:

1. How well do your experiences and/or observations support the feminist analysis concerning the underlying causes of domestic violence? Explain your answer.
2. According to Hamby, how did external domination by the United States contribute to domestic violence in many native societies?
3. How does Hamby account for the finding that disparagement of women is not linked to domestic violence among American Indians? What challenge does this finding present to majority Western cultures?
4. Do you agree that a focus on community is essential to a feminist analysis of domestic violence in American Indian societies? Explain your answer.
5. How might the ecological, feminist model be applied to understanding domestic violence in your community? (If you are a member of an American Indian community, discuss whether or not you agree with Hamby's analysis.)

There are 512 recognized native groups and 365 state-recognized Indian tribes who speak 200 different languages in the United States alone (Chester, Robin, Koss, Lopez, & Goldman, 1994). The peoples that are defined as a single "American Indian" or "Native American" entity by the majority culture are in fact composed of an extremely diverse and heterogeneous set of communities, many of whom had little or no contact with one another prior to the modern era (Groginsky & Freeman, 1994). American Indians are faced with the same oversimplifications that lump Laotians, Japanese, and others into a single "Asian" category and Puerto Ricans, Brazilians, and many others under a single "Latino" rubric (West, 1998). As with all ethnic and cultural groups, far greater attention needs to be paid to the form and context of individual native communities to advance our understanding of how community structure and identity affect community problems, particularly for American Indians who reside on reservations. This appreciation is especially needed among non-Indian outsiders, who are most likely to see native peoples as a single homogeneous group. While a more community-oriented analysis is needed in a wide range of areas, this paper will focus on how an appreciation of inter-tribal differences enhances a feminist analysis of domestic violence in native North America.

Feminist Analysis of Domestic Violence

Feminism has contributed much to the understanding of the causes and perpetuation of domestic violence in American, Canadian, and European cultures (e.g., Dobash & Dobash, 1979; Pence & Paymar, 1993). The most important contribution has been to emphasize that the primary cause of domestic violence is the gendered nature of power and control in intimate relationships. In Western culture, violence against wives historically occurred in a rigid patriarchal structure that offered almost no legal or social redress to battered wives. According to a feminist analysis, violence against wives is not a problem with anger, but a behavior that has a goal of maintaining male dominance of the social climate. In recent times, Western societal changes have reduced but not eliminated the patriarchal structure (Dobash & Dobash, 1979; Pence & Paymar, 1993). Socialization into gender roles that produce male domination, male violence, and female subordination remains a powerful force. It is still acceptable for men to behave possessively toward their partners and to demand domestic labor. The belief in the sanctity of the family is still valued and produces an unwillingness to intervene in family affairs that helps create a context in which domestic violence can still occur without punishment. This theoretical analysis acknowledges that not all men batter women, and that not all batterers are the same, but the root cause of violence is seen as gendered definitions of privilege (Pence & Paymar, 1993). Nonetheless, significant gains have been made and evidence suggests that rates of domestic violence may be falling over time, at least in the United States (Straus & Kaufman, Kantor, 1994).

More recent feminist analysis has included class along with gender and dominance as crucial to the understanding of domestic violence. Early feminist accounts paid little attention to socioeconomic issues and tended to focus on upper middle class European American females (Ptacek, 1997; Richie, 1996). Domestic violence advocates frequently went even one step further and insisted that there was no association between class and violence in an effort to make clear that domestic violence crosses all class boundaries (e.g., Davidson, 1978). Although it has been repeatedly demonstrated that domestic violence occurs in all socioeconomic groups, it is increasingly acknowledged that economic stresses both increase the likelihood of violence occurring and severely curtail victims' abilities to effectively respond to violence once it has occurred (Cazenave & Straus, 1990; Ptacek, 1997).

The Importance of Community Context

The success of the social movement against domestic violence in American and European countries rests largely on the success of the critique of the status quo that emerged at the beginning of the movement (e.g., Davidson, 1978; Dobash & Dobash, 1979). That critique was successful because feminists accurately identified the common threads of experience in the lives of White, middle class, European American women. Some of those common threads included the isolation produced by the suburban nuclear family, an increasingly secular culture that was heavily influenced by Protestant roots, and traditional patriarchal gender roles. Current efforts to extend this movement to other cultural groups face considerable obstacles due to significant religious, social, economic, and cultural differences between those groups and the generally liberal, secular, and middle-class values of most American antiviolence advocates (Richie, 1996; Timmins, 1995).

Many authors with cross-cultural experience have noted that the ability to extend domestic violence awareness into new communities is dependent on the ability to appreciate, understand, and respect the cultural values of those communities (cf. Timmins, 1995). There are many factors, some centuries old, that are specific to particular tribal groups and that affect the context and definition of domestic violence in native communities (Chester et al., 1994).

Additionally, contemporary disparities in land bases, varying geographic locations of reservations, and differences between tribes with reservations and tribes without them, have created new sources of diversity. For example, some reservations, such as Gila River near Phoenix, Arizona, are located near modern urban centers. As a result, the economic marginalization of its members, who have improved access to jobs and casino profits, is not as extreme as found on more geographically isolated reservations. Contrary to popular conceptions among non-Indians, tribal membership is a key defining aspect of most native communities and an important feature of personal identity.

It should also be noted that American Indians have multilayered identities, just as others do. This often does include an identity of "American Indian," and many organizations such as Inter Tribal Councils, the UNITY youth organization, and the Gathering of Native Americans (GONA) promote common political interests and fellowship. The need for respecting tribal differences is emphasized in this paper both because that is the identity most commonly lost to outsiders and because of the need to find local solutions to the domestic violence problem. Just as the original analysis of domestic violence in the majority U.S. culture focused on commonalties among the community of middle-class White females, so a comprehensive analysis of domestic violence in native North America must start with an appreciation of community identity. Further, although it might be useful to apply the main tenet of a feminist analysis of domestic violence, that of the role of male power and control, to native groups, such application must be sensitive to ethnic differences in the meaning and expression of the concept.

Domestic Violence in Native North America

Existing survey data indicate that rates of domestic violence are currently quite high in most native communities. Within a generally elevated range, there is also evidence for significant variability, although unfortunately most data are not tribal specific. A study of women who had sought various programs for American Indians in the Rocky Mountain region showed 46% had a history of domestic violence (Norton & Manson, 1995). A survey of pregnant native women in Minnesota indicated that 60% were currently with an abusive partner (Bohn, 1993). Both of these studies took place in centralized health care centers that provide services to many tribes in those regions. A qualitative study of three Alaska communities found that informants believed domestic violence to be occurring in 15–36% of the homes in their community (Shinkwin & Pete, 1983). Unfortunately, though, this studied relied on publicly known incidents. The only community-based study of domestic violence victimization found a yearly incidence rate of 48% and a relationship prevalence rate of 75% for female residents of an Apache reservation (Hamby & Skupien, 1998). Other lifetime estimates range from 50–80% (West, 1998).

Medical and shelter data also suggest that rates of domestic violence are high. A study on the Hualapai Indian Reservation in Arizona showed that domestic violence accounted for 56% of all female assault victims who received medical attention (Kuklinski & Buchanan, 1997). In Minnesota, American Indians comprise less than 1% of the population but 11–14% of women in shelters (Bohn, 1989; Wolk, 1982). There are some data suggesting that domestic violence rates are higher for American Indians than for other U.S. ethnic groups. One national study found that rates of severe domestic violence were higher for American Indians than for European Americans (Bachman, 1992), while another found that lifetime rates of all physical assault and rape were higher for American Indians than any other U.S. ethnic group (Tjaden & Thoennes, 1998). In New Mexico, statewide data showed that domestic violence-related homicide rates were higher for American Indians than for others (Arbuckle et al., 1996).

Although these data suggest that rates of domestic violence are generally higher in most native communities compared to other U.S. communities, the quality of information is sometimes poor. Much of this limitation is due to the use of telephone or mail surveys that are appropriate for middle-class suburban homes, but do not include homes that are too poor or isolated to have telephones, or communities whose members have relatively low levels of English fluency. Other methodological drawbacks include a tendency to focus on clinic samples, use of measures with unknown properties in Native populations, and use of interviewers who are unfamiliar with the community (Chester et al., 1994). Data based on nationally representative surveys often include very few American Indians with which to make group comparisons. Much of the literature is still impressionistic and anecdotal (West, 1998). Further, even studies of groups who are primarily American Indian (e.g., Maguire, 1987) may attend little to issues of race or culture. There is a great need for more investigations of domestic violence among American Indians that takes into account the culture and context of Indian life (LaFramboise, Choney, James, & Running Wolf, 1995b).

It is debated whether domestic violence is a new problem in American Indian communities. Some authors believe that domestic violence has been present for a long time, while others assert it dates after the introduction of Western European influences. Many state that while domestic violence did occur prior to Western contact, it was rare and severely sanctioned. Documented cases do date from the mid-1860's but these also postdate missionary contact (Chester et al., 1994), although it seems possible that European influence on communities at the time of first contact was modest. Assessments of native cultures before Western contact are difficult because of the lack of written or visual records (DeBruyn, Wilkins, & Artichoker, 1990), and oral histories have received insufficient attention. It is likely that, as in other areas, there was considerable variability among tribes, and that unrecognized cultural differences account for some of the disagreement. The one area of agreement is that rates of domestic violence appear to have risen dramatically in the last 150 years (Chester et al., 1994; DeBruyn et al., 1990; Gunn Allen, 1990; LaFramboise et al., 1995b). Contact with Westerners has had many negative consequences, including increased domestic violence rates, probably due in part to profound losses in the traditional statuses and roles of both men and women (Wolk, 1982). Participants in one study reported an increase in domestic violence during a 10-year period of oil business development (Durst, 1991). There are anecdotal accounts of U.S. agents forcing violent couples to remain married (Levinson, 1989). While there has been little formal examination of the influence of Western contact and oppression, few question that the poverty and social and economic marginalization of many American Indian communities has contributed to the severity of the current domestic violence problem.

The Role of Dominance in Domestic Violence among American Indians

There is some research evidence, unfortunately rather limited, that the feminist analysis of domestic violence has relevance for American Indian communities. One recent quantitative study found that ratings of partner's control over finances was associated with increased physical assault and injury victimization for Apache females (Hamby & Skupien, 1998). There have been several feminist efforts to intervene against domestic violence in native communities (e.g., DeBruyn et al., 1990; Maguire, 1987; National Training Project, 1997). Although some advocates believe that power and control models have an even deeper meaning for native communities that are also faced with external domination by U.S. society (DeBruyn et al., 1990), in general data on the relevance of a feminist analysis have not been offered. The historical record is composed primarily of qualitative ethnographic accounts, which unfortunately often contain only sparse descriptions of marital relationships (Bohn, 1989). Observers in some native communities have reported that punishment for infidelity was a major control technique and closely tied to domestic violence. Apache tradition, at least in the 19th century, permitted men to cut off the noses of unfaithful wives (Cochise, 1971; Stockel, 1991). Disfigurement was also sometimes the punishment for female infidelity among the Dakota and Ojibway (Bohn, 1989). Many tribes encouraged women to stay in violent marriages if they had children by their husbands (LaFramboise, Berman, & Sohi, 1995a). On

the other hand, abuse that was perceived as unjustified was not tolerated by Ojibway extended family (Bohn, 1989).

Levinson's (1989) seminal cross-cultural work is still the main source of quantified information in this area. His results indicate that patterns of dominance between husbands and wives can help explain both high and low levels of domestic violence. He reviewed the ethnographic records of 90 societies worldwide. Of these, 17 were native communities in North America. Of those 17, 3 were found to have no or minimal levels of family violence: Iroquois, Fox, and Papago (also known as Tohono O'Odham). The others, such as the Arapaho, showed evidence of domestic violence at least back to the 19th century. Societies that lacked family violence were generally characterized by shared decision making, wives' control of some family resources, equally easy divorce access for husbands and wives, no premarital sex double standard, monogamous marriage, marital cohabitation, peaceful conflict resolution within and outside the home, and immediate social responses to domestic violence. Some of these, such as shared decision making, clearly represent authority aspects of dominance, whereas others, such as divorce access and lack of sexual double standards, indicate that societies that do not restrict or disparage women tend to be less violent. In general, his findings support the feminist conclusion that higher levels of male dominance are associated with high rates of domestic violence. Levinson's work is also consistent with the proposition that variation among native communities exists and can be partly attributed to differences in dominance dynamics.

Although the literature that focuses on domestic violence among American Indians is quite small, there is considerable literature on gender roles and gender dynamics. This body of knowledge can help to illustrate the importance of tribal context in an analysis of domestic violence. While much of this literature has focused on the period before Western domination, the dramatic effects of Western contact indicate that both the traditional and modern eras need to be examined to fully understand today's domestic violence problems. The following discussion first takes up the issue of gender and power using feminist and community psychology principles. Although class issues have received less attention, they are also critical to an analysis of the contemporary situation. A section is devoted to the issues of class and domestic violence. This is followed by conclusions and recommendations for addressing domestic violence in Indian country.

Gender and Dominance

Gender and dominance have been topics of increasing visibility in literature about native peoples. Unfortunately, much of the literature is heavily politicized. Early literature on native communities has been criticized for overly negative and skimpy portrayals of native women that were often excessively colored by colonial and missionary attitudes (c.f. Klein & Ackerman, 1995). In recent years, however, the political pendulum has swung in the other direction and American Indians are often idealistically held up as examples of egalitarian or matriarchal societies (e.g., Guemple, 1995; Gunn Allen, 1990). The implication of these portrayals is that violence was not part of male-female relations in matriarchal societies.

Neither portrayal is accurate and both extreme views tend to paint in broad strokes the gender roles in individual tribes and often for all of Indian country. Current slogans about domestic violence like "It's

Not Cultural" (DeBruyn *et al.*, 1990) or "It's Not Traditional" are meant to apply equally well to the Apache as to the Lakota when there are large and important differences in gender roles in these and other native communities. Even more problematically, analyses of single communities are often colored by predetermined conclusions. For example, Guemple (1995) details how Inuit men "exercise ultimate control over decision making in domestic matters" (p. 22), how wives are reprimanded if their housework is not acceptable to their husbands, and how husbands can even arrange sexual exchanges with other men without their wives' consent. She further reports that Inuit women do not have similar reciprocal powers, yet nonetheless concludes that "men and women in Inuit society enjoy relatively equal status, power, and prestige" (p. 27), primarily because the division of labor is so gender specific that they have relatively independent social roles. Although it is important to acknowledge variations in power dynamics among Inuit tribes, as with any other community, such a biased analysis of social relations is doomed to failure despite the authors' apparent good intentions. A more complete analysis would incorporate nonegalitarian features of power dynamics into the authors' final assessment of women's status. Some authors at least acknowledge that their redefinition of reality does not correspond to current attitudes in many tribes. For example, DeBruyn et al. (1990) discuss the current problem, common in some tribes, of using the term "Indian love" as a slang term for domestic violence.

In fact, the analysis of gender relations in native communities is a complex and challenging task. There are many frameworks that might be applied, but a feminist analysis of the gendered nature of power relations is key to understanding how gender relations can promote or at least permit domestic violence. The association of gender and dominance will be explored using a tripartite typological model of dominance (Hamby, 1996) to elucidate some of the variations in dominance within and across native groups. The types of dominance that are most closely associated with domestic violence in existing literature can be grouped into three main categories: authority, restrictiveness, and disparagement (Hamby, 1996). An appreciation of the distinctions among forms of dominance has been noted in previous literature (e.g., Pence & Paymar, 1993), but this framework is the first formal organization of dominance types. While the existing empirical literature on the dominance-violence link consists primarily of studies with European Americans, the framework provides a beginning place to explore these issues in native communities and highlight areas that need to be changed or adapted in different communities.

Many writers emphasize the complementarity of gender roles in many native communities (cf. Klein & Ackerman, 1995). In native societies with highly specialized gender roles, there was often little overlap in work and sometimes even little contact between men and women. Unfortunately, past scholarship has seldom concentrated on areas of overlap, and in particular, on areas of conflict and how conflict was handled. Thus, it is possible to emphasize matrilineal descent or some other feature of women's lives without focusing on their risk for being abused or mistreated, which likely involves their interactions with their husbands and their community at least as much as it involves segregated aspects of their lives.

Gender and Authority

The notion of authority is closely related to decision-making power. In this form of dominance, instead of both partners in a relationship having equal input on decisions about the relationship, one partner holds a majority of decision-making power. He or she is "in charge" of the relationship. Authority is also related to social roles and social status, and is often obtained through wealth, occupational status, or other forms of prestige. The association between authority and domestic violence has been studied extensively, although much Western research has relied on a rather poor measure of decision making. Thus, the size of the association between authority and domestic violence has been found to be only moderate (although positive) in most U.S. and European studies (Hamby & Sugarman, 1996). In his comprehensive cross-cultural study, however, Levinson (1989) found that male household decision-making power was one of the most important predictors of rates of violence.

Male and female authority is also the form of dominance that has been most extensively studied in native communities. In scholarship about native communities, it is most often discussed using the anthropological terms for social organization: matriarchy/patriarchy, matrilineal/patrilineal, and matrilocal/patrilocal. Matriarchal societies, in contrast to patriarchal ones, are ones in which the mother is the head of the family, clan, or tribe. Final decision-making power rests with the mother or possibly other senior females in this kind of organization. Most matriarchal societies are also matrilineal; that is, the line of descent or clan membership is passed through the mother. There are, however, far more matrilineal societies than matriarchal ones, both in and out of Indian country. Matrilocal societies are those in which living and social arrangements focus on the woman's family of origin, as when newlyweds reside near the bride's parents. Female authority associated with matrilineal and matrilocal societies is often indirect.

Many outsiders believe that all traditional native cultures are matriarchal and often refer to native women as particularly empowered, but this is an overgeneralization that does not reflect variations from one tribal culture to another and even within single tribes (Klein & Ackerman, 1995). Many observers do not distinguish between matriarchal and matrilineal organization, as well. In fact, gender roles and social organization differ greatly from one tribe to the next (LaFramboise et al., 1995a). The status of women probably varies from one context to another in many tribes more than in most Western cultures. For example, a tribe may be matrilineal while at the same time limiting women's access to political positions and religious ceremonies. Most studies focus on the precolonial period, but contact with European Americans has eroded female-centered social organization in many parts of Indian country. Christian marriage conventions influence many American Indian tribes today, and patriarchal, patrilineal patterns are far more prevalent today than in the past. Boarding schools often participated in the indoctrination of Western values by offering less education to girls than boys and making girls clean the schools (LaFramboise et al., 1995b). Most observers (e.g., Gunn Allen, 1990; Wolk, 1982) believe native women have lost status due to Western patriarchal influences, but at least one study attributed a very recent rise in domestic violence to the increasing status of females (Durst, 1991). Informants in those Canadian native communities cited increased tendencies for women to work outside the home and become the primary wage earners as causes of domestic violence.

Although it is not possible to describe all 512 groups in this paper, some flavor of the differences and similarities across tribes can be suggested with a few examples. The San Carlos Apache are traditionally matrilineal and matrilocal. In their case, matrilocal social organization is better preserved than matrilineal clan identity. The Iroquois, Hopi, and Zuni tribes are also matrilineal (Chester et al., 1994). In contrast, the Omaha (V. Phillips, Omaha tribal member, personal communication, 1997), Ojibway (Bohn, 1989), Pima, and Cheyenne (Chester et al., 1994) are all patrilineal. Whereas many matrilineal societies are not matriarchal, most patrilineal societies are patriarchal. Some native societies practiced pure forms of neither and the common categorizations do not easily fit all native cultures. For example, the Pomos of the west coast traditionally practiced both matrilocal and patrilocal residence, with the same couple often alternating between families, at least for a time (Patterson, 1995). Klein (1995) has described how the Tlingit have both a matrilineal and avunculocal (residing near one's uncle) system that is further complicated by a common cross-cousin marriage pattern.

The Iroquois, a confederacy of tribal nations, are a good example of the complexity and variability of social organization. Traditional Iroquois societies are often described as matriarchal (e.g., Chester *et al.,* 1994; Gunn Allen, 1986) and approach matriarchy more closely than most societies. Historically, Iroquois women had significant arenas of power, including land ownership, control over horticultural production, and the ability to nominate chiefs. Important powers were reserved for men, however. Women could not be chiefs although the line of descent passed through women. Women influenced who became leaders but were not in direct leadership roles. They influenced but did not control war making. Thus, they do not represent a full matriarchy (Bilharz, 1995). Rather, traditional Iroquois society may best be described as one with complementary gender roles, matrilineal descent, and matrilocal residence (Bilharz, 1995). The Seneca, one nation of the Iroquois, illustrate some of the changes that modified traditional society during the colonial period. By the late 1800's, Quakers and Federal officials had transformed their matrilineal society into a patrilineal one that emphasized the nuclear family (Bilharz, 1995; Gunn Allen, 1986). The reservation system and disagreements with the United States led to political changes that disenfranchised women. Only men could hold tribal offices and vote. Women did not gain the vote until 1964. At that time, the aftereffects of a flood provided Seneca women opportunities to influence relief programs and obtain more paid employment. More recently, women have held elective offices, but not president (Bilharz, 1995). Thus, some of the status lost in the last 150 years has been regained, although outside patriarchal influences continue.

The complexity of gender status among the Seneca and other tribes needs greater recognition. As best as can be determined, few tribes were absolute matriarchies and an overly simplistic portrayal of them as such can mask important gender issues. Even further caution should be exercised in concluding that domestic violence is absent from societies with matriarchal, matrilineal, or complementary social organization. Male and female authority is only one aspect of gender roles. Authority probably best represents what resources women can access to help stop domestic violence. Matrilineal descent or matrilocal residence may speak little to the question of how much freedom women have to choose their friends, take on the roles they want, or divorce as they wish. A broader analysis of

dominance can shed more light on the role of gender in domestic violence. Other forms of dominance are more centrally tied to the dynamics of domestic violence in European American countries (Hamby & Sugarman, 1996), and deserve some exploration in native contexts as well.

Gender and Disparagement

Disparagement occurs when one partner fails to equally value the other partner and has an overall negative appraisal of his or her partner's worth. For example, one partner may feel that he or she is more deserving, skilled, and attractive than the other is. Typical beliefs include "My partner is not a very good person." The egalitarian opposite occurs when both partners in a relationship equally value each other's worth and personal attributes (Hamby, 1996). Spousal disparagement is correlated with frequency of conflict and divorce (Shackelford & Buss, 1997) as well as with abusive behavior (Hamby, 1996; Shackelford & Buss, 1997). Although this aspect of dominance has been less studied than authority and restrictiveness, it appears to be linked to authority and at least moderately related to violence (Hamby & Sugarman, 1996).

Many accounts of native communities suggest that disparagement was not historically common. Observers often note the valuation of both male and female contributions to the maintenance of the social fabric of tribal communities. The complementarity of gender roles and the necessity of many forms of labor to the success of a community tend to promote an appreciation for each person's contribution. Descriptions of the Tlingit (Klein, 1995), Inuit (Guemple, 1995), Blackfoot (Kehoe, 1995), Lakota (Wolk, 1982), and many other groups emphasize the value of both men's and women's contributions to family and society. Women's role as bearers of children are also typically honored. Spirituality is an extremely important aspect of most American Indian cultures and typically also emphasizes respect and honor. This aspect of egalitarian social relations appears to be a strength of many native cultures.

There is very little written on contemporary patterns of disparagement, but it is likely that the loss of traditional roles has led to less mutual valuation of the roles of men and women. Anecdotally, the devaluation of both male and female status has been much commented upon (e.g., Gunn Allen, 1990). Men's traditional roles have eroded more than women's traditional roles in many communities, as jobs outside the home have become scarce and hunting and fishing activities are sometimes restricted (Wolk, 1982). It has been noted that role loss and internalized oppression have had a profound negative impact on men's self-esteem and contributes to the level of violence in native communities (Duran, Duran, Woodis, & Woodis, 1998). Meanwhile, women's roles as caregiver and food preparer may be better preserved. It is possible that the relatively greater devaluation of men's roles has led to frustration and jealousy of women, perhaps especially those who have paying jobs. This could be one mechanism for the increase in domestic violence found by Durst (1991) during a period when women increased outside employment. One qualitative study found that some battered Navajo women felt men could not handle their wives' success when faced with unemployment or similar stresses (Maguire, 1987). These outside pressures may contribute to a sharpening of gender-based distinctions and contribute to the increases in disparagement and domestic violence of the last 150 years.

Gender and Restrictiveness

Restrictiveness refers to the extent to which one partner feels the right to control and limit the other's behavior. For example, the restrictive partner may prohibit their partner from spending time with certain individuals or going certain places. The restrictive partner usually feels that he or she has a right to know and be involved with everything his or her partner does. The egalitarian opposite of restrictiveness occurs when both partners in a relationship respect the other's right to some individual autonomy concurrent with their mutual commitment (Hamby, 1996). Jealousy is often a main cause of restrictiveness. Restrictiveness is a prominent feature of many clinical descriptions of battering (e.g., Pence & Paymar, 1993). A meta-analysis showed that restrictiveness had the strongest association with domestic violence of the three dominance types (Hamby & Sugarman, 1996). These studies consisted of primarily European American participants. Restrictiveness has received less attention in the literature on gender and native communities, yet the importance of the construct in Western samples suggest it may have potential to contribute to an understanding of domestic violence in native communities.

As with other aspects of native communities, an appreciation of marked variation across groups is the key to understanding restrictiveness. Individual autonomy, which is the opposite of restrictiveness, is highly valued among the Blackfoot (Kehoe, 1995). As a result, Blackfoot women could potentially depart from traditional gender roles of submissiveness and docility and seek other lifestyles. There is a concept called *ninauposkitzipxpe,* or "manly hearted woman" in traditional Blackfoot society. Such women owned property, tended to be active in religious ceremonies, and were assertive in public, in their homes, and as sexual partners. The term "manly hearted" derived from gender stereotypes that considered boldness and ambition to be ideal male attributes, but the designation was available to many, especially older, women (Kehoe, 1995). Among the Ojibway (Wolk, 1982) and Apache (Stockel, 1991), some women became healers and warriors, but it was not generally accepted for men to take on women's roles.

Modern attitudes toward restrictiveness in intimate relationships are affected by a complicated interplay of many issues. Many tribes currently show the influence of Christianity with resultant restrictions on women's behavior, particularly access to divorce. For example, members of Pueblo tribes, which are heavily Catholic, are often very resistant to women's efforts to leave abusive relationships and may be told that they should tolerate such abuse (DeBruyn et al., 1990; LaFramboise et al., 1995a). In one study, Navajo women reported that their own parents and their inlaws frequently encouraged reconciliation after violence (Maguire, 1987). Women who work to help domestic violence victims on some reservations have received death threats in efforts to intimidate them (DeBruyn et al., 1990).

Rigidity in gender roles is one aspect of restrictiveness, and is the only aspect that has been extensively described in the literature. There are many other important aspects of restrictiveness, however. Control over social contacts and movements outside the home are two primary characteristics in many cultures, including those influenced by Christian and Muslim religions. It seems possible that they are important to native communities as well. Some Inuit women had no control over their own bodies (Guemple, 1995). Jealousy was apparently common among the Apache around the

time of early Western contact, supported by social prohibitions restricting access between married men and women. A man whose wife was unfaithful was considered unmanly if he did not take strong action, which usually meant beating and often disfiguring his wife (Opler, 1941/1996). A more recent study of battered Navajo women found that they often thought jealousy or the desire for control was the motive for violence (Maguire, 1987). Anecdotally, today many native battered women report such control tactics as being locked in their homes, forbidden to speak with their friends or even family of origin, and not being allowed to have money. Whether these are general patterns in some tribes needs further study.

Socioeconomic Organization and Domestic Violence

Violence in male-female relationships comes not just from gender roles, but also from the stresses that are placed on both genders. American Indian and other ethnic minorities continue to be disadvantaged in a society in which race determines access to economic resources. Current poverty rates of American Indian communities range from 20–47%, compared with 12% of the total U.S. population (LaFramboise et al., 1995b). Numerous sources document the lower income, education, and employment of American Indians in contrast to European Americans and even compared to some other minority groups (West, 1998). There is consistent evidence that lower socioeconomic status places one at greater risk for domestic violence (Ptacek, 1997). Racism also makes it more difficult for American Indian victims to access the resources they need to escape domestic violence, such as assistance from legal and social services agencies (Maguire, 1987). Other communities beset by extreme poverty and racial discrimination, such as Black women in ghetto communities, also have high rates of battering (e.g., Richie, 1996). No study of American Indians can be complete without an acknowledgment of their socioeconomic situation.

Socioeconomic change has been dramatic in the last 150 years. Many native tribes were hunting and gathering societies prior to Western contact, but others, such as the Pueblo tribes, were primarily agriculturally based farming communities (Wolk, 1982). In some societies, such as the Apache, raiding held significant economic importance (Opler, 1941/1996). Most communities did not adhere to a concept of individual land ownership. Some tribes moved seasonally to maintain the best access to food and water, but others lived in single locations with year-round access to food. Lack of food and other necessities was not unknown, but differential lack of resources was fairly uncommon. There were not marked disparities between the wealth of different tribes that approach the differences between Anglo and Indian communities today. Nonetheless, the individual accumulation of wealth and the consequent ability to be generous were important in some tribes, such as the Tlingit, and women with greater socioeconomic status enjoyed greater freedoms in some groups (Klein, 1995).

In the last century, increases in poverty rates and changes in socioeconomic organization are thought to have contributed to the current high rates of domestic violence. The forced transition from hunting, gathering, and farming to a cash-based economy threw most native groups into a cycle of poverty and indebtedness from which most have not emerged (Bohn, 1989; Chester et al., 1994; DeBruyn et al.,

1990). The ability to develop economically strong communities has been severely damaged by other forms of economic and social marginalization. These include the removal of Indian peoples from their ancestral lands, prohibitions against traditional religious practices, frequent removal of Indian children into foster homes and boarding schools, and a drastic reduction in the native population from the time of Western contact until the creation of the reservations. Some authors also believe that stereotypical images of Indians, which emphasized the physical threat that Indians posed to U.S. residents, have become a self-fulfilling prophecy over time and have affected native peoples despite their struggles to oppose them (Gunn Allen, 1990). In fact, the persistence of these images contributes to some reluctance to provide more data on domestic violence that potentially could be misused to reinforce negative stereotypes (Wolk, 1982). This is another reason why it is extremely important to provide textured, contextualized accounts of domestic violence that avoid racist stereotypes.

Socioeconomic problems, including the loss of social roles due to unemployment and lifestyle restrictions, have also promoted alcoholism in native communities (Duran et al., 1998). Although most participants in one study saw alcohol as a major cause of domestic violence (Hamby & Skupien, 1998), it also seems likely that both problems stem from the social conditions created by Western oppression. It should also be noted that the use of alcohol and other drugs varies considerably from one native community to another (Koss & Chester, 1997; Pego, Hill, Solomon, Chisolm, & Ivey, 1996), and, as with other areas, blanket generalizations should be avoided.

Despite the importance of socioeconomic issues and the effects they have on many aspects of native life, the association between socioeconomic status and domestic violence has been even less studied in native communities than the link between male dominance and violence. In a rare study of socioeconomic factors, Durst (1991) found mixed effects in a study of two native Arctic communities. He reported that domestic violence rates appeared to increase with industrial development but also that the communities' willingness to discuss and respond to the problem increased. Norton and Manson (1995) did not find socioeconomic differences within their native sample, but differences between violence levels in native and nonnative communities are often attributed to socioeconomic differences (Chester et al., 1994). In other minority communities, poverty often helps create violent situations and keeps women in them (Richie, 1996). Thus, it likely that American Indians are not inherently more violent than other groups, but are more likely to be overrepresented in demographic categories that are at greater risk for violence.

Summary and Implications

Many factors contribute to the current domestic violence situation in Indian country. Although there is evidence that current rates of domestic violence are very high in Indian country, insufficient attention has been paid to tribal differences in rates, causes, and contexts of violence. The several hundred communities that are identified as American Indian by the majority United States and Western culture encompass the gamut from matriarchal, matrilineal societies to patriarchal, patrilineal societies and many forms in between. Possible responses to domestic violence will also depend on specific tribal cultures and the varying degrees of Western influence.

Contextualized, community-oriented feminist analyses need to take these differences into account. In addition, class, another important element of an ecological, feminist analysis, is a hugely important factor in tribal communities that have often lost their traditional sources of sustenance and wealth. The stress of poverty contributes to the high rates of domestic violence and should be part of any contextualized or ecological analysis.

The implications of such an analysis are numerous.

1. Although it may seem frustrating to outsiders to have to individually approach each community, many of which are fractions of their precolonial size, this is nonetheless needed. The feminist analysis of gender, class, and power will vary tremendously from cultures such as the Iroquois, who traditionally gave women considerable power, to the Pueblos, who have been influenced by Catholicism and its patriarchal ideology for over 400 years. The frequency of domestic violence and the ability to respond to it will vary from the Fox, who have historically experienced low levels of domestic violence, to the Apache, for whom domestic violence was sometimes an acceptable punishment. Analyses of these communities need to be as accurate and culturally congruent as the critiques that initiated the domestic violence movement in European American cultures, or they will have little impact. For example, in one Apache community, presentations on the historic lack of domestic violence in Indian country are often greeted by questions about the Apache practice of cutting off a nose for infidelity. These questions may not be offered to the

speaker but discussed only among community members. Overgeneralizations, no matter how positive, diminish the credibility of both speaker and intervention.

2. As with most nonmajority communities, we need more information on prevalence rates, antecedents, and outcomes of domestic violence (West, 1998). Research should assess tribal identification, residence (on and off reservation), and should not aggregate data across diverse groups.

3. The small postcolonial size of most American Indian communities affects what interventions will be seen as congruent with preserving community identity. According to the 1990 census, only nine tribes have more than 50,000 members. While the 1990 census is generally considered an undercount of tribal populations, this still illustrates how tribal survival is a real issue for many American Indians. The choice of marriage partners from one's own tribe may be quite limited. Although many interracial marriages occur, some women may be reluctant to marry outside their tribe and especially to marry a non-Indian. The dilution of bloodlines is a sensitive issue in some communities (Sprott, 1994). A contextualized analysis suggests that divorce—a recommendation of many domestic violence advocates—may be viewed quite differently by American Indians who will not have the same options for intraracial remarriage that most other women have. Advocates from other ethnic groups may see such attitudes simply as prejudice against interracial marriages rather than as cultural survival issues.

4. Local cultures should be viewed as resources and potential sources of strength (Trickett, 1996). For example, autonomy, highly valued among Blackfoot (Kehoe, 1995), could play a central role in formulating community-based domestic violence interventions. Other values are more central to other native groups. Among the Apache, strength, especially in the sense of endurance, and respect are primary values and any community intervention would do well to emphasize those attributes. The importance of making specific tribal adaptations is increasingly recognized by groups such as National Training Project (1997), which address this issue when they share a batterers program developed among the Lakota with other native groups. The lack of disparagement that characterizes many American Indian cultures is also a resource.

5. Interventions in American Indian communities need to be sensitive to the history of oppression and domination by outsiders. Using materials or resources developed for the majority culture can raise issues of domination. At the same time, tribal communities should not be forced to reinvent the wheel in some outsider's interest of developing an emic approach. Starting from scratch may seem like a luxury of academic privilege, and many American Indian communities are interested in more immediate solutions. They may be happy to borrow from existing work if they feel that will be effective and efficient. There can also be advantages to outsider participation; for example, some tribal members perceive greater confidentiality with outsiders. Such factors should be considered and be openly acknowledged.

How can these goals be accomplished? It is mostly among outsiders that more attention needs to be paid to these recommendations. Feminist standpoint theory (e.g., Hartsock, 1998) points out that subordinate groups have information about social relations that are not available to members of the dominant group, as subordinate members must learn the social mores of both groups. One Blackfoot woman expresses this idea by calling American Indians " bicultural warriors" (Newbreast, 1998). Oppression should not be romanticized, but members of subordinate groups may be less likely to see themselves as "universal man." Standpoint theorists also discuss how achievement of a standpoint is not an automatic byproduct of group membership, but often intentionally sought (Hartsock, 1998). Although no European American can entirely escape his or her dominant ethnic position, it is perhaps possible to at least increase one's awareness of what that means. Most American Indian reservation communities have distinct cultures. They offer unique opportunities to get away from the White experience of being perceived as the universal norm—to get away from the overwhelming experience of being treated as lacking race or culture that is so pervasive in American society.

Unfortunately, most non-native researchers and providers interact with American Indian cultures from a position of power and privilege. They spend only brief periods, sometimes hours, on reservations, interact only as professionals, and leave. It is possible to do otherwise. In the spirit of community psychology, one can become involved in antidomestic violence movements, or one can attend community social activities. Unlike other U.S. minority communities, tribes typically have their own government and one can often attend political rallies or town meetings. European

Americans can experience first hand what it is like to be a statistical minority, what it is like to not know the appropriate social behavior or catch all of the jokes, what it is like to be regarded with uncertainty or suspicion about the reasons for your presence, and what it is like to hear frequent references to the problems caused by your own cultural group. European Americans who are willing to do so will learn that they indeed have a culture and an ethnic identity. This will hopefully promote more culturally congruent violence research and more active domestic violence programs with American Indians.

References

Arbuckle, J., Olson, L., Howard, M., Brillman, J., Anctil, C., & Sklar, D. (1996). Safe at home? Domestic violence and other homicides among women in New Mexico. *Annals of Emergency Medicine, 27,* 210–214.

Bachman, R. (1992). *Death and violence on the reservation: Homicide, family violence, and suicide in American Indian populations.* Westport, CT: Auburn House.

Bilharz, J. (1995). First among equals? The changing status of Seneca women. In L. Klein & L. Ackerman (Eds.), *Women and power in native North America* (pp. 101–112). Norman: University of Oklahoma Press.

Bohn, D. K. (1989). *Roles, status, and violence: Ojibway women in historical perspective.* Unpublished manuscript.

Bohn, D. K. (1993). Nursing care of American Indian battered women. *AWHONN's Clinical Issues, 4,* 424–436.

Cazenave, N. A., & Straus, M. A. (1990). Race, class, network embeddedness, and family violence: A search for potent support systems. In M. Straus & R. Gelles (Eds.), *Physical violence in American families: Risk factors and adaptations to violence in 8,145 families* (pp. 321–340). New Brunswick, NJ: Transaction Publishers.

Chester, B., Robin, R. W., Koss, M. P., Lopez, J., & Goldman, D. (1994). Grandmother dishonored: Violence against women by male partners in American Indian communities. *Violence and Victims, 9,* 249–258.

Cochise, C. N. (with Griffith, A. K.). (1971). *The first hundred years of Niño Cochise.* New York: Pyramid Books.

Davidson, T. (1978). *Conjugal crime: Understanding and changing the wifebeating pattern.* New York: Hawthorn Books, Inc.

DeBruyn, L., Wilkins, B., & Artichoker, K. (1990, November). *"It's not cultural": Violence against American Indian women.* Paper presented at the 89th American Anthropological Association Meeting, New Orleans, LA.

Dobash, R. E., & Dobash, R. P. (1979). *Violence against wives: A case against patriarchy.* New York: The Free Press.

Duran, E., Duran, B., Woodis, W., & Woodis, P. (1998). A postcolonial perspective on domestic violence in Indian country. In R. Carillo & J. Tello (Eds.), *Family violence and men of color: Healing the wounded male spirit* (pp. 95–113). New York: Springer.

Durst, D. (1991). Conjugal violence: Changing attitudes in two northern native communities. *Community Mental Health Journal, 27,* 359–373.

Groginsky, L., & Freeman, C. (1994). Domestic violence in American Indian Indian and Alaskan Native communities. *Protecting Children, 11,* 13–16.

Guemple, L. (1995). Gender in Inuit society. In L. Klein & L. Ackerman (Eds.), *Women and power in native North America* (pp. 17–27). Norman: University of Oklahoma Press.

Gunn Allen, P. (1986). *The sacred hoop: Recovering the feminine in American Indian tradition.* Boston: Beacon.

Gunn Allen, P. (1990, July). Violence and the American Indian woman. *Newsletter: Common Ground—Common Planes,* 186–188. The Women of Color Partnership Program.

Hamby, S. L. (1996). The Dominance Scale: Preliminary psychometric properties. *Violence and Victims, 11,* 199–212.

Hamby, S. L., & Skupien, M. B. (1998). Domestic violence on the San Carlos Apache Indian Reservation: Rates, associated psychological symptoms, and current beliefs. *The Indian Health Services Provider, 23,* 103–106.

Hamby, S. L., & Sugarman, D. B. (1996, August). Power and partner violence: A meta-analytic review. In S. L. Hamby (Chair), *Theorizing about gender socialization and power in family violence.* Symposium conducted at the American Psychological Association Annual Meeting, Toronto, Ontario.

Hartsock, N. C. M. (1998). *The feminist standpoint revisited and other essays.* Boulder, CO: Westview Press.

Kehoe, A. B. (1995). Blackfoot persons. In L. Klein & L. Ackerman (Eds.), *Women and power in native North America* (pp. 113–125). Norman: University of Oklahoma Press.

Klein, L. F. (1995). Mother as clanswoman: Rank and gender in Tlingit society. In L. Klein & L. Ackerman (Eds.), *Women and power in native North America* (pp. 28–45). Norman: University of Oklahoma Press.

Klein, L. F., & Ackerman, L. A. (Eds.). (1995). *Women and power in native North America.* Norman: University of Oklahoma Press.

Koss, M. P., & Chester, B. (1997). *Alcoholism prevalence and gene/environment interactions in American Indian tribes.* Unpublished manuscript.

Kuklinski, D. M., & Buchanan, C. B. (1997). Assault injuries on the Hualapai Indian Reservation: A descriptive study. *The Indian Health Services Provider, 22,* 60–64.

LaFramboise, T. D., Berman, J. S., & Sohi, B. K. (1995a). American Indian women. In L. Comas-Diaz & B. Greene (Eds.), *Women of color: Integrating ethnic and gender identities in psychotherapy* (pp. 30–71). New York: Guilford Press.

LaFramboise, T. D., Choney, S. B., James, A., & Running Wolf, P. R. (1995b). American Indian women and psychology. In H. Landrine (Ed.), *Bringing cultural diversity to feminist psychology: Theory, research, and practice* (pp. 197–239). Washington, DC: American Psychological Association.

Levinson, D. (1989). *Family violence in cross-cultural perspective.* Newbury Park, CA: Sage.

Maguire, P. (1987). *Doing participatory research: A feminist approach.* Amherst: University of Massachusetts.

National Training Project. (1997). *Walking in balance: A native approach to domestic violence.* Duluth, MN: Author.

Newbreast, T. (1998, January). *The challenge of FAS in Native American communities.* Presented at FAS: Train the Trainer, San Carlos Apache Reservation, AZ.

Norton, I. M., & Manson, S. M. (1995). A silent minority: Battered American Indian women. *Journal of Family Violence, 10,* 307–318.

Opler, M. E. (1941/1996). *An Apache life-way: The economic, social, and religious institutions of the Chiricahua Indians.* Lincoln: University of Nebraska Press.

Patterson, V. D. (1995). Evolving gender roles in Pomo society. In L. Klein & L. Ackerman (Eds.), *Women and power in native North America* (pp. 126–145). Norman: University of Oklahoma Press.

Pego, C. M., Hill, R. F., Solomon, G. W., Chisolm, R. M., & Ivey, S. E. (1996). Tobacco, culture, and health among American Indians: A historical review. *The Indian Health Services Provider, 21,* 19–28.

Pence, E., & Paymar, M. (1993). *Education groups for men who batter. The Duluth model.* New York: Springer.

Ptacek, J. (1997, July). *Racial politics, class politics, and research on woman battering.* Paper presented at the 5th International Family Violence Research Conference, Durham, NH.

Richie, B. E. (1996). *Compelled to crime: The gender entrapment of battered black women.* Florence, KY: Routledge.

Shackelford, T. K., & Buss, D. M. (1997). Spousal esteem. *Journal of Family Psychology, 11,* 478–488.

Shinkwin, A. D., & Pete, M. C. (1983). *Homes in disruption: Spouse abuse in Yupik Eskimo society.* Unpublished doctoral dissertation, University of Alaska, Fairbanks.

Sprott, J. E. (1994). "Symbolic ethnicity" and Alaska Natives of mixed ancestry living in Anchorage: Enduring group or sign of impending assimilation? *Human Organization, 53,* 311–322.

Stockel, H. H. (1991). *Women of the Apache nation: Voices of truth.* Reno: University of Nevada Press.

Straus, M. A., & Kaufman Kantor, G. (1994, July). *Change in spousal assault rates from 1975 to 1992: A comparison of three national surveys in the United States.* Presented at the 13th World Congress of Sociology, Bielefeld, Germany.

Timmins, L. (1995). *Listening to the thunder: Advocates talk about the battered women's movement.* Vancouver: Women's Research Centre.

Tjaden, P., & Thoennes, N. (1998). *Prevalence, incidence, and consequences of violence against women: Findings from the National Violence Against Women Survey.* Washington, DC: U.S. Department of Justice (NCJ 172837).

Trickett, E. J. (1996). A future for community psychology: The contexts of diversity and the diversity of contexts. *American Journal of Community Psychology, 24,* 209–234.

West, C. M. (1998). Lifting the "political gag order": Breaking the silence around partner violence in ethnic minority families. In L. Williams & J. Jasinski (Eds.), *Partner violence: A 20 year review and synthesis* (pp. 184–209). Newbury Park, CA: Sage.

Wolk, L. E. (1982). *Minnesota's American Indian battered women: The cycle of oppression.* Saint Paul, MN: St. Paul American Indian Center.

17

Separation and Socialization: A Feminist Analysis of the School Shootings at Columbine

Rebecca Y. Mai and Judith L. Alpert

In this reading, Mai and Alpert make a connection between gender and school violence—which is typically committed by boys. Using both feminist psychodynamic theory and socialization theory, they discuss how typical patterns of male development may have affected the perpetrators of the tragic shootings at Columbine High School. While Mai and Alpert acknowledge that violent crimes do not occur *because* the perpetrators are boys, they nevertheless claim that there is something about their being boys that contributes to this type of violence **(gender role effects).**

Mai and Alpert first explore how feminist psychodynamic theory may be used to explain the role of gender in school violence. This theory argues that beginning in infancy, when a boy is encouraged to distance himself from his mother in order to

form a masculine gender identity, boys are directed toward autonomy and separateness. The result is often a sense of disconnection that extends into later relationships, and contributes to a sense of morality that is based on rules and justice rather than caring and connection with others. Mai and Alpert argue that this sense of disconnection may have contributed to the Columbine perpetrators' feelings of isolation, their lack of close family relationships, and their withdrawal from peers. The lack of connection with others enabled these boys to see their actions in abstract terms—as justified retribution—without taking into account how they would affect the lives of individual people. Mai and Alpert also discuss the ways that socialization theory may be used to explain the link between gender and school violence. They review socialization literature which describes powerful social forces at home and at school that push boys to be stoic and withdrawn, to hide their true feelings, to be traditionally masculine, and to believe that weakness is shameful and violence is honorable **(defined norm)**. Mai and Alpert argue that such gender role socialization may have also been an important factor in the actions of the Columbine perpetrators.

Questions to Consider:

1. According to Mai and Alpert, how do autonomy and separateness contribute to male violence?
2. How well does the description of male development provided by Mai and Alpert match your own experience (or if you are female, the experience of a male that you know)? Does it contribute to your understanding of your own experiences of violence (or if you are female, does it help you understand the experiences of violence of a male that you know)?
3. Mai and Alpert explain male violence as a social and psychological problem. Using the dialectical model, how could biological influences on violence—such as testosterone levels or genetic predispositions—be incorporated into their explanation?
4. Mai and Alpert conclude by saying that there is a need to translate a theoretical understanding of the effects of rigid gender socialization into practical awareness. What are your suggestions for changes in the family and in school that will enable boys to feel more connected, less stoic, and more willing to share their feelings?
5. Imagine that you are conducting a research project to test the explanation

of school violence presented by Mai and Alpert. You have the opportunity to interview the families, school mates, and schools officials involved in the shootings at Columbine. Who would you interview, and what would you ask them?

Last fall, just seven months after the incredible tragedy that left 15 members of their school community dead and 23 wounded, the Columbine High School Rebels won the Colorado state football championships for the first time. All of the players wore the number 70 on their helmets, in honor of their teammate Matt Kechter, who was one of the students killed in the April 20, 1999 tragedy. Matt himself should have worn the number 70 this fall in what would have been his senior year. The crowd chanted "We are Columbine" as the Rebels played the Bruins of Cherry Creek ("Columbine Wins"). It became a slogan of victory and reclamation.

Mike Sheehan, president of the Columbine High School student body in the year following the massacre, greeted a gathering of 2,700 students and parents on the first morning of school at a "Take Back our School Rally:" "Good morning, Columbine! It's so great to see so many of you out here today to take back our school." He drew the crowd's attention to a sign restored over the entrance to the school that reads: "Through these halls pass the finest kids in America, the students of Columbine High School" (Olinger et al. 8A). At the same rally, principal Frank DeAngelis said, amidst cheers from the crowd, "I have waited for months to say this, and I say it with great pride: Columbine, we are back" (Janofsky 21).

Re-entry to the school in September was framed as reclamation: "We are Columbine" and "We are back." What does that mean? What *were* they as a school and as a community prior to the tragic massacre on April 20? What *are* they now? "How could it happen here?" is a question often asked in communities like Columbine where school violence seems unthinkable. Clearly, many factors contributed to the crimes: some unique to Eric and Dylan and the Littleton community and others more broadly representative of boys and school communities.

In this paper, we will focus on the gender components that may have contributed to the crimes. There is an incontestable relationship between gender and school violence: school shootings are committed by boys. The perpetrators don't commit violence at school *because* they are boys. But what about their being boys contributes to their committing the violence? It is this question that we will attempt to answer in this paper. We will use feminist psychodynamic theory to address relational differences in boys and girls that may have played a role in this tragedy. Also, we will consider how males and females are socialized differently in our society, in their homes, and in their schools and their communities, and how this difference made Eric and Dylan, because they were boys, vulnerable to rage and violence. Further, because these boys didn't fit into the "myth" of masculinity, they may have been more likely than their peers to attempt to prove their manhood through active violence.

The Feminist Psychodynamic Perspective

Nancy Chodorow, Carol Gilligan, and other feminist authors hold that for women, development, moral reasoning, and the construction of knowledge are relationship-centered while for men they are independent, autonomous pursuits. Women center their lives around a web of relationships, while men value autonomy. Whereas the socialization literature holds that boys' emotional disconnection is learned rough-out childhood and adolescence as boys are shown in countless ways that emotional vulnerability is shameful, the feminist psychodynamic theory situates boys' distancing from emotionality in infant attachments to the mother. We will explore gender differences in conceptions of relationship and morality, core elements of feminist theory, and consider how their gendered orientations toward autonomy and separateness may have helped lead Dylan and Eric to the violent consummation of their rage.

Relationship

The feminist psychodynamic position that girls and women are driven by relationship while boys and men are driven by autonomy and separateness was outlined in the 1970s and '80s by such authors as Nancy Chodorow, Carol Gilligan, and Jean Baker Miller. Some of these theories look at the nature of attachment during infancy as a way to explain fundamental differences in relationship between men and women. Chodorow asserts that a crucial reason for the difference in male and female development comes out of the fact that mothers are for the most part responsible for early child care. Chodorow writes that mothers of daughters, because they are of the same gender, tend not to experience their infants as separate from them in the way that mothers of sons do. The sense of connection is strong in both cases, but a sense of "oneness and continuity" (*Reproduction* 109) is stronger with infant daughters than it is with infant sons. Boys thus experience themselves as separate from the mother, their earliest attachment, yielding an orientation toward separateness that will persist throughout their lives.

Like many boys, Eric and Dylan were raised in two-parent families where the primary care-giving was probably done by their mothers. They most likely learned, as the theory suggests, independence and differentiation at a very young age. Each boy experienced himself as different from his mother, his earliest attachment, and had to distance himself from her in order to achieve a masculine gender identity. Girls, by contrast, have less need to separate. They identify closely with the role of their mother and later "reproduce" mothering and nurturing in their own daughters (Chodorow, *Reproduction*). Miller writes that, as a result of this early identification with their mothers, women "stay with, build on, and develop in a context of connections with others" (83). Their sense of self is centered around their ability to make and sustain relationship.

Chodorow writes that a boy must replace his primary identification with his mother in order to achieve masculine gender identification. This new masculine identification is most often based on identification with the father, or father-figure. Because the father is generally more distant than the mother (physically and emotionally), the boy's identification is often with a fantasized masculine gender role. According to Chodorow, a boy identifies with "aspects of his father's role, or what he fantasies to be a male role, rather than with his father as a person involved in a relationship with him" ("Family" 50). Additionally, because of the societal devaluation of women, a boy will define his masculinity in opposition to femininity; masculinity is "that which is not feminine or involved with women" (50). Internally, he tries to deny his attachment to and dependence on his mother, while externally he represses the feminine side of himself.

How might this theory relate to Eric Harris and Dylan Klebold? According to reports, both boys seemed emotionally withdrawn (e.g., Gibbs and Roche 45), suggesting isolation. Further, they spoke specifically about separation in the videos they made about their plan. Eric quoted Shakespeare: "Good wombs hath borne bad sons" (Gibbs and Roche 48–9), articulating a parallel to the infant and child's need to distance from the mother and all that she represents. He needed to distance himself from his mother in order to form his ultimate masculine, and violent, identity. He had to reject the connected nurturing relationship offered by the mother (the "good womb") in order to embrace the "bad son" who would commit this evil act. At another point, Eric apologized to his parents for the "hell" his actions were going to put them through and talked about his necessary withdrawal from them, for their own good, before his final terrorist act. He said, "I don't want to spend any more time with them. I wish they were out of town so I didn't have to look at them and bond more" (Gibbs and Roche 50). Eric's withdrawal from his parents served also to distance himself from the full repercussions of his actions. If he didn't "bond" with them, he wouldn't need to be fully cognizant, in the present moment, of how evil his plan was. It was as if the emotional connection with his parents brought an emotional and ethical reality to the plan that Eric knew he had to eliminate in order to carry the plan through.

On the videotapes, Eric and Dylan showed remorse, in advance, about how their actions were going to effect their parents. It was the only remorse they were to indicate. Eric says about the plan, "It f___ing sucks to do this to them. . . . They're going to be put through hell once we do this." He speaks directly to them on the tape: "There's nothing you guys could've done to prevent this" (Gibbs and Roche 50). Eric points to his parents' disconnection as inconsequential to his actions. Could they have prevented "this" if they were aware of his rage? Would his rage be so intense if he felt connected, and understood, by his parents? Would he have a more complex understanding of the impact of his actions on his parents than "It f___ing sucks?" Dylan goes further than Eric to tell his mother and father that they have been "great parents" who taught him "self-awareness, self-reliance." He adds "I always appreciated that," and says "I'm sorry I have so much rage'" (Gibbs and Roche 50). Similarly to Eric, he saw himself as so separate from his parents that he distanced them from this violent vein of his development. What if he had felt more connected to them? Would he have talked about their impact on him? Would they have had an impact on him? Would he conceive of his actions as having the devastating, insurmountable effects on them that they surely have had? Did Dylan get power out of the secrecy of his feelings, because in secrecy he felt autonomous?

Dylan, according to a *Time* article, came "across as the bashful, nervous type who could not lie very well." However, he managed to hide a great deal from his friends and family. "People have no clue," he said on one videotape (Gibbs and Roche 45), referring to his inner rage and life. In hiding himself from others, Dylan actively constructed a "separate" life and within this isolated world was able to construct his violent and dangerous plan. Both boys masked their inner rage, which they felt was unacceptable to their families, and consequently lived in inauthentic relationships with them. A connectedness could have fostered the authenticity that Dylan and Eric lost in their familial relationships as they pursued autonomy. Obviously, separateness doesn't necessarily bring violence. However, connectedness makes violence less likely.

Terrence Real builds on Chodorow's theories about a boy's loss of connection to the mother in infancy and writes that boys suffer from a broader "loss of the relational" (137) which has three parts: diminished connections to the mother, the self, and others. The disconnection from the mother starts in infancy and is perpetuated throughout a boy's childhood in subtle and not-so-subtle messages about what it means to be masculine. Real writes that the early disconnection from the mother "is a particular manifestation of the disavowal of all things deemed feminine, including many of the most emotionally rich parts of the self" (144). Thus, the loss of relationship that begins in infancy is the beginning of series of losses that continues throughout development. In a later section of this paper, we describe how Eric and Dylan are socialized by their peers into a strict masculine gender role. They reacted to assaults and name-calling (like "reject" and "homo") (Gibbs and Roche 50–51) that urged them to "disavow" any shred of femininity in the most masculine way possible: with violence. Further, we see in the boys a withdrawal from their peers that suggests the broader withdrawal from relationships that Real writes about.

William Pollack asserts that boys learn that being a man means being strong and not expressing vulnerability. As Chodorow writes, boys identify with a fantasized male. When inevitably he feels vulnerable, a boy is ashamed. In order to deal with this shame, Pollack writes that boys "mask their emotions and ultimately their true selves" (xxiv), leaving them feeling disconnected from their families and, ultimately, from themselves. According to Pollack, boys can react to such isolation by feeling "alone, helpless, and fearful" (xxiv). By feeling these emotions, which society tells him are not acceptable, a boy feels that he is not measuring up to the masculine ideal. He can't talk about this "failure," nor can he talk about his shame. Pollack writes that boys ultimately lose touch with themselves as they learn to ignore their feelings of vulnerability and shame.

Violence is not a necessary implication of the nonrelationally oriented development we see in boys. But how does it relate to such development? The devaluing of relationship among males that begins, according to Chodorow, in infancy, is translated into their emotional isolation, which can in turn lead to depression and violence (Real; Garbarino). When rather rigid sex-role standards are added to a non-relational orientation, men, feeling isolated and lacking emotional resources, hide their depression, for it is considered a symptom of weakness and thus too painful to reveal. Instead, they demonstrate their depression in what they believe are more socially acceptable ways: workaholism, drug and alcohol abuse, physical abuses, and rage (Real 24). Dylan and Eric, feeling rejected, isolated, and disconnected, recoiled from the less masculine reactions of depression and translated their isolation into violence. The translation of these feelings into violence is certainly not assured. However, when boys and men are not allowed more authentic avenues for expressing their feelings, they may revert to methods that more closely fit the masculine ideal. Eric and Dylan chose violence.

These boys, Eric in particular, illustrate how a disconnection from the mother can allow a disconnection from the self and then from others. Both boys assert that despite the fact that their parents had met their needs, that they couldn't prevent the anger that led to their violence. According to Dylan, though his mom and dad were "great parents," he remains filled with rage. The emotional disconnection that boys experience from infancy can make it very difficult for them to receive and integrate the nurture that both boys claim their parents provided. If, as Chodorow asserts, they defined themselves from infancy as autonomous from and in opposition to their mothers while identifying with a fantasized father, they might conceive of themselves as so separate that they are untouchable by their parents' care. Their parents cannot penetrate their very individuated and autonomous selves. Dylan says that he is thankful to his parents for giving him "self-reliance." It is this quality (along with others) that prevents him from experiencing the important sense of connection with his parents and others. Such a connection could have allowed him to feel acceptance rather than rejection by his peers.

Morality

Another basic insight of the feminist psychodynamic literature concerns the differences in conceptions of morality among males and females. Carol Gilligan writes that boys and girls conceptualize morality in different ways: relationship and connection is central for girls, while a more abstract, autonomous set of rules is central for boys (*Different* 57).

One of us recently led a discussion with a group of fourth graders about friendship issues. The five students in the group chose to talk about the conflicts they were having. The three girls in the group were chatty and analytical. The boys were silent. The leader pointed out this difference. Libby, a talkative girl with a big space between her two front teeth, said matter-offactly, "They don't care about our problems and we don't care about theirs." "Are your problems different?" the leader asked. Libby answered immediately: "We fight about who's friends with who, and they fight about who cheated in the soccer game."

This difference, so obvious to Libby, was a ground-breaking notion when Gilligan wrote about it in her influential book *In a Different Voice.* As Libby said, at the heart of conflict for girls are relationship issues, while for boys, conflict arises when a set of rules is violated. Males build their moral frameworks according to an "ethic of justice," while females organize their moral systems around an "ethic of care" (Gilligan, *Different*).

The orientations toward separation and autonomy learned in infancy in boys would seem to breed the moral differences that Gilligan writes about. A look at the games children play in childhood demonstrates how boys and girls further learn and perpetuate these different orientations through play. Lever, in a study of fifth graders, found that boys played organized, competitive games in large groups. Girls, on the other hand, played in smaller groups and in games like jump-rope and hopscotch, where competition is indirect and turn-taking is fundamental. Boys learn rules, while girls learn relationships. Jean Baker Miller asserts that boys' games and their later correlates like the military, prepare men to operate in the "games" of "business, politics, and power" (192). As Gilligan states, boys learn to play by the rules, whereas women don't. She writes that "the logic underlying an ethic of care is a psychological logic of relationships, which contrasts with the formal logic of fairness that informs the justice approach" (73). Nonviolence is fundamental to the ethic of care: no one should be hurt. In contrast, fairness is the underlying premise to the ethic of justice: everyone should be treated the same.

Within a framework of care and responsibility, the ramifications of aggressive actions are measured in terms of the victims' experience as well as by the possible damage to the relationship between the aggressor and the victim. Within a framework of rules and a hierarchy of rights, aggressive actions can be justified in the abstract as "fair" retribution.

What was the boys' view of their situation in the school? Did they see themselves on the bottom rung of the Columbine High School social ladder? How was their violent reaction justified by their view? What might a girls' view be? How might it be different? These are all questions to consider when looking at the role of gender in these boys' violent actions. It was Dylan and Eric's view that they were victimized by their peers and their school: their peers taunted them and the school allowed it to happen. The taunts and the teasing de-masculinized the boys in many ways and relegated them to the position of the weak victim. Their reaction was to take power back violently, and in their view they were justified in doing so. They did not think about the complicated web of relationships they had within the school in the ways that a girl would likely have. In Eric and Dylan's judgment, it was their "right" to fight back. They were not in relationship with their "enemies," where their actions would have complex ramifications; instead, they were in a game, with rules, though very skewed ones. They were "dissed" so they retaliated, in a deadly way. In their very distorted thinking, Eric and Dylan could have conceived of their act as part of the "game" they were losing. Their assumption of power was an effort to win in the competitive social atmosphere of the school.

These boys clearly formulated their views of the situation in the school, and their plan to deal with it, in a vacuum. They showed profound disconnection from their families and peers. Belenky, Clinchy, Golberger, and Tarule theorize in *Women's Ways of Knowing* that women form knowledge in a collaborative, empathic fashion, whereas men form knowledge much more autonomously. Dylan and Eric formulated knowledge, and their conception of reality, only as it related to themselves, which made possible their very skewed view of their situation.

If they formed their identities modeled after a fantasized male (as Chodorow asserts boys do), Eric and Dylan would have modeled themselves after a stereotype of how they should be rather than after an actual example. Within this framework, they do not allow themselves to experience a range of emotions but rather a few, very extreme ones on which they felt they needed to act. If their moral orientation was one of a "hierarchy of rules" (as Gilligan asserts), the boys would have conceived of their actions in terms of an abstract set of rules and not in terms of the people and the relationships they would affect. The results were catastrophic.

Sex-Role Socialization Perspective

Feminist literature, including works by Deem and Donovan, outlines and analyzes the corrupt process of socialization that teaches girls and women weakness, insecurity, and subordination. Yet boys and men are also enslaved by a corrupt process of socialization. Boys are taught that they have fewer emotional needs than girls. As a result, they cultivate few emotional resources. Added to a stunted emotional education is the strong message to boys that "toughness" is desirable. According to authors who write

on boys' socialization such as Real, Pollack, and Kindlon and Thompson, when a boy is faced with a complex emotional situation, he has few resources to direct toward its resolution.

The sex-role socialization literature is very broad. We have reviewed selected literature that is relevant to the crimes at Columbine High School and present a brief summary of our review in two sections: socialization in the home and socialization at school, by both the institution and the peers within it.

Learning Gender at Home

While anecdotal evidence about parental socialization is strong, reviews of the literature on sex-role socialization present conflicting evidence on whether, and the extent to which, parents treat their sons and daughters differently. Maccoby and Jacklin concluded, from their literature search of studies of differential socialization, that parental socialization of boys and girls is remarkably similar (339). They found, however, that parents reinforce some sex-typed behaviors—most notably, they reward sex-typed play activities and choice of toys. They found that boys are more pressured *not* to engage in "sex-inappropriate" behaviors (328), while girls have a much more loosely defined set of inappropriate behaviors. Lytton and Romney present a meta-analysis of the literature on parents' differential socialization of boys and girls. Their findings are consistent with those of Maccoby and Jacklin: they find surprisingly uniform socialization of boys and girls except in the area of encouragement of sex-typed activities. Criticisms of these analyses include the point that there may be flaws and limitations in the primary literature, that meta-analyses do not detect subtle differences in treatment, and that there is variability in the studies for which the meta-analyses do not account.

Individual studies, however, speak loudly to the existence and quality of parental socialization. Real, Pollack, and Kindlon and Thomson write about a socialization process that begins at the earliest stage of life and occurs within the context of home and school and under the grand umbrella of society's expectations. One research study looked at the effect of a newborn's gender on parents' responses to him or her in the first 24 hours of life. The newborns were selected so that there were no significant differences between boys and girls in terms of weight, length, alertness, and strength. The study found that parents saw newborn sons as "more alert, stronger, larger featured, more coordinated, and firmer" (Real 121). By contrast, they saw their newborn daughters as "less attentive, weaker, finer featured, less coordinated, softer, smaller, more fragile and prettier" (121). This example illustrates the very beginning of a process of parenting and schooling in which boys are seen to be more emotionally independent and less needy than girls. Ultimately they try to live up to such false expectations, often at great expense to their inner, and outer, lives.

We have little information about the family lives of Dylan Klebold and Eric Harris. We know that they came from two-parent middle-class households in which they were both the younger of two brothers. Eric grew up as an "army brat," moving frequently from base to base, until his father retired as a major in the Air Force in 1993 and the family moved to Denver. In Plattsburgh, NY, where the Harrises lived from 1991 to 1993, neighbors and friends described the Harris boys as "Scouts and Little Leaguers" and their parents as being involved in the community and their children (Belluck A14). Wayne Harris, Eric's fa-

ther, who worked at a company that develops flight training simulators, was described by a friend as a "*Leave it to Beaver* dad" (Belluck A14). His mother Kathy worked at a catering company.

We can only speculate on the existence and degree of sex-role socialization that took place in Eric's home. Was his crying discouraged? Were expressions of vulnerability ridiculed? Were discussions of feelings looked down upon? One could conjecture that Eric, growing up on an air-force base, was surrounded by a traditional view of sex-roles in his household.

Dylan Klebold's parents are likewise described as "good parents" involved in their son's life. Dylan was raised in the suburbs of Denver and attended confirmation classes at the Lutheran church and observed Jewish rituals at home. Tom Klebold, Dylan's father, runs a small real estate business from his home. Susan, Dylan's mother, is an employment counselor at a local community college. She had previously worked with disabled students at the college. Though Dylan exhibited an early and intense interest in guns, his parents prohibited them, even toy guns, in their house. According to friends of the family, the Klebolds tried to quell Dylan's interest in guns and violence, for example, having a "big conversation" (the friends did not elaborate on the contents, details, or outcome of this conversation) when he brought home violent movies in the fourth grade (Belluck A14). Shortly after the massacre, the Klebolds wrote letters to the families of their son's victims. They said:

> We'll never understand why this tragedy happened, or what we might have done to prevent it. We did not see anger or hatred in Dylan until the last moments of his life, when we watched in helpless horror with the rest of the world. (Belluck A14).

Dylan's interest in guns and violence seems to have been actively discouraged by his parents; are there other ways in which they encouraged "masculine" attitudes? What was the climate in the household that may have led to Dylan's interest in guns? Was he praised for his strength and chastised for weakness?

Dylan spoke of how his "popular" older brother Byron and his friends "ripped" on him (Gibbs and Roche 44). Likewise, Eric's older brother Kevin was a popular A-student who was admired as a leader. He was a football player with varsity letter jackets. To what extent were Dylan and Eric "socialized" by their older brothers into a world where popularity is of the utmost importance and is gained by showing strength and avoiding weakness? Or did they have to find a different, equally powerful role for themselves, in reaction to the socialization?

Many people, trying to explain the atrocity at Columbine High School, want to believe that the families were deviant, abusive, and neglectful of their sons. This, however, does not appear to be the case with the Klebold and Harris families. The families may have contributed to the tragedy, however, through messages about sex-role which can be subtly (or not subtly but socially acceptably) sent at home. Few, if any, reporters would find deviance in a mother's applauding the strength and toughness of her son when he was a toddler. Or abuse in a father's disapproval, however strong, of an interest in a "feminine" pursuit like poetry. Outsiders would not perceive parents as being removed when they dismissed their son's moodiness and withdrawal during an adolescent stage of development. However, these acts are messages that go far in teaching boys to be stoic and withdrawn, to hide their true feelings and develop a mythic counterpart who is strong and unemotional. We cannot fully know the atmosphere of the Harris and Klebold homes. However, in most homes in our society, sex-role socialization thrives as boys are taught to send their weaknesses and vulnerabilities underground (Kindlon and Thompson; Real). These are the messages that quite probably were being relayed in the homes of Dylan Klebold and Eric Harris as well.

Columbine High School: Learning Gender at School

Boys experience "shaping" of gender at school from peers, teachers, and curricula. Some research suggests that peers play an important role in socialization, particularly during adolescence (Hibbard and Buhrmester; Beal; Maccoby; and Berndt). Further, research has indicated that males may be more rigid with each other in their demands of conformity to sex-role norms than girls are (Sucker et al.; Fagot). Similarly, some research suggests that teachers and curricula play a major role in the socialization process (Andersen, Deem). While we will treat the social climate in the school most extensively, we also note briefly the more institutional role of the school in sex-role socialization. At the time of the massacre, in April 1999, Columbine had won 32 statewide sports championships in the preceding 10 years. According to reports, athletes and cheerleaders are the elite of the school, recognized as such by their peers, their teachers, and themselves. Scott Schulte, described in a magazine as "golden-boy track and football star" (Pooley par. 16) at Columbine High School said that it's "the greatest school with the greatest kids. . . . We are perfect, and the atmosphere is perfect" (Pooley par. 16). The school participates in the athletic leagues that raise the athlete to a role of honor. Pep rallies and heavily attended football games send a message to athletes that they are valued. To gawky, introverted boys, it may send the message that their qualities are less valuable.

Andersen observes that schools are so influential in "teaching" gendered attitudes and behavior that learning gender might be considered a "second curriculum" in schools (43). In classrooms, teachers are likely to perpetuate stereotyped gender roles, treating boys and girls who "act out" in class differently (American Association of University Women). Textbooks, similarly, portray a narrow view of gender roles (Andersen 43). To Dylan and Eric, the sum of these messages may have been that their less traditionally masculine qualities were unacceptable, even shameful.

We have previously noted the differences between boys' and girls' play and its role in socialization. Brown and Gilligan write about how girls "monitor each other" (45) in the socialization process, where girls lose their "authentic selves" and are required to become "nice." They write that "'whispering,' 'telling secrets,' 'making fun of,' and 'laughing at' others are ways to prevent girls from resisting too much or acting in ways that are too threatening, too different" (45). Boys, too, monitor each other in a socialization process that demands that they be strong and stoic. They tease each other mercilessly for being weak or a "sissy." Kindlon and Thompson describe the "psychological warfare" (73) that takes place in the peer culture of boys in which the older, stronger boys pick on their younger, weaker counterparts. The younger boys, in turn, imitate these older models, creating a "conformity-driven 'boy pack' against the boy who fails in any way to conform with pack expectations" (73).

According to Kindlon and Thompson, at about 10 years of age, boys become more aware of themselves and their status within the peer group (73). As a result, boys be-

come more competitive with each other. Competition is based largely on traditional ideals of masculinity: who is stronger, smarter, a better athlete. In addition, boys in adolescence are separating from their parents, becoming more autonomous and less supervised. They willingly enter the peer culture that demands a conformity to traditional gender roles. Boys ridicule each other in this culture: any deviation from the masculine ideal is a subject for teasing. Most boys hide the hurt that results from such ridicule, because hurt shows weakness that is not acceptable in this culture.

Kindlon and Thompson call the social culture of adolescent boys a "culture of cruelty" (75) in which nobody is safe from being the target, though some are picked on more than others. Everybody is vulnerable to attack. They write of a "popular" boy who says:

> Everybody thinks you've got it so easy when you're on top, but being on top just means that you have to worry all the time about slipping or somebody gaining on you. All it takes is one mistake or a bad day, and all sorts of people are waiting to take you down. (75)

For the boy on the bottom of the social hierarchy, things are worse: he can be teased and abused constantly, which can result in serious emotional problems that can lead to violence toward himself or others. According to Kindlon and Thompson, these boys, because they are afraid that they too will be the target of cruel behavior, are always on the defensive against appearing weak. In this defensive mode, they are more likely to be cruel to others and assert power. They can move themselves out of a position of weakness by belittling others.

Reports about Columbine High School indicate that the cliques that made up its social hierarchy were not limited simply to the jocks and the non-jocks. Though the great majority of Columbine's 1,935 students are white and middle to upper-middle class, there are many easily identifiable subgroups. Students in the school identify cliques made up of "hockey kids (a separate group), preppies, stoners, gangbangers (gang-member wannabes), skaters (skateboarders) and . . . nerds" (Cohen par. 3). While some of the groups co-existed quite peacefully, others were targeted by groups of athletes. Among those targeted was the "Trench Coat Mafia," the clique with which Dylan and Eric were associated.

Eric Harris and Dylan Klebold were described by fellow students as "stereotype geeks" (Gibbs par. 11), on the low end of the social spectrum. They defined themselves in angry opposition to the more "popular" groups of athletes. One student, a hockey player, said, "They hate us because we're like the social elite of the school" (Gibbs par. 12). As the story goes, members of the "Trench Coat Mafia" were taunted by athletes. One would hurl insults such as "dirt bag" or "nice dress" as they passed. Jocks called Eric and Dylan "dirt-bag" and "faggot." Jocks threw bottles at Dylan and Eric from moving cars (Gibbs, par. 13). Evan Todd, a 255-lb. football player who was wounded in the attack, justifies the abuse by saying,

> Sure we teased them. But what do you expect with kids who come to school with weird hairdos and horns on their hats? It's not just jocks; the whole school's disgusted with them. They're a bunch of homos, grabbing each other's private parts. If you want to get rid of someone, usually you tease 'em. So the whole school would call them homos, and when they did something sick, we'd tell them, "You're sick and that's wrong" (Gibbs and Roche 50–51).

The picture painted of the school indicates a split into powerful and powerless groups. Leon Botstein, educational theorist and president of Bard College, writes that high school is "a world defined by insiders and outsiders, in which the insiders hold sway because of superficial definitions of good looks and attractiveness, popularity and sports prowess" (A16). Such a depiction certainly holds true of Columbine, where groups of athletes were bestowed power by acceptance, praise, and tradition. Other groups, like the "nerds" with whom Dylan and Eric associated, were marginalized, told by their peers and sometimes even teachers and administrators that they were less acceptable and desirable than their stronger, better looking, more athletic peers.

On a day-to-day level, some in the group tried to ignore the insults, while others "fought back:" one flashed a shotgun and several made a video for class in which kids in trench coats hunted down their enemies with guns (Gibbs par. 14). Brooks Brown, a classmate of Eric and Dylan who had once been the object of threats from Eric, told his parents just 5 days before the shootings that Eric and Dylan weren't so bad, they were "bright, maladjusted kids united in their intelligence and disdain for the jock culture of Columbine High" (Pooley par. 5). Their disdain quite probably stemmed from the abuse they received from this culture, which can be called, in the words of Kindlon and Thompson, a "culture of cruelty" (75).

In this culture, boys are judged on the strength or weakness of their actions. Their peers insulted their masculinity, their strength, by calling them names such as "faggot" and "homo" (Gibbs and Roche 50–51). They were continually teased for their weakness. What better way to combat such teasing than to react with strength?

James Gilligan writes that "the male gender role generates violence by exposing men to shame if they are not violent, and rewarding them with honor when they are" (233). When a boy's masculinity is in question, he may try to prove himself, and his manhood, with violent actions.

On a more chronic level, the boys internalized these taunts. They mentioned being teased in the tapes that they made to explain their actions. In one of the tapes, Eric talked about how, in moving frequently, he always had to start over "at the bottom of the ladder" and how people made fun of him, "my face, my hair, my shirts" (Gibbs and Roche 44). Likewise, Dylan spoke of how his "popular" brother Byron, along with his friends, "ripped" on him. He said, "Being shy didn't help. . . . I'm going to kill you all. You've been giving us s___ for years" (Gibbs and Roche 44). The boys talked about being teased, which suggests that they felt that others saw them as falling short of the masculine ideal. Schooled in a culture that tells boys to follow a code of behavior in which they are stoic when faced with pain and powerful in the face of shame, Dylan Klebold and Eric Harris reacted to the hostile attacks from their peers and "defended themselves" with the violence that this culture sanctions for them. And they were certainly hardened as they withdrew and translated this hurt into violent anger and, ultimately, horrific violence.

Research indicates that the least "popular" boy is likely to be the most aggressive. Richard Tremblay at the University of Montreal studied a large group of boys from the time they were in kindergarten. His findings indicated that the boys who had been consistently rated as the most aggressive by both teachers and students also tended to be boys who were unpopular and struggling academically (Kindlon and Thompson 225). Kindlon and Thompson write that boys, to preserve their "honor," feel the need to defend themselves from being "dissed." Because these boys have been teased and taunted so often, they become continually "on guard" against attack. Kindlon and Thompson liken this process to the process of psychological conditioning; in this case, boys learn to associate peer relationship with hostility and attacks (228). Dylan and Eric, two unpopular boys, were likely to have learned that peer relationships are associated with verbal abuse. They ultimately formed such an exaggerated view of their peers that they could justify this attack.

Brooks Brown said shortly after the massacre:

> Did they snap? I think they snapped a bunch of times. Every time someone slammed them against a locker and threw a bottle at them, I think they'd go back to Eric or Dylan's house and plot a little more—at first as a goof, but more and more seriously over time. It's a theory, but it makes sense to everyone who knew them. (Pooley par. 17)

The plan may have begun as a fantasy to defend against the humiliation that the boys faced at the taunting by their peers. Brown's assessment, that the boys matched the assaults of others with additions to their violent plan, illustrates the psychological conditioning that Kindlon and Thompson write about. At some point, though, the fantasy turned into reality, yielding tragic consequences.

We have written about the theories that assert that weakness is shameful for boys while violence is honorable. Dylan and Eric saw in their plan not only a payback to those who had hurt them, but also a glorified, cult-like conquest. The extremity of their scheme strongly suggests a pursuit of honor. In one of the videos, Dylan and Eric claimed that they were aiming for casualties of 250 in their "Judgment Day" massacre. In this video, Eric picks up a shotgun and makes shooting noises, asking, "Isn't it fun to get the respect that we're going to deserve?" (Gibbs and Roche 44). Such details indicate that the boys were looking not only for revenge but also for glory. Dylan predicted, "Directors will be fighting over this story" (Gibbs and Roche 42). Eric wondered who would be the best man for the job, Spielberg or Tarantino. The movie, according to Eric, should be full of "a lot of foreshadowing and dramatic irony" (Gibbs and Roche 46–7). These details strongly suggest that the boys were aiming for a dramatic effect, that they wanted to make a very strong, lasting, original statement. They wanted their revenge to be powerful.

After they had concocted their ideal, Eric and Dylan fueled their anger in order to keep up enough momentum of rage to enact it. In a video Eric says, "More rage. More rage. . . . Keep building it on," with an emphasizing motion of his hands (Gibbs and Roche 44). Their anger was something they cultivated: they wanted to make themselves cult heroes but needed to keep their anger levels up in order to do so. In one video, Dylan sits in a tan La-Z-Boy, a toothpick in his mouth. Eric adjusts his video camera a few feet away, then sits in his own chair; he has a bottle of whiskey and a sawed-off shotgun in his lap. He takes a drink and tries to hide the sting. One viewer said he was "like a small child playing grown-up" in the video (Gibbs and Roche 40–41). He certainly seems to have been a boy assuming a part; in his case the part was a boy with a violent identity.

Eric and Dylan lived immersed in a world of violence: they loved movies like *Reservoir Dogs*, and they tailored gory, violent video games like Doom, to their violent fantasies (Gibbs and Roche 44; Pooley 23). Eric called himself "Reb," short for rebel, while Dylan took VoDKa as a nickname (a combination of his initials and his favorite liquor) (Gibbs and Roche 44). These two boys created identities of violence which then birthed the idea of the massacre. Were these identities defenses against a culture that called them weak? As the theorists on boys' development note, for adolescent boys, being weak is shameful, while being violent is being "a man." Eric and Dylan found agency through violence; they lived in a world that gave them few options for dealing with their complicated emotions and shamed them for feeling vulnerable. They went to a school where their masculinity was constantly called into question, where they were humiliated frequently, where they had little sense of power. Dylan and Eric took their quest for strength to the extreme.

During the massacre, students overheard the shooters saying, "Oh, you f___ing nerd. Tonight's a good night to die" (Gibbs par. 26). In calling their victims "nerds," a label they seem to have carried themselves, the boys were putting their victims into the role they had been given by their peers. They were then assuming power over them. Ironically, their frightening strength is what is most likely to be remembered from the massacre; not their loneliness, isolation, and feelings of weakness.

Conclusions and Implications

Most boys experience the separation in infancy and the socialization in childhood and adolescence that we have addressed in this paper. Yet few boys take their anger and isolation to the extreme the way Eric Harris and Dylan Klebold did when they planned and executed their complicated plan to kill on April 20, 1999. What about these two boys led them to the deadly violence? The analysis we have presented here does not by any means provide a complete answer. It considers the boys as a unit, not as unique individuals. It does not address the extremity of their actions. However, when seen within a context of a society in which school shootings are becoming far too common, it does provide evidence that boys' psychodynamic separation issues and ensuing socialization are important factors to consider when trying to explain and prevent such violence.

We propose that there is something about their being boys that contributed to Dylan and Eric's violent actions. Their gender is inseparable from their crime. The socialization of boys to be autonomous and stoic comes out of a predisposition to such separateness that is gained in infancy. Socialization is not likely to change radically. However, a theoretical awareness of the potentially disastrous effects that come from rigid gender socialization must be translated into a practical awareness among administrators, teachers, and students.

Works Cited

American Association of University Women. *How Schools Short-change Girls*. New York: Marlowe, 1992.

Andersen, Margaret L. *Thinking About Women: Sociological Perspectives on Sex and Gender,* Third Edition. New York: Macmillan, 1993.

Beal, C. R. *Boys and Girls: The Development of Gender Roles*. New York: McGraw-Hill, 1979.

Belenky, Mary Field, Blythe McVicher Clinchy, Nancy Rule Goldberger, and Jill Mattuck Tarule. *Women's Ways of Knowing*. New York: Basic Books, 1986.

Belluck, Pam and Wilgoren, Jodi. "Caring Parents, No Answers, In Columbine Killers' Pasts." The *New York Times* 29 June 1999, early ed.: A1+.

Berndt, Thomas J. "Developmental Changes in Conformity to Peers and Parents." *Develop-mental Psychology* 15 (1979): 608–616.

Betcher, R. William and William S. Pollack. *In a Time of Fallen Heroes: The Re-Creation of Masculinity*. New York: Guilford, 1993.

Bingham, Janet. "Students Given Help Forming Ties." The *Denver Post* 17 Aug. 1999: 1B+.

Botstein, Leon. "Let Teen-Agers Try Adulthood." The *New York Times* 17 May 1999: A16.

Brown, Lyn Mikel and Carol Gilligan. *Meeting at the Crossroads: Women's Psychology and Girls' Development*. New York: Ballantine Books, 1992.

Chodorow, Nancy. "Family Structure and Feminine Personality." *Woman, Culture, and Society*. Ed. Michelle Zimbalist Rosaldo and Louise Lamphere. Stanford: Stanford UP, 1974, 43–66.

———. *The Reproduction of Mothering: Psychoanalysis and the Sociology of Gender*. Berkeley: U of California P, 1979.

Clatterbaugh, Kenneth. *Contemporary Perspectives on Masculinity: Men, Women, and Politics in Modern Society*. Boulder, CO: Westview P, 1990.

Cloud, John and Andrew Goldstein. "The Principal: Could He Have Done More?" *Time* 20 Dec. 1999: 48–49.

Cohen, Adam. "A Curse of Cliques." *Time* 3 May 1999.

"Columbine Wins State Championship." The *New York Times* 5 Dec. 1999, early ed., sec. 8: 13.

Deem, Rosemary. *Women and Schooling*. London: Routledge & Kegan Paul, 1978.

DeFalco, Beth. "Task Force Hears Ideas." The *Denver Post* 23 July 1999. 29 Aug. 1999.

Donovan, Josephine. *Feminist Theory: The Intellectual Traditions of American Feminism*. New York: Continuum, 1997.

Entwisle, Doris R. "Schools and the Adolescent." *At the Threshold: The Developing Adolescent*. Ed. S. Shirley Feldman and Glen R. Elliott. Cambridge, MA: Harvard UP, 1990, 197–224.

Fagot, Beverly I. "Consequences of Moderate Cross-Gender Behavior in Children." *Child Development* 48 (1977): 902–907.

Garbarino, James. *Lost Boys: Why Our Sons Turn Violent and How We Can Save Them*. New York: Free P, 1999.

Gibbs, Nancy. "In Sorrow and Disbelief." *Time* 3 May 1999.

Gibbs, Nancy and Timothy Roche. "The Columbine Tapes." *Time* 20 Dec. 1999: 40–51.

Gilligan, Carol. "The Hollow Men." *The New York Times* 16 February 1997, 1 June.

———. *In a Different Voice*. Cambridge: Harvard UP, 1982.

Gilligan, James. *Violence: Reflections on a National Epidemic*. New York: Vintage, 1996.

Goldstein, Andrew. "The Victims: Never Again." *Time* 20 Dec. 1999: 52–57.

Hibbard, David R. and Duane Buhrmester. "The Role of Peers on the Socialization of Gender-Related Social Interaction Styles." *Sex Roles* 39 (1998): 185–202.

Janofsky, Michael. "A Fresh Coat of Paint and a New Start." The *New York Times* 15 Aug. 1999, early ed.: 21.

Jordan, Judith V., Alexandra G. Kaplan, Jean Baker Miller, Irene P. Stiver, and Janet L. Surrey. *Women's Growth in Connection*. New York: Guilford P, 1991.

Kindlon, Dan and Michael Thompson. *Raising Cain: Protecting the Emotional Life of Boys*. New York: Ballantine, 1999.

Lever, Janet. "Sex Differences in the Games Children Play." *Social Problems* 23 (1976): 478–487.

———. "Sex Differences in the Complexity of Children's Play and Games." *American Sociological Review* 43 (1978): 471–483.

Lytton, Hugh and David M. Romney. "Parents' Differential Socialization of Boys and Girls: A Meta-Analysis." *Psychological Bulletin* 109 (1991): 267–296.

Maccoby, Eleanor Emmons and Carol Nagy Jacklin. *The Psychology of Sex Differences*. Stanford: Stanford UP, 1974.

Maccoby, Eleanor Emmons. "Gender and Relationships: A Developmental Account." *American Psychologist* 45 (1990): 513–520.

———. *The Two Sexes: Growing Up Apart, Coming Together*. Cambridge, MA: Harvard UP, 1998.

Miller, Jean Baker. "The Construction of Anger in Women and Men." *Women's Growth in Connection*. Ed. Judith V. Jordan, Alexandra G. Kaplan, Jean Baker Miller, Irene P. Stiver, and Janet L. Surrey. New York: Guilford, 1991.

———. *Toward a New Psychology of Women*. Boston: Beacon, 1976.

Olinger, David, Patricia Callahan, and Janet Bingham. "School's Opening Day a Bittersweet Event." *The Denver Post* 17 Aug. 1999: 1A+.

Pollack, William. *Real Boys: Rescuing Our Sons from the Myths of Boyhood*. New York: Henry Holt, 1998.

Pooley, Eric. "Portrait of a Deadly Bond." *Time* 3 May 1999.

Prothrow-Stith, Deborah. *Deadly Consequences: How Violence is Destroying our Teenage Population and a Plan to Begin Solving the Problem*. New York: Harper, 1991.

Real, Terrence. *I Don't Want to Talk about It: Overcoming the Secret Legacy of Male Depression*. New York: Fireside, 1997.

Ryckman, Lisa Levitt. "A New Start: Columbine Sophomores Talk about Returning to School." *Denver Rocky Mountain News* 15 Aug. 1999: 26A+.

Schrof, Joannie M. "Unhappy Girls and Boys." *U.S. News & World Report* 119 October 1995: 86–7.

Tobias, Sheila. Introduction. *Faces of Feminism: An Activist's Reflections on the Women's Movement*. Westview P, 1997. 23 June 1999.

Viadero, Debra. "Behind the 'Mask of Masculinity.'" *Education Week* May 1998. 13 May 1999.

———. "Their Own Voices." *Education Week* May 1998. 10 June 1999.

Walsh, Mary Roth, ed. *Women, Men, and Gender: Ongoing Debates*. New Haven: Yale UP, 1997.

Weiler, Kathleen. *Women Teaching for Change: Gender, Class and Power*. Massachusetts: Bergin & Garvey, 1988.

Zucker, Kenneth J., Debra N. Wilson-Smith, Janice A. Kurita, and Anita Stern. "Children's Appraisals of Sex-Typed Behavior in their Peers." *Sex Roles* 33 (1995): 703–725.

*Chapter 8: Putting It All Together*_____

1. How might feminist psychodynamic theory and socialization theory contribute to our understanding of domestic violence?
2. Based on these readings, what suggestions do you have for reducing the incidence of male violence?
3. Given what you have learned in this chapter, how would you respond to someone who argued that men are naturally violent?

9

Gender and Caregiving

The readings in this chapter question our cultural ideals for both motherhood and fatherhood, arguing that these ideals are unrealistic and do not reflect the variety of circumstances in which children are parented. The first reading contends that the gendered division of childcare is not a biological given, but rather develops out of particular physical and social environmental conditions. Children need at least one adult who consistently cares for them in an emotionally positive way, but this adult can be male or female, and effective parenting can take place in a variety of family structures. The authors advocate for an expanded view of fathering, one that makes the father-child bond as important as the mother-child bond. The second reading explores the cultural values that surround mothering by interviewing substance-abusing women. Although these women are not generally seen as "ideal" mothers, they see themselves as caring and committed parents. While acknowledging the detrimental effects of their drug abuse on their children, substance-abusing mothers also describe parenting behaviors which meet cultural ideals, and they attempt to broaden these cultural ideals through their own definitions of good parenting.

18

Deconstructing the Essential Father

Louise B. Silverstein and Carl F. Auerbach

Because of a recent surge in research on fathering, fathers are now recognized as playing an important role in their children's psychological lives. According to the essentialist perspective, children need their fathers because biological differences in reproduction create different parenting roles for women and men. Without a father, a child is deprived of a unique, masculine contribution that is important for healthy development. The essentialist perspective also assumes that men are most likely to be motivated to be responsible fathers when they are involved in a heterosexual marriage **(defined norm).** Silverstein and Auerbach argue that the essentialist position on fathering is oversimplified and incorrect. They contend that a gendered division of childcare is not the result of biological sex differences, but rather develops as a response to a particular bioecological context **(dialectical model).** They cite cross-species, cross-cultural, and social science research to support

the view that neither fathers nor mothers are essential to healthy child development, and that effective fathering can take place in a variety of family structures. They conclude with social policy recommendations for encouraging men in all types of family structures to be responsible fathers.

Questions to Consider:

1. According to Silverstein and Auerbach, why are neither fathers nor mothers essential to healthy child development?
2. The essentialist positions holds that fathers are necessary for the development of a psychologically healthy masculine gender identity in boys. In your view, what does a psychologically healthy masculine gender identity look like? Is it important to have a father in

L. B. Silverstein & C. F. Auerbach (1999). Deconstructing the essential father. *American Psychologist, 54,* (6), 397–407. *Copyright (c) 1999 by the American Psychological Association. Reprinted with permission.*

order to develop such an identity? Why or why not?

3. Why do Silverstein and Auerbach believe that it is important to define the father-child bond as independent of the father-mother relationship? Do you agree with them? Why or why not?

4. Discuss how a dialectical model of the relationship between biology, society, and gender (see Introduction and Chapter 1) would explain gendered differences in parenting.

In the past two decades, there has been an explosion of research on fathers (see Booth & Crouter, 1998; Lamb, 1997: Phares, 1996, for recent reviews). There is now a broad consensus that fathers are important contributors to both normal and abnormal child outcomes. Infants and toddlers can be as attached to fathers as they are to mothers. In addition, even when fathers are not physically present, they may play an important role in their children's psychological lives. Other important issues about fathers and families remain controversial. For example, scholars continue to debate the extent to which paternal involvement has increased over the past 20 years (Pleck, 1997). Similarly, researchers are only beginning to study the ways that fathering identities vary across subcultures (Auerbach, Silverstein, & Zizi, 1997; Bowman & Forman, 1998; Roopnarine, Snell-White, & Riegraf, 1993), and the effects of divorce on fathers and their children are not yet clearly understood (Hetherington, Bridges, & Insabella, 1998).

Overall, this explosion of research on fathering has increased the complexity of scholarly thinking about parenting and child development. However, one group of social scientists (e.g., Biller & Kimpton, 1997; Blankenhorn, 1995; Popenoe, 1996) has emerged that is offering a more simplis-

tic view of the role of fathers in families. These neoconservative social scientists have replaced the earlier "essentializing" of mothers (Bowlby, 1951) with a claim about the essential importance of fathers. These authors have proposed that the roots of a wide range of social problems (i.e., child poverty, urban decay, societal violence, teenage pregnancy, and poor school performance) can be traced to the absence of fathers in the lives of their children. Biller and Kimpton (1997, p. 147) have even used the term "paternal deprivation" in a manner parallel to Bowlby's (1951) concept of maternal deprivation. In our view, the essentialist framework represents a dramatic oversimplification of the complex relations between father presence and social problems.

We characterize this perspective as essentialist because it assumes that the biologically different reproductive functions of men and women automatically construct essential differences in parenting behaviors. The essentialist perspective defines mothering and fathering as distinct social roles that are not interchangeable. Marriage is seen as the social institution within which responsible fathering and positive child adjustment are most likely to occur. Fathers are understood as having a unique and essential role to play in child development, especially for boys who need a male role model to establish a masculine gender identity (see Table 1 for a definition of the essentialist perspective).

Our research experience has led us to conceptualize fathering in a way that is very different from the neoconservative perspective. Over the past six years, we have studied the fathering identities of men who are actively involved with their children (Auerbach & Silverstein, 1997; Auerbach et al., 1997; Silverstein, 1996; Silverstein, Auerbach, Grieco, & Dunkel, in press;

TABLE 1   *The Essentialist Paradigm*

Essentialist belief	Explanation
Biological sex differences construct gender differences in parenting	The biological experiences of pregnancy and lactation generate a strong, instinctual drive in women to nurture. In the absence of these experiences, men do not have an instinctual drive to nurture infants and children.
The civilizing effects of marriage	Because a man's contribution to reproduction is limited to the moment of conception, active and consistent parenting on the part of men is universally difficult to achieve.
	The best way to ensure that men will consistently provide for and nurture young children is to provide a social structure in which men can be assured of paternity (i.e., the traditional nuclear family). Without the social institution of marriage, men are likely to impregnate as many women as possible, without behaving responsibly toward their offspring.
The importance of a male role model	If men can be induced to take care of young children, their unique, masculine contribution significantly improves developmental outcomes for children. This is especially true for boys who need a male role model to achieve a psychologically healthy masculine gender identity.

Silverstein & Phares, 1996; Silverstein & Quartironi, 1996). To date, approximately 200 men from 10 different subcultures within U.S. society have participated in this qualitative research. Our research participants include Haitian Christian fathers; Promise Keeper fathers; gay fathers; Latino fathers; White, nongay divorced fathers: Modern Orthodox Jewish fathers; and Greek grandfathers.

In contrast to the neoconservative perspective, our data on gay fathering couples have convinced us that neither a mother nor a father is essential. Similarly, our research with divorced, never-married, and remarried fathers has taught us that a wide variety of family structures can support positive child outcomes. We have concluded that children need at least one responsible, caretaking adult who has a positive emotional connection to them and with whom they have a consistent relationship. Because of the emotional and practical stress involved in child rearing, a family structure that includes more than one such adult is more likely to contribute to positive child outcomes. Neither the sex of the adult(s) nor the biological relationship to the child has emerged as a significant variable in predicting positive development. One, none, or both of those adults could be a father (or mother). We have found that the stability of the emotional connection and the predictability of the caretaking relationship are the significant variables that predict positive child adjustment.

We agree with the neoconservative perspective that it is preferable for responsible fathers (and mothers) to be actively involved with their children. We share the concern that many men in U.S. society do not have a feeling of emotional connection or a sense of responsibility toward their children. However, we do not believe that the data support the conclusion that fathers are essential to child well-being and that heterosexual marriage is the social context in which responsible fathering is most likely to occur.

Many social scientists believe that it is possible to draw a sharp distinction between scientific fact and political values. From our perspective, science is always structured by values, both in the research questions that are generated and in the interpretation of data. For example, if one considers the heterosexual nuclear family to be the optimal family structure for child development, then one is likely to design research that looks for negative consequences associated with growing up in a gay or lesbian parented family. If, in contrast, one assumes that gay and lesbian parents can create a positive family context, then one is likely to initiate research that investigates the strengths of children raised in these families.

The essentialist theoretical framework has already generated a series of social policy initiatives. For example, a 1998 congressional seminar recommended a series of revisions to the tax code that would reward couples who marry, and end taxes altogether for married couples with three or more children (Wetzstein, 1998). Other federal legislation has emerged with a similar emphasis on the advantages of marriage. The 1996 welfare reform law begins by stating, "Marriage is the foundation of a successful society" (Welfare Reform Act, 1996, p. 110). Similarly, a housing project in Hartford, Connecticut now provides economic supports to married couples and special opportunities for job training to men (but not to women) who live with their families (LaRossa, 1997). In 1997, Louisiana passed a Covenant Marriage Act (1997) that declared marriage a lifelong relationship and stipulated more stringent requirements for separation and divorce.

The social policy emerging out of the neoconservative framework is of grave concern to us because it discriminates against cohabiting couples, single mothers, and gay and lesbian parents. The purpose of the current article is to present a body of empirical data that illustrates the inaccuracy of the neoconservative argument. Throughout our discussion, we focus on the work of Blankenhorn (1995) and Popenoe (1996) because they have been most influential in structuring both public debate and social policy (Haygood, 1997; Samuelson, 1996).

Specific aspects of the neoconservative paradigm have been critiqued elsewhere. For example, McLoyd (1998) has pointed out that families without fathers are likely to be poor, and it is the negative effects of poverty, rather than the absence of a father, that lead to negative developmental outcomes. Similarly, Hetherington et al. (1998) have made the point that divorce does not always have negative consequences for children. However, the neoconservative argument as a whole has not been deconstructed. Thus, it tends to be absorbed in a monolithic fashion, buttressed by unconscious gender ideology and traditional cultural values. Therefore, we think that a systematic counterargument is necessary. We cite research indicating that parenting roles are interchangeable, that neither mothers nor fathers are unique or essential, and that the significant variables in predicting father involvement are economic, rather than marital. We also offer an alternative framework for encouraging responsible fathering.

We acknowledge that our reading of the scientific literature supports our political agenda. Our goal is to generate public policy initiatives that support men in their fathering role, without discriminating against women and same-sex couples. We are also interested in encouraging public policy that supports the legitimacy of diverse family structures, rather than policy that privileges the two-parent, heterosexual, married family.

We also realize that some of the research we cite to support our perspective will turn out to be incorrect. Haraway (1989) pointed out that as research paradigms evolve to reflect diverse gender, ethnic, class, and cultural perspectives, much of the established body of "scientific fact" has turned out to be science fiction. Fischhoff (1990) identified two options for psychologists in the public arena: helping the public define their best interests or manipulating the public to serve the interests of policymakers. Thus, despite the fact that new data will inevitably prove some aspects of our argument wrong, we hope that by stimulating scholarly debate, we will contribute to the process by which the public more accurately defines its best interests.

We begin by presenting cross-species and cross-cultural data that contradict the claim that parenting behaviors are constructed by biological differences. We argue that parenting involves a series of caregiving functions that have developed as adaptive strategies to specific bioecological contexts. These caregiving functions can be performed by parenting figures of either sex, whether or not they are biologically related to the child.

We then review the research on marriage and divorce. This body of data suggests that the poor psychological adjustment observed in some children in divorcing families is caused by the disruption of the child's entire life circumstances, rather than simply by the dissolution of the marriage or the absence of a father. We present data illustrat-

ing that emotionally connected, actively nurturing, and responsible fathering can occur within a variety of family structures.

Finally, we examine why the neoconservative perspective has been so widely accepted within popular culture. We speculate that the appeal of neoconservative ideology is related to two social trends: a genuine concern about children and a backlash against the gay rights and feminist movements. We then offer social policy recommendations that support men in their fathering role, without discriminating against women and same-sex couples.

The Essentialist Position

Biological Sex Differences Construct Gender Differences in Parenting

One of the cornerstones of the essentialist position is that biological differences in reproduction construct gender differences in parenting behaviors. This theoretical framework proposes that the biological experiences of pregnancy and lactation generate a strong instinctual drive in women to nurture. This perspective assumes that men do not have an instinctual drive to nurture infants and children.

The neoconservative perspective relies heavily on evolutionary psychology to support this argument. Evolutionary psychologists cite Trivers's (1972) sexual-conflict-of-interest hypothesis to explain sex differences in mating strategies. Trivers's hypothesis states that all other things being equal, male mammals will maximize their evolutionary fitness by impregnating as many females as possible, while investing very little in the rearing of any individual offspring. Female mammals, in contrast, invest a great deal of physiological energy in pregnancy and lactation and thus are motivated to invest a corresponding amount of time and energy in parenting.

Trivers's (1972) hypothesis accurately predicts behavior in many mammalian species. However, Smuts and Gubernick (1992) have shown this hypothesis to be inaccurate in predicting male involvement with infants among nonhuman primates. Unfortunately, Smuts and Gubernick's critique of the relevance of Trivers's hypothesis for primate behavior has not been integrated into evolutionary psychological theory.

Evolutionary psychology has recently gained prominence within psychology and other social sciences (e.g., Archer, 1996; Buss, 1995). Because the formal academic training of most social scientists does not include cross-species research and evolutionary theory, many social scientists have accepted evolutionary psychologists' use of Trivers's (1972) hypothesis in relation to primate behavior. However, many scholars within the natural science community have been critical of evolutionary psychology (see, e.g., the more than 20 negative commentaries on Thornhill & Thornhill's, 1992, article or Gould's, 1997, critique of evolutionary psychology).

Blankenhorn (1995) and Popenoe (1996), like many social scientists, have incorrectly assumed that Trivers's (1972) theory is true of all primates and is universally applicable across many different ecological contexts. However, all other things have generally not been equal over the course of evolutionary history. As bioecological contexts change, so do fathering behaviors, especially among male primates.

Marmosets are an extreme example of primates who live in a bioecological context that requires males to become primary caretakers (Smuts & Gubernick, 1992). Because marmosets always have twins, female marmosets must nurse two infants simultaneously. This generates nutritional pressure for the mother to spend all of her time and energy feeding herself. Therefore, the father most commonly performs all parenting behaviors. Thus, these animals do not conform to Trivers's (1972) hypothesis about the universality of nonnurturing male primates. Male marmosets behave like full-time mothers.

Marmosets illustrate how, within a particular bioecological context, optimal child outcomes can be achieved with fathers as primary caretakers and limited parenting involvement by mothers. Human examples of this proposition include single fathers (Greif & DeMaris, 1990), two-parent families in which the father is the primary caretaker (Pruett, 1989), and families headed by gay fathers (Patterson & Chan, 1997).

Another cornerstone of the essentialist position is that the traditional division of labor characteristic of Western, industrialized societies has been true throughout human evolutionary history. Popenoe (1996) stated that our hominid ancestors "had a strong division of labor in which males did most of the hunting and females did most of the gathering" (p. 167). Zihlman (1997), in contrast, has pointed out that for most of our evolutionary history, human societies were nomadic. This bioecological context required both men and women to travel long distances, hunt, gather food, and care for older children and other members of their community. Similarly, in contemporary foraging and horticultural societies, women perform the same range of tasks as men do and add infant care to their other responsibilities. Cross-cultural research illustrates that women are capable of traveling long distances, carrying heavy loads, and participating in hunting. Thus, the assertion that a rigid sexual division of labor existed over most of our evolutionary history is not supported either by what is known about human society in prehistory or by contemporary preagricultural cultures.

The neoconservative perspective has also assumed that providing has been a universal male role. Yet Nsa-menang (1992) pointed out that in many West African rural cultures, tradition places the sole responsibility for providing food on mothers. Similarly, in hunting–gathering cultures, women typically provide 60% of a family's nutritional requirements (Zihlman, 1997). Thus, in most preindustrial cultures, fathers have never been sole providers, and in some cultures they do not participate at all in the provider role.

The neoconservative perspective has also claimed that mothers are more "natural" caregivers than fathers. Yet, more than a decade ago, Lamb (1987) reported that research on mothers and fathers during the newborn period yielded no differences in parenting behaviors. Neither mothers nor fathers were natural parents. Because mothers tended to spend so much more time with their infants, they became much more familiar with their biological rhythms, visual and behavioral cues, and so forth. Therefore, when observations were repeated after a year, mothers appeared as much more competent caregivers than fathers. Many subsequent studies have shown that when fathers assume the primary caretaking role, they are as competent and as sensitive as mothers (Lamb, 1997).

In summary, the neoconservative position is simply wrong about the biological basis of observed differences in parenting behaviors. Cross-species and cross-cultural data indicate that fathering can vary from a high level of involvement to a total lack of involvement. Given these wide variations in paternal behaviors, it is more accurate to conclude that both men and women have the same biological potential for nurturing and that the sexual division of labor

in any culture is defined by the requirements of that culture's specific bioecological context.

Marriage Matters

The neoconservative perspective has argued that without a biological basis for nurturing in men, the best way to ensure that men will behave responsibly toward their offspring is to provide a social structure in which men can be assured of paternity (i.e., the traditional nuclear family).

Nonhuman Primate Behavior

This point of view is based on a corollary of Trivers's (1972) sexual-conflict-of-interest hypothesis, the paternity hypothesis. Trivers reasoned that without paternity certainty, male primates would not risk investing time and energy in another male's offspring, thereby decreasing their own evolutionary fitness.

However, Smuts and Gubernick (1992) have demonstrated that Trivers's (1972) paternity hypothesis is not generally predictive of fathering behavior among nonhuman primates. If paternity certainty were the most significant variable, then male primates should show greater paternal involvement in species where several females live with only one breeding male. In species where several males and several females live together (and therefore multiple mating opportunities make paternity uncertain), males should have lower paternal involvement.

The paternity hypothesis does correctly predict male care of infants in most monogamous species. In most monogamous mating pairs, males provide a high level of care. However, the paternity hypothesis does not accurately predict male care in other primate social groupings. With the exception of mountain gorillas, males in one-male groups (where paternity is certain) show less paternal involvement than males in multimale groups (where paternity is uncertain).

Smuts and Gubernick (1992) found that the amount of time and energy males invest in nurturing and protecting infants varies depending on the mutual benefits that males and females have to offer each other within a particular bioecological context. These authors offered an alternative hypothesis, the "reciprocity hypothesis," to account for variations in male care of infants. The reciprocity hypothesis predicts that male care of infants will be low when either males or females have few benefits to exchange. The probability of high male care of infants increases when females have substantial benefits to offer males (e.g., when females can offer to mate more frequently with specific males or can provide males with political alliances that enhance their status within the male dominance hierarchy).

Smuts and Gubernick (1992) found that male care of infants is lower in one-male groups because this system of reciprocal benefits does not exist. Each female has no alternative except to mate with the single male, whether or not he cares for her infants. Because she has no other mating possibilities, she cannot offer preferential mating opportunities in exchange for infant care. Similarly, in a one-male group, the breeding male does not have to compete for a place within a male dominance hierarchy. He is the only male in the group. Therefore, females cannot offer political assistance to enhance his dominance ranking. Because females lack benefits to offer males in exchange for infant care, male involvement, in contrast to what would be predicted by the paternity hypothesis, is low in one-male groups.

Overall, a very large body of animal research points to the importance of an array of variables, which we refer to as bioecological context, in determining parenting behaviors. Low levels of infant care do not characterize all male primates, nor is biological paternity the most significant variable in increasing the probability of high male involvement. Other feminist anthropologists and sociobiologists have similarly deconstructed Trivers's (1972) theory (e.g., Gowaty, 1997; Hrdy, 1997). In contrast to Trivers's emphasis on universal sex differences and the relative fixity of behaviors, these feminist researchers have pointed to the overlap of behaviors between the sexes and the relative flexibility of complex human behaviors. Unfortunately, this feminist scholarship has not been integrated into most social science literature.

Human Primate Behavior

Smuts and Gubernick (1992) have made a strong case for the power of the reciprocity hypothesis to predict male involvement among nonhuman primates. However, does their hypothesis predict human primate behavior? We argue that the reciprocity hypothesis does predict male involvement among human primates.

In cultures where women have significant resources to offer men in exchange for child care, paternal involvement should be higher than in cultures where women have fewer resources. In line with this prediction, paternal involvement in the United States, Sweden, and Australia is higher than in more traditional cultures, such as Italy and Spain, where women's workforce participation is less widespread (Blossfeld, 1995). Similarly, Haas (1993) reported that a survey of more than 300 Swedish families indicated that fathers participated more in child care if their partners made as much or more money than they did.

Erikson and Gecas (1991) have provided examples of how paternal involvement varies on the basis of the benefits men have to exchange. These authors pointed out that the least amount of father involvement in U.S. society has been observed in two groups of fathers: poor, unmarried teenage fathers and upper-class fathers in traditional nuclear families. Teen dads in U.S. society are often undereducated and underemployed. Therefore, they cannot make a meaningful contribution to the economic security of their children. Poor teen fathers do not have meaningful benefits to offer their child's mother. As the reciprocity hypothesis would predict, these fathers are often minimally involved in the lives of their children.

In upper-class families, in contrast, it is most often the wives who have few benefits to exchange. The family's high income is the result of the husband's earning capacity. The wife's additional economic contribution is rarely meaningful to the family's economic security. Most of the wives do not participate in paid employment. Thus, the upper-class wives have few benefits to offer in exchange for direct paternal involvement. Within this context, the fathers in these families use their income to pay for other-than-mother child care but do little active caregiving themselves.

The fathers with the highest level of active child-care involvement are in dual-shift, working-class families. Pleck (1993) has estimated that fathers in this family context are responsible for, on average, 30% of child care. Working-class, dual-shift families are the context in which mothers and fathers are most evenly matched in terms of the resources they have to exchange. Both parents' incomes are significant to family stability. Because they work opposite shifts, involvement in child care by

the at-home parent is necessary for child well-being. From the perspective of the reciprocity hypothesis, the parity of resources between husband and wife within this family structure generated the high level of paternal involvement.

Stier and Tienda (1993) have provided other data that support the link between father involvement and economic benefits. Using interviews from more than 800 resident and nonresident fathers living in poor neighborhoods in Chicago, these authors examined the relations between paternal support and several background variables. The researchers found that the only significant predictors of which fathers would pay child support were those that reflected the father's economic status. Fathers who were currently employed were three times more likely to support their nonresident children compared with fathers who were not working.

In summary, these data on human parenting behaviors conform to the predictions of the reciprocity hypothesis. In social contexts where either the fathers or the mothers have few benefits to exchange, paternal involvement is low. When both fathers and mothers have benefits that contribute to family well-being, paternal involvement is relatively high. Thus, improving employment opportunities for women, as well as men, is crucial to increasing father involvement. These findings suggest that in our current cultural context, it is economics, not marriage, that matters.

The Civilizing Effects of Marriage

The essentialist position has also proposed that marriage has a civilizing effect on men. Popenoe (1996), reflecting this point of view, has stated that "all successful societies have imposed social sanctions on men . . . the most important of these is the institution of marriage" (p. 164). Similarly, Blankenhorn (1995) declared that "marriage constitutes an irreplaceable life support system for effective fatherhood" (p. 223).

Blankenhorn (1995) further asserted that marriage protects women and children from domestic violence (p. 34). He reported that as the percentage of men living within the confines of marriage has declined over the past two decades, domestic violence has increased. However, a recent report on intimate violence published by the U.S. Department of Justice (1998) indicated that as marriage has declined over the past two decades, so has intimate violence. This report stated that murders of women by their intimate partners decreased 40%, from 3,000 in 1976 to 1,800 in 1996. Similarly, nonlethal violence (sexual assault, robbery, aggravated and simple assault) declined from 1.1 million reported incidents in 1993 to 840,000 in 1996 (U.S. Department of Justice, 1998).

Blankenhorn (1995) and Popenoe (1996) have also argued for the protective effect of biological fatherhood within the context of marriage. Citing a study by Daly and Wilson (1985), Blankenhorn claimed that children are more frequently abused by stepfathers than by biological fathers. However, Sternberg (1997) pointed out that Daly and Wilson specified only that the more frequently abused children lived in households with stepfathers. They could not specify whether the perpetrator of the abuse was the stepfather, the biological mother, or another adult in the household. Malkin and Lamb (1994), in an attempt to correct for this design flaw, included information about the perpetrator's gender and relationship to the child. They found that biological caretakers, in both stepfamilies and biological families, were more likely to engage in serious physical abuse than stepparents. Nonbiological caretakers, in contrast, committed minor abuse.

These findings are confirmed by the Third National Incidence Study of Child Abuse and Neglect (Sedlak & Broadhurst, 1996). This study reported that the majority (78%) of children who suffered maltreatment, both neglect and abuse, were maltreated by a birth parent. Parent substitutes (foster, adoptive, step) were responsible for the abuse in only 14% of reported cases. In terms of sexual abuse, 46% of children were sexually abused by a stranger. Birth parents were about as likely to be sexually abusive (29%) as were parent substitutes (25%). These statistics do not support the neoconservative contention that stepfathers or mothers' boyfriends abuse children more frequently than biological fathers (and mothers).

In a comprehensive article reviewing the nature, causes, and consequences of abuse, Emery and Laumann-Billings (1998) have identified multiple variables that lead to abuse. These include personality of the perpetrator (such as low self-esteem or poor impulse control), characteristics of the immediate family context (such as job loss), and qualities of the broader ecological context (such as poverty or high levels of violence in the community). Stepchildren, unplanned children, and children in large families are all at greater risk for abuse. Thus, high levels of child abuse are associated with a broad array of biopsychosocial variables. In summary, we do not find any empirical support that marriage enhances fathering or that marriage civilizes men and protects children.

Fathers Make a Unique and Essential Contribution to Child Development

The neoconservative perspective has proposed that if men can be induced to take care of young children, their unique, masculine contribution significantly improves the developmental outcomes for children. From the essentialist perspective, "fatherhood privileges children. . . . Conversely, the primary consequences of fatherlessness are rising male violence and declining child well-being and the underlying source of our most important social problems" (Blankenhorn, 1995, pp. 25–26).

These claims represent an oversimplification of the data. On average, children from divorced families have been shown to be at greater risk for a range of problems than are children from nondivorced families. However, it is also true that 75% of children from divorced families exhibit no negative effects (see Hetherington et al., 1998, for a review). Furthermore, the size of the negative effect of divorce is considerably reduced when the adjustment of children preceding divorce is controlled. For many of these children, the problems attributed to divorce were actually present prior to the divorce. In addition, divorce does not affect all children negatively. Amato, Loomis, and Booth (1995) reported that, although children from low-conflict marriages were stressed by divorce, the adjustment of children in high-conflict marriages actually improved after divorce. Overall, the research suggests that divorce does not irretrievably harm the majority of children.

Hetherington et al. (1998) have pointed out that divorce is not a single event, but rather a cycle of negative events. The cycle begins with marital conflict, followed by dissolution of the current family structure, and culminates with the formation of separate households. In the majority of families, at least one parent remarries, forming a new, blended stepfamily. In addition, divorce occurs more frequently in second marriages, reinitiating the disruptive cycle of loss and conflict. This cycle entails economic stress, disrupted attachments, and often separation from the family home and neighborhood.

In his deconstruction of Bowlby's (1951) maternal deprivation hypothesis, Rutter (1974) illustrated that the negative developmental outcomes observed in institutionalized infants were caused by the disruption of the child's entire life circumstances, rather than simply by separation from the mother. Likewise, it seems more probable that the link between marital transitions and negative developmental outcomes is due to the disruption of the children's entire lives, rather than simply to the absence of their fathers.

Blankenhorn's (1995) and Popenoe's (1996) reliance on the father-absence research paradigm is surprising, because the limitations of this approach have been documented by many researchers over the past two decades (see Phares, 1996, for a review). Father absence covaries with other relevant family characteristics (i.e., the lack of an income from a male adult, the absence of a second adult, and the lack of support from a second extended family system). McLoyd (1998) has pointed out that because single-mother families are overrepresented among poor families, it is difficult to differentiate the effects of father absence from the effects of low income.

Another major limitation to this paradigm is that father absence is not a monolithic variable. Qualitative research has shown that relationships between absent fathers and their children can vary widely. Weil (1996) studied 22 divorced fathers who were recruited from a self-help fathers' rights group. These middle-class, suburban, mostly White fathers used a variety of settings (e.g., school, day care, extended-family events) to increase their interaction with their children above the limited contact specified in their visitation arrangements. In another study, Way and Stauber (1996) interviewed 45 urban adolescent girls about their relationships with their fathers. Of the 26 girls who did not live with their fathers, 7 reported weekly contact with them, 10 reported occasional contact, and only 9 reported almost no contact. Thus, father involvement exists on a continuum, whether or not fathers live with their children. Fathers can be absent even when they reside with their children and can be present despite nonresident status.

The essentialist position also fails to acknowledge the potential costs of father presence. Engle and Breaux (1998) have shown that some fathers' consumption of family resources in terms of gambling, purchasing alcohol, cigarettes, or other nonessential commodities, actually increased women's workload and stress level.

The Importance of a Male Role Model

Another aspect of the neoconservative perspective is the argument that "key parental tasks belong essentially and primarily to fathers" (Blankenhorn, 1995, p. 67). Fathers are seen as essential role models for boys, relationship models for girls, and "protectors" of their families (Popenoe, 1996, p. 77). However, there is a considerable body of empirical evidence that contradicts these claims.

The essentialist perspective assumes that boys need a heterosexual male parent to establish a masculine gender identity. Pleck (1995) has demonstrated that empirical research does not support this assumption. Similarly, a significant amount of research on the children of lesbian and gay parents has shown that children raised by lesbian mothers (and gay fathers) are as likely as children raised in heterosexual, two-parent families to achieve a heterosexual gender orientation (Patterson, 1995; Patterson & Chan, 1997). Other aspects of personal development and social relation-

ships were also found to be within the normal range for children raised in lesbian and gay families.

However, persistent, although inconsistent, findings suggest that the negative impact of divorce is more significant for boys than for girls. After reviewing the divorce and remarriage research, Hetherington et al. (1998) concluded that "the presence of a father may have positive effects on the well-being of boys" (p. 178). These authors also pointed out that the research is not clear about how father presence acts as a protective factor for boys. Lytton and Romney (1991), in a meta-analysis of 172 studies, found very few significant differences in the ways that mothers and fathers treated girls and boys. Similarly, Lamb (1997) concluded that "very little about the gender of the parent seems to be distinctly important" (p. 10). Thus, the relation between father presence and better developmental outcomes for boys remains correlational, not causal.

We speculate that the larger cultural context of male dominance and negative attitudes toward women may interfere with the ability of many single mothers to establish an authoritative parenting style with male children. Within patriarchal culture, boys know that when they become adult men, they will be dominant to every woman, including their mother. This cultural context, unmediated by a male presence, may undermine a single mother's authority with her sons. Qualitative research is needed to explore the subjective experiences of boys in single-mother, single-father, and two-parent nuclear families in order to understand these persistent but unclear findings.

Taken as a whole, the empirical research does not support the idea that fathers make a unique and essential contribution to child development. From our perspective, it is not the decline of marriage that is discouraging responsible fathering. Rather, various social conditions inhibit involved parenting by unmarried and divorced men. For example, unmarried teen fathers typically have low levels of education and job training. Thus, they lack the ability to contribute significantly to the economic security of their offspring. Similarly, many divorced fathers cannot sustain a positive emotional connection to their children after the legal system redefines their role from parenting to visitation.

Social policy is needed that removes the impediments to paternal involvement for never-married and divorced fathers. Rather than privileging the institution of heterosexual marriage at the expense of other family structures, it is essential to strengthen the father-child bond within all family contexts, especially nonmarital contexts.

Change and the Change-Back Reaction

If the essentialist paradigm is not supported by empirical data, why has it been so widely accepted? We believe that the appeal of the essentialist position reflects a reaction against the rapid changes in family life that have taken place in the past three decades. Since the 1960s, family-formation strategies have changed dramatically in Western, industrialized cultures (Blossfeld, 1995). The cultural norm of early and universal marriage has been reversed. Fertility rates have declined overall, and age at the birth of a first child has risen across all cohorts. More couples are choosing to live together outside the context of marriage, and a first pregnancy more frequently precedes rather than follows marriage. Previously rare family types (e.g., single mothers by choice,

dual career families, and gay or lesbian parents) are increasingly more common.

Industrialized cultures are in the process of changing from a context in which child development could flourish with fathers as the sole or primary provider to a context in which two providers are now necessary in the vast majority of families. In a survey of 1,502 U.S. families, 48% of married women reported that they provided half or more of the family income (Families and Work Institute, 1995). Given this commitment to breadwinning, women can no longer shoulder the sole responsibility for raising children.

In this context of rapid change, the neoconservative position reflects a widespread societal anxiety about who will raise the children. Mothers are no longer at home, and society has not embraced other-than-mother care. The United States, in contrast to other Western countries, has not yet developed a social policy agenda designed to help women and men integrate their work and family responsibilities. Thus, many people believe that a return to the traditional nuclear family structure with its gendered division of labor would be preferable to large numbers of neglected and unsupervised children.

In addition to an authentic concern about the welfare of children, we believe that the appeal of the essential father also reflects a backlash against the gay rights and feminist movements. In the past two decades, the employment of women has dramatically increased, whereas the employment of men has declined significantly (Engle & Breaux, 1998). Many more women than in past historical periods can now choose to leave unsatisfactory marriages or to have children on their own, outside of the context of a traditional marriage. Two of three divorces are now initiated by women (Rice, 1994).

Just as the feminist movement created new opportunities for women, the gay rights movement has encouraged many more gay men and lesbians to live an openly homosexual lifestyle. Many gay men and women who would previously have entered into a heterosexual marriage to have children, now see a gay family structure as a viable alternative for raising children. Parallel to these changes is the tendency emerging among heterosexual couples to live together and delay marriage until after a first pregnancy (Blossfeld, 1995). Thus, the distinctions between marital and cohabiting unions and between marital and nonmarital childbearing are losing their normative force.

These social changes require heterosexual men to relinquish certain aspects of power and privilege that they enjoyed in the context of the traditional nuclear family. Most men no longer have sole economic power over their families. Similarly, most men must accept some degree of responsibility for child care and household tasks. The majority of heterosexual men no longer have full-time wives to buffer the stress of balancing work and family roles. Within this new context of power sharing and role sharing, heterosexual men have been moved from the center to the margins of many versions of family life. In our view, the societal debate about gender differences in parenting is, in part, a reaction to this loss of male power and privilege. We see the argument that fathers are essential as an attempt to reinstate male dominance by restoring the dominance of the traditional nuclear family with its contrasting masculine and feminine gender roles.

Family systems theory (Kerr & Bowen, 1988) has proposed that natural systems (such as families and societies) fluctuate between periods of homeostasis and periods of disequilibrium. When change occurs, elements within the system react with a pressure to change the system back to its prior state of homeostasis. This cycle is called change and the change-back reaction. The current social context of multiple and diverse family structures, with their interchangeable parenting roles and more egalitarian distribution of power, challenges the dominant cultural ideology. From our perspective, the emphasis on the essential importance of fathers and heterosexual marriage represents a change-back reaction. It is an attempt to reassert the cultural hegemony of traditional values, such as heterocentrism, Judeo-Christian marriage, and male power and privilege.

An Alternative Blueprint for Social Change

We have argued that the neoconservative paradigm is based on an oversimplification of empirical research. Thus, we believe that the social policy emanating from this perspective cannot ultimately be successful in encouraging responsible fathering. Pressuring men and women to enter into or maintain unsatisfactory marriages is unlikely to enhance paternal involvement. We now present an alternative framework that we believe more accurately fits the data. Our framework has three main recommendations: reconstructing traditional masculinity ideology, restructuring societal institutions, and providing a comprehensive program of governmental subsidies to all families with children.

Because we believe that ideology defines both social policy and individual behavior, our first recommendation speaks to the necessity of reconstructing cultural ideology about gender roles. Those who support the neoconservative perspective also want to reconnect fatherhood and masculinity. Blankenhorn (1995) has stated that "being a real man [must come to mean] being a good father" (p. 223). However, within the essentialist framework, responsible fathering is inextricably intertwined with marriage. Our goal, in contrast, is to create an ideology that defines the father–child bond as independent of the father–mother relationship.

If the father–child bond were accorded the same importance as the mother–child bond, then young boys would be socialized to assume equal responsibility for the care and nurturing of their children. A father's relationship with his children could then develop and remain independent of his relationship with the child's mother. This ideological shift would encourage the development of diverse models of responsible fatherhood. Roopnarine et al. (1993) described a group of African Caribbean fathers living in a variety of relationship contexts (e.g., marital, common law, and "friending") who behaved responsibly to both biological and stepchildren. These data indicate that responsible fathering need not be dependent on a marital relationship.

We believe that this change in cultural gender ideology would be effective in maintaining a high level of paternal involvement for resident as well as nonresident fathers. Divorce and nonmarital childbirth would then be less likely to be characterized by father absence, because cultural norms would prescribe that never-married and divorced fathers remain actively involved with their children.

This ideological enhancement of the father–child bond is also necessary for restructuring societal institutions so that father involvement is encouraged, rather than inhibited. Maintaining the sacred status of the mother—child dyad continues the myth of separate (i.e., gendered) spheres of life. The cultural assumption of separate spheres links public/work/masculine and private/family/feminine. This cultural linking of family and feminine is reflected in the assumption that women, but not men, will decrease their involvement in paid work to balance the competing demands of work and family life.

Pleck (1993) found that men are reluctant to take advantage of family-supportive policies because they fear that they will be perceived as uncommitted to their job or unmasculine. Until workplace norms acknowledge that men have equivalent responsibility for child care, it is unlikely that most men will feel comfortable restructuring their commitment to work in a manner that allows more family involvement.

In the context of poor, ethnic minority families, it is often fathers rather than mothers who have no resources to exchange. More than a decade ago, Wilson (1987) pointed out that institutionalized racism caused minority men to be marginalized, first from the labor market and then from the family. Governmental policy must acknowledge the link between father absence and job absence. Men who can contribute substantially to family finances are more likely to get married and to assume financial responsibility for their children.

Our final recommendation relates to an overall governmental family policy. The United States cultural ideology of rugged individualism continues to assume that individual families can and should balance the stress of work and family without the benefits of large-scale government supports. The United States remains one of the few industrialized countries without a comprehensive family policy that provides paid parental leave, governmentally financed day care, and economic subsidies for all families with children. Without these benefits, the responsibility for child care continues to fall largely on women.

Because women continue to bear the bulk of the responsibility for the welfare of children, the goal of economic equality remains elusive. Providing families with governmental supports would not only alleviate many of the stresses of working families, it would also free women from the unequal burden of making major accommodations in their involvement in paid work. This shift would then decrease gender inequalities in the workplace, provide women with more resources to exchange, and thus contribute to higher paternal involvement.

How can these societal changes be achieved? Haas (1993) pointed to the high participation by women in politics as one of the social forces that has been significant in establishing progressive family policy in Sweden. Since the early 1970s, women have held one third or more of the seats in parliament, compared with 12% in the 1996 U.S. Congress (The World Almanac, 1998). The example of Swedish politics suggests that until more women become active in government, many of the governmental supports needed to help families may not be forthcoming.

Conclusion

We have tried to illustrate how the essentialist position does not accurately reflect relevant empirical research. We have provided an alternative explanation of the research and have generated recommendations for social policy supports to mothers and fathers that we believe will more effectively achieve the goal of reconnecting fathers and children. We hope that this article will generate scholarly debate within the psychological community and encourage a critical analysis of the essentialist paradigm.

References

Amato, P. R., Loomis, L. S., & Booth, A. (1995). Parental divorce, marital conflict, and offspring well-being during early adulthood. *Social Forces, 73,* 895–915.

Archer, J. (1996). Sex differences in social behavior: Are the social role and evolutionary explanations compatible? *American Psychologist, 51,* 909–917.

Auerbach, C., & Silverstein, L. (1997, November). *Is parenting gendered? A postmodern conversation.* Symposium conducted at the National Conference on Family Relations, Arlington, VA.

Auerbach, C., Silverstein, L., & Zizi, M. (1997). The evolving structure of fatherhood: A qualitative study of Haitian American fathers. *Journal of African American Men, 2,* 59–85.

Biller, H. B., & Kimpton, J. L. (1997). The father and the school-aged child. In M. E. Lamb (Ed.), *The role of the father in child development.* (3rd ed., pp. 143–161). New York: Wiley.

Blankenhorn, D. (1995). *Fatherless America: Confronting our most urgent social problem.* New York: Basic Books.

Blossfeld, H.-P. (Ed.). (1995). *The new role of women.* Boulder, CO: Westview.

Booth, A., & Crouter, A. C. (1998). *Men in families: When do they get involved? What difference does it make?* Mahwah, NJ: Erlbaum.

Bowlby, J. (1951). *Maternal care and mental health.* Geneva, Switzerland: World Health Organization.

Bowman, P. J., & Forman, T. A. (1998). Instrumental and expressive family roles among African American fathers. In R. Taylor, J. Jackson, & L. M. Chatters (Eds.), *Family life in Black America* (pp. 216–261). Newbury Park, CA: Sage.

Buss, D. M. (1995). Psychological sex differences: Origins through sexual selection. *American Psychologist, 41,* 164–168.

Covenant Marriage Act, LSA-R.S. 9:272, *et seq.* (1997).

Daly, M., & Wilson, M. (1985). Child abuse and other risks of not living with both parents. *Ethology and Sociobiology, 6,* 197–210.

Emery, R. E., & Laumann-Billings, L. (1998). An overview of the nature, causes, and consequences of abusive family relationships: Toward differentiating maltreatment and violence. *American Psychologist, 53,* 121–135.

Engle, P. L., & Breaux, C. (1998). Fathers' involvement with children: Perspectives from developing countries. *Social Policy Report: Society for Research in Child Development, XII,* 1–23.

Erikson, R. J., & Gecas, V. (1991). Social class and fatherhood. In F. W. Bozett & S. M. H. Hanson (Eds.), *Focus on men: Vol. 6. Fatherhood and families in cultural context* (pp. 114–137). New York: Springer.

Families and Work Institute. (1995). *Women: The new providers.* New York: Whirlpool Foundation Study.

Fischhoff, B. (1990). Psychology and public policy: Tool or toolmaker? *American Psychologist, 45,* 647–653.

Gould, S. J. (1997, July 12). Darwinian fundamentalists. *The New York Review of Books, 10,* 34–37.

Gowaty, P. A. (1997). Introduction: Darwinian feminists and feminist evolutionists. In P. A. Gowaty (Ed.), *Feminism and evolutionary biology* (pp. 1–18). New York: Chapman & Hall.

Greif, G. L., & DeMaris, A. (1990). Single fathers with custody. *Families in Society: The Journal of Contemporary Human Services, 71,* 259–266.

Haas, L. (1993). Nurturing fathers and working mothers: Changing gender roles in Sweden. In J. C. Hood (Ed.), *Men, work, and the family* (pp. 238–261). Newbury Park, CA: Sage.

Haraway, D. (1989). *Primate visions.* New York: Routledge.

Haygood, W. (1997, November 30). Underground dads. *The New York Times Magazine,* p. 156.

Hetherington, E. M., Bridges, M., & Insabella, G. M. (1998). What matters? What does not? Five perspectives on the association between marital transitions and children's adjustment. *American Psychologist, 53,* 167–184.

Hrdy, S. B. (1997). Raising Darwin's consciousness: Female sexuality and the prehominid origins of patriarchy. *Human Nature, 8,* 1–49.

Kerr, M., & Bowen, M. (1988). *Family evaluation.* New York: Norton.

Lamb, M. E. (1987). The emergent American father. In M. Lamb (Ed.), *The father's role: Cross-cultural perspectives* (pp. 3–25). Hillsdale, NJ: Erlbaum.

Lamb, M. E. (1997). Fathers and child development: An introductory overview and guide. In M. E. Lamb (Ed.), *The role of the father in child development* (3rd ed., pp. 1–18). New York: Wiley.

LaRossa, R. (Chair). (1997, November). *Perspectives for encouraging father involvement.* Symposium conducted at the National Conference on Family Relations, Arlington, VA.

Lytton, H., & Romney, D. M. (1991). Parents' differential socialization of boys and girls: A meta-analysis. *Psychological Bulletin, 109,* 267–296.

Malkin, C. M., & Lamb, M. E. (1994). Child maltreatment: A test of sociobiological theory. *Journal of Comparative Family Studies, 25,* 121–134.

McLoyd, V. C. (1998). Socioeconomic disadvantage and child development. *American Psychologist, 53,* 185–204.

Nsamenang, B. A. (1992). Perceptions of parenting among the Nso of Cameroon. In B. S. Hewlett (Ed.), *Father–child relations: Cultural and biosocial contexts* (pp. 321–343). New York: Aldine de Gruyter.

Patterson, C. J. (1995). Lesbian mothers, gay fathers, and their children. In A. R. D'Augelli & C. F. Patterson (Eds.), *Lesbian, gay, and bisexual identities over the lifespan* (pp. 262–290). New York: Oxford University Press.

Patterson, C. J., & Chan, R. W. (1997). Gay fathers. In M. E. Lamb (Ed.), *The role of the father in child development* (3rd ed., pp. 245–260). New York: Wiley.

Phares, V. (1996). *Fathers and developmental psychopathology.* New York: Wiley.

Pleck, J. H. (1993). Are "family supportive" employer policies relevant to men? In J. C. Hood (Ed.), *Men, work, and family* (pp. 217–237). Newbury Park, CA: Sage.

Pleck, J. H. (1995). The gender role strain paradigm: An update. In R. F. Levant & W. S. Pollack (Eds.), *A new psychology of men* (pp. 11–32). New York: Basic Books.

Pleck, J. H. (1997). Paternal involvement: Levels, sources, and consequences. In M. E. Lamb (Ed.), *The role of the father in child development* (3rd ed., pp. 66–103). New York: Wiley.

Popenoe, D. (1996). *Life without father.* New York: Pressler Press.

Pruett, K. D. (1989). The nurturing male: A longitudinal study of primary nurturing fathers. In S. H. Cath, A. Gurwitt, & L. Gunsberg (Eds.), *Fathers and their families* (pp. 389–405). Hillsdale, NJ: Analytic Press.

Rice, J. K. (1994). Reconsidering research on divorce, family life cycle, and the meaning of family. *Psychology of Women Quarterly, 18,* 559–585.

Roopnarine, J., Snell-White, P., & Riegraf, N. (1993). *Men's roles in family and society: Dominica, Guyana, and Jamaica.* Kingston, Jamaica: UNICEF and UWI.

Rutter, M. (1974). *The qualities of mothering: Maternal deprivation reassessed.* New York: Aronson.

Samuelson, R. J. (1996, June 17). Why men need family values. *Newsweek, 127,* 58–61.

Sedlak, A. J., & Broadhurst, D. D. (1996). *Third national incidence study of child abuse and neglect.*

Washington, DC: National Center on Child Abuse and Neglect, U.S. Department of Health and Human Services.

Silverstein, L. B. (1996). Fathering is a feminist issue. *Psychology of Women Quarterly, 20,* 3–27.

Silverstein, L. B., Auerbach, C. F., Grieco, L., & Dunkel, F. (in press). Do Promise Keepers dream of feminist sheep? *Sex Roles.*

Silverstein, L. B., & Phares, V. (1996). Expanding the mother–child paradigm: An examination of dissertation research 1986–1993. *Psychology of Women Quarterly, 20,* 39–54.

Silverstein, L., & Quartironi, B. (1996). Gay fathers. *Family Psychologist, 12,* 23–24.

Smuts, B. B., & Gubernick, D. J. (1992). Male-infant relationships in nonhuman primates: Paternal investment or mating effort? In B. S. Hewlett (Ed.), *Father–child relations: Cultural and biosocial contexts* (pp. 1–31). New York: Aldine de Gruyter.

Sternberg, K. J. (1997). Fathers, the missing parents in research on family violence. In M. E. Lamb (Ed.), *The role of the father in child development* (3rd ed., pp. 284–309). New York: Wiley.

Stier, H., & Tienda, M. (1993). Are men marginal to the family? Insights from Chicago's inner city. In J. C. Hood (Ed.), *Men, work, and family* (pp. 23–44). Newbury Park, CA: Sage.

Thornhill, R., & Thornhill, N. W. (1992). The evolutionary psychology of men's coercive sexuality. *Behavioral and Brain Sciences, 15,* 363–375.

Trivers, R. L. (1972). Parental investment and sexual selection. In B. Campbell (Ed.), *Sexual selection and the descent of man 1871–1971* (pp. 136–179). Chicago: Aldine-Atherton.

U.S. Department of Justice. (1998). *Violence by intimates: Analysis of data on crimes by current or former spouses, boyfriends, and girlfriends.* Washington, DC: Bureau of Justice Statistics.

Way, N., & Stauber, H. (1996). Are "absent fathers" really absent? Urban adolescent girls speak out about their fathers. In B. J. R. Leadbeater & N. Way (Eds.), *Urban girls: Resisting stereotypes, creating identities* (pp. 132–148). New York: New York University Press.

Weil, F. (1996). *Divorced fathers: A qualitative study.* Unpublished doctoral dissertation, Ferkauf Graduate School of Psychology, Yeshiva University, Bronx, NY.

Welfare Reform Act, 104 U.S.C. Stat. 2110 (1996).

Wetzstein, C. (1998, April 15). Congress urged to provide economic, social incentives to preserve family. *The Washington Times,* p. A2.

Wilson, W. J. (1987). *The truly disadvantaged: The inner city, the underclass, and public policy.* Chicago: University of Chicago Press.

The World Almanac. (1998). Mahwah, NJ: World Almanac Books.

Zihlman, A. L. (1997). Women's bodies, women's lives: An evolutionary perspective. In M. E. Morbeck, A. Galloway, & A. L. Zihlman (Eds.), *The evolving female: A life history perspective* (pp. 185–197). Princeton, NJ: Princeton University Press.

19

"I Take Care of my Kids": Mothering Practice of Substance-Abusing Women

Phyllis L. Baker and Amy Carson

White, middle-class, heterosexual standards of child-centered mothering require that women deliver constant care to their children and put their own needs second **(defined norm)**. This model of mothering, requiring that women devote endless amounts of time, energy, and money toward their children, is unrealistic and unattainable, yet it continues to be upheld as the ideal. In this reading, Baker and Carson explore the ways that substance-abusing mothers, who are generally seen as falling far short of these exacting standards, evaluate their own parenting. Although these mothers recognize the negative impact their drug use has had on their children, they also see themselves as caring and committed parents. They reject a portrayal of themselves as bad mothers: 1) by describing behaviors that adhere to the socially acceptable model of white, middle-class, heterosexual motherhood, and 2) by creating more inclusive standards for acceptable mothering. Baker and Carson argue that by listening to the voices of substance-abusing mothers, we see both how women internalize the standards of the defined norm (the white, middle-class, heterosexual model), and how they resist these messages **(gender role effects)**.

Questions to Consider:

1. According to Baker and Carson, what are some of the ways substance-abusing mothers follow the white, middle-class, heterosexual model of good mothering? What are some of the ways their definition of good mothering differs from this model?

2. Describe your own mother's (or other female caregiver's) model of good mothering. How does it fit with the contemporary ideology of mothering described by Baker and Carson?

P. L. Baker & A. Carson, *Gender & Society, 13,* (3), pp. 347–363. Copyright (c) 1999 by Sociologists for Women in Society. Reprinted by permission of Sage Publications, Inc.

3. Baker and Carson argue that the interpretive and qualitative methodology they employed in this study allowed them to describe participants' perspectives without imposing the views of the researchers. What are the advantages and disadvantages of such methodology?

4. What are the implications of this research for developing a more inclusive and realistic model of "good" mothering?

Research on substance abuse indicates that there are a number of characteristics unique to women. Women have a different path to addiction that requires smaller quantities of alcohol and drugs but rapidly progresses to addiction and other related health problems (Grella 1996). Women who abuse substances also report a higher incidence of anxiety, depression, and other psychiatric disorders than do men (Benishek et al. 1992). Rape and other sexual assault characterize the history of many substance-abusing women (Hanke and Faupel 1993). Women also report feelings of guilt and shame related to their drug abuse and the impact of their addiction on their families (Rosenbaum 1979). Serious, life-threatening illnesses and diseases can compromise the health status of substance-abusing women.[1] In short, substance-abusing women live in a complex social and psychological environment. What does it mean to be a substance-abusing woman and a mother?

Substance-abusing women, who also take on the responsibilities of motherhood, experience increased problems because of the demands placed on them by the contemporary ideology of mothering. Notions about mothering in the United States are based on a white, middle-class, heterosexual standard that places the biological mother as the sole parent to deliver constant care and attention to her children (Hays 1996; Hill Collins 1994; McMahon 1995; Nakano Glenn, Chang, and Forcey 1994). Although this ideology tells us that mothering is constituted by women's biological role in reproduction, a sociological perspective dictates that mothering should be seen as a social construct (Hays 1996; Nakano Glenn, Chang, and Forcey 1994). It was not until late modernity that motherhood evolved as a legal institution, became normalized, and brought with it notions of "good" and "bad" mothering as cultural boundaries for women (Smart 1996). Hays noted that

> the model of the white, native-born middle-class has long been, and continues to be, the most powerful, visible, and self-consciously articulated, while the child-rearing ideas of new immigrant groups, slaves, American Indians, and the poor and working classes have received relatively little positive press. (1996, 21)

Critics of this contemporary ideology of mothering agree that the boundaries of "appropriate" mothering practices are demanding, conflicting, and unattainable. Hays argued that the contemporary ideology of mothering dictates that mothers follow the principles of "intensive mothering," a process that is "child centered, expert guided,

AUTHORS' NOTE: *The authors thank the University of Northern Iowa for research support through project grants and a 1997 summer fellowship. A version of this article was presented at the 1997 meeting of the Midwest Sociological Society. We also thank graduate assistants Leslie Lanning and Lori Wiebold for their administrative, bibliographic, and editorial help. William Downs, Sharon Hays, and Michael Lieber made helpful comments on previous drafts.*

emotionally absorbing, labor intensive, and financially expensive" (1996, 8). The socially constructed definition of mothering requires limitless amounts of the mother's monetary and emotional resources to be directed toward the fulfillment of all the child's needs and desires, making her own needs secondary to those of her children (Hays 1996; McMahon 1995; Smart 1996).

The conventional ideology of mothering continues to be based on a model of white families, who enjoy a relatively greater degree of economic security and racial privilege (Hill Collins 1994); it fails to represent or recognize other ways of mothering that coexist with the dominant model. Blum and Deussen observed "alternative" practices in which Black mothers resisted assumptions that a deserving mother must be singularly and exclusively present and that legal marriage is required for good mothering (1996, 208). Latina immigrant domestic workers who leave their children to come to the United States for work build alternate constructions of motherhood that contradict that of the United States' white and middle-class model (Hondagneu-Sotelo and Avila 1997). Lewin showed how lesbian mothers resist the cultural opposition between "lesbian" and "mother" but experience these two dimensions of their identity as competing and interfering (1994, 343). Thus, any woman who is not white, middle-class, married, and heterosexual is a bad mother.

Substance-abusing mothers have been stigmatized, labeled as unfit, and targeted for disapproval due to their failure to meet cultural standards for mothering. Condemnation of substance-abusing mothering is common in most of the studies about them that research the effects of alcohol and illegal drug use on the fetus and the children (Chazotte, Youchah, and Comerford Freda 1995; Lawton Hawley et al. 1995), the effects of treatment on continued use (Smith et al. 1992), the predictive factors for continued use (Richman, Rospenda, and Kelley 1995), and/or drug-taking behaviors and lifestyles (Grant Higgins, Hendel Clough, and Wallerstedt 1995). Regardless of topic, these traditional studies reinforce the notion that substance-abusing women are bad mothers because they accept the dominant discourse on mothering. Recent disapproval is particularly evident in the construction of crack mothers, particularly African American and Latina mothers, as the epitome of maternal villains who actively and permanently damage their offspring (McNeil and Litt 1992, 31). These constructions of substance-abusing mothers have led to the development of a "bio-underclass" (McNeil and Litt 1992) who become victims of a cultural captivation with the "criminalization of pregnancy." There is such reproach for substance abusing mothers that a platform for fetal rights has resulted in punitive policies and legislation enhancing the ability of prosecutors to charge substance-abusing, pregnant women (mostly minority and low-income women) with offenses ranging from drug trafficking to homicide (Albertson Fineman 1995; Litt and McNeil 1997; Young 1994). These mothers are incarcerated, separated from their newborns, and lose custody of their children. Within a very punitive social, political, and economic climate, any substance-abusing woman is invariably a "bad" mother, for it is assumed that the search for, and the use of, substances makes her inattentive, self-indulgent, and negligent rather exclusively mindful of her children's needs (Ettorre 1992).

Missing from the extant literature is research in which substance-abusing mothers speak for themselves, explaining their visions of a "good" mother, and how they believe they fit into that vision. Seventeen substance-abusing mothers in residence at a substance-abuse treatment facility were directly and intimately interviewed about their lives and children to explore their cultural knowledge about mothering and their observations of their own mothering practices. The data presented in this article are unique in providing the participants' detailed perceptions of their mothering practices. Contrary to the conclusions of most of the literature on substance-abusing mothers, these women describe themselves as caring and committed moms.

Methodology

An interpretive and qualitative methodology aims to acquire the member's perspective and to report it without imposing an outsider's point of view (Neuman 1994; Sands and McClelland 1994). This differs from the vast majority of research on substance abuse that has been largely acquired through studies dominated by male researchers and male participants (Ettorre 1992), typically using quantitative methods such as cross-sectional surveys, institutionally based surveys, and rigorous experimental models. Although large-scale, quantitative research generates useful data, it fails to take into account the feelings, strengths, behaviors, and experiences of the participant. The interpretive and qualitative study reported here transgresses the boundaries of traditional methodologies by focusing on what substance-abusing women had to say about their lives.

To collect substance-abusing mother's voices, I engaged in participant observation and gave semistructured interviews at "A Place to Be,"² a comprehensive residential substance-abuse treatment program for pregnant women and women with children. The program design attempts to meet the special needs of pregnant women and women with child care responsibilities who might otherwise be denied admission into a traditional treatment program. During participant observation at several treatment groups, I made appointments with women willing to be interviewed. Once we agreed upon a suitable date and time, 17 on-site semistructured interviews were recorded. Only 15 of the interviews were later transcribed because the tape recorder malfunctioned during 2 interviews.

The interviewing environment allowed for participants to raise topics and elaborate on issues that they deemed pertinent, creating a situation for discovery of new categories of meaning. The one- to two-hour interviews focused on the residents' biographical experiences as organized around a single moment in their lives—residency in the residential treatment program. The final interview guide I developed contained 11 general topics: demographic (age, race, children, drug of choice, stage of treatment, clean date), substance-abuse story, history of previous treatment programs, mothering, drug experiences, relapse, comparison of life stages, involvement in welfare, criminal justice, child protective services, and view of future. Although mothering was not included as a topic on the initial interview guide, it soon emerged as central to the participants' lives and, therefore, became central to the data collection and analysis. Experience with, and evaluation of, treatment modes; conditions present during the etiology of use; and lifestyle changes resulting from use also emerged as important themes during the interviews. To determine patterns in the data regarding the participants' views of their mothering, I undertook a systematic content analysis of the interview transcripts and participant observation field notes. Essential to the interviewing environment was my commitment to place the women's accounts at the center of analysis.

In addition to the uniqueness of the research design, the participants were also unique. Of the study sample, 15 of the women were white and 2 were African American. The women ranged in age from 20 years to 41 years. I came to consider most of them poor or working-class because subsistence concerns dominated their lives and they were often at the mercy of the criminal justice, welfare, and human service bureaucracies. Women from more privileged classes are not as vulnerable to state intervention. Crack-cocaine and crystal methamphetamine were the drugs of choice for 14 women, alcohol was the drug of choice for 2 women, and painkillers were drugs of choice for 1 woman. The mothers addicted to crack or crystal looked sickly and had far worse problems with child protective services and the criminal justice system.

"A Place to Be" was an uncommon type of substance-abuse treatment center because residents were allowed to have their children with them while in treatment and because the center mandated attendance at parenting classes. Consequently, I assume some social desirability effects in how the respondents talked about and viewed their mothering practices. Furthermore, the sample is unique because the women self-selected for the interviews. Because of the self-selection factor and the qualitative nature of the research design, the findings are not representative of all substance-abusing women whether they be street addicts, middle-class housewives, or even working-class women in treatment at "A Place to Be." Nevertheless, the data offer us insight into a social reality about which social scientists, policy makers, and laypeople have made assumptions without much depth and understanding. Important to

note before turning to the findings is that this study focuses on women's stories about their mothering practices and not on their actual practices.

Findings

Regardless of variation among the respondents, motherhood emerged as a fundamental part of their lives. As they told stories about themselves as mothers, the women revealed a picture of a complex existence embroiled in contradictions about the quality of their mothering practices. When their drug-using lifestyle exposed their children to danger; when they were physically, financially, and emotionally unavailable for their children; and when they did not keep their children's behavior under control, they viewed themselves as bad mothers. In contrast, they viewed themselves as good mothers when they protected their children from a harmful life-style, fulfilled what they saw as their children's practical needs, and were able to cope with everyday life stresses without losing their tempers. Partner relationships and physical punishments were notably absent as themes in the interviews. This is surprising because the extant literature often cites violence as an outcome of stimulant use and partner relationships as creating and facilitating women's drug use. My guess is that they did not mention these topics in any depth because their treatment program focused on the inappropriateness of physical punishment and on the importance of self-determination rather than dependency in intimate relationships.[3] The working-class mothers in this study defined good and bad mothering practices similarly to those McMahon described in *Engendering Motherhood* (1995); that is, they defined good and bad mothering in the same ways as "typical" working-class women. These women's commitments to their children, their desires to be "intensive" mothers, and their ambivalence about the quality of their mothering were consistent throughout the interviews.

Bad Mothering Practices

A number of studies have documented the presence of parenting problems among substance-abusing parents and the risks to children posed by parental substance use. These include findings that parents who have used drugs may have difficulty providing a safe environment for their children (Bijur et al. 1992); families of drug users may lack bonding and attachment (Kumpfer and Turner 1990–1991); the parent's need to acquire drugs or alcohol may at times supersede the child's need for love, attention, supervision, food, and clothing (Inciardi, Lockwood, and Pottieger 1993). In the same way, the mothers in this study sometimes characterized themselves as victimizing their children. The women recognized and felt guilty about the times in which they failed to be good mothers. These descriptions reveal ways substance-abusing mothers accepted the constraints of the dominant ideology of good mothering and recognized themselves as bad mothers.

Exposing to danger. The women often talked about exposing their children to a dangerous lifestyle, including perinatal abuse of illegal substances. Vicki described her perinatal substance abuse:

> I smoked a lot of pot when I was pregnant with my daughter, and I did cocaine very excessively . . . . I mean, I did it every day, and then would sleep for three or four days. My daughter was born addicted. When I was going to the hospital to have

my daughter, I was so high, so high. I kept snorting, doing lines all day thinking the pain would go away.

Vicki was in the minority. Most of the women attempted to reduce or eliminate use during pregnancy. Lola, a 29-year-old white mother of one, started drinking alcohol in third grade and taking illegal substances in seventh grade. "A Place to Be" was her first treatment attempt. She reduced her use while pregnant and explained, "I didn't know I was pregnant for five months. So when I found out, I tried to quit using. I still did use, just not as much. Seth [my son] was born positive anyway." Naomi, a 41-year-old white mother of three used methamphetamine and cocaine since she was 15 years old and had been through six treatment programs. Like Lola, she attempted to quit using while pregnant and stayed clean for five months. But she said that she eventually "went on a five-day roll and used an ounce and a half of cocaine." Lola and Naomi, like most of the mothers I interviewed, attempted to reduce their substance abuse while pregnant and clearly demonstrated through those efforts that they believed perinatal use of harmful substances was a sign of a bad mom.

More generally, these women recognized their drug-abusing lifestyle as dangerous to their children. For instance, Natasha, a 23-year-old white mother of three children, who started using at age 13 and had been through two other treatment programs, spoke of her lifestyle in which "we did a lot of drinking beer and fighting and more fights and it was just terrible. It was a very bad lifestyle for Tia [her daughter] to be in. We always had fights and big parties." Similarly, Carol reported that her children saw her husband run her over with a car. At other times they "watched him kick me up and down the hallways of our house. It was real abusive." Carol was a 31-year-old white mother of five children who had used illegal substances since she was 18 years old. Her drug of choice was methamphetamine, and she had been through three other treatment programs.

In addition to viewing violence in the drug lifestyle, some of the children were direct victims of it. Carol discussed being unaware or unable to do anything about sexual and physical abuse of her children as a characteristic of a bad mother. Her second husband sexually and physically abused all her children. He was sentenced to 61 years in prison for the assaults. He passed on genital herpes to Carol's daughter. Carol wished she could have prevented this abuse from happening to her children.

Besides violence, the substance-abusing mothers acknowledged other problems associated with their lifestyle. Nettie, a 30-year-old white mother of three children was addicted to methamphetamine for 14 years and now in her first treatment program said that there would be "dirty needles and broken needles in the garbage, and my kids seen that." Linda spoke about using with her daughter: "My daughter [11 years old] wanted to experiment with it [marijuana] one night when I was drinking and using, and I let her be in the room while it was going on, and I shouldn't have." She was a 28-year-old white mother of three children, a poly-drug user, and had been in seven treatment programs. Linda told a story about a time when she was drunk and had an accident in which she hit five cars, a telephone pole, and injured someone while her baby daughter was in the car.

Being physically, financially, and emotionally unavailable.

Another theme in the women's talk about their bad parenting practices centered on their inability to be available physically, financially, or emotion-

ally. While abusing substances, many women left their children with relatives, baby-sitters, or alone. Several women also spoke about spending money on drugs, which left their children without any luxuries and, sometimes, without necessities. Finally, some women acknowledged that their substance use left them emotionally inaccessible for their children. Ultimately, then, the residents' unavailability to their children while using substances was seen as another bad mothering practice.

Ullie is a good example of someone who described behavior consistent with much of the extant literature on crack-cocaine users (Inciardi, Lockwood, and Pottieger 1993; Mahan 1996; Taylor 1993). Ullie was a 24-year-old African American pregnant mother of five children who started smoking crack-cocaine when she was 17 years old. She had been through five treatment programs for substance abuse. In the following quote, Ullie describes ways in which she was physically unavailable for her children:

> It was sick behavior. Staying out all night leaving kids with my mom when I know she has to go to work, taking her car, taking my kids on drug runs, leaving them in the car while I went into a dope house to smoke.

Vicki reported behaviors that she perceived as bad for her children, saying,

> I was never, never responsible because I could leave my kids with my grandma and take off for three days or four days or whenever I felt the need to. I would just skip on, and I knew they would be taken care of.

A 25-year-old white mother of three children, a poly-substance abuser since she was 12 years old and in her third treatment program, Greta described how she would leave her kids when she abused illegal substances.

> I ended up getting into it so much at work that I left my children at the baby-sitter, and I left for the weekend. My husband had to go pick them up. And after that I just, I left the house. It controlled my life. I forgot about my kids. I forgot about my husband. I forgot about everything. I quit my job. We [my friends and I] went on road trips; we slept in cars, slept at parks; we slept on the side of the road on the freeway.

Greta left her children for months while she immersed herself into a crack-abusing lifestyle. Each of these women described a lifestyle that was so compelling and addicting that they were willing to leave their children in order to pursue it.

A majority of the residents also spoke about their inability to financially take care of their children. Quinne said that

> Margaret [my daughter] was the one that suffered from me using because she didn't get anything extra. She didn't get anything that every little girl needs. She's 10 years old. She didn't get to go to the mall with me on Saturdays and spend money on the movies or games or little pink dresses because I was spending all that money on myself and that was not fair to her.

Quinne was a 30-year-old white mother of one who had been smoking crack-cocaine since she was 20 years old. "A Place to Be" was her first treatment program. Ullie said that she would take the welfare check meant for her children and spend it on herself. She commented, "I was spending and getting so high. I would wake up the next day knowing I spent $400. That can be really frustrating, knowing that I had to go

through the whole month with nothing." Micah was a 29-year-old white mother of two children. Her drug of choice was methamphetamine, which she had been using since she was 15 years old. Micah was in her fourth treatment program. Like Ullie and Quinne, she also felt guilty because she took a lot of things away from her children. Micah mentioned that she did not buy her children things very often but that when she did, she would often take them back and get money to buy drugs.

Finally, the women described themselves as emotionally unavailable for their children. The words "I was not there for them" were spoken often by the residents during the interviews. For instance, Carol said, "They did not have me there a lot of the times." Vicki claimed that her children were emotionally abused because she was gone so much of the time. Candie, a 24-year-old white pregnant mother of three children, who had used methamphetamine since she was 16 years old and was in her second treatment program, admitted that she was inaccessible for her baby from the time she got home from giving birth at the hospital. Candie disclosed,

> I started [using] the day I got out of the hospital. It got way crazy. I was up for four or five days, and then I would sleep for a couple. I also had postpartum depression really bad; so, from the beginning I was just out of my mind. I did not know what was going on.

Similarly, Naomi explained,

> There was a lot of expanses of time that I cannot remember my son's childhood. I know that I was *there*. I know I did not physically abuse him, but I'm sure that I neglected him a lot. I did not go to his Little League games or his school pro-

grams. I could not because I was high. I *thought* I was taking care of his emotional needs, but I'm sure I wasn't.

These women attested to their emotional unavailability for their children and considered their emotional, financial, and physical unavailability as bad mothering practices.

Lacking control over children.   As a final example of a bad mothering practice, the women frequently talked about discipline problems with their children as a primary characteristic of a problematic parenting style. Ullie described her lack of control: "I tend to let my children play the parenting role. Sometimes I tend to do what they want instead of taking control, instead of letting them know that I'm the mother." Katie, a 22-year-old white mother of two children, a methamphetamine user for 14 years, and in her second treatment program, responded to a question about her mothering by saying that she was a young mom and that "we're [my son and I] more like friends than mother and son. I let him walk on me a lot. He gets away with a lot." In another case, Quinne reported that her daughter "took *big* advantage of me when she knew that I was high, and she knew my attitude change, so she knew that all I wanted to do was be alone." At these times, Quinne's daughter would ask for things and to go places because she knew her mom would say yes.

Part of the reason that these women lacked control over their children, some mothers would tell me, is because they would send their children away from them when they did not want to be bothered with child rearing while they were high. Linda revealed as much when she said,

I used to let them [my children] get away with a lot, like go out, just so they would get away from me. And I would let them

go out and play all night until dark, and I shouldn't have. They should have been in doing their chores and getting ready for bed.

Micah also felt that she failed to keep her children's behavior under control and that her children took advantage of her. She stated,

I'm not a very strict mother, and my oldest one kinda picked up on that real quick, and I just got shoved out of the way, but I let that happen. I let them run all over me. I was *not* a very good disciplinarian at all. I let them pretty much do *what* they wanted *when* they wanted so I didn't have to *deal* with them.

Linda and Micah, like the other mothers, believed they were bad moms when they lacked control over their children because they were high and wanted their children to leave them alone. These women believed that not supervising one's children was a sign of bad mothering.

Documentation of parenting problems among substance-abusing parents confirms the existence of these forms of child-rearing practices and similarly argues that parental substance use had a negative effect on children. Rosenbaum (1981) found that heroin-using women experience difficulty managing their children along with their habit. More recently, Inciardi, Lockwood, and Pottieger (1993) graphically described the particular case of crack-addicted women. Involved in a cycle of prostitution, drug dealing, and constant drug use, cocaine-abusing women resist socially acceptable employment opportunities because they cannot financially support their drug habit and their children.

The stories told by the women in this study expand what is known about substance-abusing mothers' behaviors by illustrating, from the women's perspectives, their sense of the trouble they had integrating their substance abuse with good parenting. The residents at "A Place to Be" perceived themselves as failing to fulfill their roles as socially acceptable mothers when they put their children in danger, when they were unavailable for their children, and when they lacked control over them. The guilt these women felt indicates that they accepted, at least in part, the parameters of the dominant ideology of intensive mothering.

Good Mothering Practices

The substance-abusing women interviewed for this project avoided the cultural claim that they were bad mothers. They did this by asserting that they cared for, and were deeply committed to, their children even though they were addicts. Not much literature has been written from the substance-abusing mothers' perspectives, and even more notably absent is research on the times when substance-abusing women follow mothering practices that fall within the boundaries of the dominant ideology. Rosenbaum (1979) noted that many studies fail to recognize how these women really care about their children and try hard to balance their use and that care. As a result, these women's voices have not been heard and the depiction of their mothering practices may be inaccurate and more negative than appropriate or valid. One of the few exceptions is Colten's (1982) comparison of heroin-addicted and non-addicted mothers. Although the heroin-addicted mothers were more apt to express doubts about their adequacy as mothers, both groups shared many of the same experiences with their children, had similar relationships with their children, and expressed

similar feelings and attitudes regarding their children.

All of the residents interviewed for this project perceived themselves as good moms, in some aspect or another, even when they were using. According to the women, a substance-abusing mother can be a good mom as long as she takes care of her child(ren)'s practical needs, protects her children from harm, and copes with everyday life struggles without losing her temper. The assertion by these women that they were good mothers reveals how they avoided and manipulated the contemporary ideology of motherhood.

Fulfilling practical needs. The most pervasive theme in the residents talk about their good mothering focused on fulfilling their child(ren)'s practical needs for food, cleanliness (clothes and house), and education. Micah acknowledged that she thought she was doing a good job as a mom because "I was still cooking my daughters' meals on time. I was getting my kids to school on time. I was keeping my house clean." Quinne said, "I was functional. Margaret [her daughter] went to bed; I read her bedtime stories. I gave her baths; I did everything with her that I was supposed to do." Nettie noted that her substance abuse did not interfere with her family life: "I was there for the kids. I made sure my bills were paid and my rent was paid." Like Nettie, Naomi asserted that "I always took care of them. I knew that they were dressed right. No matter how high I got, my kids were always tended to, *always*. I cannot ever remember my kids being cold, hungry, abandoned, left unattended."

Vicki summed up these women's understandings of themselves as substance-abusing moms by saying of her children, "They're clean, they're always well-groomed, and they're well dressed." To these women, fulfilling their children's needs for food, shelter, clothing, and education was the most important role they played as mothers.

Protecting from harm. Protecting children comprises a second set of mothering practices about which the women in this study felt proud. The ways they protected their children included not abusing substances while pregnant and not doing drugs around children. Being good moms, even though they used illegal substances, meant that the women protected their children from harm.

Katie did not do methamphetamine or alcohol while pregnant because she believed the use of such substances was bad for the woman and the fetus. Despite this belief, Katie smoked marijuana to relax and to keep from going into premature labor because a doctor in California prescribed marijuana for her. Quinne also asserted that she stayed clean during her pregnancy. She said, "I didn't abuse during either pregnancy. I was able to stop using when I was pregnant." Similarly, Naomi reported,

> My son was born on December 2nd. When I found out I was pregnant, I quit using everything. I thought, "While I'm pregnant, I don't need to use." I smoked cigarettes, and that was the only thing that I didn't give up. So I quit using. I stayed clean for seven months.

Katie, Quinne, and Naomi stayed clean because they cared about the health of their fetuses and babies. Staying clean while pregnant indicated to the women in this study that they were good mothers.

Besides not using drugs while pregnant, many women protected their children by not using drugs in front of them. Ullie stated that even though her son's hair sample came back positive for crack-cocaine, she never smoked in front of him. Quinne described how she would tell her boyfriend and daughter that she had some housework to do upstairs. She would then go upstairs, smoke crack-cocaine, get rid of the smell, get herself together, and go back downstairs. Linda tried not to do drugs around her children. She said that her children did not know very much about drugs but "they do know anyway. They can usually tell when I'm high, but I don't smoke pot in front of them. But I do drink in front of them." When Candie had her intravenous use of methamphetamine under "control," she would wait until her children went to school to do her first "hit" of the day.

> I'd get up and feed my kids and get them off to school. I wouldn't do any drugs until they were gone. Then I would justify it, after they left. It was OK to do it when they weren't there.

She controlled her drug use thereby fulfilling her role as a good mother. Naomi said that her son was aware of her use but that she "never used in front of him. I never left needles or anything around where he could see it." To these women, not doing drugs in front of their children or while they were pregnant meant they were being good mothers.

Coping with stress. A third mothering practice that indicated to these substance-abusing women that they were good mothers was when they used drugs as a means to cope with everyday life pressures. The drugs were not used to "party" but to maintain emotional and physical well-being to effectively function for their children. This sort of coping happened in two ways: The women would control the amount and timing of their substance use, and they used the drugs to relieve stress they felt from their husband, children, and social service agencies.

Nettie is an example of someone who talked about her coping experiences. She said, "I could keep it under control. I mean, I didn't let it interfere with my family life. I was there for my kids; I didn't push my kids off." Candie reported that when she started using again after her fourth treatment, she had control over methamphetamine. She explained,

> I had everything under control. I didn't totally go out of control like before. I could keep my job, and I had my kids, and I could still use. I thought I was doing pretty good, even though I was still firing [intravenous drug use].

Controlling the amount of her use allowed her to maintain a relatively functional lifestyle. Similarly, Quinne said, "I wouldn't do all the things that somebody else on crack-cocaine would do. I could manage my mood swings. I could, unless I had a large amount, manage it." Each of these women coped with substance abuse by controlling the amount and time of their use to practice good mothering.

The use of drugs to relieve stress was the other way of coping. For example, Edith was a 34-year-old mother of two children who was addicted to prescription pain pills for six years and was in treatment for the first time. She described her substance-abuse experiences and reasoned that she abused pain pills because they helped her manage her children, stating,

> As far as how it made me feel, I got everything done, the housecleaning. It [pain pills] made me feel great. I managed with the kids. A lot of reason I used was to deal with my kids. Single parenting is like the hardest job in the world. It made

me feel good. I was more alert. I baked. I cooked. I cleaned. I dealt with the kids better. We played; we did all kinds of things.

Edith concluded that her use made her a better mom. Likewise, Micah contended that she would "go to the bathroom and get high to chill out" when she was angry with her children. Linda acknowledged,

> I used to get so stressed out with having so many kids at once that I just tried to drink to get out of parenting or something. I think it [my use] was just to cope with three kids. I thought if I was drunk it would be easier.

Substance use, these women argued, helped them to cope with their children.

Some of the moms contended that using helped them to deal with their partners and with social service agencies. Carol said, "That's another reason why I started using again [after treatment] because it just became too overwhelming for me. I blamed myself [for the sexual abuse of my children by my second husband]." Naomi asserted that living with her husband, who was a "big-time" marijuana dealer who strictly controlled her life, was very stressful. She said,

> I was still smoking pot *all* day, *every* day. It was my only way of coping, or so I thought at the time, because I wanted to kill this man. I would lay there at night, and I would think of ways to kill him. "Should I cut his throat? Get it over with. How can I kill him without getting caught? Make it look like an accident."

Naomi and Carol were in abusive relationships and used drugs as a way to cope with their partners.

Other women asserted that they used drugs to cope with social service and legal systems, which were placing too many demands on them. For example, Carol said that she ended up using again after treatment because

> they [Department of Human Services] were putting me under so much pressure that I said, "To hell with it. They're threatening to put me in prison. Why not use?" They were telling me I was an unfit mother. But I knew I took care of my kids.

In short, these moms asserted that substance use helped them to calm down, to deal with everyday life situations, and to be better mothers. These findings of women coping with stress support some researchers' claims that addicts use substances to self-medicate, thereby receiving relief from distressing feelings, events, and symptoms (see Abrams and Niaura 1987; Cooper et al. 1992; Lisansky Gomberg 1993; Weiss, Griffin, and Mirin 1992).

The residents of "A Place to Be" contended that they were good moms, at least part of the time. Good mothering practices included protecting children from harm, fulfilling children's practical needs, and coping with everyday life stresses while maintaining their composure. Although there is not much research to support the notion that an addict can, in some ways, be a good mother, addicted women who participated in this study described themselves as caring and committed mothers, thereby defying the dominant cultural stereotype of substance-abusing women as mothers who have little or no parenting skills, are out of control, and do not care for their children. Reports of positive mothering practices were uniform across respondents regardless of differences among them.

Conclusion

There is little dispute that parental substance abuse can have negative effects on children, physically, socially, and psychologically. What can be disputed is that drug-addicted mothers are always bad parents. Although the women in residential treatment interviewed for this study realized that their substance-abusing lifestyles had, at times, a negative impact on their children, they also insisted that they exhibited behaviors associated with socially acceptable, intensive parenting. Ambivalent about the quality of their parenting and yet cognizant of the negative impact it had on their children, the women did not see themselves as bad or unfit mothers, nor were they willing to admit that they were always incapable or less competent than other mothers. Rather, they clearly and uniformly evoked images of themselves and detailed practices that illustrated their capabilities as parents.

The women in this study described their mothering practices primarily in relation to the "needs" of the children. Missing from their talk is an explicit consideration of their parenting experiences in terms of class, gender, or race. Sometimes respondents articulated feelings of powerlessness and recognized the public assistance systems as intrusive and victimizing, noticing that they were not protected or privileged in the same way as middle-class women. The participants did not, however, claim that their class position had an impact on their parenting experiences. Similarly, an analysis of gender was also absent in their talk about mothering. This is most clear in the participants' lack of discussion of their partners during the interviews. An absence of talk about their partners is, in part, due to resocialization away from dependence on men taking place during treatment, although it also attests to an assumption that the primary care of children should be in the mothers' hands, a classic patriarchal notion. Finally, the white women in this study (15 out of 17 respondents) did not verbally locate themselves in the race hierarchy with race privilege. None of them mentioned their race in any meaningful way, exemplifying Frankenberg's (1993) idea that white women's race privilege is invisible to them. Missing from these women's talk is a socially based analysis of their "problems" and therefore no direct challenge to class, gender, and race arrangements.

Just as surely, though, their voices contained active avoidance and manipulation of the white middle-class heterosexual mothering model. Claiming to be and viewing themselves as "great" mothers illustrates that these women reject a portrayal of them as bad mothers and instead create for themselves more inclusive boundaries for acceptable mothering practices. In this way, the substance-abusing mothers in this study act similarly to other groups of marginalized women such as Hispanic, African American, lesbian, and working-class mothers, who resist the dominant discourse about mothering. In the participants' understandings of their mothering practices, we see the potency of ideology and the omnipresence of agency come alive.

This article gives substance-abusing women a voice by analyzing their visions of a "good" mother and how they think they fit into that vision. These women add one further and complicating critique to the dominant ideology of mothering. Because substance-abusing women do not fit the model of a "good woman" or of the "ideal mom" does not mean that they were not committed or were uncaring. Similar to other marginalized women, the substance-abusing women in this project reported loving their children and caring for them in many ways even when this love and caring conflicted with the women's own personal needs while using drugs.

Notes

1. For a thorough discussion of health-related problems, including sexually transmitted diseases and the human immunodeficiency virus (HIV) refer to the following sources: (1) clinical aspects: Lowinson et al. (1994), (2) practical approaches in the treatment of women who abuse alcohol and other drugs: Des Jarlais, Hagan, and Friedman (1997).
2. I used pseudonyms for all personal names, treatment centers, and locations mentioned during the interviews to ensure confidentiality.
3. Because I developed the interview guide with topics raised by the participants and because the participants did not raise partner relationships and physical punishment as topics, they were not on the interview guide. In retrospect, I should have included them. Nonetheless, it is notable that they were absent. Sometimes what the interviewees do not say is as interesting as what they do say.

References

Abrams, D., and R. S. Niaura. 1987. Social learning theory. In *Psychological theories of drinking and alcoholism,* edited by H. T. Blane and K. E. Leonard. New York: Guilford.

Benishek, L., K. Bieschke, B. Stoffelmayr, B. Mavis, and K. Humphreys. 1992. Gender differences in depression and anxiety among alcoholics. *Journal of Substance Abuse* 4:235–45.

Bijur, P., M. Kurzon, M. Overpeck, and P. Scheidt. 1992. Parental alcohol use, problem drinking, and children's injuries. *Journal of the American Medical Association* 267:3166–71.

Blum, L. M., and T. Deussen. 1996. Negotiating independent motherhood: Working-class African American women talk about marriage and motherhood. *Gender & Society* 10:199–211.

Chazotte, C., J. Youchah, and M. Comerford Freda. 1995. Cocaine use during pregnancy and low birth weight: The impact of prenatal care and drug treatment. *Seminars in Perinatology* 19:293–300.

Collins, P. Hill. 1994. Shifting the center: Race, class, and feminist theorizing about motherhood. In *Representations of motherhood,* edited by D. Bassin, M. Honey, and M. M. Kaplan. New Haven, CT: Yale University Press.

Colten, M. E. 1982. Attitudes, experiences, and self-perceptions of heroin addicted mothers. *Journal of Social Issues* 38:77–92.

Cooper, M., M. Russell, J. Skinner, M. Frone, and P. Mundar. 1992. Stress and alcohol use: Moderating effects of gender, coping, and alcohol expectancies. *Journal of Abnormal Psychology* 101:139–52.

Des Jarlais, D. C., H. Hagan, and S. R. Friedman. 1997. Practical approaches in the treatment of women who abuse alcohol and other drugs. Contact no. CSAT-93-0006, pp. 25–31. Rockville, MD: Department of Health and Human Services, Public Health Service.

Ettorre, E. M. 1992. *Women and substance use.* New Brunswick, NJ: Rutgers University Press.

Fineman, M. Albertson. 1995. *The neutered mother, the sexual family and other twentieth century tragedies.* New York: Routledge.

Frankenberg, Ruth. 1993. *White women, race matters: The social construction of whiteness.* Minneapolis: University of Minnesota Press.

Glenn, E. Nakano, G. Chang, and L. R. Forcey. 1994. *Mothering: Ideology, experience, and agency.* New York: Routledge.

Gomberg, E. S. Lisansky. 1993. Women and alcohol: Use and abuse. *Journal of Nervous and Mental Diseases* 181:211–19.

Grella, C. E. 1996. Background and overview of mental health and substance abuse treatment systems: Meeting the needs of women who are pregnant or parenting. *Journal of Psychoactive Drugs* 28 (4):319–43.

Hanke, P. J., and C. E. Faupel. 1993. Women opiate users' perceptions of treatment services in New York City. *Journal of Substance Abuse Treatment* 10:513–22.

Hawley, T. Lawton, T. Halle, R. Drasin, and N. Thomas. 1995. Children of addicted mothers: Effects of the "Crack Epidemic" on the caregiving environment and the development of preschoolers. *American Journal of Ortho-psychiatry* 65:364–79.

Hays, S. 1996. *The cultural contradictions of motherhood.* New Haven, CT: Yale University Press.

Higgins, P. Grant, D. Hendel Clough, and C. Wallerstedt. 1995. Drug-taking behaviours of pregnant substance abusers in treatment. *Journal of Advanced Nursing* 22:425–32.

Hondagneu-Sotelo, P., and E. Avila. 1997. "I'm here, but I'm here." The meaning of Latina transnational motherhood. *Gender & Society* 11:548–71.

Inciardi, J., D. Lockwood, and A. Pottieger. 1993. *Women and crack cocaine.* New York: Macmillan.

Kumpfer, K., and C. W. Turner, 1990–91. The social ecology model of adolescent substance abuse: Implications for prevention. *International Journal of Addictions* 25 (4A): 435–64.

Lewin, E. 1994. Negotiating lesbian motherhood: The dialectics of resistance and accommodation. In *Mothering: Ideology, experience, and agency,* edited by E. N. Glenn, G. Chang, and L. R. Forcey. New York: Routledge.

Litt, J., and M. McNeil. 1997. Biological markers and social differentiation: "Crack Babies" and the construction of the dangerous mother. *Health Care for Women International* 18:31–41.

Lowinson, J. H., P. Ruiz, R. B. Millman, and J. G. Langrod, eds. 1994. *Substance abuse: A comprehensive textbook.* 3d ed. Baltimore: Williams & Wilkins; Center for Substance Abuse Treatment.

Mahan, S. 1996. *Crack cocaine, crime, and women: Legal, social, and treatment issues.* Vol. 4, *Drugs, Health, and Social Policy Series.* Thousand Oaks, CA: Sage.

McMahon, M. 1995. *Engendering motherhood: Identity and self-transformation in women's lives.* New York: Guilford.

McNeil, M., and J. Litt. 1992. More medicalizing of mothers: Foetal alcohol syndrome in the USA and related developments. In *Private risks and public dangers,* edited by S. Scott, G. Williams, S. Platt, and H. Thomas. Ashgate, VT: Ashgate.

Neuman, W. L. 1994. *Social research methods: Qualitative and quantitative approaches.* 2d ed. Needham Heights, MA: Allyn & Bacon.

Richman, J. A., K. M. Rospenda, and M. A. Kelley. 1995. Gender roles and alcohol abuse across the transition to parenthood. *Journal of Studies on Alcohol* 56:553–57.

Rosenbaum, M. 1979. Difficulties in taking care of business: Women addicts as mothers. *American Journal of Drug and Alcohol Abuse* 6:431–46.

———. 1981. Women addicts' experience of the heroin world: Risk, chaos, and inundation. *Urban Life* 10 (1): 65–81.

Sands, R. G., and M. McClelland. 1994. Emic and etic perspectives in ethnographic research on the interdisciplinary team. In *Qualitative research in social work,* edited by E. Sherman, and W. J. Reid. New York: Columbia University Press.

Smart, C. 1996. Deconstructing motherhood. In *Good enough mothering? Feminist perspectives on lone motherhood,* edited by E. B. Silva. New York: Routledge.

Smith, I. E., D. Z. Dent, C. D. Coles, and A. Falek. 1992. A comparison study of treated and untreated pregnant and postpartum cocaine-abusing women. *Journal of Substance Abuse Treatment* 9:343–48.

Taylor, C. S. 1993. *Girls, gangs, women and drugs.* East Lansing: Michigan State University Press.

Tutty, L., M. Rothery, and R. Grinnell Jr. 1996. *Qualitative research for social workers: Phases, steps, & tasks.* Needham Heights, MA: Allyn & Bacon.

Weiss, R. D., M. L. Griffin, and S. M. Mirin. 1992. Drug abuse as self-medication for depression: An empirical study. *American Journal of Drug Alcohol Abuse* 18 (2): 121–29.

Young, I. M. 1994. Punishment, treatment, empowerment: Three approaches to policy for pregnant addicts. *Feminist Studies* 20:33–57.

*Chapter 9: Putting It All Together*_____

1. How does the ideology of fathering and mothering support a patriarchal social structure? How would our social structure change if fathering and mothering roles changed?
2. Who do you (or have you) had caregiving responsibility for? Have your caregiving behaviors been affected by your gender? Explain.
3. How has your view of the ideal mother and father been shaped by your class, race, and sexual orientation?

10

Gender and Work

The readings in this chapter explore two key issues in the psychology of gender and work: sex segregation of employment and the glass ceiling. The research presented in the first reading demonstrates the important role that gender stereotypes may play in reflecting and promoting the gendered division of labor. This research also provides evidence that such stereotypes may play a role in justifying social and economic inequality between men and women. The second reading describes the different perceptions on corporate mobility and success held by male and female corporate presidents and CEOs. Men above the glass ceiling see corporate success as due to hard work, talent, and individual effort, and are less likely to recognize sexism as a factor. Women above the glass ceiling, on the other hand, saw male-dominated networks and peer similarities as barriers to success.

20

Gender-Stereotypic Images of Occupations Correspond to the Sex Segregation of Employment

Mary Ann Cejka and Alice H. Eagly

Despite a dramatic influx of women into the labor market, sex segregation in employment continues. The research reported in this reading explores the role that gender stereotypes may play in justifying this gendered division of labor. Cejka and Eagly found that jobs dominated by females were thought by research participants to require stereotypically feminine personality (e.g., gentle, nurturing, helpful) or physical qualities (e.g., pretty, cute, petite), while jobs dominated by men were thought to require stereotypically masculine personality (e.g., competitive, dominant, aggressive) or physical qualities (e.g., muscular, physically vigorous). Further, female participants reported greater attraction to jobs that were seen as requiring feminine qualities for success, while male participants were more attracted to jobs that were seen as requiring masculine qualities for success. Cejka and

Eagly argue that gender stereotyping may promote sex segregation in employment by producing gendered expectations about which occupations are appropriate for each sex, and influencing women's and men's tendencies to choose particular occupations. They also found that occupations that were seen as requiring masculine personal characteristics had higher prestige and earnings **(defined norm)**. Thus, gender stereotypes may not only serve to promote a gendered division of labor, they may also serve to justify a hierarchical social structure in which males have more power than females **(gender role effects)**.

Questions to Consider:

1. Have you chosen a career that is sex segregated? What qualities do you see

as necessary for success in the career you have chosen? Do these qualities follow the gender-stereotypic dimensions described in Table 1? Explain.

2. According to this research, what role do gender stereotypes play in the sex segregation of employment? How do gender stereotypes justify inequality in the social system?

3. According to Cejka and Eagly, is reducing the sex segregation of employment an effective way to improve women's status? Explain.

4. This research was conducted with participants who were introductory psychology students. In your opinion, can the findings be generalized to the wider population? Why or why not?

This study addresses stereotypes' justification of inequality in the social system as a whole, which is a function that has been termed *system justification* by Jost and Banaji (1994). Although stereotypes have long been thought to serve important motivational functions in terms of preserving one's personal status and justifying one's ingroup, their function in justifying the social system more generally has received little empirical attention. If gender stereotypes justify existing social arrangements, they must support the division of labor between the sexes, which is a profoundly important feature of social structure that scholars have long argued is the root cause of the subordination of women (e.g., Lerner, 1986). In modern nations, this division of labor manifests itself not merely in the assignment of the majority of domestic work to women but also in the sex segregation of the employed workforce. The present research addresses the extent to which gender stereotypes reflect and promote sex segregation in employment.

To understand how gender stereotypes may justify the division of labor in employment, this study examines the extent to which people believe that success in occupations dominated by one sex requires personal characteristics typical of that sex. Such beliefs would foster the segregation of employment, just as beliefs that the domestic role requires feminine qualities and that employment roles require masculine qualities foster the assignment of domestic work to women and paid employment to men (Eagly & Steffen, 1984). Even though employment roles may be thought in general to require characteristics that are more masculine and less feminine than the characteristics required by the domestic role, employment roles are likely to be quite heterogeneous in the qualities that they are believed to require. Female-dominated occupations, such as the domestic role, may be thought to require attributes that are stereotypically feminine, and male-dominated occupations may be thought to require attributes that are stereotypically masculine. Moreover, if gender stereotypes justify women's subordination, prestige and income should be associated with occupations being thought to require masculine characteristics.

To appreciate the importance of the issues addressed by this research, it is necessary to understand how effectively occupational sex segregation has been maintained. The dramatic increase in women's paid employment in the 20th century may falsely give the impression that the sexual division of labor is fast disappearing. However, de-

Authors' Note: Our thanks are extended to Antonio Mladinic and Patrick Kulesa for assistance in data analysis and to Patrick Kulesa and Amanda Diekman for comments on a draft of the article.

spite some decline in the segregation of employment in recent decades in industrialized countries, 53% of women would have to change occupations in the United States if women were to be distributed into occupations as men are distributed (Reskin & Padavic, 1994). Many occupations are almost totally dominated by one sex: For example, dental hygienists and secretaries are at least 98% women, whereas automobile mechanics and carpenters are at least 98% men (U.S. Bureau of Labor Statistics, 1998). Moreover, individual jobs within occupations (e.g., the job of dining hall manager rather than the general occupation of manager) are more highly segregated than the occupations themselves, with contemporary estimates of the proportion of women who would have to change jobs to be distributed as men running as high as 77% (Tomaskovic-Devey, 1995). Suggesting that this sex segregation is not about to disappear is Lippa and Connelly's (1990) (see also Lippa, 1995) successful prediction of the sex of 90% of their student research participants from their occupational preferences.

The idea that the sex ratios of occupations should be strongly related to gender stereotypic images of occupations follows from a central claim of Eagly's (1987) social role theory of sex-correlated differences in social behavior. This theory maintains that ideas about gender are shaped by observations of women and men in the roles that they commonly play in daily life. Consistent with the general principle of correspondence bias (Gilbert & Malone, 1995), perceivers thus reason that people have the psychological characteristics that are demanded by their family and occupational roles. Considered as a social group, women are believed to possess attributes suited for the roles they generally occupy, and men are likewise believed to possess role-appropriate attributes. Because perceivers thus infer people's characteristics from observing what they do in their daily lives, gender stereotypes can be regarded as emergents from perceivers' observations of the work that each sex commonly does (see also Yount, 1986).

Although the assignment of domestic work primarily to women is no doubt an important contributor to gender stereotyping (Eagly & Steffen, 1984), the increase in women's labor parce participation in industrialized countries means that perceivers may increasingly derive their ideas about the sexes from the different types of paid work that women and men perform. Despite some authors' claims that women's increased labor force participation should bring a sharp decline in the extent to which men and women are perceived to be different (e.g., Lueptow, Garovich, & Lueptow, 1995), this prediction is not reasonable to the extent that women's paid occupations are perceived as similar to the domestic role.

Prior research has not provided a strong test of the hypothesis that the qualities thought to be required for occupational success correspond to the gender stereotype of the female or male group that is numerically dominant in the occupation, even though other studies have shown a relation between occupations' sex ratios and the ascription of some gender-stereotypic attributes to job holders in these occupations (e.g., Kalin, 1986; McLean & Kalin, 1994; Shinar, 1978). For example, there is evidence of a positive relationship between the rated masculinity versus femininity of occupations and their sex ratio (Beggs & Doolittle, 1993; Shinar, 1975). Other research has demonstrated that occupations dominated by women, compared with those dominated by men, were perceived to require a higher level of feminine personality traits for job success and a lower level of masculine personality traits (Glick, 1991). However, given that gender stereotypes include physical and cognitive characteristics as well as personality attributes (Deaux & Lewis, 1983, 1984; J. E. Williams & Best, 1982), the gender-stereotypic characteristics that are relevant to employment should encompass a wide range of attributes. Therefore, in this research, we predict occupations' sex ratios from three classes of gender-stereotypic attributes that can be relevant to occupational success: personality traits, physical attributes, and qualities of cognition and cognitive style. Although student respondents judged occupations' stereotypic qualities in this study, their judgments should differ little from those of other citizens in view of evidence that stereotypes of social groups are widely shared in society (see Deaux & Kite, 1993; Hamilton & Sherman, 1994).

In this research, the distributions of the sexes into occupations are assessed subjectively by participants' estimates of occupations' sex distributions and objectively by census data. A closely related variable is sex differences in attraction to occupations, which is also assessed subjectively and objectively. For the subjective assessment, participants rated whether men or women are more attracted to the occupations. For the objective assessment, participants indicated their own attraction to the occupations, and men's and women's ratings were differenced to yield estimates of sex differences in actual attraction. According to social role theory (Eagly, 1987), people should tend to prefer situations, including occupations, that favor qualities thought to typify their own gender, assuming that to some extent gender roles become internalized in self-concepts (Cross & Madson, 1997). Therefore, both women and men should be attracted to gender-stereotypic occupations. Indeed, theories of occupational choice

(e.g., Gottfredson, 1981) maintain that individuals' occupational aspirations tend to become limited to alternatives regarded as appropriate for their gender.

Integral to the study's focus on the system-justifying implications of gender stereotypes is its examination of the extent to which beliefs about the gender-stereotypic qualities required for success in occupations predict occupational prestige and earnings. The study thus predicts both prestige and earnings from measures of the gender-stereotypic personality, physical, and cognitive characteristics believed to be essential for success in occupations. If social structure is patriarchal, rewards such as prestige and high wages should be associated with occupations that favor masculine characteristics. Consistent with this prediction, Glick (1991) found that prestige and earnings are associated with the extent to which occupations are thought to require masculine personality traits (see also Glick, Wilk, & Perreault, 1995). The weak negative relation that Glick (1991) reported between earnings and the belief that occupations require feminine personality traits is consistent with England, Herbert, Kilbourne, Reid, and Megdal's (1994) finding that earnings relate negatively to the perception that occupations involve nurturance. It is thus possible that system justification is reflected in both a positive relation of masculine qualities to earnings and a weaker negative relation of feminine qualities to earnings.

Method

Participants and Procedure

Participants were 189 introductory psychology students (81 men, 108 women) who volunteered for a study on perceptions of occupations to fulfill a course requirement.

These students completed questionnaires and then were thanked, debriefed, and dismissed.

To minimize context effects among the measures, these participants were divided into two groups who completed different measures. One group, consisting of 144 of the 189 participants, rated occupations on gender-stereotypic attributes and then rated either the average woman or the average man on these same attributes. These participants were divided into eight subgroups ($n \geq 17$), each of which rated 10 of the 80 occupations included in the study. The second group, consisting of the remaining 45 of the 189 participants, rated other aspects of all 80 occupations (attraction to them, prestige, earnings, sex distribution). Because the unit of analysis in the research was occupations rather than participants, all ratings were aggregated across the participants who rated each occupation (see the section on measuring instruments below).

In addition, 191 other undergraduates (123 men, 68 women) participated in the pretesting required to select the occupations (42 of these participants) and to construct measures of occupations' gender-stereotypic attributes (149 of these participants).

Selection of Occupations

A preliminary group of 335 occupations consisted of all occupations that the U.S. census indicated had more than 25,000 employees (Bergmann, 1986, Appendix A). To ensure that students had at least some knowledge of these occupations, they were pretested for their familiarity. Using a 5-point Likert-type scale ranging from 1 (*nothing at all*) to 5 (*a lot*), the 42 pretest participants rated how much knowledge they had about the people employed in each occupation. From among occupations receiving relatively high familiarity ratings

(≥ 2.80), 80 were selected to be as evenly spaced as possible along a continuum that ranged from extremely male dominated to extremely female dominated. Examples of occupations are airline pilot, architect, barber, bus driver, computer programmer, hotel clerk, psychologist, mail carrier, speech therapist, telephone operator, and elementary school teacher. These 80 occupations were distributed among the eight versions of the questionnaire so that each version included 10 occupations ranging from male dominated to female dominated. For each version, there were two different orders of the 10 occupations.

Measurement of Belief in Gender-Stereotypic Attributes' Importance to Occupational Success

Using a 5-point Likert-type scale (1 = *not at all important*, 5 = *essential*), each participant rated the 10 occupations included in his or her version of the questionnaire on the extent to which each of 56 attributes would be necessary for success in the occupation. As shown in Table 1, these 56 attributes constituted six gender-stereotypic dimensions, which were derived on the basis of a factor analysis of pretest data. Each dimension was represented by eight attributes, with the exception of the feminine personality dimension, which was represented by 16 attributes. This larger number of attributes for the feminine personality dimension stemmed from exploratory factor analyses performed on the 149 pretest participants' ratings of nine occupations on 83 gender-stereotypic attributes chosen from research by J. E. Williams and Best (1982) and Deaux and Lewis (1984). These pretest data yielded a seven-factor solution (masculine and feminine versions of personality, physical, and cognitive attributes, with feminine personality attributes loading on two separate factors). However, in the subsequent study, the two feminine personality dimensions that had appeared in the pretest results were highly correlated, $r(78) = .89$, $p < .0001$, and thus were combined.[1]

Because the unit of analysis in the research was occupations, means were computed for participants' ratings of each occupation on each attribute. These means were then averaged across the attributes included in each dimension to produce an overall value representing the extent to which each occupation was perceived to require masculine or feminine personality, physical, or cognitive attributes for success. The ratings were thus aggregated across the participants and across the individual attributes that were constituents of each dimension.

To establish that aggregation across the individual attributes making up each dimension was appropriate, alpha coefficients were calculated (in the Attributes × Occupations matrix for each gender-stereotypic dimension) with the data aggregated across the participants. These alpha coefficients, which assessed the homogeneity of each of these six dimensions across the attributes included in it, were appropriately high (see Table 1). To establish that aggregation across the participants who rated each occupation was appropriate, alpha coefficients were also calculated (in the Participants × Occupations matrix for each dimension) with the data aggregated across the attributes. This second set of calculations was performed separately for each of the eight subgroups of participants, each of which rated 10 occupations, and the resulting alphas were then averaged over the subgroups. These alpha coefficients, which assessed the homogeneity of each of the six dimensions across the participants who performed the ratings, were also appropriately high (see Table 1).

The gender stereotypically of each dimension was established by comparing the participants' ratings of the average man and woman on each dimension. On a 5-point likelihood scale, these participants thus rated the likelihood that the average man or the average woman would possess each of the 56 traits. These ratings were averaged across the attributes in each dimensions. As shown in Table 1, men were perceived as significantly more likely than women to have masculine cognitive, physical, and personality attributes, and women were perceived as significantly more likely than men to have feminine cognitive, physical, and personality attributes. The difference on the masculine cognitive dimension was relatively small although significant.[2]

Finally, the discriminant validity of the gender-stereotypic dimensions was established by showing that they were not highly intercorrelated when the mean values for the occupations were correlated across the 80 occupations (see Table 2).

Other Measuring Instruments

Attraction to occupations. Using 5-point Likert-type scales (1 = *not at all attracted*, 5 = *extremely attracted*), participants rated each occupation according to how much they themselves were attracted to it. These ratings were aggregated separately across the male and female participants to produce measures of the extent to which men were attracted to each occupation and the extent to which women were attracted. The across-participant alpha coefficients were .92 for the male participants and .88 for the female participants. The sex-related difference in attraction to each occupation was estimated by subtracting the mean score for female participants' attraction to each occupation from the mean score for males' attraction. Participants also rated on a 5-point scale (1 = *women much more attracted*, 5 = *men much more attracted*) the degree to which they believed that women or men

TABLE 1 *Description of Gender-Stereotypic Dimensions*

Characteristics of Dimension	Gender-Stereotypic Dimension					
	Masculine Physical	*Feminine Physical*	*Masculine Personality*	*Feminine Personality*	*Masculine Cognitive*	*Feminine Cognitive*
Attributes in dimension	Athletic Burly Rugged	Pretty Sexy Gorgeous	Competitive Daring Unexcitable	Affectionate Sympathetic Gentle	Analytical Mathematical Good with numbers	Imaginative Intuitive Artistic
	Muscular Tall	Dainty Soft voice	Dominant Adventurous	Sensitive Nurturing	Exact Good at reasoning	Expressive Perceptive
	Physically vigorous	Cute	Stands up under pressure	Sentimental	Good at abstractions	Verbally skilled
	Brawny	Petite	Aggressive	Warm in relations with others	Good at problem solving	Creative
	Physically strong	Beautiful	Courageous	Helpful to others Sociable Understanding of others Cooperative Kind Supportive Outgoing	Quantitatively skilled	Tasteful
Mean rating of average man[a]	3.45	2.39	3.75	3.31	3.44	3.21
Mean rating of an average woman[a]	2.31	3.54	3.06	4.14	3.26	3.77
t for average man versus woman	11.41****	−13.70****	7.92****	−9.44****	1.99**	−6.68****
Alpha across attributes	.95	.90	.84	.95	.90	.85
Alpha across raters	.96	.81	.89	.96	.94	.93

a. Ratings were on a 5-point scale on which higher numbers indicated greater likelihood that the average man (or woman) had the attributes in the dimension.

**p < .05 ****p < .001

TABLE 2: *Intercorrelations Between Variables Characterizing Occupations (N = 80)*

Variable	1	2	3	4	5	6	7	8	9	10	11	12	13
Importance of gender-stereotypic dimensions to success													
1. Masculine physical	—												
2. Feminine physical	-.31***	—											
3. Masculine personality	.41****	.12	—										
4. Feminine personality	-.39****	.62****	.06	—									
5. Masculine cognitive	-.27**	-.14	.21*	.04	—								
6. Feminine cognitive	-.47****	.48****	.27**	.56****	.31***	—							
Other characteristics													
7. Estimated sex distributions	-.58****	.54****	-.29***	.60****	-.03	.38****	—						
8. Actual sex distribution	-.56****	.59****	-.33****	.63****	-.08	.26**	.92****	—					
9. Perceived sex difference in attraction	-.59****	.57****	-.30***	.62****	-.04	.40****	.99****	.93****	—				
10. Actual sex difference in attraction	-.40****	.47****	-.26**	.65****	-.18*	.25**	.75*****	.76*****	.77****	—			
11. Prestige	-.29***	.02	.41****	.26**	.62****	.50****	.05	-.06	.03	-.16	—		
12. Estimated earnings	.18*	-.04	.47****	-.09	.12	.04	-.14	-.22**	-.18*	-.26**	.53****	—	
13. Actual earnings	.17	-.04	.42****	-.01	.12	.01	-.13	-.20*	-.16	-.22**	.53****	.94****	—

NOTE: On the gender-stereotypic dimensions (Variables 1 to 6), higher scores indicated that the attributes comprising the dimension were thought more essential for success in an occupation. On Variables 7 to 9, higher scores indicated greater estimated or actual percentages of women in an occupation or greater female than male attraction to an occupation. On Variables 11, 12, and 13, higher scores indicated greater prestige or larger estimated or actual earnings.

*p < .10. **p < .05. ***p < .01. ****p < .001.

would be attracted to each occupation. The across-participant alpha coefficient was .99 for this measure.

Prestige and earnings. Participants rated each occupation's prestige on a 5-point Likert-type scale (1 = *extremely low*, 5 = *extremely high*). They also estimated yearly earnings for each occupation. The across-participant alpha coefficients were .99 for prestige and .92 for earnings. Actual earnings were obtained from census data (U.S. Department of Labor, 1993).

Sex distribution into occupations. Participants' perceptions of the occupations' sex distribution were assessed by their estimates of each occupation's percentage of employees who are women. The across-participant alpha coefficient was .99 for this measure. The actual sex distributions of the occupations were obtained from census data (U.S. Bureau of the Census, 1993).

Results

Prediction of the Distribution of the Sexes Into Occupations From Belief in Gender-Stereotypic Attributes' Importance to Occupational Success

The main dependent variables of this study directly or indirectly index the sexual division of labor in the paid workforce: participants' estimates of occupations' sex distribution, the actual sex distribution, participants' perceptions of sex differences in attraction to the occupations, and the actual sex difference in attraction (constructed by differencing the male and female participants' attraction). As the correlation matrix in Table 2 shows, these four variables were strongly intercorrelated: Perceptions of the distribution of the sexes into occupations were highly related to the actual distribu-

tion, and these variables were in turn highly related to perceived sex differences in attraction to occupations and actual sex differences in attraction. The relationships of the actual sex difference in attraction to the other three distributional variables were, however, somewhat weaker than the other relationships.

To examine the extent to which gender-stereotypic representations of occupations mirror the distribution of women and men into occupations, each of these four distributional variables was regressed onto the six dimensions that represent occupations' gender-stereotypic attributes. As indexed by the very substantial multiple Rs, prediction was quite successful in all cases, and the results were similar across the four variables. As shown in Table 3, the personality and physical feminine dimensions related positively to female dominance of occupations, and the personality and physical masculine dimensions related negatively to female dominance (i.e., positively to male dominance). All of these relationships were significant except for the two physical dimensions as predictors of the actual sex difference in attraction. In contrast, the masculine and feminine cognitive dimensions failed to relate significantly to any of the distributional variables, with the exception of a negative relationship of the feminine cognitive dimension to actual sex distribution. Because this relationship was opposite to prediction and did not replicate across the other three distributional variables, we do not attempt to interpret it.

Importance of Gender-Stereotypic Attributes to Occupational Success, Compared Across the Dimensions

Belief in the contribution that gender-stereotypic qualities make to occupational success also varied substantially across the

TABLE 3   *Prediction of Sex Distribution in Occupations and Sex Difference in Attraction to Occupations From Belief in Gender-Stereotypic Attributes' Importance to Occupational Success (N = 80)*

Predictor Dimension and Multiple R	Estimated Sex Distribution		Actual Sex Distribution		Perceived Sex Difference in Attraction		Actual Sex Difference in Attraction	
	B	β	B	β	B	β	B	β
Masculine physical	-9.10**	-.30	-13.78***	-.31	-0.33**	-.28	0.10	-.13
Feminine physical	21.10**	.27	42.84****	.37	0.92***	.30	0.21	.11
Masculine personality	-9.32*	-.21	-13.49**	-.21	-0.41**	-.24	-0.20*	-.20
Feminine personality	10.56***	.34	10.27****	.42	0.41***	.34	0.45****	.61
Masculine cognitive	-1.34	-.04	-0.52	-.01	-0.06	-.04	-0.11	-.14
Feminine cognitive	-0.53	-.01	-13.03**	-.24	0.01	.01	-0.10	-.12
Multiple R	.76****		.82****		.79****		.74****	

NOTE: On the predictor variables, higher scores indicated that the attributes comprising the dimension were thought more essential for success in an occupation. On the criterion variables, higher scores indicated greater estimated or actual percentage of women or greater perceived or actual female than male attraction to careers. β = unstandardized regression coefficient; β = standardized regression coefficient.

*p < .10. **p < .05. ***p < .01. ****p < .001.

six dimensions of gender stereotypes: Some types of characteristics were judged to be generally more important than others. To display this variation overall and within male- and female-dominated occupations, we classified the occupations as male dominated if their incumbents were 75% or more male (e.g., construction laborer, truck driver, civil engineer), female dominated if their incumbents were 75% or more female (e.g., bank teller, dental hygienist, typist), and integrated if their incumbents were less than 75% but more than 25% female (manager/administrator, bartender, pharmacist). A mixed analysis of variance (ANOVA) was then calculated, treating the three levels of sex distribution as a between-occupations variable and the six gender-stereotypic dimensions as a within-occupations (i.e., repeated measures) variable. The means associated with this analysis are displayed in Table 4. Although the sex distribution did not produce a significant main effect, both the main effect of dimension, $F(5, 385) = 141.49$, $p < .001$, and the Distribution $\times$ Dimension interaction, $F(10, 385) = 13.56$, $p < .001$, were highly significant.

Consistent with the contrasts across the dimensions that are displayed in Table 4, occupations were not thought to be generally very demanding of physical characteristics. Feminine physical characteristics were perceived as least important to occupational success in general, with masculine physical traits somewhat more important. The most important dimension overall was masculine cognitive abilities, with feminine cognitive abilities and personality characteristics being next most important, followed by masculine personality characteristics. Yet, the ordering of these requisites changed substantially when viewed within occupations that were relatively dominated by one sex. For male-dominated occupations, masculine cognitive

characteristics were rated as most important, followed by feminine cognitive, masculine personality, masculine physical, feminine personality, and feminine physical characteristics. For female-dominated occupations, feminine personality attributes were rated as most important, followed by masculine cognitive, feminine cognitive, masculine personality, feminine physical, and masculine physical.

Prediction of Occupations' Prestige and Earnings From Belief in Gender-Stereotypic Attributes' Importance to Occupational Success

As shown in Table 5, occupations gained prestige to the extent that they were thought to require masculine personality or cognitive qualities. Feminine personality and cognitive qualities made only smaller, nonsignificant contributions to prestige. Not surprisingly, occupations lost prestige to the extent that masculine or feminine physical qualities were thought essential for success. As also shown in Table 5, only masculine qualities of personality were significantly related to estimated and actual earnings. Occupations were thus well paid to the extent that they were believed to require masculine qualities of personality for success.

Occupations' sex distributions related to earnings but not to prestige (see Table 2). Consistent with prior research showing that occupations' prestige bears an uncertain relation to their sex ratios (see Jacobs, 1989),[3] the four variables representing the distribution of the sexes into occupations were unrelated to prestige. However, occupations' estimated and actual earnings showed consistently negative relationships to the four sex-distributional variables, indicating that male dominance of occupations was associated with higher wages.

TABLE 4   *Mean Belief in Gender-Stereotypic Attributes' Importance to Success in Male-Dominated, Integrated, and Female-Dominated Occupations*

Sex Distribution in Occupation	n	Gender-Stereotypic Dimension					
		Masculine Physical	Feminine Physical	Masculine Personality	Feminine Personality	Masculine Cognitive	Feminine Cognitive
Male dominated	30						
M		2.46$_{bc}$	1.16$_a$	2.63$_{bc}$	2.40$_b$	3.27$_d$	2.72$_c$
SD		0.88	0.15	0.60	0.64	0.76	0.60
Integrated	28						
M		1.58$_a$	1.41$_a$	2.50$_b$	2.87$_c$	3.19$_d$	3.22$_d$
SD		0.46	0.29	0.46	0.68	0.77	0.66
Female dominated	22						
M		1.40$_a$	1.55$_a$	2.13$_b$	3.39$_c$	3.12$_c$	3.07$_c$
SD		0.30	0.32	0.38	0.65	0.44	0.54
All occupations	80						
M		1.86$_b$	1.35$_a$	2.45$_c$	2.84$_d$	3.20$_e$	2.99$_d$
SD		0.78	0.30	0.53	0.76	0.69	0.64

NOTE: Means are on a 5 point Likert type scale on which higher numbers indicate that attributes in dimension were believed more necessary for success in the occupations. Contrasts between dimensions were computed overall and within levels of sex distribution; means having the same subscript are not significantly different at the Bonferroni adjusted alpha level of .0033.

Discussion

This research demonstrates that gendered mental images of occupations correspond to the sex segregation of the occupations and, moreover, that high prestige and wages are associated with masculine images. Our research participants thus thought that, to the extent that occupations are female dominated, success in them requires feminine qualities of personality and/or feminine physical qualities; they similarly thought that, to the extent that occupations are male dominated, success in them requires masculine qualities of personality and/or masculine physical qualities. That prediction of occupations' sex distributions on the basis of gender-stereotypic qualities was very successful, as indexed by relatively high multiple correlation coefficients, and shows how profoundly the occupational structure has been shaped by gender.

It is highly informative to examine which stereotypic dimensions best predicted the distribution of the sexes into occupations. The strongest predictor in all four of the analyses on the variables assessing occupations' sex ratios (see Table 3) was feminine qualities of personality—the niceness-nurturance cluster of traits that appear as stereotypic of women in virtually all studies of gender stereotypes (e.g., De Lisi & Soundranayagam, 1990; J. E. Williams & Best, 1982; see review by Ashmore, Del Boca, & Wohlers, 1986). Thus, success in female-dominated (vs. male-dominated) occupations was associated considerably more with qualities such as being gentle, nurtur-

TABLE 5:   *Prediction of Occupations' Prestige and Earnings From Belief in Gender-Stereotypic Attributes' Importance to Occupational Success (N = 80)*

Predictor Dimension and Multiple R	Prestige		Estimated Earnings		Actual Earnings	
	B	β	B	β	B	β
Masculine physical	−0.33***	−.31	−5,530.17	−.15	−5,924.59	−.13
Feminine physical	−0.69**	−.25	−4,381.91	−.05	−10,784.61	−.09
Masculine personality	0.67****	.43	29,843.96****	.57	35,766.00****	.52
Feminine personality	0.18	.17	−3,588.84	−.10	3,483.04	.07
Masculine cognitive	0.43****	.36	−424.69	−.01	993.85	.02
Feminine cognitive	0.20	.16	−4,526.63	−.10	−10,963.60	−.19
Multiple R	.78****		.49***		.45**	

NOTE: On the predictor variables, higher scores indicated that the attributes comprising the dimension were thought more essential for success in an occupation. On the criterion variables, higher scores indicated greater prestige or larger estimated or actual earnings. *B* = unstandardized regression coefficient; β = standardized regression coefficient.

**p < .05. ***p < .01. ****p < .001.

ing, helpful to others, sociable, kind, cooperative, and supportive. Masculine personality attributes were important as well: Success in male-dominated occupations was associated with masculine qualities of personality (e.g., being competitive, dominant, aggressive) to a greater extent than was success in female-dominated occupations.

The prediction from stereotypic physical attributes to the distribution of the sexes into occupations is also notable. Success in male-dominated (vs. female-dominated) occupations was more strongly associated with masculine physical attributes (e.g., muscular, physically vigorous), whereas success in female-dominated (vs. male-dominated) occupations was more strongly associated with feminine physical attributes (e.g., pretty, cute, petite). These two classes of physical characteristics were reliably associated with occupations' sex distributions despite the lesser overall importance ascribed to physical attributes as determinants

of occupational success. Specifically, physical attributes were thought to be generally rather unimportant to occupational success in comparison with personality attributes and cognitive attributes (see Table 4). Nonetheless, masculine and feminine physical attributes related in the predicted manner to the distribution of women and men into occupations, with the exception of the actual sex difference in attraction, which was computed as a difference between the male and the female participants' self-reported attraction to the occupations. This failure of physical attributes to predict the actual sex difference in attraction is not surprising, because our participants were university students—most of whom aspire to professional and managerial occupations—for which physical characteristics are thought to be quite unimportant.

By identifying the types of gender-stereotypic requisites of occupational success that are correlated with sex differences in occupational preferences, the present study goes beyond the simple generalization that each sex's occupational preferences are related to the sex ratio of occupations. The most important predictor of the male and female participants' differential attraction to occupations was belief that success requires feminine qualities of personality, and the belief that success requires masculine personality attributes was the next most important predictor. With respect to attraction to occupations on other gender-stereotypic bases, sex similarity prevailed. These findings are generally consistent with Pratto, Stallworth, Sidanius, and Siers's (1997) demonstration that men tend to have occupations that enhance group-based inequality and that women tend to have occupations that attenuate inequality. They showed that interest in hierarchy-enhancing careers was associated with valuing outcomes, such as leadership opportunities and being famous, that are generally compatible with the present study's stereotypically masculine qualities of personality; interest in hierarchy-attenuating careers was associated with valuing outcomes, such as working with people and helping others, that are compatible with the present study's stereotypically feminine qualities of personality. Partially consistent with the present research is Lippa's (1998) argument that women are relatively more attracted to occupations that are oriented toward people and men are relatively more attracted to occupations that are oriented toward things. Although in the present research women's caring and nurturing orientation toward people was reflected in their attraction to occupations believed to require feminine personality attributes, men's more controlling and dominating orientation toward people may have been reflected in their attraction to occupations believed to require masculine personality attributes. Although

male-dominated occupations may be in some sense oriented toward things, they may also favor a type of orientation toward people that is different from what typifies female-dominated occupations.

Another noteworthy feature of our findings is the general weakness of prediction of occupations' sex distributions from the cognitive dimensions of gender stereotypes. Judgments of the gender-stereotypic cognitive attributes required for success in occupations failed to show gender-congruent relations to occupations' sex ratios.[4] The absence of such prediction may in part reflect the lesser stereotypicality of the masculine cognitive dimension (see Table 1). Nonetheless, these findings suggest that the sex segregation of employment may not be importantly related to requirements of mathematical and analytical competence in male-dominated occupations, although much discussion of employment segregation has focused on the cognitive abilities that may be necessary for success in male-dominated occupations (see Betz & Fitzgerald, 1987).

Although this study was not designed to test causal relations, the findings are consistent with reasonable assumptions about reciprocal causal links between the sex segregation of occupations and gender stereotyping. As social role theory (Eagly, 1987) argues, people derive their images of women and men from observing their sex-typical work. Both direct and indirect observation (e.g., through the media) provide exposure to women's and men's roles in the private and public spheres. From this perspective, occupational distributions are causes of gender stereotypes. However, the reciprocal causal link is suggested by our findings on actual sex differences in attraction to occupations: Gender-stereotypic images of occupations would foster sex segregation of employment by producing gendered expectations about the occupations appropriate for each sex and influencing women's and men's tendencies to aspire to particular occupations. Relevant to these processes is research showing that people in gender-incongruent occupations tend to experience role conflict (e.g., Luhaorg & Zivian, 1995; C. L. Williams, 1989) and that personal difficulties are thought to plague such people, especially women in male-dominated fields (C. L. Williams, 1989; Yoder & Schleicher, 1996). Other research suggests that gendered occupational stereotypes mediate sex discrimination in hiring decisions (Glick, Zion, & Nelson, 1988). Thus, the causal relationships between occupational sex ratios and gender stereotypes are no doubt bidirectional, and research in various paradigms has demonstrated relevant mediational processes.

Accuracy of Perceptions of Occupations

Whether beliefs about occupations are accurate is important to our research because of the possibility that perceivers might use the sex ratio of occupations as a heuristic to suggest the extent to which job holders need to display masculine or feminine qualities to be successful. Consistent with this view, Krefting, Berger, and Wallace (1978) argued that the sex ration of occupations and not actual job content is the most important predictor of beliefs that occupations require feminine or masculine qualities. However, less congenial to this interpretation is the considerable variability in the attributes ascribed to male-dominated and female-dominated occupations and the overall perceived importance of masculine cognitive characteristics to occupational success, even in female-dominated occupations (see Table 4). Thus, participants did not in simple fashion assume that, regardless of job content, female-dominated occupations require a full range of feminine qualities and that male-dominated occupations require a full range of masculine qualities. Had participants used sex ratios as a simple heuristic, the strength of the prediction of the occupational division of labor from our six gender-stereotypic dimensions should have mirrored the relative stereotypicality of the dimensions (see Table 1). Although it is more likely that perceivers have at least a somewhat accurate understanding of the qualities required for success in differing occupations, our study does not yield a formal test of the accuracy of perceivers' beliefs about the qualities required for success in occupations.

One aspect of the accuracy of perceiving occupations can be examined empirically by this study—namely, perceptions of occupations' sex ratio and earnings. Participants' estimates of the distribution of men and women into each occupation were thus related to the actual distributions reported in census data, producing a correlation consistent with overall accuracy, $r(78) = .91$, $p < .001$. Nonetheless, confirming research by McCauley and his colleagues (McCauley & Thangavelu, 1991; McCauley, Thangavelu, & Rozin, 1988), participants' errors reflected systematic underestimates of the extent to which male-dominated and female-dominated occupations were segregated. The percentage of women in the female-dominated occupations (i.e., 75% or more female) was underestimated by 9.30%, and the percentage of women in the male-dominated occupations (i.e., 75% or more male) was overestimated by 17.14%.[5] Although this finding fits other research showing that stereotypes, including gender stereotypes, often underestimate group differences (see Eagly & Diekman, 1997; McCauley, 1995; Swim, 1994), in the present study the underestimation of segregation may reflect a more general contraction bias against extreme judgments of magnitude (Poulton, 1989). This interpretation becomes especially plausible in view of the additional tendency we obtained for participants to underestimate high wages and overestimate low wages, despite overall accuracy of participants' estimates of occupations' earnings as shown by the correlation of the estimated and the actual wage variables, $r(78) = .94$.

Improving Women's Status by Reducing the Sex Segregation of Employment

This research followed from our assumption that the division of labor between men's work and women's work is the key to understanding the causes of women's subordination (e.g., Lerner, 1986). Women are positioned in the social structure to have greater domestic responsibility than men regardless of their employment status (e.g., Blair & Lichter, 1991; Shelton, 1992). Also very important, as illustrated by this research, is the tendency of women and men to be concentrated in different types of occupations. Regardless of the accuracy of perceivers' beliefs about occupations' demands, success in female-dominated occupations (compared with male-dominated occupations) is thought to follow relatively more from feminine qualities of personality and from feminine physical attributes; success in male-dominated occupations (compared with female-dominated occupations) is thought to follow relatively more from masculine qualities of personality and masculine physical attributes. Perceivers thus assume a degree of fit between the sex of job holders and the requirements of occupations, and this gender congruence would tend to foster sex segregation. Nonetheless,

they also perceive some commonality in the qualities occupations require regardless of their sex ratios. Cognitive skills, both masculine and feminine, were generally important, although feminine qualities of personality were also very important for female-dominated occupations.

Our findings on occupations' prestige and earnings suggest that movement by women into stereotypically masculine roles is a possible route to raising women's status in society. The critical findings are that earnings related positively to the belief that occupations require masculine personality characteristics,[6] and prestige related positively to the beliefs that occupations require masculine personality characteristics and cognitive characteristics. However, the male-stereotypic qualities associated with highly paid, prestigious occupations can discourage women's entry into such occupations, because competence and comfort in such occupations might require that women view themselves as possessing a greater measure of masculine qualities. Yet, if large enough numbers of women enter an occupation that it becomes female dominated rather than male dominated, its wages might lag because of the wage penalty associated with feminized occupations (Anker, 1997), and its image might be redefined along more feminine lines. However, any such redefinitions probably occur very slowly, as suggested by the small magnitude of the shifts that have occurred in the qualities thought to be required for success in the managerial role (e.g., Brenner, Tomkiewicz, & Schein, 1989; Frank, 1988; Russell, Rush, & Herd, 1988), which has become far less male dominated. Women thus face the daunting reality of a social structure in which high wages and prestige are associated with occupations that are thought to require masculine personal characteristics.

Notes

1. These dimensions were not equated for their evaluative content. Consistent with evidence that the female stereotype is somewhat more evaluatively positive than is the male stereotype (Eagly, Mladinic, & Otto, 1991), the feminine dimensions may have somewhat more positive valence than would the masculine dimensions.

2. The mean ratings of the female and male participants were compared on all of the dependent variables for all 80 occupations. Because these analyses revealed few significant differences, the data were combined across female and male participants (with the exception of ratings of attraction to occupations).

3. As Jacobs (1989) discussed, various methodological problems have limited understanding of the relation between occupations' prestige and their sex ratios. These difficulties may include a tendency of respondents to use different, sex-specific standards of comparisons when rating the prestige of occupations that are dominated by one sex (see Biernat, 1995).

4. Because of the possibility that the effects of gender-stereotypic cognitive attributes might relate to occupations' sex distributions only for higher prestige occupations, prestige was examined as a potential moderator. However, no such effects emerged.

5. Very similar findings have been reported by Beyer and Finnegan (1997).

6. A tendency for occupations that are perceived to require feminine personality characteristics to have lower earnings would be consistent with sociologists' demonstrations of lower wages in occupations perceived to require nurturance (England, Herbert, Kilbourne, Reid, & Megdal., 1994; see also Kilbourne, England, Farkas, Beron, & Weir, 1994). The absence of this finding in the present study may reflect our broader definition of feminine personality characteristics and differences between our sample of 80 occupations and the much larger sample used in sociological studies. The sociological studies have not investigated the relation between earnings and beliefs that occupations require masculine personality characteristics.

References

Anker, R. (1997). Theories of occupational segregation by sex: An overview. *International Labour Review, 136,* 315–339.

Ashmore, R. D., Del Boca, F. K., & Wohlers, A. J. (1986). Gender stereotypes. In R. D. Ashmore & F. K. Del Boca (Eds.), *The social psychology of female-male relations: A critical analysis of central concepts* (pp. 69–119). Orlando, FL: Academic Press.

Beggs, J. M., & Doolittle, D. C. (1993). Perceptions now and then of occupational sex typing: A replication of Shinar's 1975 study. *Journal of Applied Social Psychology, 23,* 1435–1453.

Bergmann, B. R. (1986). *The economic emergence of women.* New York: Basic Books.

Betz, N. E., & Fitzgerald, L. F. (1987). *The career psychology of women.* Orlando, FL: Academic Press.

Beyer, S., & Finnegan, A. (1997, August). *The accuracy of gender stereotypes regarding occupations.* Paper presented at the meeting of the American Psychological Association, Chicago.

Biernat, M. (1995). The shifting standards model: Implications of stereotype accuracy for social judgment. In Y. Lee, L. J. Jussim, & C. R. McCanley (Eds.), *Stereotype accuracy: Toward appreciating group differences* (pp. 87–114). Washington, DC: American Psychological Association.

Blair, S. L., & Lichter, D. T. (1991). Measuring the division of household labor: Gender segregation of housework among American couples. *Journal of Family Issues, 12,* 91–113.

Brenner, O. C., Tomkiewicz, J., & Schein, V. E. (1989). The relationship between sex role stereotypes and requisite management characteristics revisited. *Academy of Management Review, 32,* 662–669.

Cross, S. E., & Madson, L. (1997). Models of the self: Self-construals and gender. *Psychological Bulletin, 122,* 5–37.

Deaux, K., & Kite, M. (1993). Gender stereotypes. In F. L. Denmark & M. A. Paludi (Eds.), *Psychology of women: A handbook of issues and theories* (pp. 107–139). Westport, CT: Greenwood Press.

Deaux, K., & Lewis, L. L. (1983). Components of gender stereotypes (Manuscript No. 2583). *Psychological Documents, 73,* 25.

Deaux, K., & Lewis, L. L. (1984). Structure of gender stereotypes: Interrelationships among components and gender label. *Journal of Personality and Social Psychology, 46,* 991–1004.

De List, R., & Soundranayagam, L. (1990). The conceptual structure of sex role stereotypes in college students. *Sex Roles, 23,* 593–611.

Eagly, A. H. (1987). *Sex differences in social behavior: A social-role interpretation.* Hillsdale, NJ: Lawrence Erlbaum.

Eagly, A. H., & Diekman, A. B. (1997). The accuracy of gender stereotypes: A dilemma for feminism. *Revue Internationale de Psychologie Sociale/International Review of Social Psychology, 10*(2), 11–30.

Eagly, A. H., Mladinic, A., & Otto, S. (1991). Are women evaluated more favorably than men? An analysis of attitudes, beliefs, and emotions, *Psychology of Women Quarterly, 15,* 203–216.

Eagly, A. H., & Steffen, V. J. (1984). Gender stereotypes stem from the distribution of women and men into social roles. *Journal of Personality and Social Psychology, 46,* 735–754.

England, P., Herbert, M. S., Kilbourne, B. S., Reid, L. L., & Megdal, L. M. (1994). The gendered valuation of occupations and skills: Earnings in 1980 census occupations. *Social Forces, 73,* 65–99.

Frank, E. J. (1988). Business students' perceptions of women in management. *Sex Roles, 19,* 107–118.

Gilbert, D. T., & Malone, P. S. (1995). The correspondence bias. *Psychological Bulletin, 50,* 21–38.

Glick, P. (1991). Trait-based and sex-based discrimination in occupational prestige, occupational salary, and hiring. *Sex Roles, 25,* 351–378.

Glick, P., Wilk, K., & Perrcault, M. (1995). Images of occupations: Components of gender and status in occupational stereotypes. *Sex Roles, 32,* 565–582.

Glick, P., Zion, C., & Nelson, C. (1988). What mediates sex discrimination in hiring decisions? *Journal of Personality and Social Psychology, 55,* 178–186.

Gottfredson, L. (1981). Circumscription and compromise: A developmental theory of occupational aspirations. *Journal of Counseling Psychology, 28,* 545–579.

Hamilton, D. L., & Sherman, J. W. (1994). Stereotypes. In R. S. Wyer, Jr., & T. K. Srull (Eds.), *Handbook of social cognition* (2nd ed., Vol. 2, pp. 1–68). Hillsdale, NJ: Lawrence Erlbaum.

Jacobs, J. A. (1989). *Revolving doors: Sex segregation and women's cariers.* Stanford, CA: Stanford University Press.

Jost, J. T., & Banaji, M. R. (1994). The role of stereotyping in system-justification and the production of false consciousness. *British Journal of Social Psychology, 33,* 1–27.

Kalin, R. (1986, August). *The role of gender in occupational images.* Poster presented at the meeting of the American Psychological Association, Washington, DC.

Kilbourne, B. S., England, P., Farkas, G., Beron, K., & Weir, D. (1994). Returns to skill, compensating differentials, and gender bias: Effects of occupational characteristics on the wages of white women and men. *American Journal of Sociology, 100,* 689–719.

Krefting, I. A., Berger, P. K., & Wallace, M. J. (1978). The contribution of sex distribution, job content, and occupational classification to job sex-typing: Two studies. *Journal of Vocational Behavior, 13,* 181–191.

Lerner, G. (1986). *The creation of patriarchy.* New York: Oxford University Press.

Lippa, R. (1995). Gender-related individual differences and psychological adjustment in terms of the Big Five and circumplex models. *Journal of Personality and Social Psychology, 69,* 1184–1202.

Lippa, R. (1998). Gender-related individual differences and the structure of vocational interests: The importance of the "people-things" dimension. *Journal of Personality and Social Psychology, 74,* 996–1009.

Lippa, R., & Connelly, S. (1990). Gender diagnosticity: A new Bayesian approach to gender related individual differences. *Journal of Personality and Social Psychology, 59,* 1051–1065.

Lueptow, L. B., Garovich, L., & Lueplow, M. B. (1995). The persistence of gender stereotypes in the face of changing sex roles: Evidence contrary to the sociocultural model. *Ethology and Sociobiology, 16,* 509–530.

Luhaorg, H., & Zivian, M. T. (1995). Gender role conflict: The interaction of gender, gender role, and occupation. *Sex Roles, 33,* 607–620.

McCauley, C. (1995). Are stereotypes exaggerated? A sampling of racial, gender, academic, occupational, and political stereotypes. In Y. Lee, L. J. Jussim, & C. R. McCauley (Eds.), *Stereotype accuracy: Toward appreciating group differences* (pp. 215–243). Washington, DC: American Psychological Association.

McCauley, C., & Thangavelu, K. (1991). Individual differences in sex stereotyping of occupations and personality traits. *Social Psychology Quarterly, 54,* 267–279.

McCauley, C., Thangavelu, K., & Rozin, P. (1988). Sex stereotyping of occupations in relation to television representations and census facts. *Basic and Applied Social Psychology, 9,* 197–212.

McLean, H. M., & Kalin, R. (1994). Congruence between self-image and occupational stereotypes in students entering gender-dominated occupations. *Canadian Journal of Behavioural Science, 26,* 142–162.

Poulton, E. C. (1989). *Bias in quantifying judgements.* Hillsdale, NJ: Lawrence Erlbaum.

Pratto, F., Stallworth, L. M., Sidanius, J., & Slers, B. (1997). The gender gap in occupational role attainment: A social dominance approach. *Journal of Personality and Social Psychology, 72,* 37–53.

Reskin, B., & Padavic, I. (1994). *Women and men at work.* Thousand Oaks, CA: Pine Forge Press.

Russell, J. E. A., Rush, M. C., & Herd, A. M. (1988). An exploration of women's expectations of effective male and female leadership. *Sex Roles, 18,* 279–287.

Shelton, B. A. (1992). *Women, men, and time: Gender differences in paid work, housework, and leisure.* New York: Greenwood Press.

Shinar, E. H. (1975). Sexual stereotypes of occupations. *Journal of Vocational Behavior, 7,* 99–111.

Shinar, E. H. (1978). Person perception as a function of occupation and sex. *Sex Roles, 4,* 679–693.

Swim, J. K. (1994). Perceived versus meta-analytic effect sizes: An assessment of the accuracy of gender stereotypes. *Journal of Personality and Social Psychology, 66,* 21–36.

Tomaskovic-Devey, D. (1995). Sex composition and gendered earnings inequality: A comparison of job and occupational models. In J. A. Jacobs (Ed.), *Gender inequality at work* (pp. 23–56). Thousand Oaks, CA: Sage.

U.S. Bureau of the Census. (1993). *Statistical abstract of the United States, 1993* (113th ed.). Washington, DC: Author.

U.S. Bureau of Labor Statistics. (1998). *Labor force statistics from the current population survey* (Annual average tables from the January 1998 issue of Employment and Earnings: Table 11) [on-line]. Available from the World Wide Web: ftp://ftp.bls.gov/pub/special.requests/lf/aat11.txt.

U.S. Department of Labor. (1993). *Occupational outlook handbook.* Washington, DC: Bureau of Labor Statistics.

Williams, C. L. (1989). *Gender differences at work: Women and men in nontraditional occupations.* Berkeley: University of California Press.

Williams, J. E., & Best, D. L. (1982). *Measuring sex stereotypes: A thirty-nation study.* Beverly Hills, CA: Sage.

Yoder, J. D., & Schleicher, T. L. (1996). Undergraduates regard deviation from occupational gender stereotypes as costly for women. *Sex Roles, 34,* 171–188.

Yount, K. (1986). A theory of productive activity: The relationships among self-concept, gender, sex role stereotypes, and work-emergent traits. *Psychology of Women Quarterly, 10,* 63–88.

21

Women Above the Glass Ceiling Perceptions on Corporate Mobility and Strategies for Success

Sally Ann Davies-Netzley

Although women are more likely to hold managerial and professional positions, they continue to be overrepresented at the bottom of organizational hierarchies. There is a "glass ceiling," where invisible barriers to advancement keep women from achieving the top positions in their professions. In this reading, Davies-Netzley describes the experiences of a small number of women who have made it "above the glass ceiling." She interviewed white male and female corporate presidents and CEOs regarding their views on corporate mobility and success. She found that the white men she interviewed supported the standards of the defined norm and believed that success was the result of individual effort, talent, hard work and competition **(defined norm)**. These men did not see themselves as privileged in the corporate world and denied that sexism was a barrier to moving up the corporate ladder. The white women she interviewed however, felt that intelligence, talent, and hard work were not sufficient for success, and pointed to external barriers such as male-dominated networks and peer similarities that kept them from advancing **(gender role effects)**. In order to succeeed, these women employed strategies such as advanced education, developing similarities with male peers, establishing networks with other women, and resolving work and family conflicts.

Questions to Consider:

1. According to Davies-Netzley, who do the women in her study hold different

S.A. Davies-Netzley, *Gender & Society, 12* (3), pp. 339–356, copyright (c) 1998 by Sociologists for Women in Society. Reprinted by Permission of Sage Publications, Inc.

AUTHOR'S NOTE: *I thank Leo Chavez, Judith Stepan-Norris, and Judith Treas for their suggestions throughout this study, as well as Beth Schneider and the anonymous reviewers for their useful comments.*

views of corporate mobility and success than the men?

2. Based on these interviews, would you say that the "old boys" network continues to play a role in corporate success? Why or why not?

3. What suggestions do you have for making it more possible for women to break through the glass ceiling?

4. If you were to conduct a similar study of women and men of color who have made it to top executive positions, what questions would you ask them? Explain your choices.

In recent decades women have increasingly entered managerial and professional occupations. In 1994, 29 percent of all working women were employed in executive, managerial, or professional positions, which exceeded the comparable figure for men (U.S. Department of Labor 1995). But these broad occupational categories mask the fact that women continue to cluster near the bottom of organizational and professional hierarchies and have lower earnings, authority, and advancement potential in comparison with men. Viewing women as a broad, homogeneous group also masks the fact that the U.S. labor force is gender and race segregated. Compared with women of color, white women have made the greatest gains in achieving upper management and professional positions. Women and men of color face the additional constraints of racial discrimination and informal barriers to occupational advancement (Collins 1989; Higginbotham 1994; Martin 1994).

Considerable sociological and feminist work has been conducted on why women remain in work positions with lower pay and authority compared to men. But what happens when women attain elite positions within business? This article focuses on a small number of white women who have reached above the glass ceiling to top leadership positions in corporate America. The metaphor of a glass ceiling has often been used to describe invisible barriers through which women can see elite positions but cannot reach them.

The number of women who have attained elite positions in corporate offices and boardrooms in the United States remains considerably low. Women comprise roughly 4 percent of directors and 2 percent of corporate officers in Fortune 500 companies (Von Glinow and Krzyczkowska-Mercer 1988). More progress has been made in corporate boardrooms. In the mid-1970s, only 13 percent of the 1,350 major corporations in the United States had a female director on their board. By 1985, that figure rose to 41 percent (*The Wall Street Journal* 1986).

Some scholars interpret these gains as dismal progress for women and emphasize the lack of substantial numbers of women at the top. Others characterize women in elite corporate positions as token workers who are less integrated in the large, influential central circles of power (Kanter [1977] 1993; Moore 1988). While we can point to a limited number of studies discussing elite women as "outsiders on the inside," there is a lack of research focusing on women's experiences in elite corporate positions and their perspectives on corporate mobility and success.

Drawing on interviews with 16 corporate elites in Southern California, I examine the ways in which women corporate presidents and chief executive officers (CEOs) function in male-dominated elite circles of power. I compare these women's perceptions of corporate mobility and success with those of men in similar positions. How might women's views of corporate mobility differ from those of white men who have traditionally held top corporate positions?

What strategies do women use to maneuver within such elite positions of power?

Women above the Glass Ceiling

Many studies on women in management have engaged in the debate concerning gender differences in styles of management. Some suggest that women naturally display a more interactive, caring leadership style (Rosener 1990); others argue that focusing on gender differences only reinforces gender stereotyping (Epstein 1991). While this debate has significance for understanding the ways women lead, it is crucial to place women's experiences in management within the context of gendered power relations. As Michel Foucault contends, "[T]he exercise of power itself creates and causes to emerge new objects of knowledge" (1980, 51). Some partial, located knowledges, such as white men's, have become privileged over others in gendered and racially stratified ways. These ideologies are embedded in the structures and practices of organizations and constitute a "regime of truth" with which women managers engage (Martin 1994).

Women managers often confront patriarchal ideologies that link womanhood with unpaid work, marriage, and the family, and justify women in lower management positions with limited authority and opportunity (Crowly and Himmelweit 1992). Furthermore, business management has been constructed in terms of objectivity, rationality, and logic, competencies traditionally associated with masculinity (Swan 1994). The social constructs of gender and management have implications for women managers who are often the highly visible other, marginalized by ideology, and "kept controlled within the spaces of specialized 'female' roles and lower ranks" (Swan 1994, 107).

While engaging with ideologies that frame womanhood in terms of family, home, and unpaid or lower paid work, women managers also are marginalized by a work situation characterized by mostly male peers. This is especially true of women in senior management positions who often lack peer support and mentoring. Boundary heightening, the act of a dominant group exaggerating differences between themselves and tokens, appears to be a significant concern for these women (Kanter [1977] 1993; Martin 1994). Rosabeth Moss Kanter notes that by the 1990s, "In executive offices and on Board of Directors, women and minorities were still scarce, but it was likely that at least one served in a significant position, bringing the X-O dynamics of tokenism to the boardroom" ([1977] 1993, 298). Kanter argues that women token workers, the few Os among mostly Xs, experience unique pressures, including high degrees of visibility, isolation, and gender-stereotyped roles (Kanter [1977] 1993). Janice Yoder (1991) also contends that women token workers are often faced with sexual harassment, blocked mobility, and wage inequities.

Similarly, Gwen Moore (1988) finds that women who have reached the highest corporate or political positions are isolated in comparison to male counterparts and are best characterized as "outsiders on the inside." Drawing on national surveys from 1971 to 1981 (54 women and 1,361 men) from the United States, West Germany, and Australia, Moore finds that women in national elite positions are less integrated in informal discussion networks and outside the influential, central circle of high-level position holders. Such isolation, Moore concludes, hampers women's performance in top-level positions. Moore's findings support those of other scholars, who indicate that women occupying senior positions are rarely allowed entry into informal networks that may assist with career success and advancement (Epstein 1975; Freeman 1990; Kaufman and Fetters 1983; Zweigenhaft 1987).

This study builds on the existing literature on women in management in several ways. First, I question the extent to which men and women in elite corporate positions offer similar perspectives on corporate success and mobility. Second, I examine how women presidents and CEOs respond to a work situation that, ideologically, has been associated with masculinity and continues to be characterized by mostly men. What strategies do women use to succeed in their elite positions above the corporate glass ceiling?

Methodology

In the fall of 1995 and 1996, I interviewed men and women who occupy elite corporate positions in Southern California. I considered those in elite positions to be at the top of the corporate hierarchy. Consequently, I limited my sample to individuals who hold the title of president or chief officer. Participants were selected from a wide range of industries: a midsize law firm, a private university, a local bank, and one of the largest local hospitals. The financial and advertising companies have been reported among the top 25 of their industries in terms of employees and revenues, which ranged from $250,000 to $500,000. The bio- and high-technology firms had revenues exceeding 1 million annually, and some ranked in the top 10 of their industries.

Initially, I interviewed three individuals in elite positions whom I contacted through my own social networks. I then asked each of these initial three interviewees to suggest several other individuals

who also hold top positions in southern California corporations. The process of snowball sampling proves an effective technique in studying small or difficult-to-contact populations such as elite groups.[1] By asking the CEOs who participated in the study to identify other top executives in the area, I was able to interview people who otherwise would have been inaccessible. On more than one occasion, I was told that I was granted an interview because I knew their colleague.

Most interviews were conducted face-to-face in the offices of the informants and lasted about one hour. Questions were open-ended and focused on the respondents' social origins, education, career path, business and social affiliations, characterization of social networks, and factors assisting them in their rise to the top and their ability to successfully function in their position. Respondents also were asked to characterize their views concerning social relationships between people in elite positions and the extent to which gender was a significant factor in influencing an individual's success.

Sixteen informants were interviewed. Nine were white women, and 7 were white men. Considering the small size of my sample and that most corporate CEOs and presidents are white, it is not surprising that snowball sampling produced an all-white sample. An obvious drawback of this sample is that it does not allow for direct comparisons to men and women of color. The median age was 52 for men and 50 for women. In addition, all of the interviewees had earned bachelor's degrees. Six of the men and five of the women had degrees beyond the bachelor's level. The median years in current position was eight for men and seven for women. Six of the men and five of the women were presently married. All of the men and five of the women had children.[2]

Ideology at Work: Elite Men's Perspectives

I start with a look at the men in my sample and their attitudes toward corporate mobility and their own success. Most of the men in the sample had obtained graduate degrees and then entered the workforce in middle- or upper-management positions. Four described themselves as moving quickly up the ladder, two reaching vice president positions while still in their 20s. The other men described the process of "growing up" with the corporation.

When discussing what it takes to make it to the top, the men primarily attribute their success and elite status to their own individual qualities.[3] These men uphold the dominant stratification ideology in the United States by emphasizing that success and economic reward come from individual talent and effort.

Overall, the men ranked hard work as the most important element for success. Douglas Strickland, president of a biotechnology corporation, comments, "Everyone in the game is smart enough. It takes hard work." In thinking about what is most important in achieving and maintaining a top position, Strickland notes, "Hard work is first, timing/luck, cold honest appraisal, and good, useful ideas."

Strickland mentions luck as the second factor in achieving success. Four other men also mention luck as one factor in success, but they always place luck after individual effort. For instance, Steven Putnam, a law firm partner, notes, "I think luck has something to do with it, but I don't think luck is a major factor." He continues, "It's a matter of some internal drive people develop." For Putnam, this inner drive, possessed by some but not all individuals, is important for a successful career. Similarly, Matthew Gilbert, president of a scientific institute, and John Holden, CEO for a private university, emphasize the importance of an individual's inner qualities, particularly leadership skills, in becoming successful.

The men highlight competitive qualities needed to succeed in business, and several drew parallels between being a corporate elite and an athlete. For instance, Holden makes the connection between sports and the business world:

> I don't think you'll find a successful CEO that doesn't thrive on competition. . . . To use a sports analogy, think of the person who wants the ball at the last of the game. A lot of people who don't want the ball say, "What if I miss?" I think competitors say, "What if I make it?"

Likewise, Strickland uses a football analogy, comparing a president of a company to a quarterback: "The quarterback has got to do his job, even though he knows that within a split second of throwing the football, he's going to get creamed."

These men define their success in terms of performance and winning, dominant values of organized sports. The analogy they draw between business and organized sports is significant, because sports are an important organizing institution for the embodiment of masculinity and represent "a practice through which men's separation from and power over women is embodied and naturalized" (Messner 1989, 73). These elite men discuss the qualities needed to function in business and sports, such as competitiveness, but they do not acknowledge the male-dominated nature of these institutions.

When thinking about their own success and what it takes to make it to the top, all of the men downplay the importance of an "old boys' network" or peer similarities among men and underscore the significance of individual qualities. A good example of undermining the importance of all-male, elite networks is provided by Strickland. He initially denies the existence of an old boys' network but acknowledges that many boardrooms are occupied primarily by men: "Oftentimes I'll go to a meeting and it will be all white men in the room." Still, he undermines the assertion that gender plays an important role: "But I know these men and they don't give a damn. If there's a woman in there who can give them an edge, then get in there." For Strickland, the old boys' network does not explain success: "It isn't an old boys' network—but it is, it's an old boy network of 'successful' people, it has nothing to do with men and women, or black and white."

Likewise, Holden discusses the relationship between gender and board of directors' membership of his corporation. He states that while in 1989 the board was all white men, today it includes several women and ethnic minorities. The reason for this demographic shift? Holden argues that, just as in the past, individuals hold seats on the board because "they are persons who are successful." Similar to Strickland, Holden asserts that individual qualities are most important in explaining the demographic changes at the top.

The significance of peer similarities for success also is downplayed in favor of one's individual talents and qualities. Andrew Norton, president of a hospital, admits that in some organizations commonalities with those in higher positions, such as leisure activities, can be significant. However, when describing his own career, Norton argues that his success is based on his ability to deliver results.

> My approach to my whole career is that I wasn't going to play the politics. I'm not a golfer and I'm not going to go out and play golf with people and hustle board members and all of that. My thing was that I'd do my job, and I'd deliver tremendous results.

Above all, Norton upholds the significance of being able to achieve results. When discussing his relationships with other CEOs, Holden acknowledges that they have shared interests. However, just as with Norton, Holden downplays the significance of these social activities for his own success: "When I see other executives socially, the last thing I want to talk about is our work. . . . It's never been that important to me to have contact with other executives." Both men elevate individual qualities while failing to recognize the less obvious benefits of socializing among their peers. They legitimate their own rise to success by reinforcing the individualism of America's hegemonic culture.

In addition to asking the men about success, I also asked for their thoughts on the paucity of women at the top. Assumptions inherent in patriarchal gender ideology were used by the men to explain why women are underrepresented in elite positions. Three men felt that women's lack of necessary skills and know-how had prevented them from attaining elite positions. James Olson, president of a financial institution, describes the recent addition of the first woman to the bank's board: "We talked about having a woman in the past but had been unable to settle on someone who we thought could make a major contribution." According to Olson, until recently, many women did not have the skills to contribute meaningfully at the board level.

Similarly, when discussing the recent addition of women to his company's board of directors, Holden states that women are now developing the skills and talent necessary to make it in business: "It wasn't because their gender offers something special. It was because they were the most qualified." He asserts that it has always been about choosing the most talented person, and "as more women come out prepared, more pressure is going to come because that CEO is going to have to go for the most talented person." They reinforce the belief that we have a system of meritocracy that will recognize women as they develop the necessary skills.

Family conflict also was suggested by four of the men as the most significant reason why few women are at the top. These men equate women primarily with the homemaker role, asserting that because women's family responsibilities are paramount, they are often unable to commit the time needed in an elite position. Gilbert comments,

> No matter how much you want to fight it, there is this underlying thing for women that they always have to be the wife, the mother. The male, well, they're supposed to be the father and husband, but that doesn't mean quite the time commitment.

He states that married women do not perform as well because they can't commit the time that male counterparts can. Norton also argues that there is still conflict between work and home for women in senior positions that require 12- to 14-hour workdays. These four men view single women without children as better suited to corporate elite positions than wives and mothers. And while they felt it was problematic for women at the top to have families, they did not view their own family responsibilities as a hindrance for their work in elite positions.

Five men in the sample had wives who stayed at home for most of their children's school-age years. The two men with wives working in the paid workforce relied more heavily on paid child care. All of the men (all have children) state that they have sacrificed family time for work; however, they all underscore the benefits of an elite position for their families: private school attendance, a "nice home in a nice area," and recreational opportunities. Although it ap-

pears that men in the United States have shifted their attitudes toward the provider role in a more egalitarian direction (Wilkie 1993), the men in my sample typify primary breadwinning men who view their parental contribution in terms of income and financial support.

Success from the Standpoint of Elite Women

Unlike the men who describe moving up the ladder quickly or growing with the company, all of the women offered examples of experiencing gender discrimination in their corporate careers—whether it be in the form of comments from men colleagues questioning their ability to have a career and family or feeling left out of informal networking opportunities. To advance their careers, five of the women talked of fleeing larger corporations, working in smaller firms, networking in the local corporate community, and then moving into higher positions in more established corporations. The act of leaving large corporations and moving to "smaller, more hospitable organization[s]" is a common response among professional women experiencing workplace discrimination (Rosener 1995, 113). This is illustrated by Marie Johnson, president of a consulting company, who left a lucrative position in a large company because her advancement opportunities were blocked. She explains,

> I told my boss that I wanted to be more involved with customers. I wanted to take the next step. He said to me that he didn't think that women with children could do "marketing." I decided at that point to move on.

Likewise, advertising president Jennifer Anderson recalls gender discrimination in her previous place of business.

I've been in meetings where men haven't listened to leadership from a woman. But women are needed and should be valued. You have to prove yourself more as a woman. There's a kind of silent hostility out there toward women in business. I think there's this anger that men have to share "what belongs to them" with women.

Having experienced workplace discrimination and glass ceilings, the women's perspectives on corporate mobility contrast considerably with those of men peers. An immediate difference emerges in the role played by hard work. In contrast to men, all of the women assert that hard work alone, or even intelligence or talent, is not enough to succeed, and that opportunities are often blocked to individuals who are not white males. All of the women assert that external barriers exist to hinder a hardworking woman from achieving upward corporate mobility. Tracy Newton, CEO of a biotechnology company, illustrates this point: "Some people feel it's just hard work, do a good job, and you'll get promoted. That might be true to a certain point and that point is wherever the glass ceiling is."

This is not to say that the women did not acknowledge individual qualities as factors for success. Overall, the women agreed that an individual's inner drive, high self-esteem, and communication skills are important for success. They also felt that women were just as capable as men in displaying such qualities. Ultimately, however, the women emphasize that corporate mobility to the top does not depend primarily on individual-level variables such as inner drive or work ethic. Their views on corporate mobility and success are different from the men's.

Male-Dominated Networks

Whereas the men legitimize their positions through the ideology of individualism, all the women I spoke with explain their success by referring to social-structural variables. They emphasize social networks as most significant for success at elite levels and argue that the existence of an old boys' network continues to make it more difficult for women to succeed. They assert that success depends largely on how entrenched male networks are and how willing elite men are to accept the women into the networks.

Most of the women talk of experiencing old boys' networks within more established corporations when attempting to make their way up the corporate ladder. Newton describes the corporate atmosphere of a former workplace: "It was a male dominated culture with a good old boys' network. The only women they wanted at the top were the ones they placed there as tokens." Newton also adds that if women want to reach senior positions, they need to network with men in power positions. Newton argues, "The power is still in the males 50-plus years old. If you want to reach the top, those are the people you have to network with."

Even after having reached an elite corporate position, all of the women still consider themselves outsiders to a system that accommodates men. They speak of encountering an old boys' network composed of elites from other companies, which at times makes it difficult to function. Marsha Wagner, president of a manufacturing company, exemplifies this point: "Fund-raising is tougher for women in business because they don't have the network of 'good old boys' to put in money." Joan Miller, a former CEO who sits on several boards of directors, comments, "There is an old boys' network, and I have no doubt that there probably are opportunities [I've] missed, there probably are certain positions that I never could be in." Even though Miller and Wagner have obtained top corporate positions, they still feel excluded from business opportunities because of the existing old boys' network. This echoes the sentiments of Nancy Harrison, president of a high-technology corporation, who still does not consider herself "part of the group."

> The people at the top of this industry are still mostly men. I try not to let it bother me. I think they respect me as a professional, but I don't feel like I'm part of the group. I don't feel like I belong.

Likewise, Carrie Hughes, president of an investment corporation, describes feeling like an outsider after becoming a newly appointed board member:

> It doesn't occur to some men that a woman would be there to contribute to the board. There was this one incident when this board member thought I was part of the hotel staff and tried to pick me up. I introduced myself and he immediately backed off.

Such statements reinforce Moore's (1988) findings that even after reaching elite positions, women are still "outsiders on the inside" and often feel invisible or excluded from informal relationships and networks of all-men colleagues. Some of these women do believe, however, that it is only a matter of time before women are integrated into elite circles. Wagner states, "The network will break down. Younger men are different. They respect your leadership more." Hughes adds, "The weight of the numbers in business are now such that they won't be able to use excuses for much longer."

Peer Similarities

Women in elite positions also highlight the importance of peer similarities for achieving success. They recognize that similar interests among men, such as leisure activities, enhance their relationships and increase the likelihood they will be promoted over others. Newton elaborates, describing the time she asked for promotion:

> I told my boss I wanted a promotion and he just looked at me, flabbergasted, and said, "The guy I've got up there now has been my running partner and it's taken me two years to get him to that position." And it was sort of like, "I'm not doing that for you."

While in this example both Newton and her boss recognize the importance of developing similar interests for achieving success, the men I interviewed down-played the significance of such activities.

These women also note that the rapport between elite men often hinders women's pathways to success. Feeling like outsiders, they recognize that the nature of the relationships developed between elite males is fundamentally different from that between men and women in elite positions. Katherine Frost, president of a scientific corporation, made this point:

> There is definitely a different rapport between men. It's subtle, but they can say to each other, "Hey, could you wait a minute, I'd like to talk over some ideas with you after the meeting." With me, I think there's the hesitation of, well, she might think I'm coming onto her.

Rather than promoting the ideology of individualism, these white women primarily point to all-male networks and peer similarities as most significant in determining upward corporate mobility, a pathway that white men overwhelmingly experience. An obvious question remains: How do these women make sense of their own mobility and overcome external obstacles to enter such power positions?

Women's Survival Strategies at the Top

The women in the sample reveal several strategies for making it to, and succeeding in, top corporate positions. Among them are attaining further educational training, developing similarities with male peers, establishing networks with other women, and reconciling work and home responsibilities.

Earning advanced degrees and credentials (higher than those of most men) appears to be a way that women compete with men for elite positions. Three of the women purposefully returned to school to increase their credentials and make themselves more competitive for top positions. Hughes asserts, "I got an MBA in marketing 10 years after my MA in communication because it was apparent that I wasn't going to go higher in the corporate world without it." Master's degrees in business and law degrees are most closely related to entry into elite positions (Ward, Orazem, and Schmidt 1992). A total of five women in my sample had graduate degrees but mentioned difficulties during their graduate programs with being taken seriously by male faculty. Miller talks of one dissertation committee member: "He thought they shouldn't waste graduate positions on women because they would just marry, have children, and not be as professional."

The women also emphasize the need to develop similarities with male peers to be successful. Rather than highlighting hard work, the women talk primarily of strategies they use for fitting in: altering appearance to fit the proper business attire and changing speech and behaviors to conform to situations with other elites. Frost notes, "There are certain ways of acting in these meetings, I mean for business investors or advisory meetings, I pull my hair back, wear a suit, don't act giggly . . . because you need to fit in." When meeting with other elites, Frost puts on a calculated performance. She modifies her appearance, wears her hair differently, and dresses differently, because she knows that this is the expected way to look and behave. Likewise, this conscious modification spills over into social situations with other corporate elites. Hughes discusses avoiding some country club activities with male peers. She jokes, "It's too tough to be taken seriously when you're wearing a tennis skirt!"

These modifications are predictably influenced by gendered expectations. For instance, one man I interviewed, Douglas Strickland, comments on appropriate behavior in board meetings: "If you're going to be a frilly little sweetheart and have people open your doors . . . that isn't what it's about. I mean it has its place." Encountering such kinds of attitudes, the women attempt to downplay their own feminine qualities to fit in. Newton makes this point: "I talk sports, politics, read the *Wall Street Journal*. I talk what the guys do. I have to. My belief is 'when in Rome, do as the Romans do.'" Newton consciously brings up topics she feels will be of interest to other male elites, topics she would not otherwise discuss outside these circles. Hughes also talks of "speaking 'their' language in board meetings." And Miller also notes, "There certainly is an old boys' network, but I've also found that you can enter it, I think, so long as you are sort of, not the word, asexual, but if you don't act like a female."

A productive way to frame this discussion is in terms of cultural capital, a concept developed by French sociologist Pierre Bourdieu. Bourdieu's definition of cultural capital includes two major forms: (1) dispositions, mannerisms, tastes, and the consumption of cultural goods; and (2) education, including institutional credentials and informal training and skills (Bourdieu 1986). According to Bourdieu, cultural capital can be used to accumulate additional social and economic advantages and "yield profits of distinction for its owner" (Bourdieu 1986, 245). This study illustrates that such cultural capital is gendered. In addition to attaining higher levels of education, women attempt to display the forms of cultural capital that fit best with the male-dominated corporate scene. As I have illustrated, fitting in socially, being compatible with others, and displaying similar tastes and interests are deemed as crucial for success by the women.

Cultural capital in business is also linked to race and ethnicity. The white women in this sample have not experienced the additional burden of racial discrimination. Only two of the women were aware of these factors. Katie Mitchell, president of a personnel firm, recognizes that she has the "same ethnic experience" as men colleagues, which she argues is important because "race is still very much an issue." Similarly, Jennifer Anderson notes,

> I will walk into a room, whether advisors or investors, and at times it will be all white men. I think, "Thank God I'm white because if I wasn't, and I'm a woman, there's no way, no way I could function."

In gender- and race-conscious corporations, being white carries certain advantages for women and men. Linda Martin's (1994) study of women managers in Great Britain also supports this point by revealing that Black women managers are without exception defined as Black and female before being defined as managers by the language and actions of white men and women managers.

The women also talk of networking with other elite women as a strategy for their success. Most describe a feeling of comradeship they have with other elite women because of a shared history and common experiences of blocked opportunities and gender discrimination. This sentiment is echoed by Miller: "I think relationships with other female professionals are slightly different than with men." Miller sees that "there is a bit of a girlfriend kind of attitude that goes on, it's a little friendlier" between women. This comradeship appears to assist these women when negotiating elite circles of power. Frost describes a mentoring relationship she has with another woman who has been in an elite position for a longer period of time: "I admire her because she has an incredible network. She has offered me advice and warned me when I was going to be torn apart in meetings." Hughes, Anderson, and Johnson also underscore the importance of organized efforts designed to create networks of women in business. While understanding the significance of networking with male elites for their success, these three women also believe that all-women business groups can help other women to reach elite positions and might eventually merge with male networks.

Finally, I questioned what strategies these women use to survive in such an elite position and reconcile their family lives. Two women made a conscious decision not to have children with such a demanding career. Hughes emphasizes that with her busy travel schedule and 12-hour days, she could not devote the time necessary to raising children. "My career goals have definitely influenced my decision not to have children. I think for me, I just don't think it would be fair to have children and this kind of schedule." In addition, Mitchell argues,

> There is no way I could do this with young kids. So many times I have worked late into the night. There are just so many times you can do that and call home and say, "Sorry honey, business is more important."

As with the men, these two women question a woman's ability to hold such a position and have a family with young children.

Nancy Harrison, mother of three school-age children, has encountered this attitude:

> Now people say, "Oh, are you really going to be able to handle this presidency because you have kids and it's not like you can just go and have your wife take care of them." Now that I am, by any accounts, the business person in the company, they just are a little bit more skeptical about my ability to do it.

By the time most women reach elite positions, more often than not their children are already adults themselves.

Five of the women in my sample have children, two with school-age children, three with adult children. They all acknowledge that work and family have conflicted at some point in their careers. Newton reflects on how her extensive travel schedule affected her children as they grew up:

> In the evening I would be on the phone with them for hours. Their friends would call and want to come over with no one else there. If you have an 8-hour-a-day job, it's not that bad. But if you have a high-power position with 12-hour days, things are more difficult. I know you can do it, though.

Miller also discusses balancing the responsibilities of having a child and working in a high-power position. "It's had a lot of inconveniences," she states. "But," she continues, "it's never impossible because [my husband and I have] always been able to work it out."

While these women comment on work and family conflicts, they also are quick to suggest that they can juggle such responsibilities. As with all working parents, they talk of methods for reconciling work and family such as day care facilities and modifying schedules with partners to accommodate child care. They also are able to pay for live-in help, something most other American families cannot afford. The women with children in the sample assume both breadwinner and homemaker roles. While they stress the monetary rewards of their position for their families, they also talk of the importance of making time for activities with their children, going to school meetings, and organizing child care and household chores. Harrison notes, "The kids know I'm happy and it doesn't occur to them that maybe Mom should be home at 3:00 P.M. making chocolate chip cookies. And so I make them at 11:00 P.M." While perhaps rationalizing the limited time with their children, these women still take a more active role in the nurturing of their children than the men in the sample.

Conclusions

Most of the top executive positions and directorships in corporate America continue to be held by white men of upper- or upper-middle-class origin. In recent years, however, there has been an increase of women, particularly white upper-middle- to upper-class women, in top corporate positions. Most studies of women at the top have addressed their numbers in the leadership of the entire nation, using survey data to examine their gains within major national corporations and the U.S. government (Dye 1995; Moore 1988). This study provides a unique, detailed look at men and women who comprise part of a local community-based elite, how they think about corporate mobility, and women's strategies for success at the top.

Explanations provided by elites for corporate mobility and success are gendered and racialized. The white men, and most of the white women, appear to take race for granted. Top Black executives, in contrast, are often marginalized in race-oriented jobs and recognize more readily the race-conscious system of upward mobility in corporate America (Collins 1989). My sample does not include men and women of color, but prior research suggests that ethnic minorities, sharing a history of marginalization in white corporations, identify similar social-structural barriers to upward mobility and success described by the white women in my sample (Collins 1989).

The white men in this sample endorse the dominant stratification ideology that underscores the significance of individual effort and talent. Corporate success and mobility can be primarily achieved through hard work and competition. They downplay the degree to which their competition is primarily upper-class, American-born, white men, and they do not acknowledge significant race or gender barriers, perhaps because they themselves have never experienced them. As Linda Martin aptly suggests, "[I]t is primarily white and male denial that such power issues exist; avoidance of responsibility for dominating behavior and covert and overt exercising of power to resist change . . . [that] constitute continuing barriers to Black and white women within organizations" (Martin 1994, 122).

In contrast, the women in this study believe that individual qualities are but one component of success. White women in corporate America share a similar history as outsiders. In the words of Dorothy Smith, "[W]hat we [women] have in common is the organization of social relations that has accomplished our exclusion" (1987, 78). It is from this shared history that these women question excessive emphasis on individualism and confirm the importance of social networks and peer similarities in "making it to the top."

This tendency to resort to different ideologies of success came through clearly in interviewees' explanations for why so few women make it into elite corporate positions. While the men used assumptions from the dominant gender ideology, including women's primary commitments to their families, elite women indicated that the paucity of women in elite positions has much to do with gender discrimination reinforced by all-male networks and peers similarities.

My finding that men are less sensitive to external barriers facing women and minorities is supported by a recent survey of 325 men CEOs conducted by Catalyst (Townsend 1996). Eighty-two percent cited a lack of general management experience as the reason women are held back from corporate leadership (Townsend 1996). In contrast, among the 461 women in vice president or higher positions, male stereotyping of women was the number-one cited obstacle to women's advancement, with exclusion from informal ("old boy") networks the next most serious deterrent (Townsend 1996). This article also reveals strategies women use in maintaining their elite positions, such as displaying cultural capital in the form of advanced degrees or in modification of appearance and speech.

Future research might examine ideological rifts not only between, but possibly among, elite men and women. Under what circumstances might women emphasize individual explanations for success and might men be more conscious of networks and peer similarities? While not evident in my sample, it could be that elite men who establish closer relationships with women in similar positions are privy to their "outsider's" view and, as a result, are more aware of gender barriers. In addition, further research might explore more deeply how individual and collective strategies used by women work to secure their elite positions. How do feelings of solidarity and shared history described by the women in my sample lead to collective action assisting more women to break through the glass ceiling? Do these feelings of solidarity and practical actions include women of color?

In continuing to look at the movement of women into elite positions, it is valuable to focus on local corporate communities because it is at this level that they are making the greatest gains. All-male, white networks appear to be less entrenched within local corporations than in larger national corporations. Of the individuals I interviewed, two men and five women are in local high-technology and biotechnology corporations considered to be "sunrise industries" (Dolbeare 1989). Rising to the top of local corporations in sunrise industries might be an effective avenue for women and ethnic minorities to reach national elite positions.

This study has revealed perspectives of white men and women in top corporate positions; future work must assess explicitly and directly the dynamics of gender, race, and class for moving above the glass ceiling. Women's work experiences are not only affected by gender but also by race, ethnicity, nationality, and class. It is little surprise that women privileged within race and class hierarchies in the United States are moving up the corporate ladder. Understanding their perceptions of corporate mobility, and those of both women and men in ethnic minorities, continues to be crucial for revealing how outsiders climb the corporate ladder and break through the glass ceiling.

References

Bernard, H. Russell. 1994. *Research methods in anthropology: Qualitative and quantitative approaches.* Thousand Oaks: Sage Publications.

Bourdieu, Pierre. 1986. *The forms of capital. In Handbook of theory and research for the sociology of education,* edited by John Richardson. New York: Greenwood.

Collins, Sharon M. 1989. The marginalization of Black executives. *Social Problems* 36:317–31.

Crowly, Helen, and Susan Himmelweit. 1992. Discrimination, subordination and difference: Feminist perspectives. In *Knowing women,* edited by Helen Crowly and Susan Himmelweit. Cambridge, MA: Polity.

Deaux, Kay. 1976. *The behavior of men and women.* Monterey, CA: Brooks/Cole.

Dolbeare, Kenneth. 1989. The nature of the economic transformation. In *The reshaping of America,* edited by D. Stanley Eitzen and Maxine Baca Zinn. Englewood Cliffs, NJ: Prentice Hall.

Dye, Thomas. 1995. *Who's running America? The Clinton years.* Englewood Cliffs, NJ: Prentice Hall.

Epstein, Cynthia Fuchs. 1975. Institutional barriers: What keeps women out of the executive suite? In *Bringing women into management,* edited by F. Gordon and M. Strober. New York: McGraw-Hill.

———. 1991. Debate: Ways men and women lead. *Harvard Business Review* 69(January–February)1: 150–60.

Foucault, Michel. 1980. *Power/knowledge: Selected interviews and other writings, 1972–1977,* edited by Colin Gordon. New York: Pantheon Books.

Freeman, Sue. 1990. *Managing lives: Corporate women and social change.* Amherst: University of Massachusetts Press.

Higginbotham, Elizabeth. 1994. Black professional women: Job ceilings and employment. In *Women of color in U.S. society,* edited by Maxine Baca Zinn and Bonnie Thornton Dill. Philadelphia: Temple University Press.

Kanter, Rosabeth Moss. [1977] 1993. *Men and women of the corporation.* New York: Basic Books.

Kaufman, Debra, and Michael L. Fetters. 1983. The executive suite: Are women perceived as ready for the managerial climb? *Journal of Business Ethics* 2:203–12.

Martin, Linda. 1994. Power, continuity and change: Decoding Black and white women managers' experience in local government. In *Women in management: A developing presence,* edited by Morgan Tanton. London: Routledge.

Messner, Michael. 1989. Masculinities and athletic careers. *Gender & Society* 3:71–88.

Moore, Gwen. 1988. Women in elite positions: Insiders or outsiders? *Sociological Forum* 3:566–85.

Rosener, Judy B. 1990. Ways women lead. *Harvard Business Review* 68(November–December)6: 119–125.

———. 1995. *America's competitive secret: Utilizing women as a management strategy.* New York: Oxford University Press.

Smith, Dorothy E. 1987. *The everyday world as problematic: A feminist sociology.* Boston: Northeastern University Press.

Swan, Elaine. 1994. Managing emotion. In *Women in management: A developing presence,* edited by Morgan Tanton. London: Routledge.

Sweeney, Paul D., Richard Moreland, and Kathy L. Gruber. 1982. Gender differences in performance attributions: Students' explanations for personal success or failure. *Sex Roles* 8:359–73.

Townsend, Bickley. 1996. Room at the top for women. *American Demographics* 18(July)7: 28–37.

U.S. Department of Labor. 1995. *Employment and earnings.* Washington, DC: Government Printing Office.

Von Glinow, M. A., and A. Krzyczkowska-Mercer. 1988. Women in corporate America: A caste of thousands. *New Management* 6:36–42.

The Wall Street Journal. 1986. The board game: More women are becoming directors but it's still a token situation. 24 March, section 4, 290.

Ward, Patricia A., Peter F. Orazem, and Steffen W. Schmidt. 1992. Women in elite pools and elite positions. *Social Science Quarterly* 73:31–45.

Wiley, Mary Glenn, Kathleen Crittenden, and L. D. Birg. 1979. "Why a rejection?" Causal attribution of a career achievement event. *Social Psychology Quarterly* 42:214–22.

Wilkie, Jane Riblett. 1993. Changes in U.S. men's attitudes toward the family provider role, 1972–1989. *Gender & Society* 7:261–79.

Yoder, Janice D. 1991. Rethinking tokenism: Looking beyond numbers. *Gender & Society* 5:178–92.

Zweigenhaft, Richard. 1987. Minorities and women of the corporation: Will they attain seats of power? In *Power elites and organizations,* edited by G. William Domhoff and Thomas Dye. Newbury Park, CA: Sage.

Notes

1. Studies using snowball sampling and other nonprobability sampling techniques have low external validity and their findings cannot be generalized beyond the sample (Bernard 1994). While this study's findings are not suggestive of elite groups in general, they still offer a detailed look at a small sample of elite men and women in Southern California and can be used to inform future research questions relating to elite newcomers.

2. All names of the interviewees and some biographical details have been changed.

3. Social psychologists also have found that American men in achievement situations tend to internalize and take credit for their successes, illustrated by male college students when passing an exam (Sweeney, Moreland, and Gruber 1982). For social psychologists, socialization is an important explanation for this internal attributional style among men. Contradictory evidence has been found with respect to women's attributions of success (Deaux 1976; Wiley, Crittenden, and Birg 1979). In response to the social psychology literature, I argue that it is important to keep in mind that attributional patterns are based on men's and women's social experiences and responsive to social context and cultural ideology.

Chapter 10: Putting It All Together

1. Based on the research presented in this chapter, what are your suggestions for ending inequality in the workplace?

2. How might Cejka and Eagly's research on occupational gender stereotypes help explain the glass ceiling?

3. The two readings in this chapter focus on the social and cultural processes (stereotyping, male-dominated networks, and peer similarities) that contribute to gender differences in employment. How might biological processes influence these social and cultural processes, and how might these social and cultural processes influence biology?